Gacha Gacha

THE NEXT REVOLUTION

4

Hiroyuki Tamakoshi

Translated and adapted by
David Ury

Lettered by
North Market Street Graphics

DEL REY
BOOKS • NEW YORK

Gacha Gacha: The Next Revolution volume 4 is a work of fiction. Names, characters, places, and incidents are the products of the author's imagination or are used fictitiously. And resemblance to actual events, locales, or persons, living or dead, is entirely coincidental.

A Del Rey Trade Paperback Original

Published in the United States by Del Rey Books, an imprint of The Random House Publishing Group, a division of Random House, Inc., New York.

Publication rights arranged through Kodansha Ltd.

First published in Japan in 2005 by Kodansha Ltd., Tokyo

ISBN 978-0-345-49322-4

Printed in the United States of America

www.delreymanga.com

9 8 7 6 5 4 3 2 1

Translator—David Ury
Lettering—North Market Street Graphics

CONTENTS

著者近影…

THE "ROCK STOCK CAFÉ"
THAT APPEARS IN THIS SERIES
WAS NAMED AFTER ONE OF
MY FAVORITE MOVIES.

A MEANING-
LESS MESSAGE
FROM THE
AUTHOR.

Honorifics Explained

Throughout the Del Rey Manga books, you will find Japanese honorifics left intact in the translations. For those not familiar with how the Japanese use honorifics and, more important, how they differ from American honorifics, we present this brief overview.

Politeness has always been a critical facet of Japanese culture. Ever since the feudal era, when Japan was a highly stratified society, use of honorifics—which can be defined as polite speech that indicates relationship or status—has played an essential role in the Japanese language. When addressing someone in Japanese, an honorific usually takes the form of a suffix attached to one's name (example: "Asuna-san"), is used as a title at the end of one's name, or appears in place of the name itself (example: "Negi-sensei," or simply "Sensei!").

Honorifics can be expressions of respect or endearment. In the context of manga and anime, honorifics give insight into the nature of the relationship between characters. Many translations into English leave out these important honorifics and therefore distort the feel of the original Japanese. Because Japanese honorifics contain nuances that English honorifics lack, it is our policy at Del Rey not to translate them. Here, instead, is a guide to some of the honorifics you may encounter in Del Rey Manga.

-san: This is the most common honorific and is equivalent to Mr., Miss, Ms., or Mrs. It is the all-purpose honorific and can be used in any situation where politeness is required.

-sama: This is one level higher than "-san." It is used to confer great respect.

-dono: This comes from the word "tono," which means "lord." It is an even higher level than "-sama," and confers utmost respect.

-kun: This suffix is used at the end of boys' names to express familiarity or endearment. It is also sometimes used by men among friends, or when addressing someone younger or of a lower station.

-chan: This is used to express endearment, mostly toward girls. It is also used for little boys, pets, and even among lovers. It gives a sense of childish cuteness.

Bozu: This is an informal way to refer to a boy, similar to the English terms "kid" and "squirt."

Sempai/
Senpai: This title suggests that the addressee is one's senior in a group or organization. It is most often used in a school setting, where underclassmen refer to their upperclassmen as "sempai." It can also be used in the workplace, such as when a newer employee addresses an employee who has seniority in the company.

Kohai: This is the opposite of "sempai" and is used toward underclassmen in school or newcomers in the workplace. It connotes that the addressee is of lower station.

Sensei: Literally meaning "one who has come before," this title is used for teachers, doctors, or masters of any profession or art.

-[blank]:This is usually forgotten in these lists, but it is perhaps the most significant difference between Japanese and English. The lack of honorific means that the speaker has permission to address the person in a very intimate way. Usually, only family, spouses, or very close friends have this kind of permission. Known as *yobisute*, it can be gratifying when someone who has earned the intimacy starts to call one by one's name without an honorific. But when that intimacy hasn't been earned, it can be very insulting.

Gacha Gacha

THE NEXT REVOLUTION

gachagacha

4

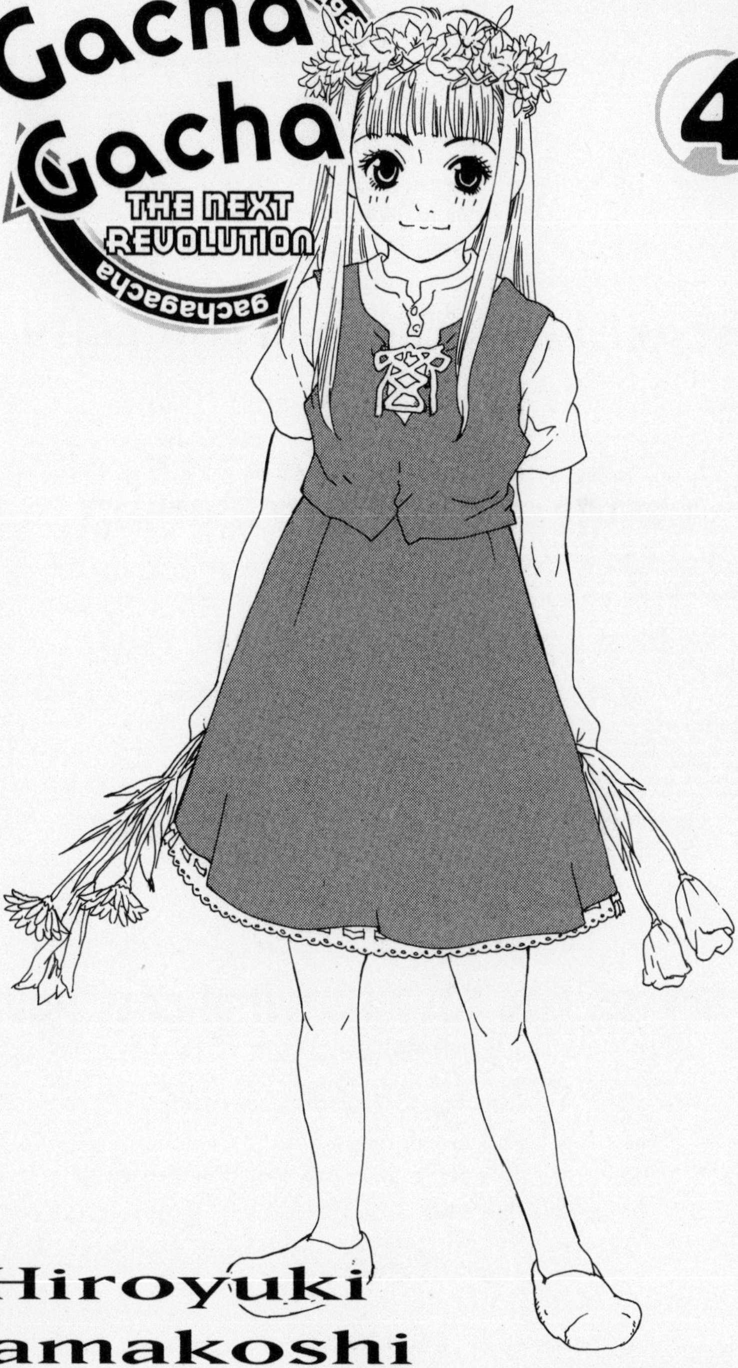

Hiroyuki Tamakoshi

THE NEXT REVOLUTION 4

CONTENTS

Gacha Gacha

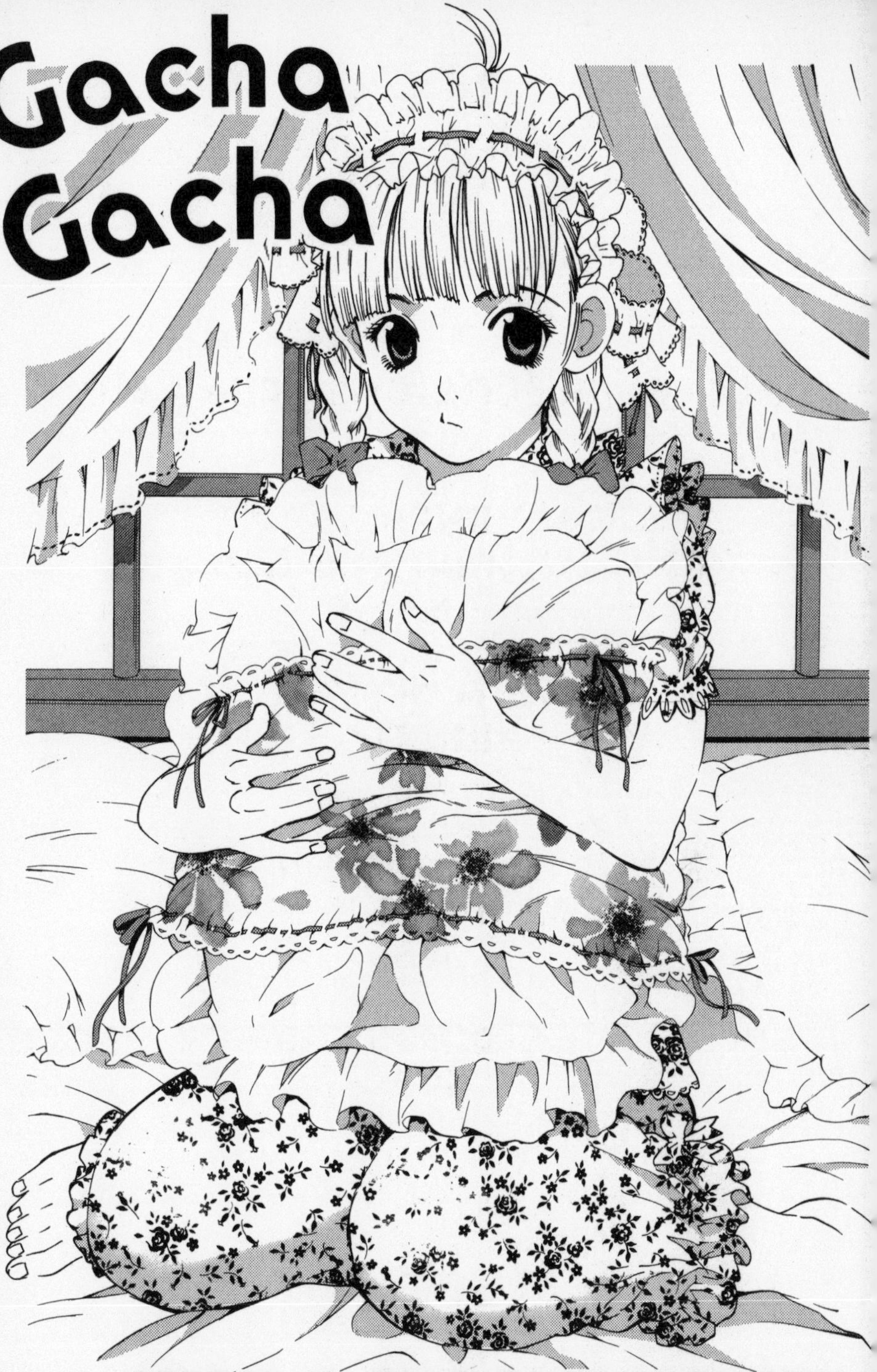

Secret 16: Forbidden Curiosity

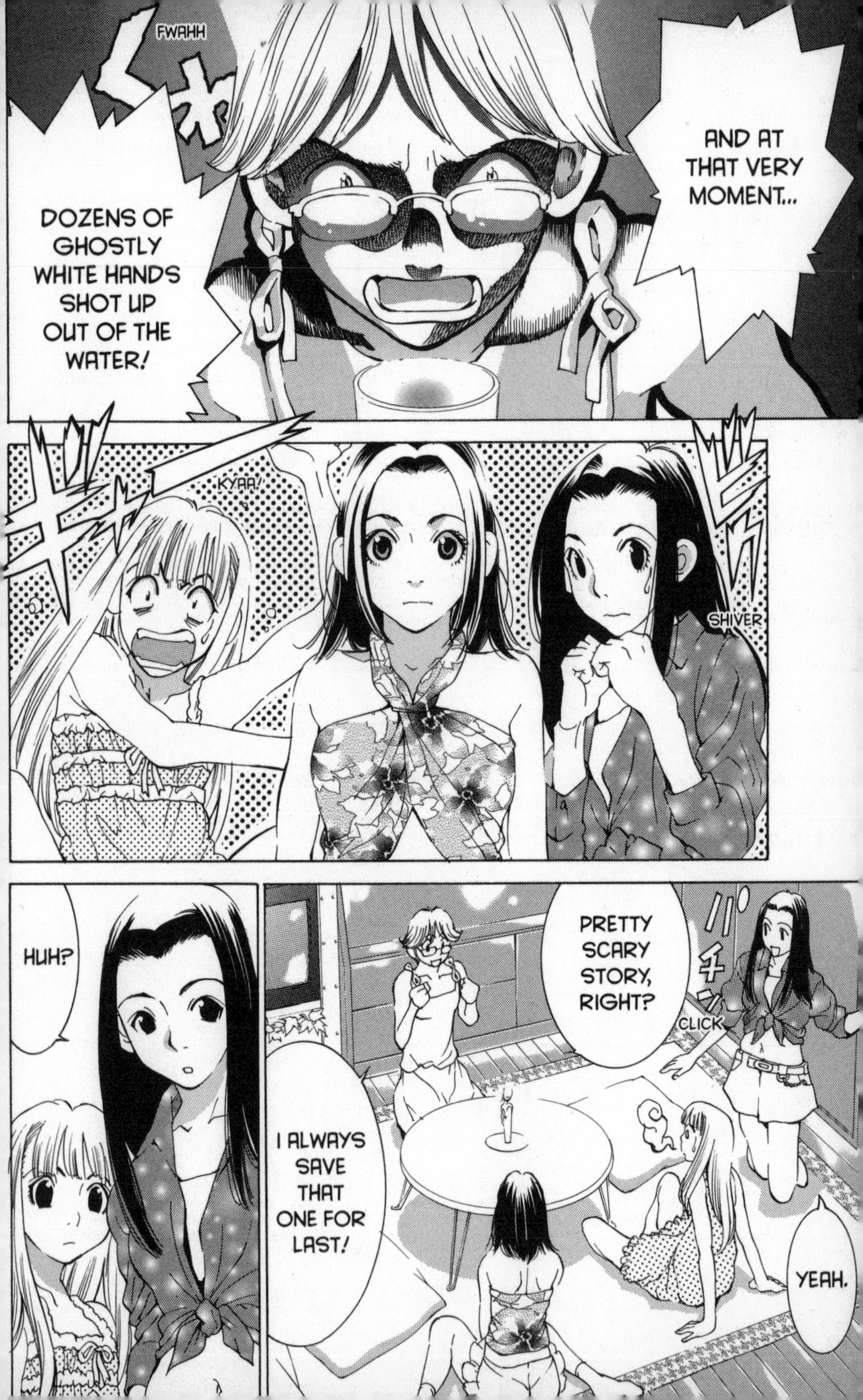
AND AT THAT VERY MOMENT...
FWAHH
DOZENS OF GHOSTLY WHITE HANDS SHOT UP OUT OF THE WATER!
SHIVER
KYAA!
PRETTY SCARY STORY, RIGHT?
CLICK
I ALWAYS SAVE THAT ONE FOR LAST!
YEAH.
HUH?

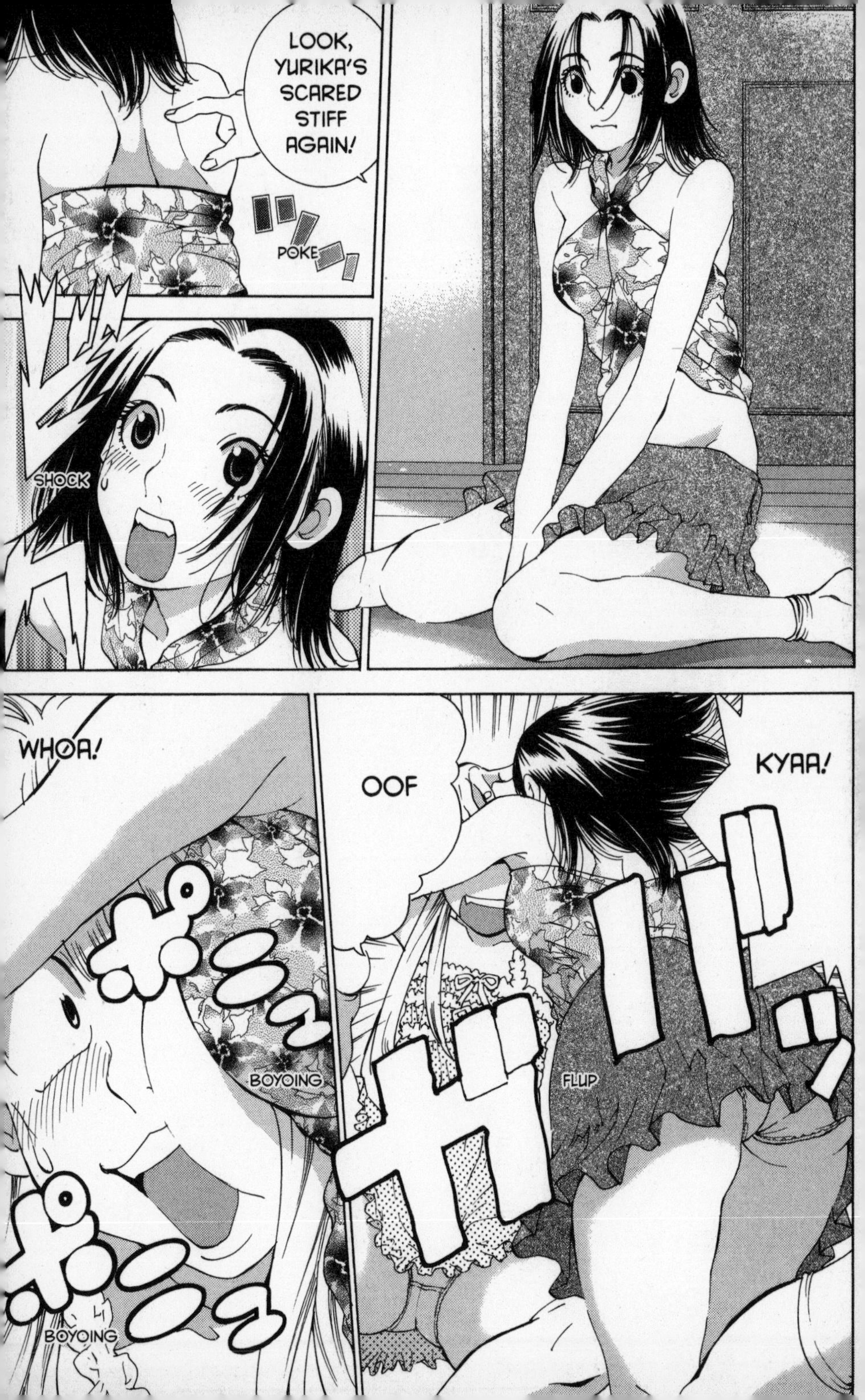
LOOK, YURIKA'S SCARED STIFF AGAIN!
POKE
SHOCK
KYAA!
OOF
FLUP
WHOA!
BOYOING
BOYOING

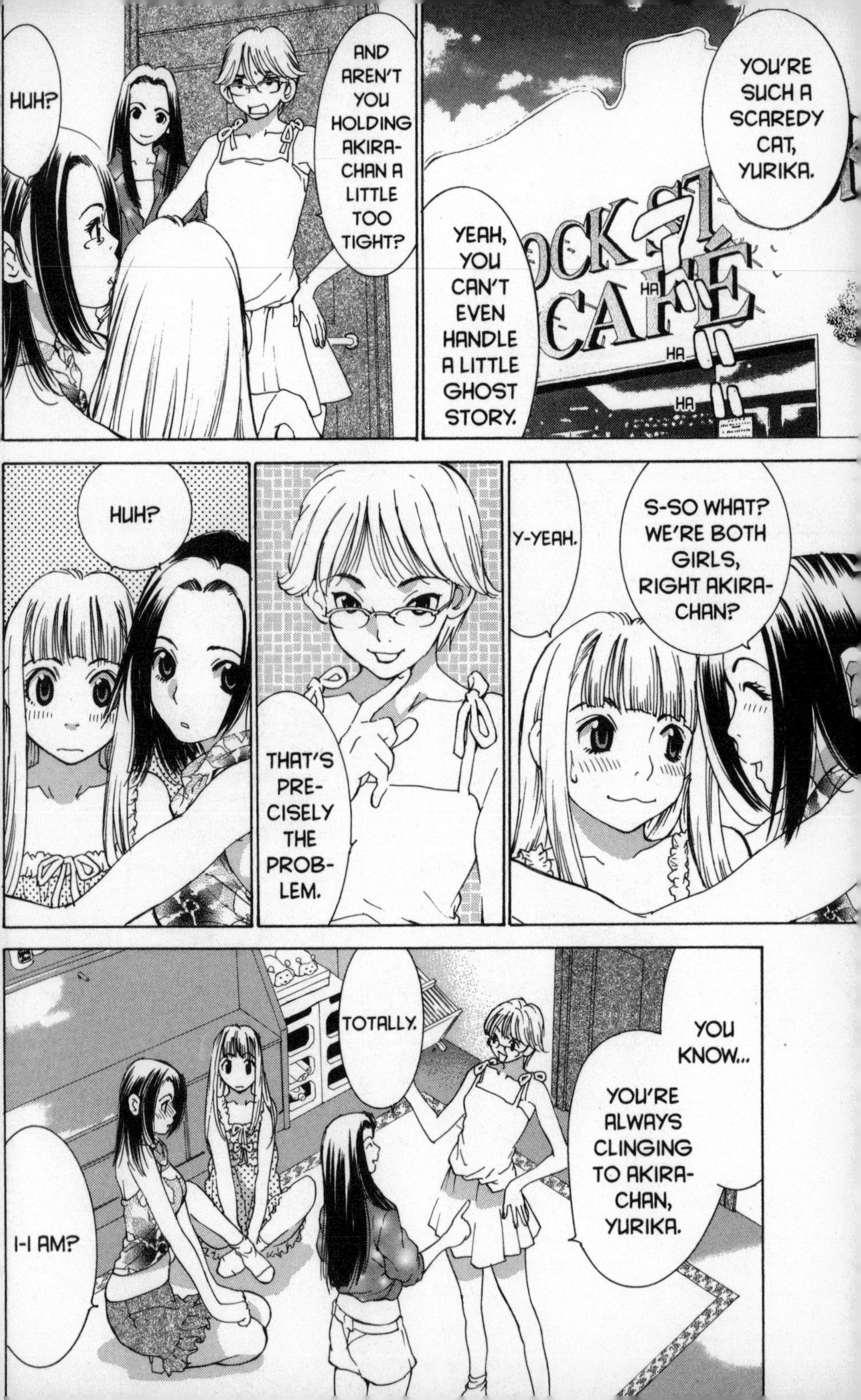
YOU'RE SUCH A SCAREDY CAT, YURIKA.
YEAH, YOU CAN'T EVEN HANDLE A LITTLE GHOST STORY.
CAFÉ
HA
HA
HA
AND AREN'T YOU HOLDING AKIRA-CHAN A LITTLE TOO TIGHT?
HUH?
S-SO WHAT? WE'RE BOTH GIRLS, RIGHT AKIRA-CHAN?
Y-YEAH.
THAT'S PRECISELY THE PROBLEM.
HUH?
YOU KNOW...
YOU'RE ALWAYS CLINGING TO AKIRA-CHAN, YURIKA.
TOTALLY.
I-I AM?

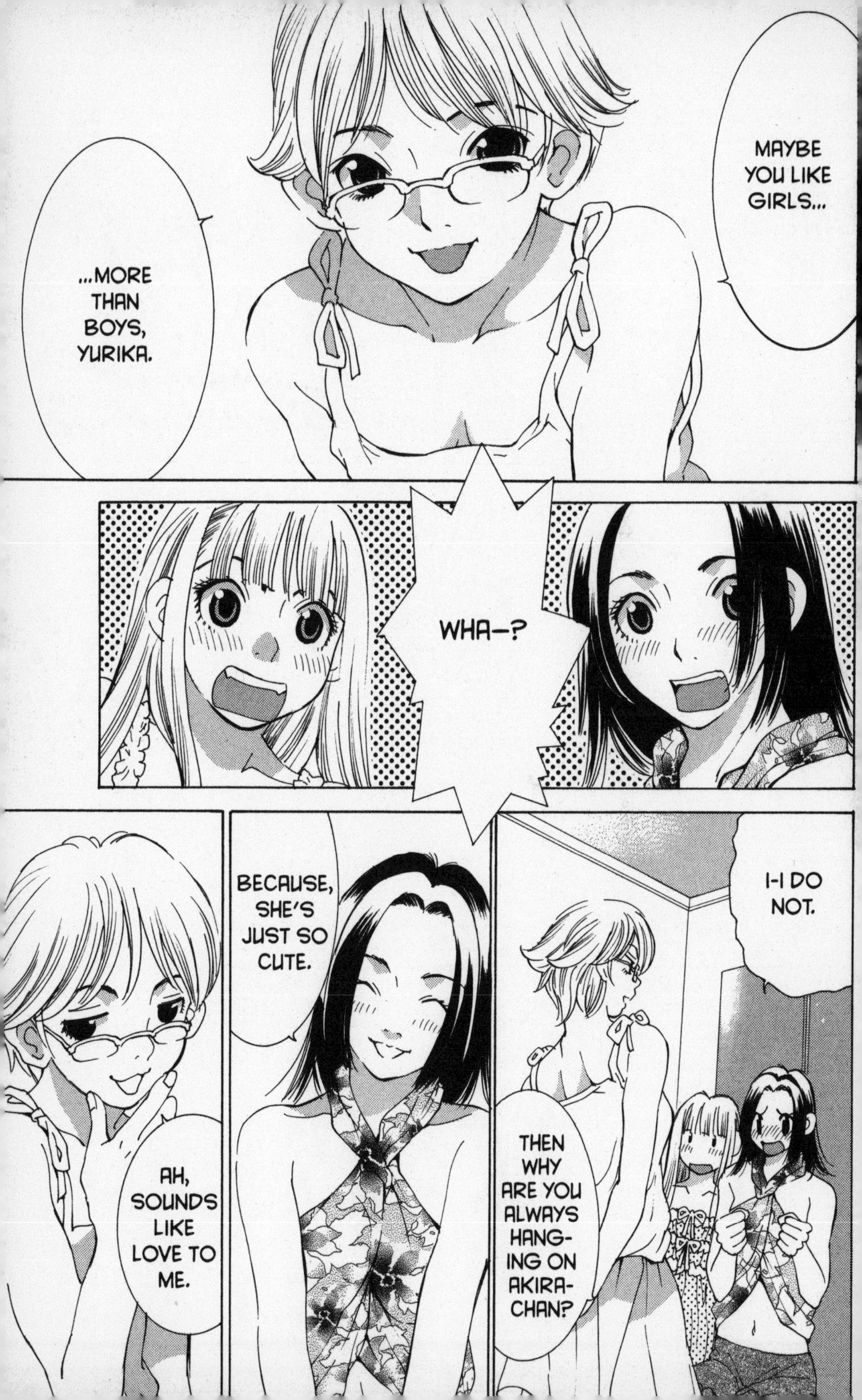
MAYBE YOU LIKE GIRLS...
...MORE THAN BOYS, YURIKA.
WHA-?
I-I DO NOT.
THEN WHY ARE YOU ALWAYS HANGING ON AKIRA-CHAN?
BECAUSE, SHE'S JUST SO CUTE.
AH, SOUNDS LIKE LOVE TO ME.

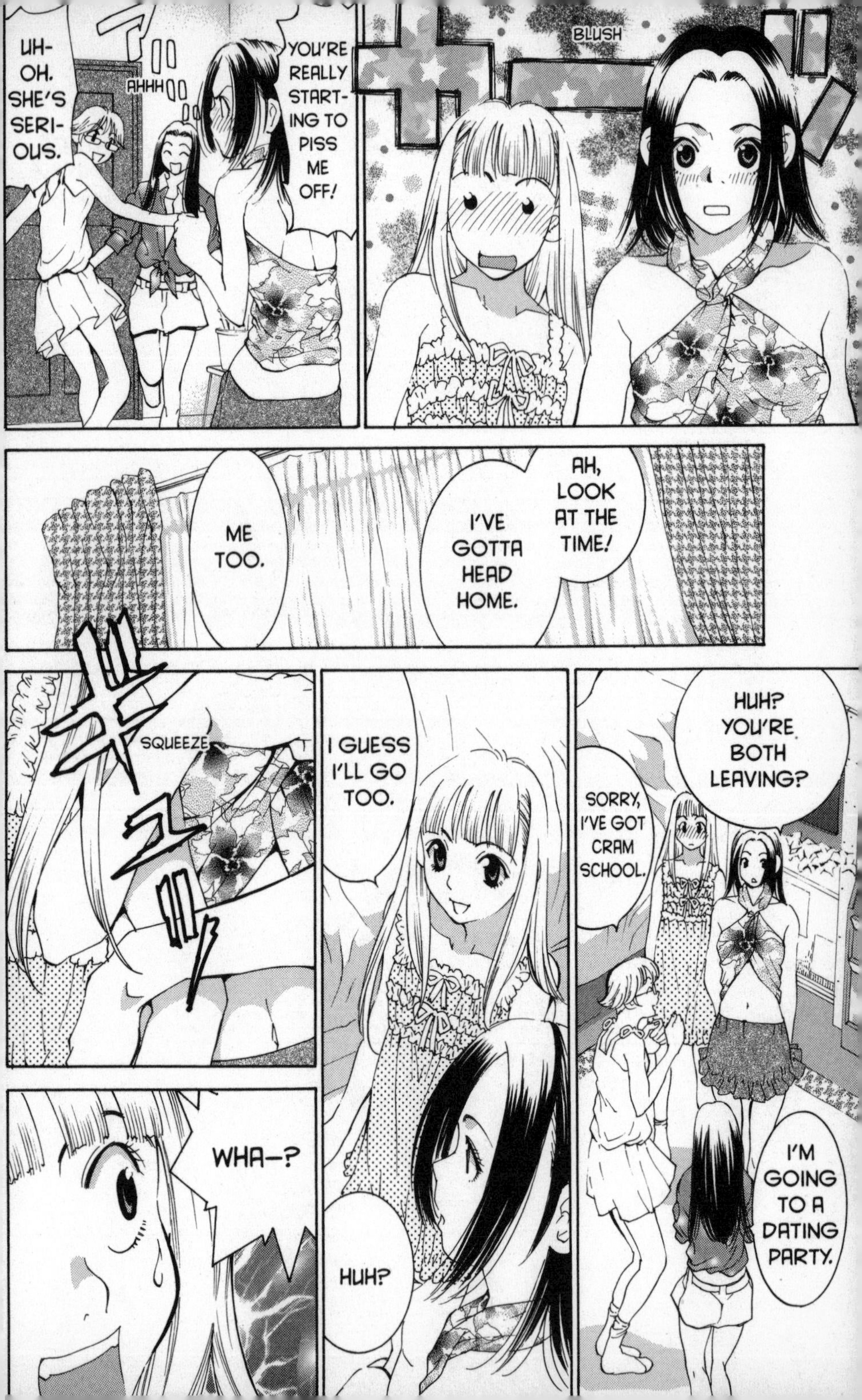

BLUSH
YOU'RE REALLY STARTING TO PISS ME OFF!
AHHH
UH-OH. SHE'S SERIOUS.
AH, LOOK AT THE TIME!
I'VE GOTTA HEAD HOME.
ME TOO.
HUH? YOU'RE BOTH LEAVING?
SORRY, I'VE GOT CRAM SCHOOL.
I'M GOING TO A DATING PARTY.
I GUESS I'LL GO TOO.
HUH?
SQUEEZE
WHA-?

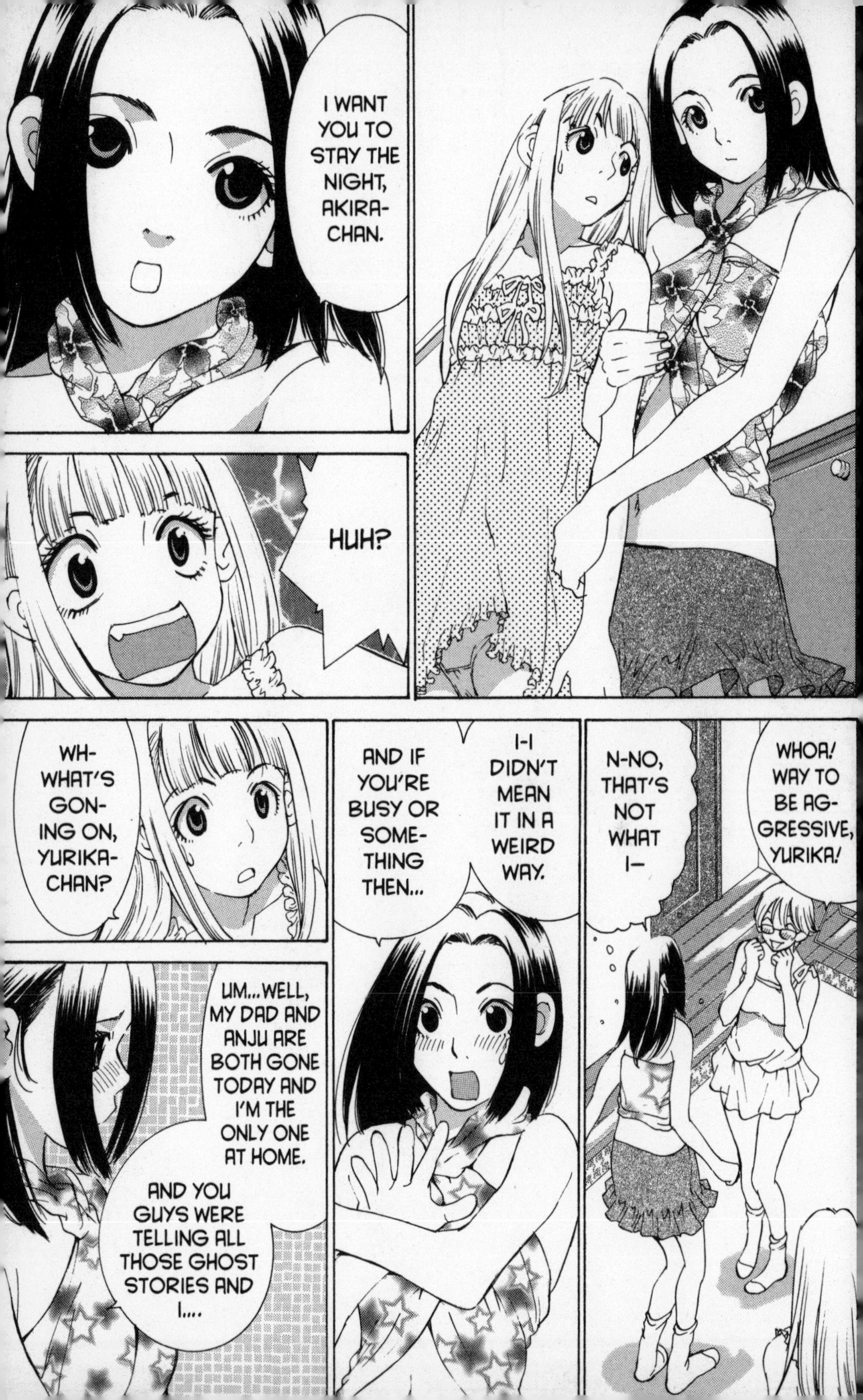
I WANT YOU TO STAY THE NIGHT, AKIRA-CHAN.
HUH?
WHOA! WAY TO BE AGGRESSIVE, YURIKA!
N-NO, THAT'S NOT WHAT I—
I-I DIDN'T MEAN IT IN A WEIRD WAY.
AND IF YOU'RE BUSY OR SOMETHING THEN...
WH-WHAT'S GONING ON, YURIKA-CHAN?
UM...WELL, MY DAD AND ANJU ARE BOTH GONE TODAY AND I'M THE ONLY ONE AT HOME.
AND YOU GUYS WERE TELLING ALL THOSE GHOST STORIES AND I....

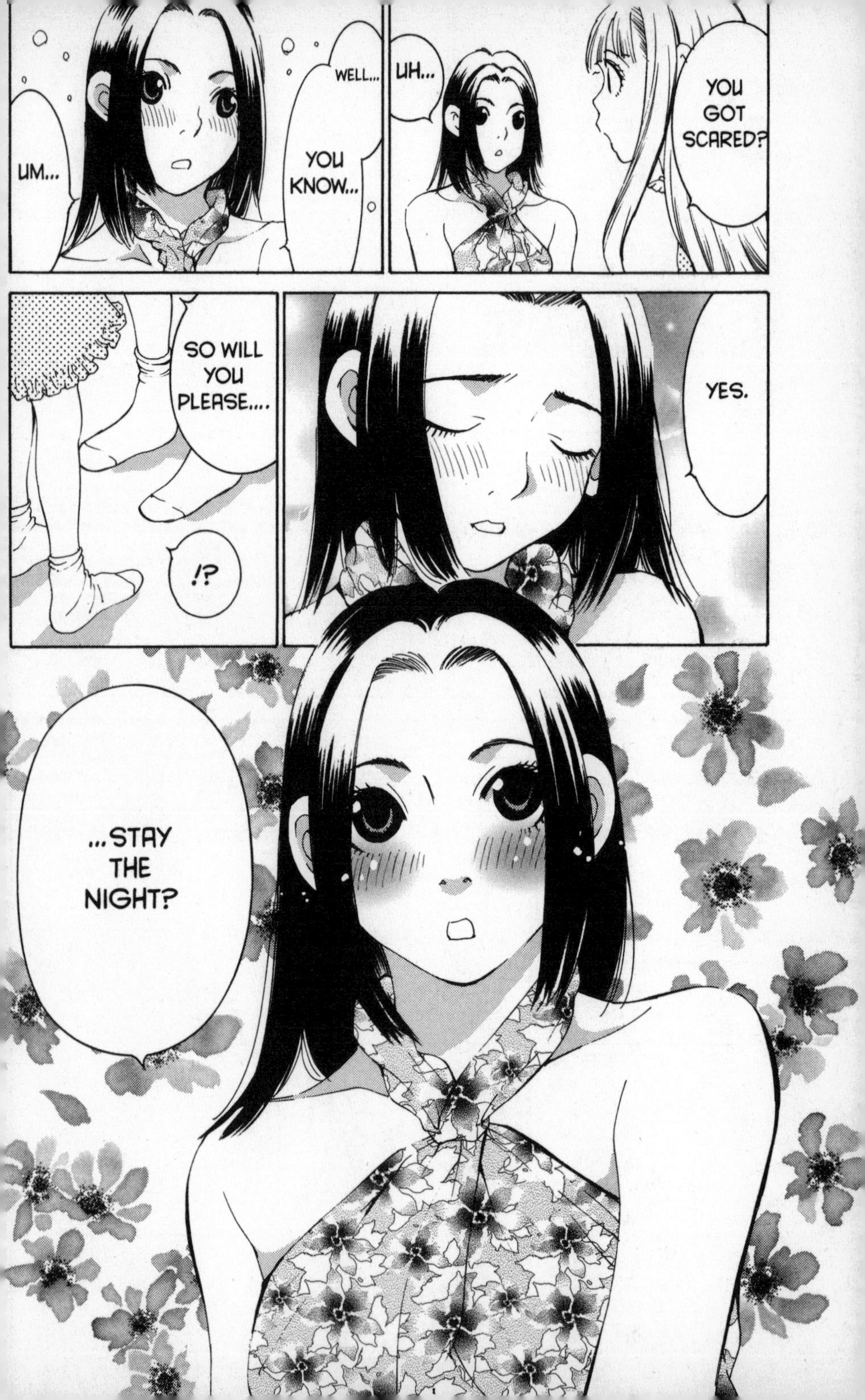
YOU GOT SCARED?
UH...
WELL... YOU KNOW...
UM...
YES.
SO WILL YOU PLEASE....
!?
...STAY THE NIGHT?

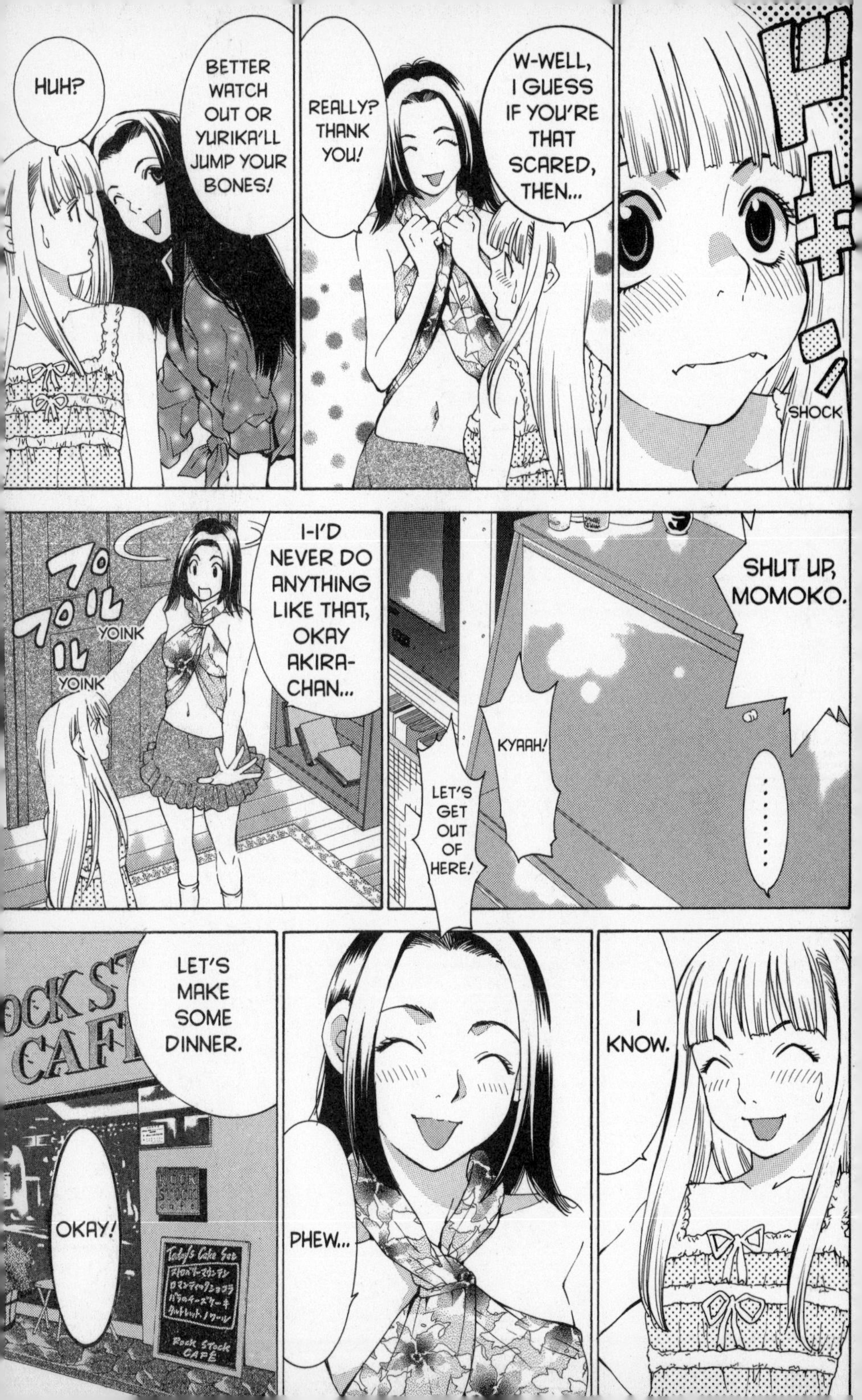
SHOCK
W-WELL, I GUESS IF YOU'RE THAT SCARED, THEN...
REALLY? THANK YOU!
BETTER WATCH OUT OR YURIKA'LL JUMP YOUR BONES!
HUH?
SHUT UP, MOMOKO.
KYAAH!
LET'S GET OUT OF HERE!
......
I-I'D NEVER DO ANYTHING LIKE THAT, OKAY AKIRA-CHAN...
YOINK
YOINK
I KNOW.
PHEW...
LET'S MAKE SOME DINNER.
OKAY!
Rock Stock CAFÉ

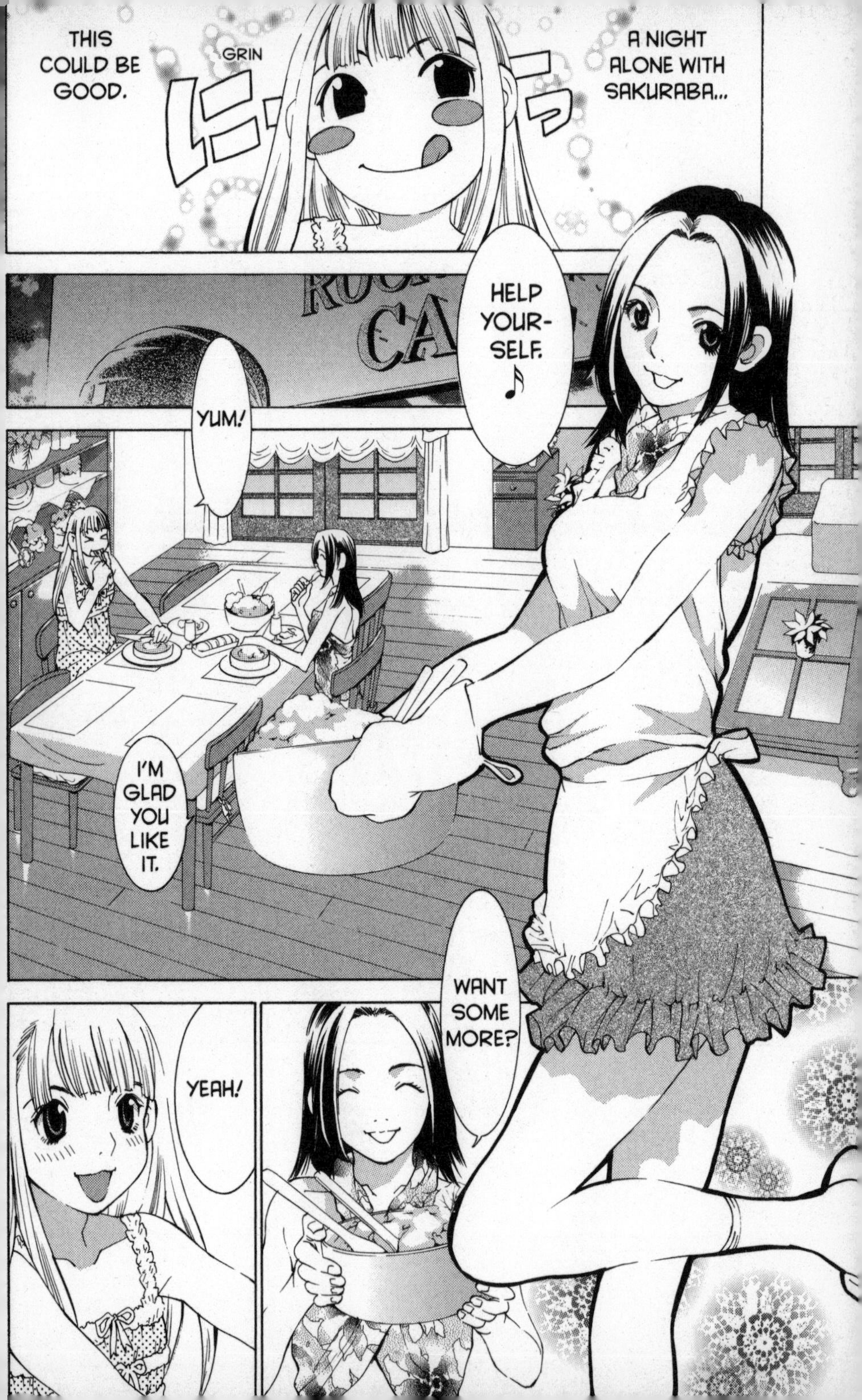
A NIGHT ALONE WITH SAKURABA...
GRIN
THIS COULD BE GOOD.
HELP YOUR-SELF. ♪
YUM!
I'M GLAD YOU LIKE IT.
WANT SOME MORE?
YEAH!

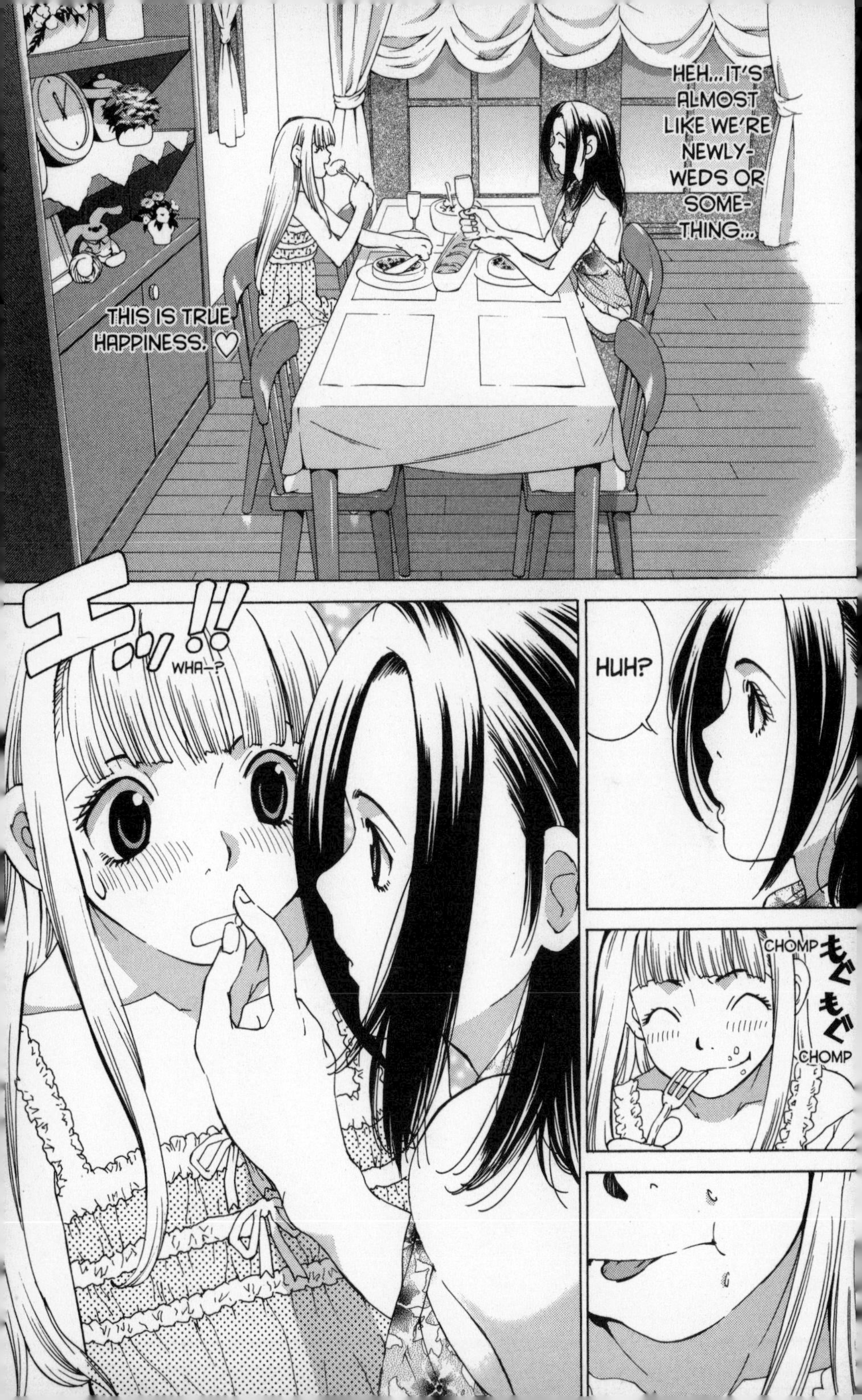
HEH...IT'S ALMOST LIKE WE'RE NEWLY-WEDS OR SOME-THING...
THIS IS TRUE HAPPINESS. ♡
HUH?
CHOMP もぐ
もぐ CHOMP
エッ!!
WHA-?

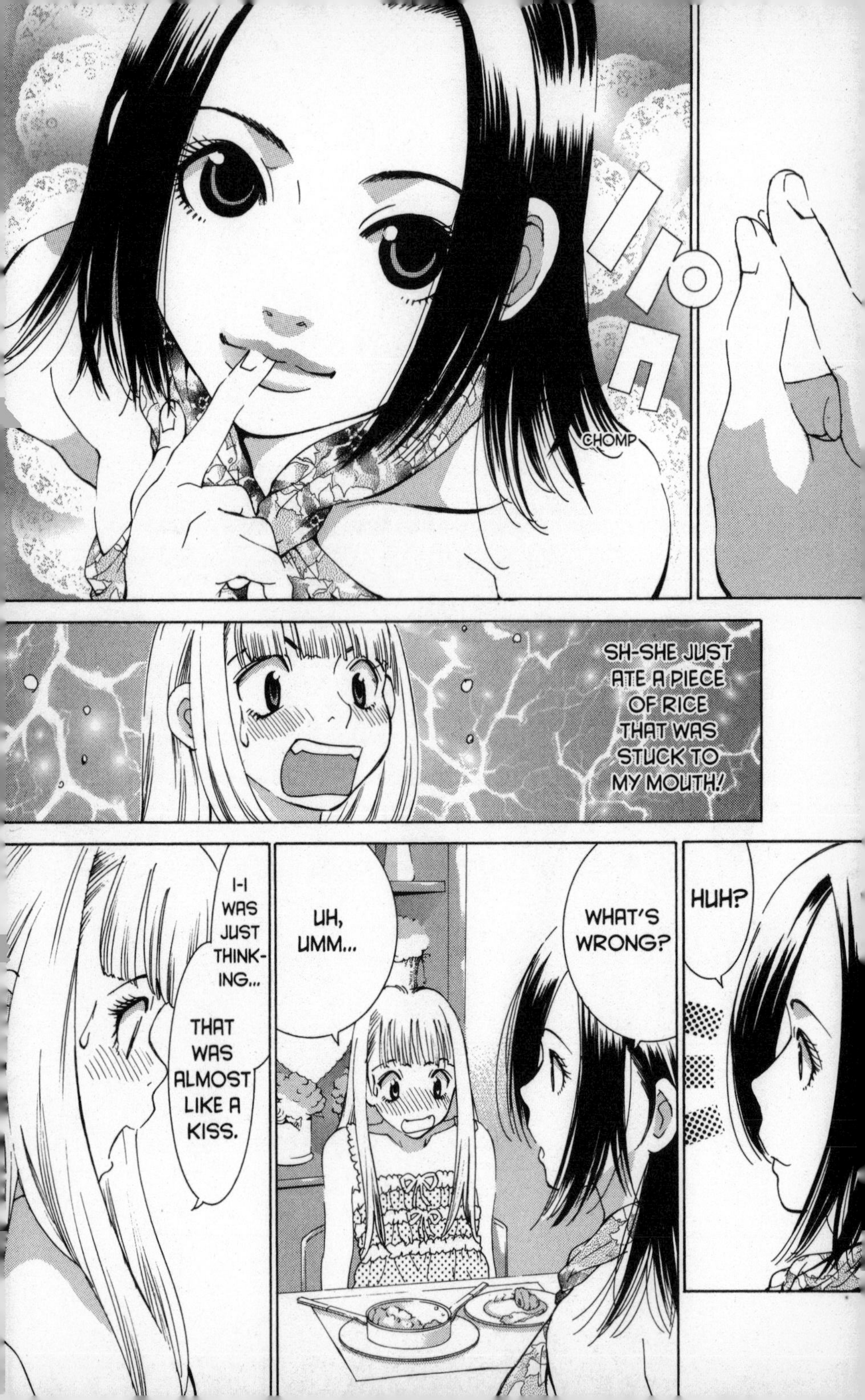
CHOMP
SH-SHE JUST ATE A PIECE OF RICE THAT WAS STUCK TO MY MOUTH!
HUH?
WHAT'S WRONG?
UH, UMM...
I-I WAS JUST THINKING...
THAT WAS ALMOST LIKE A KISS.

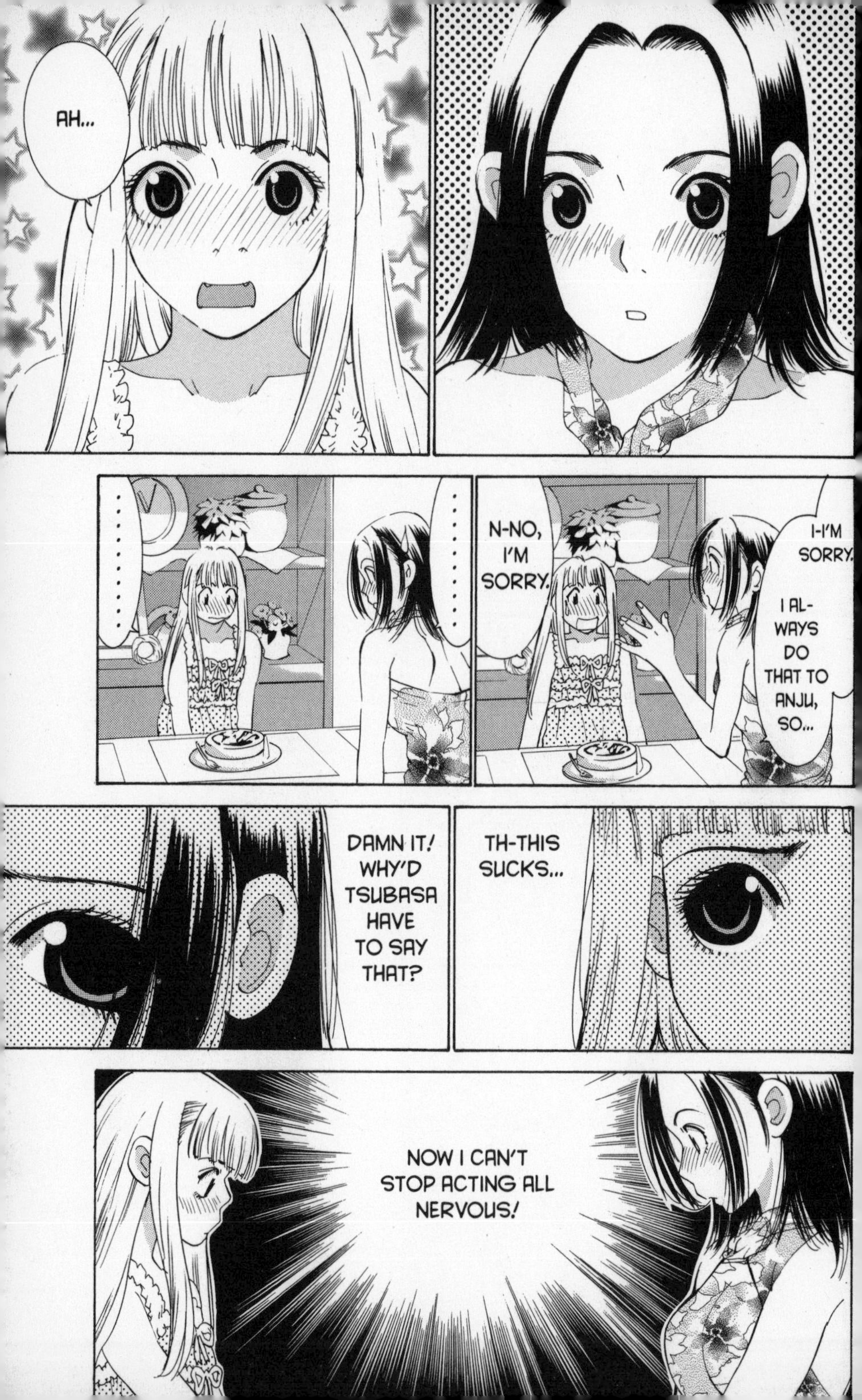
AH...
I-I'M SORRY.
I AL-WAYS DO THAT TO ANJU, SO...
N-NO, I'M SORRY.
......
......
TH-THIS SUCKS...
DAMN IT! WHY'D TSUBASA HAVE TO SAY THAT?
NOW I CAN'T STOP ACTING ALL NERVOUS!

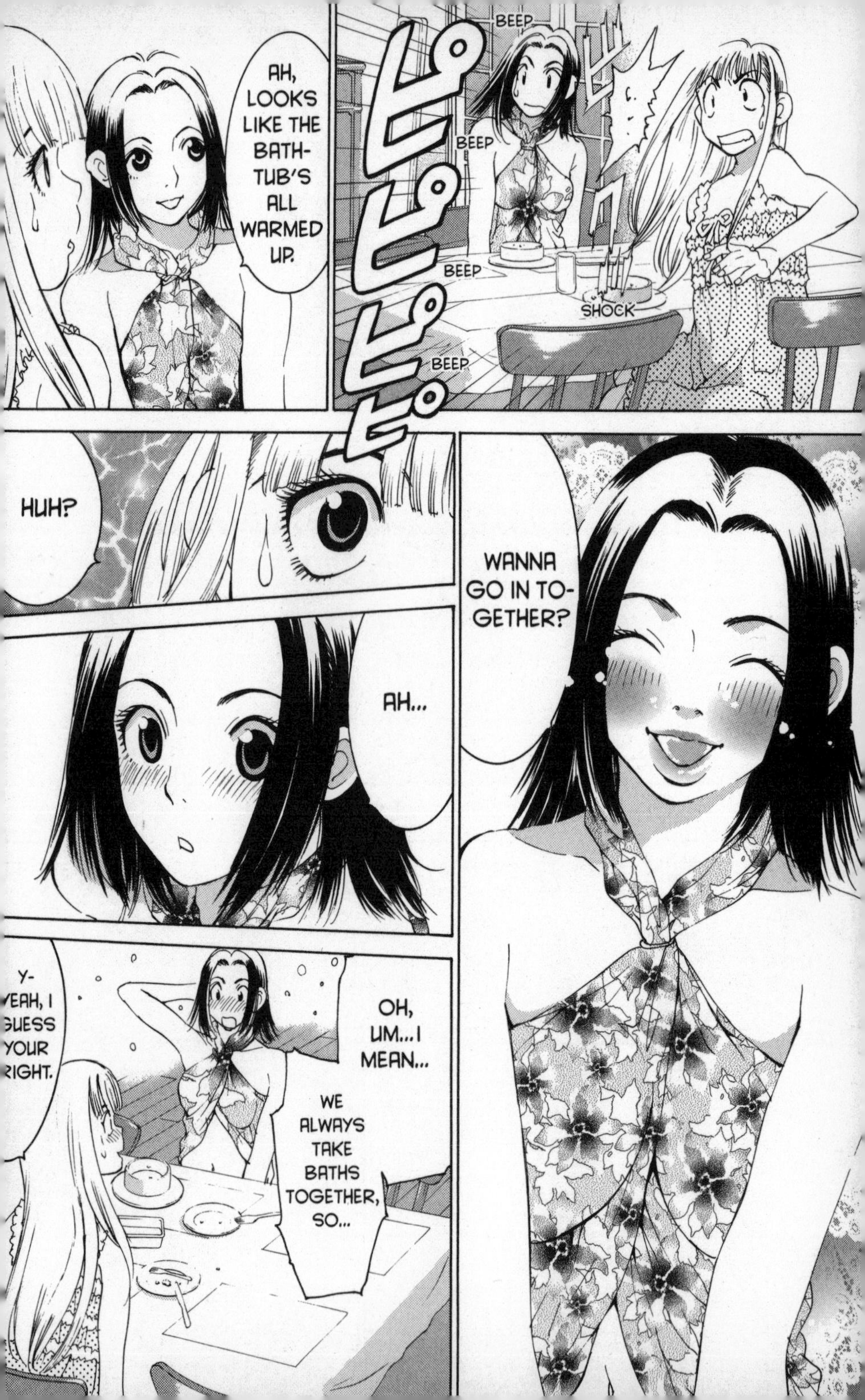
BEEP
ピピピピ
BEEP
BEEP
BEEP
SHOCK
AH, LOOKS LIKE THE BATH-TUB'S ALL WARMED UP.
WANNA GO IN TO-GETHER?
HUH?
AH...
OH, UM...I MEAN...
WE ALWAYS TAKE BATHS TOGETHER, SO...
Y-YEAH, I GUESS YOUR RIGHT.

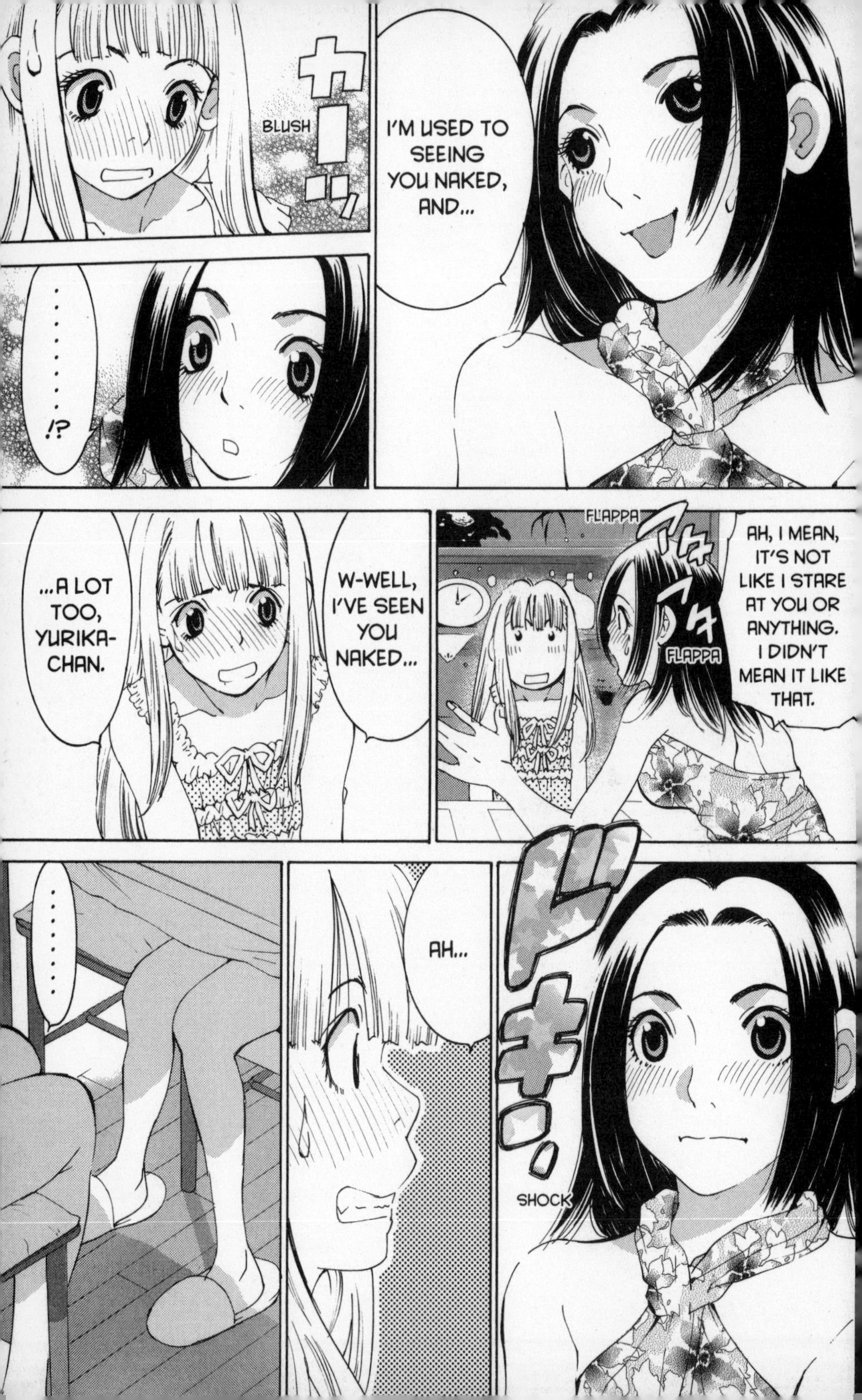
I'M USED TO SEEING YOU NAKED, AND...
BLUSH
......!?
FLAPPA
FLAPPA
AH, I MEAN, IT'S NOT LIKE I STARE AT YOU OR ANYTHING. I DIDN'T MEAN IT LIKE THAT.
W-WELL, I'VE SEEN YOU NAKED...
...A LOT TOO, YURIKA-CHAN.
SHOCK
AH...
....

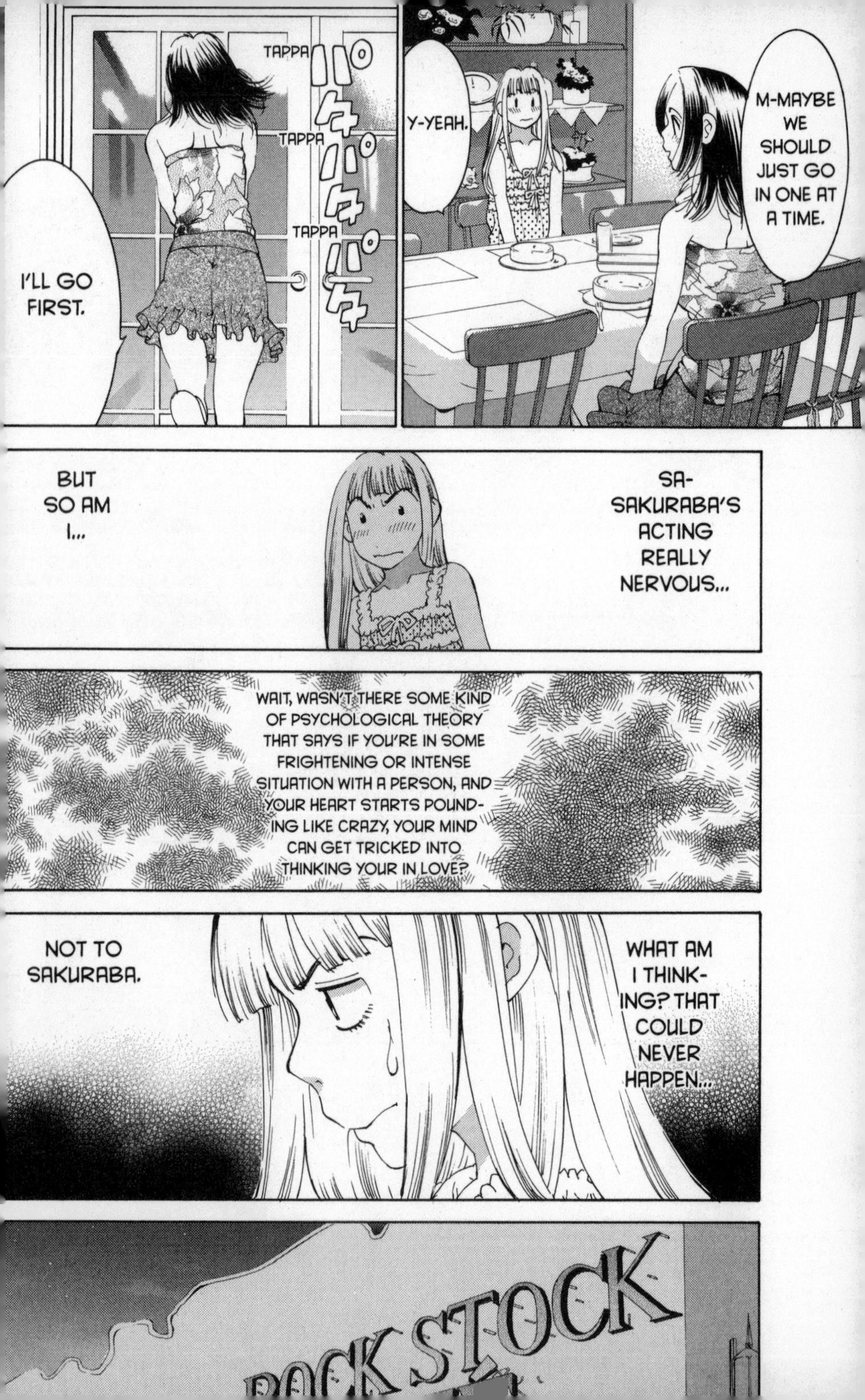
M-MAYBE WE SHOULD JUST GO IN ONE AT A TIME.
Y-YEAH.
TAPPA
TAPPA
TAPPA
I'LL GO FIRST.
SA-SAKURABA'S ACTING REALLY NERVOUS...
BUT SO AM I...
WAIT, WASN'T THERE SOME KIND OF PSYCHOLOGICAL THEORY THAT SAYS IF YOU'RE IN SOME FRIGHTENING OR INTENSE SITUATION WITH A PERSON, AND YOUR HEART STARTS POUNDING LIKE CRAZY, YOUR MIND CAN GET TRICKED INTO THINKING YOUR IN LOVE?
WHAT AM I THINKING? THAT COULD NEVER HAPPEN...
NOT TO SAKURABA.
ROCK STOCK

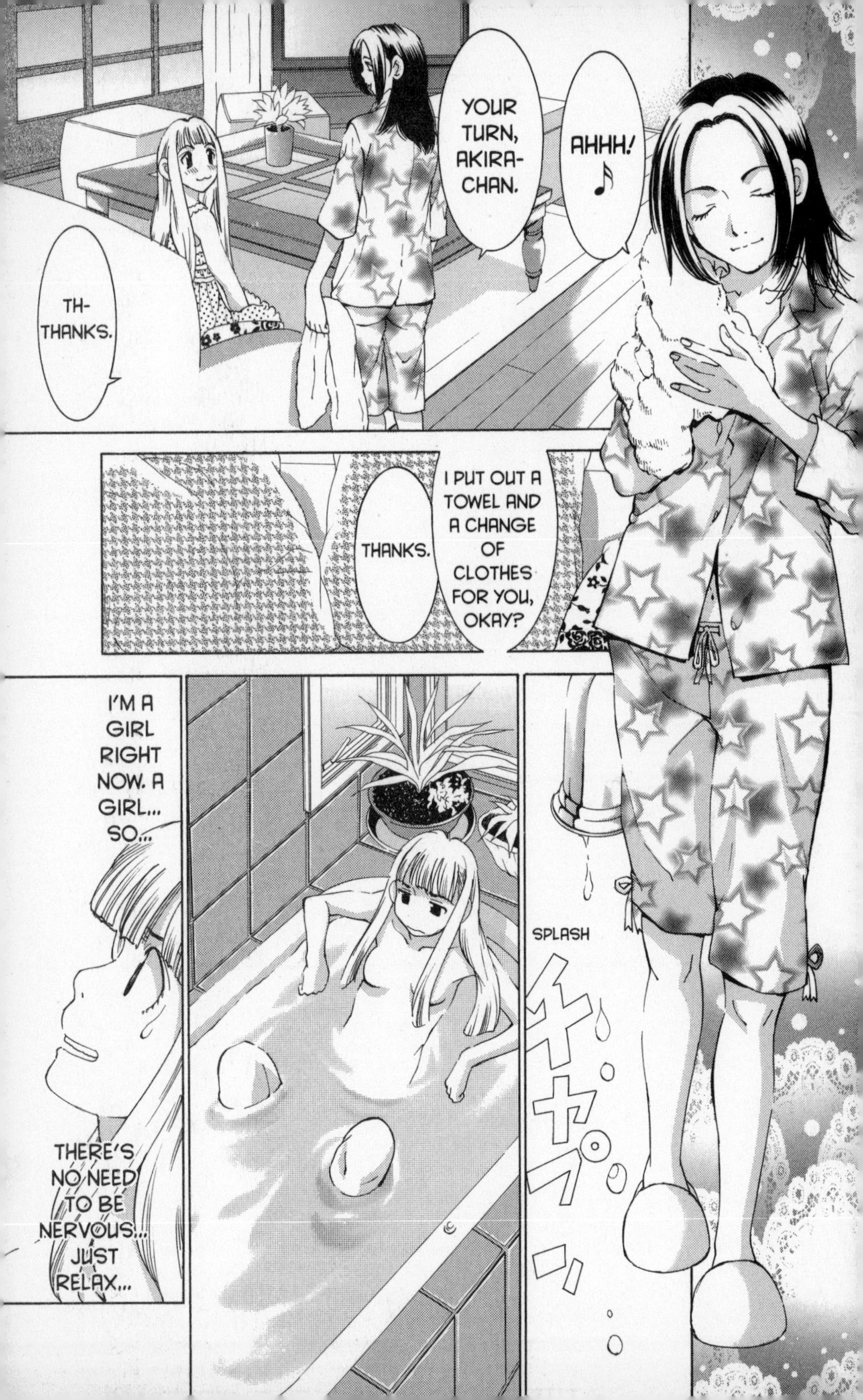
AHHH! ♪
SPLASH
YOUR TURN, AKIRA-CHAN.
TH- THANKS.
I PUT OUT A TOWEL AND A CHANGE OF CLOTHES FOR YOU, OKAY?
THANKS.
I'M A GIRL RIGHT NOW. A GIRL... SO...
THERE'S NO NEED TO BE NERVOUS... JUST RELAX...

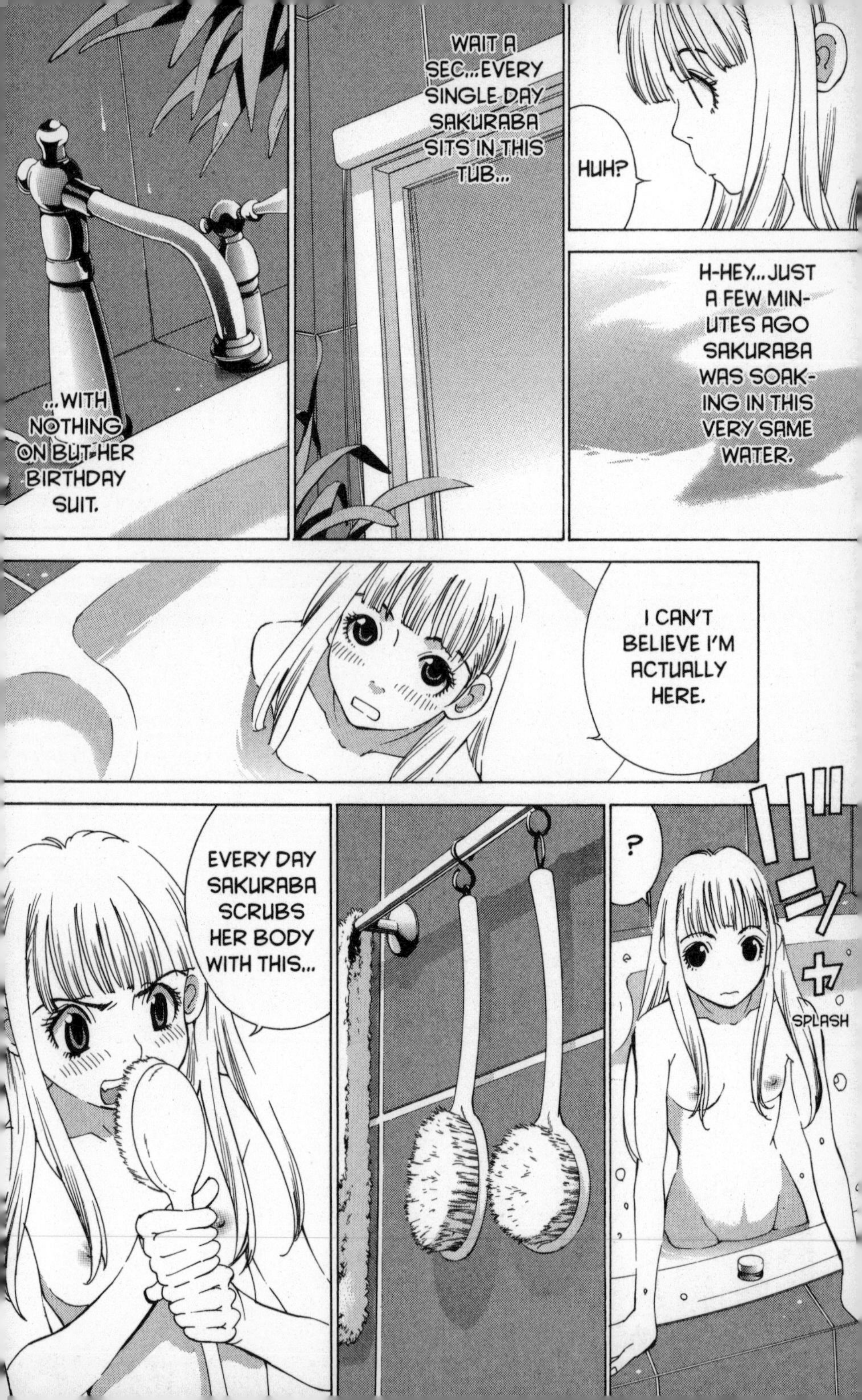
HUH?
H-HEY... JUST A FEW MIN-UTES AGO SAKURABA WAS SOAK-ING IN THIS VERY SAME WATER.
WAIT A SEC... EVERY SINGLE DAY SAKURABA SITS IN THIS TUB...
...WITH NOTHING ON BUT HER BIRTHDAY SUIT.
I CAN'T BELIEVE I'M ACTUALLY HERE.
?
SPLASH
EVERY DAY SAKURABA SCRUBS HER BODY WITH THIS...

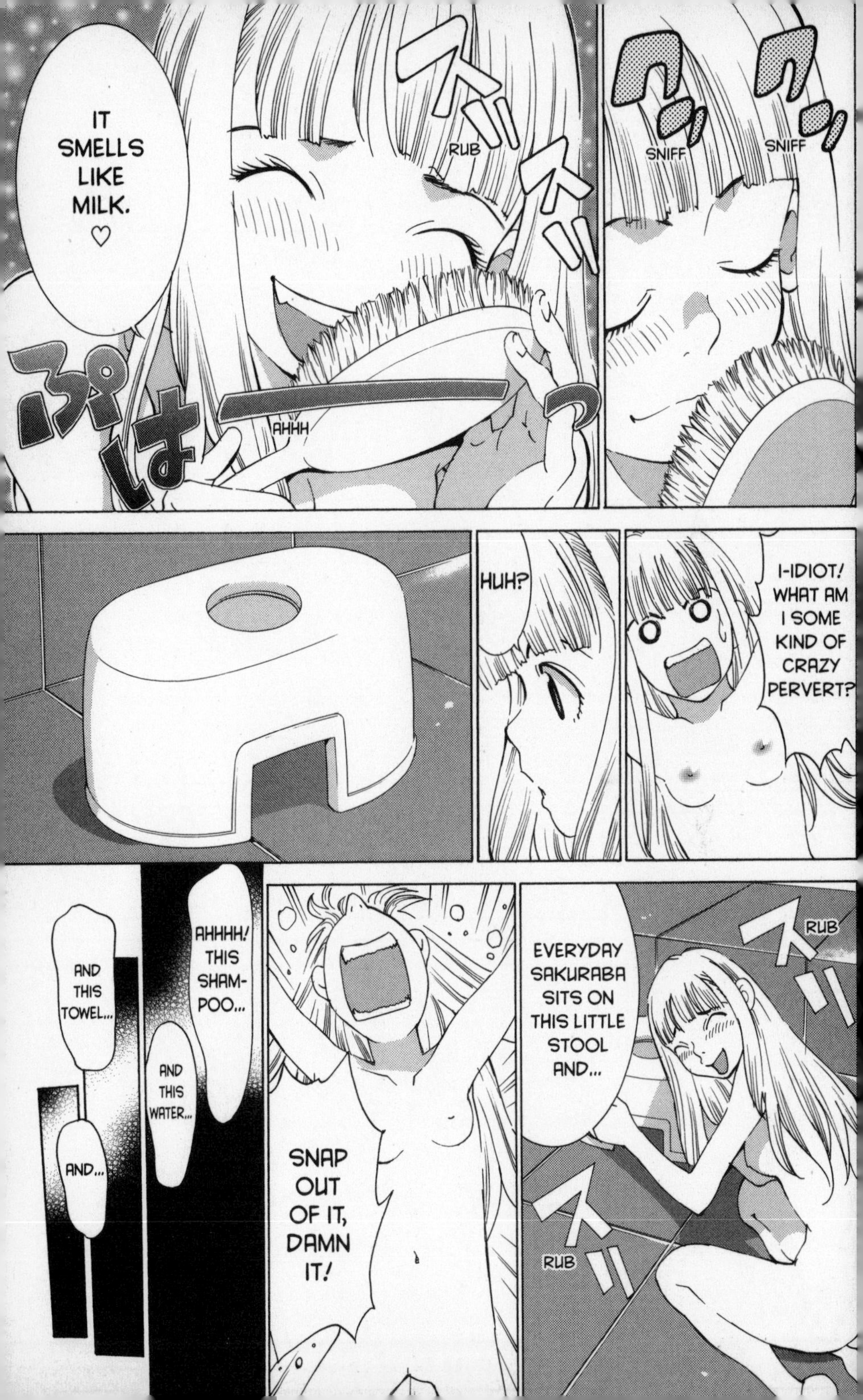
SNIFF
SNIFF
スリスリ
RUB
IT SMELLS LIKE MILK. ♡
ぷはーっ
AHHH
I-IDIOT! WHAT AM I SOME KIND OF CRAZY PERVERT?
HUH?
RUB
EVERYDAY SAKURABA SITS ON THIS LITTLE STOOL AND...
RUB
SNAP OUT OF IT, DAMN IT!
AHHHH! THIS SHAM-POO...
AND THIS TOWEL...
AND THIS WATER...
AND...

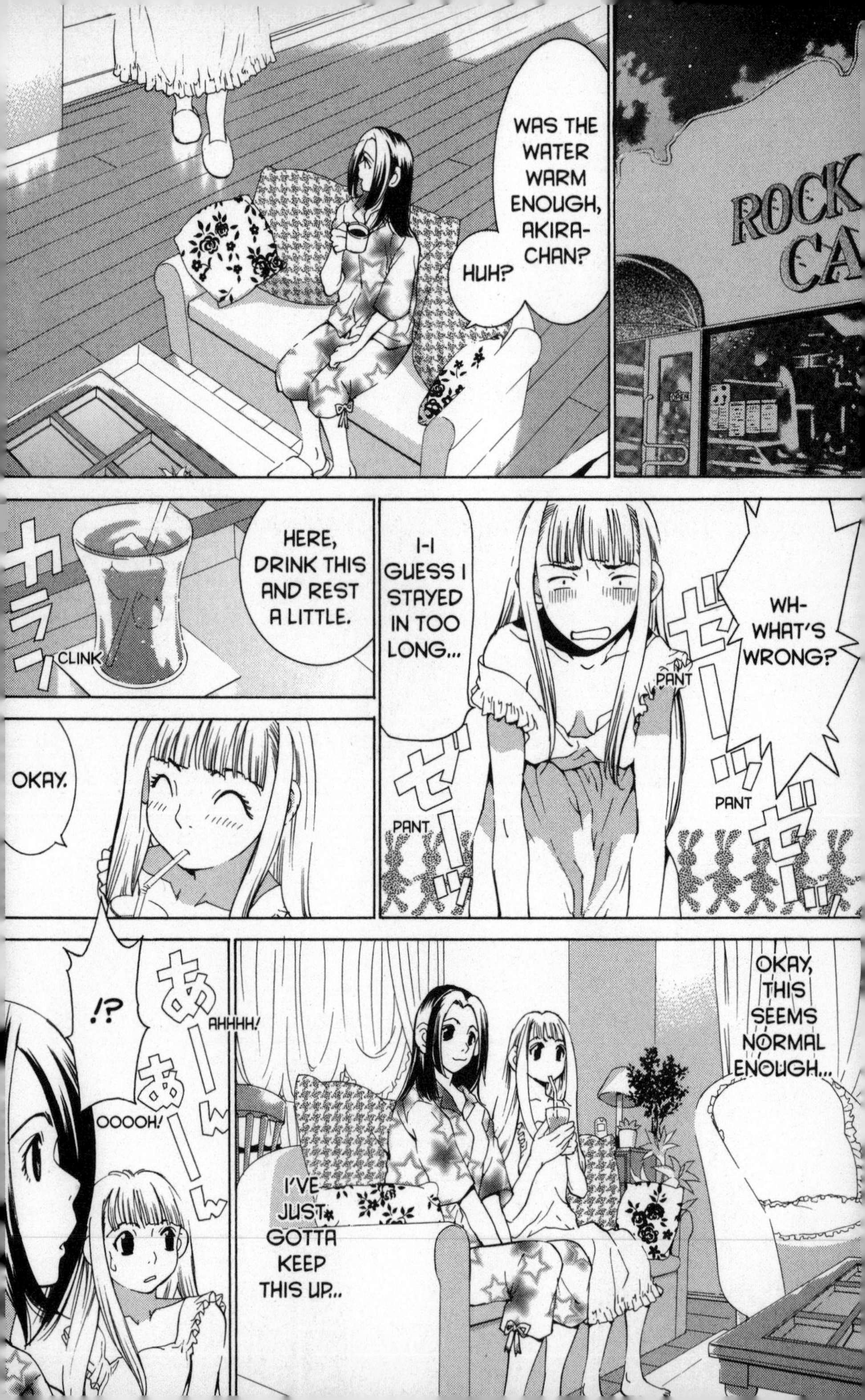
WAS THE WATER WARM ENOUGH, AKIRA-CHAN?
HUH?
WH-WHAT'S WRONG?
ぜーッ ぜーッ ぜー
PANT
PANT
PANT
I-I GUESS I STAYED IN TOO LONG...
HERE, DRINK THIS AND REST A LITTLE.
カラン
CLINK
OKAY.
OKAY, THIS SEEMS NORMAL ENOUGH...
I'VE JUST GOTTA KEEP THIS UP...
あーん
AHHHH!
あーん
OOOOH!
!?

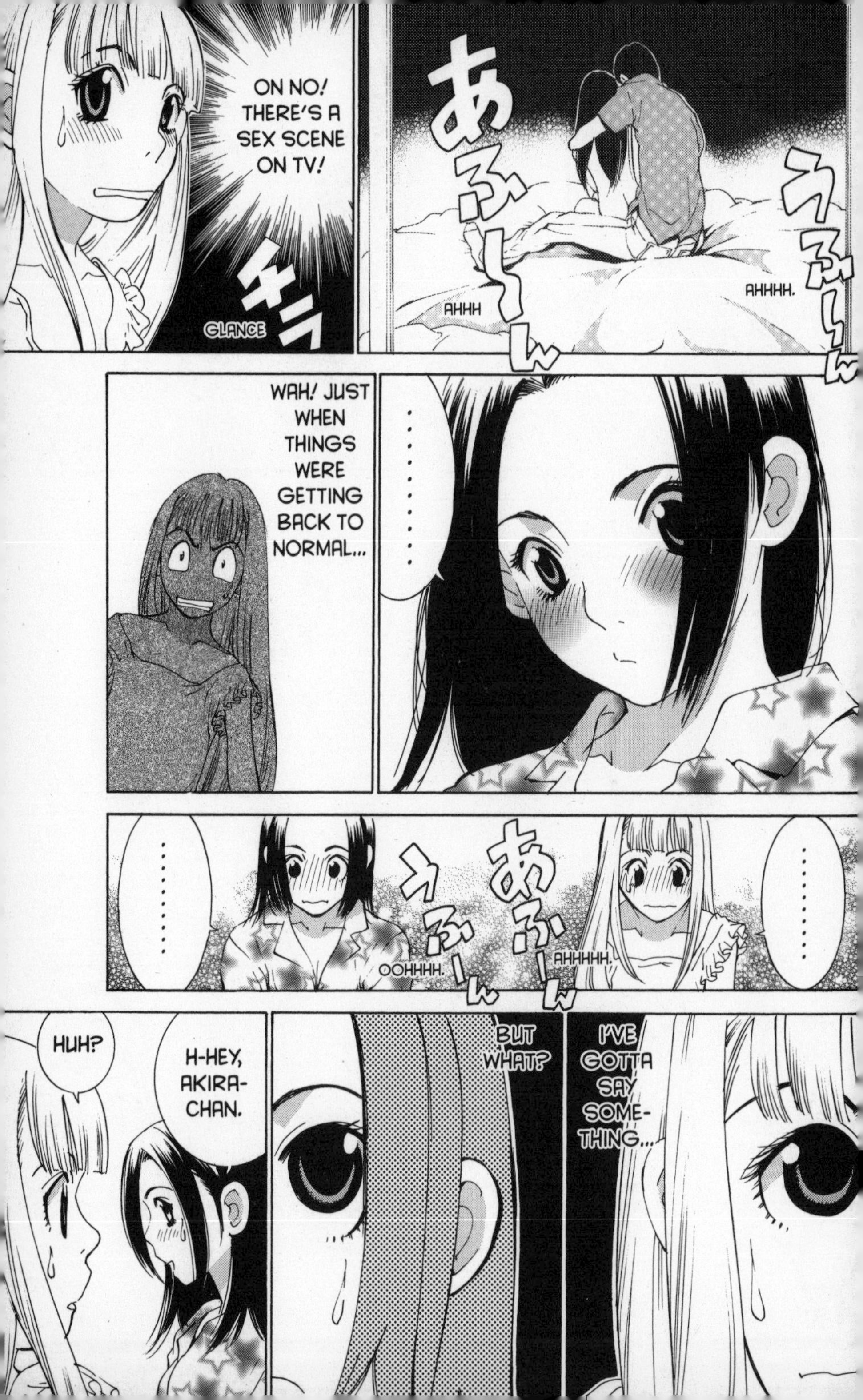
うふ〜〜ん
AHHHH.
あふ〜ん
AHHH
ON NO! THERE'S A SEX SCENE ON TV!
チラ
GLANCE
......
WAH! JUST WHEN THINGS WERE GETTING BACK TO NORMAL...
......
あふ〜ん
AHHHHH.
うふ〜ん
OOHHHH.
......
I'VE GOTTA SAY SOMETHING...
BUT WHAT?
H-HEY, AKIRA-CHAN.
HUH?

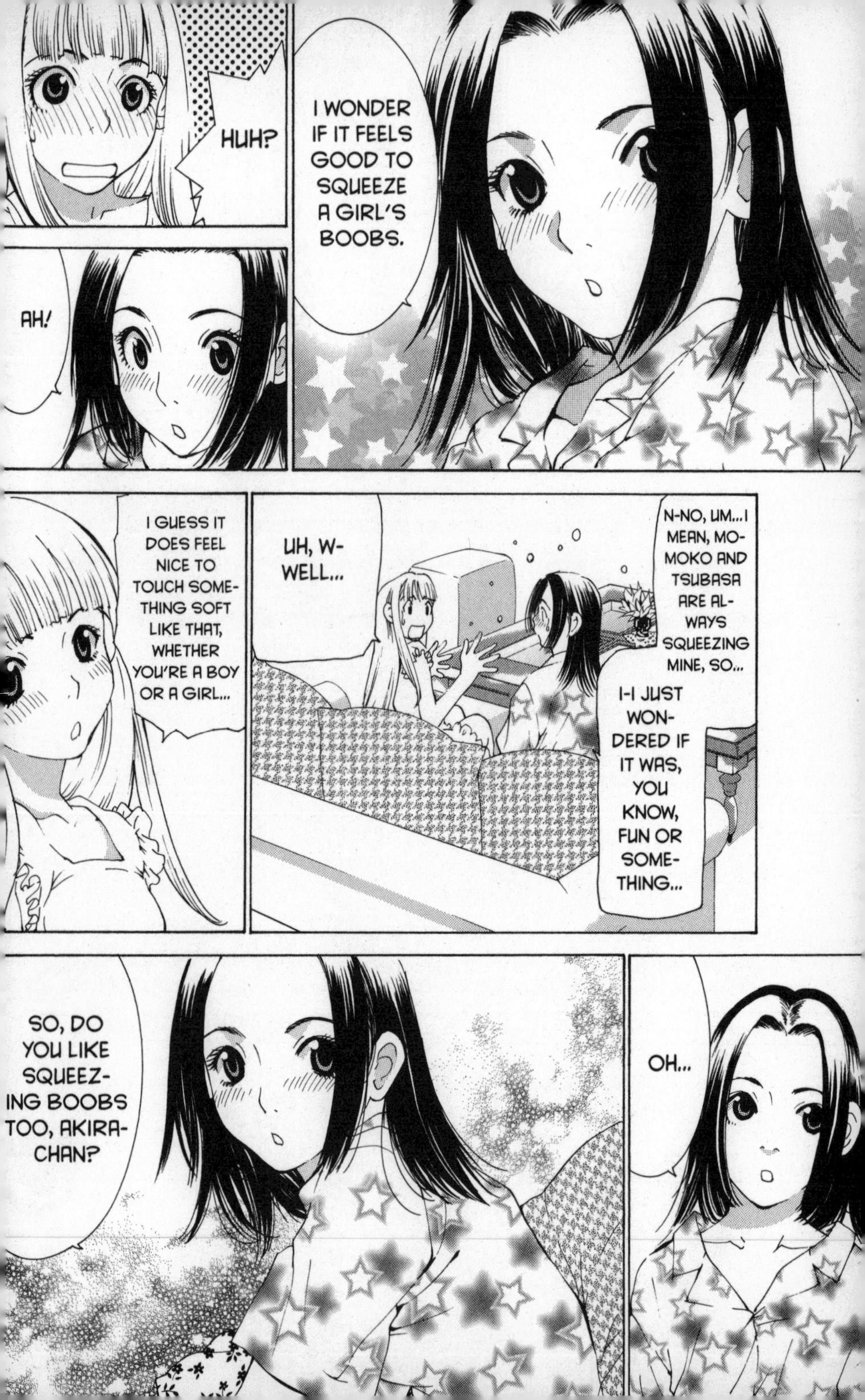
I WONDER IF IT FEELS GOOD TO SQUEEZE A GIRL'S BOOBS.
HUH?
AH!
N-NO, UM...I MEAN, MOMOKO AND TSUBASA ARE ALWAYS SQUEEZING MINE, SO...
I-I JUST WONDERED IF IT WAS, YOU KNOW, FUN OR SOMETHING...
UH, W-WELL...
I GUESS IT DOES FEEL NICE TO TOUCH SOMETHING SOFT LIKE THAT, WHETHER YOU'RE A BOY OR A GIRL...
OH...
SO, DO YOU LIKE SQUEEZING BOOBS TOO, AKIRA-CHAN?

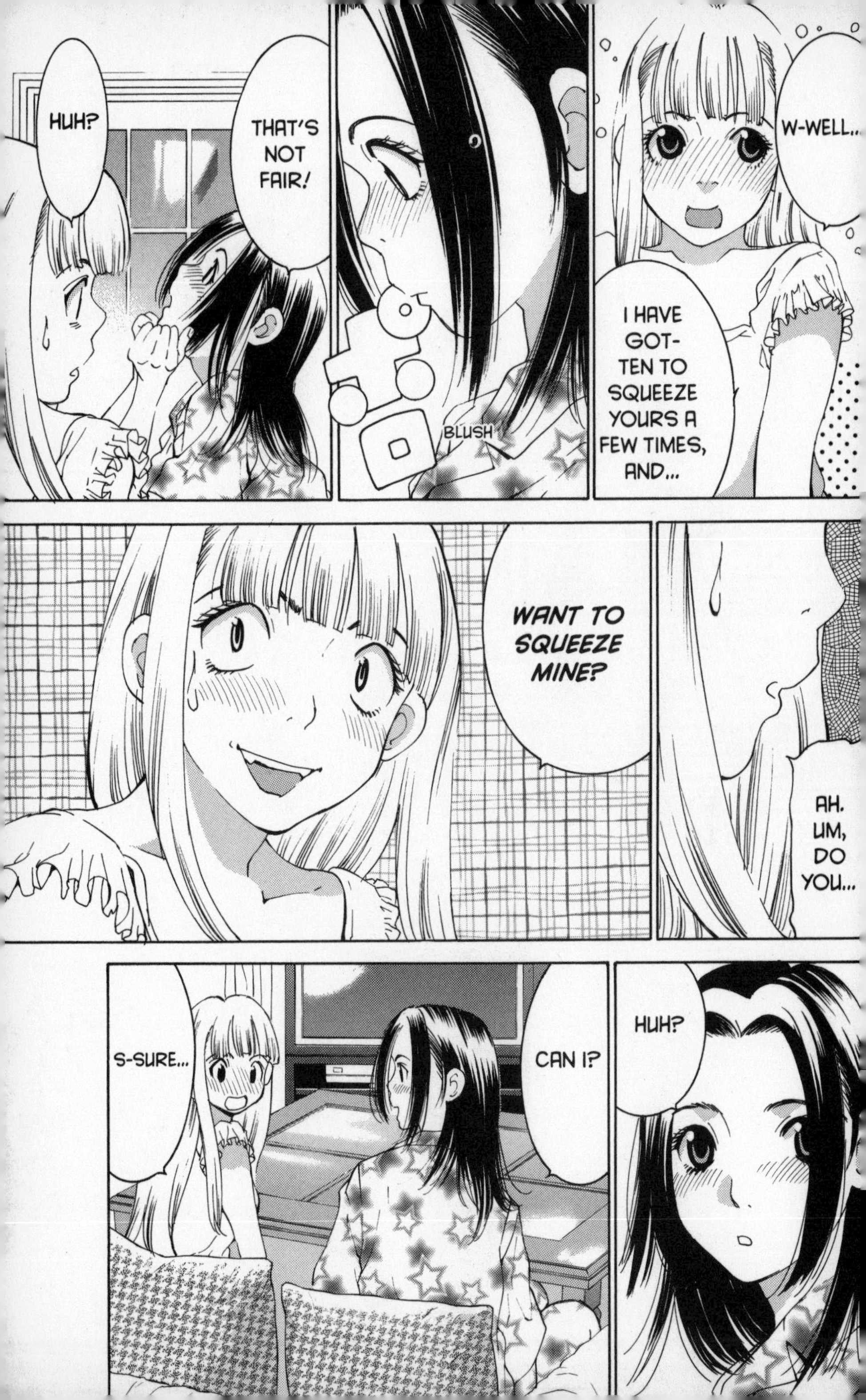
W-WELL...
I HAVE GOT-TEN TO SQUEEZE YOURS A FEW TIMES, AND...
BLUSH
THAT'S NOT FAIR!
HUH?
AH. UM, DO YOU...
WANT TO SQUEEZE MINE?
HUH?
CAN I?
S-SURE...

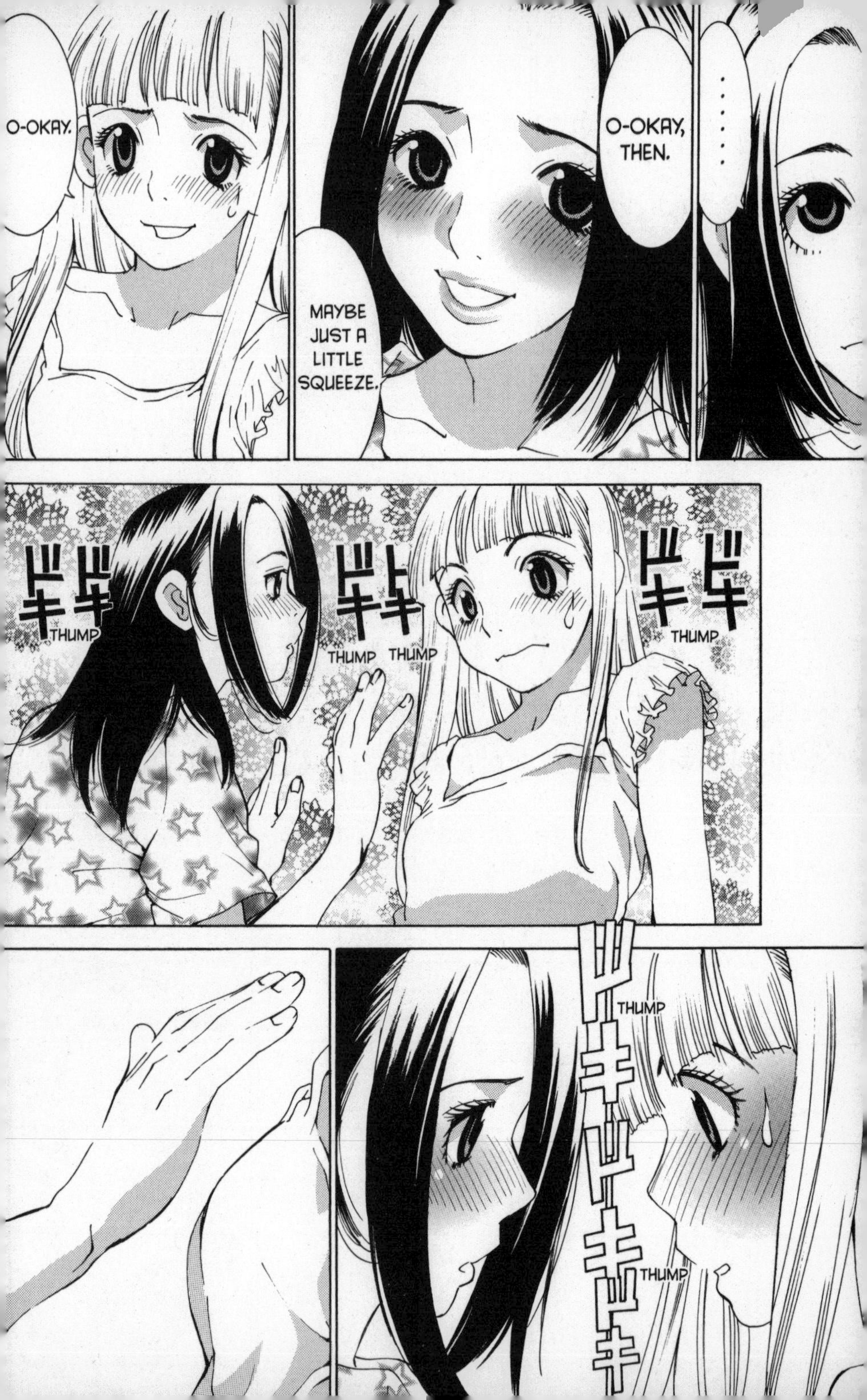
……
O-OKAY, THEN.
MAYBE JUST A LITTLE SQUEEZE.
O-OKAY.
ドキドキ
THUMP
ドキドキ
THUMP THUMP
ドキドキ
THUMP
ドキドキ
THUMP
ドキドキ
THUMP

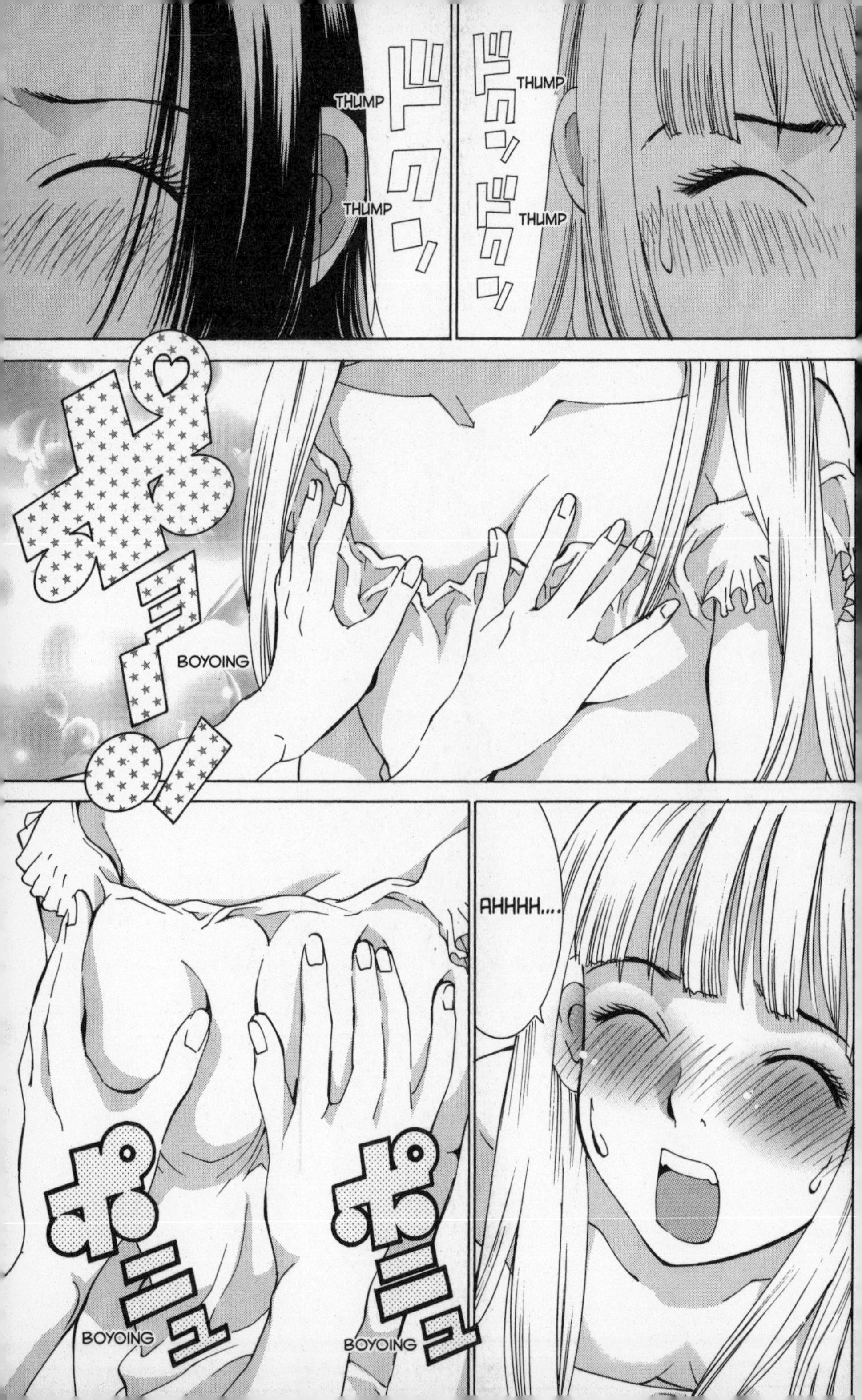
THUMP
THUMP
THUMP
THUMP
BOYOING
AHHHH....
BOYOING
BOYOING

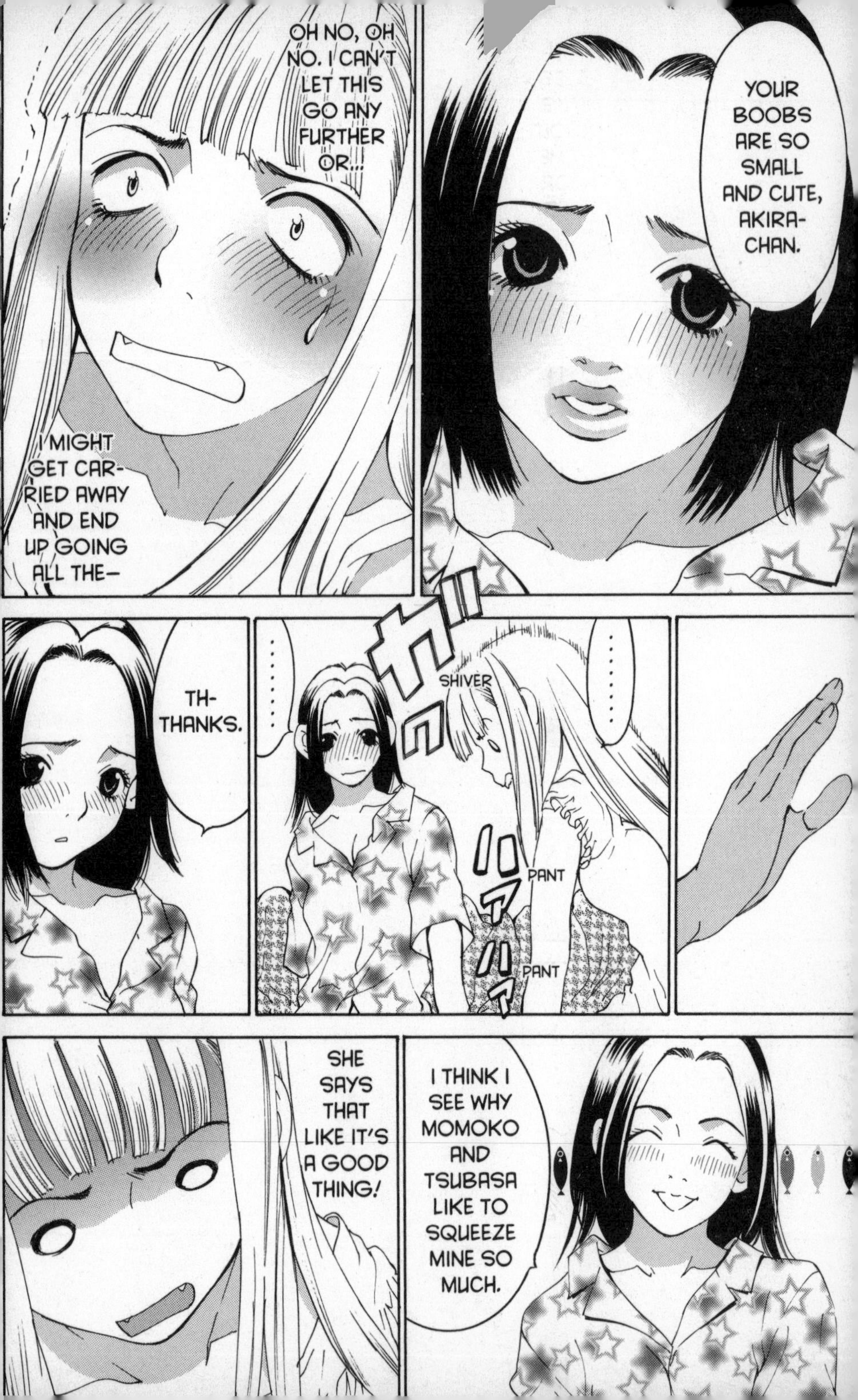
YOUR BOOBS ARE SO SMALL AND CUTE, AKIRA-CHAN.
OH NO, OH NO. I CAN'T LET THIS GO ANY FURTHER OR...
I MIGHT GET CAR-RIED AWAY AND END UP GOING ALL THE—
......
SHIVER
PANT
PANT
......
TH-THANKS.
I THINK I SEE WHY MOMOKO AND TSUBASA LIKE TO SQUEEZE MINE SO MUCH.
SHE SAYS THAT LIKE IT'S A GOOD THING!

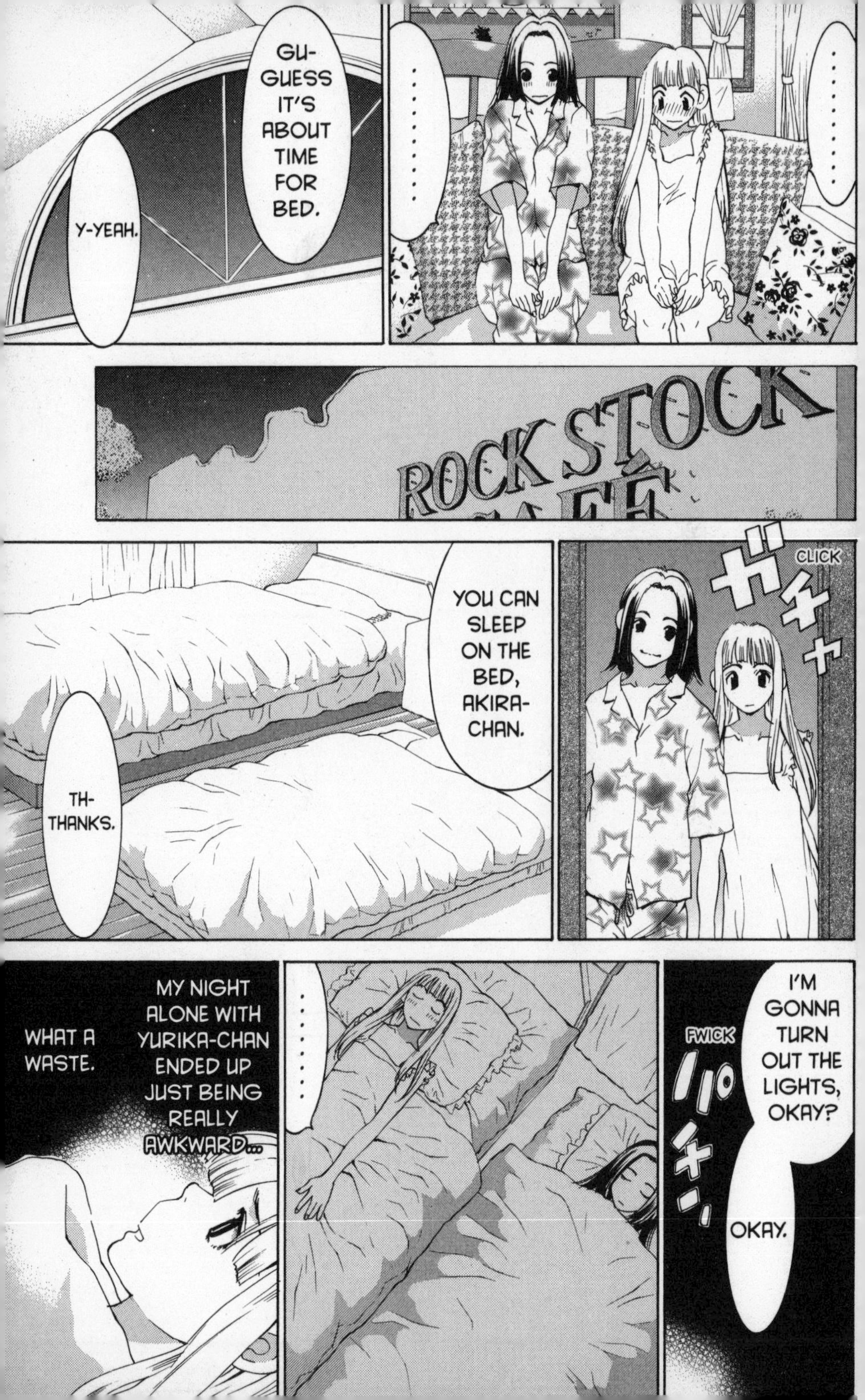
. . . .
. . . .
GU-GUESS IT'S ABOUT TIME FOR BED.
Y-YEAH.
ROCK STOCK
ガチャ
CLICK
YOU CAN SLEEP ON THE BED, AKIRA-CHAN.
TH-THANKS.
I'M GONNA TURN OUT THE LIGHTS, OKAY?
パチッ
FWICK
OKAY.
. . . .
MY NIGHT ALONE WITH YURIKA-CHAN ENDED UP JUST BEING REALLY AWKWARD...
WHAT A WASTE.

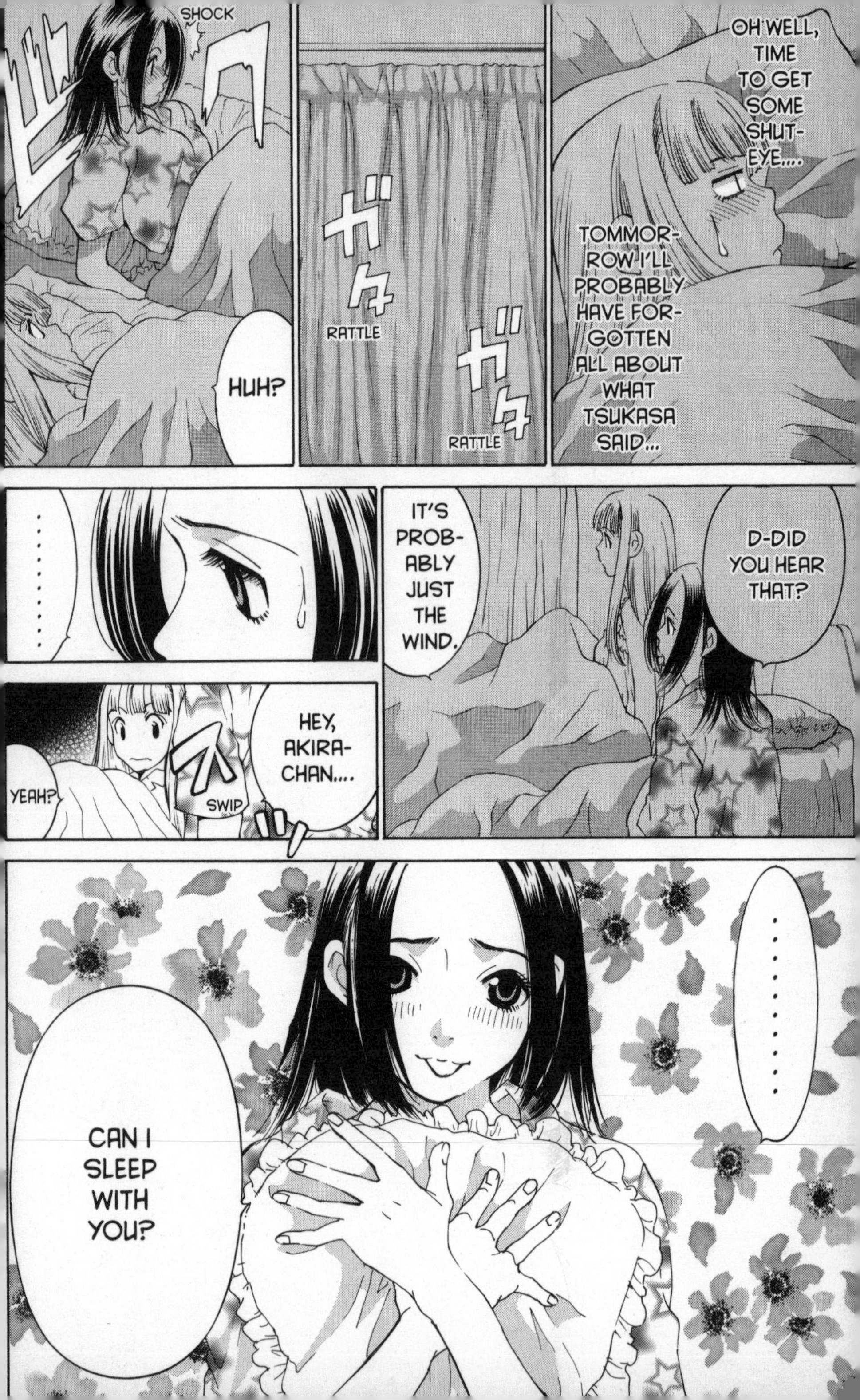

OH WELL, TIME TO GET SOME SHUT-EYE....
TOMMOR-ROW I'LL PROBABLY HAVE FOR-GOTTEN ALL ABOUT WHAT TSUKASA SAID...
RATTLE
RATTLE
SHOCK
HUH?
D-DID YOU HEAR THAT?
IT'S PROB-ABLY JUST THE WIND.
....
HEY, AKIRA-CHAN....
SWIP
YEAH?
....
CAN I SLEEP WITH YOU?

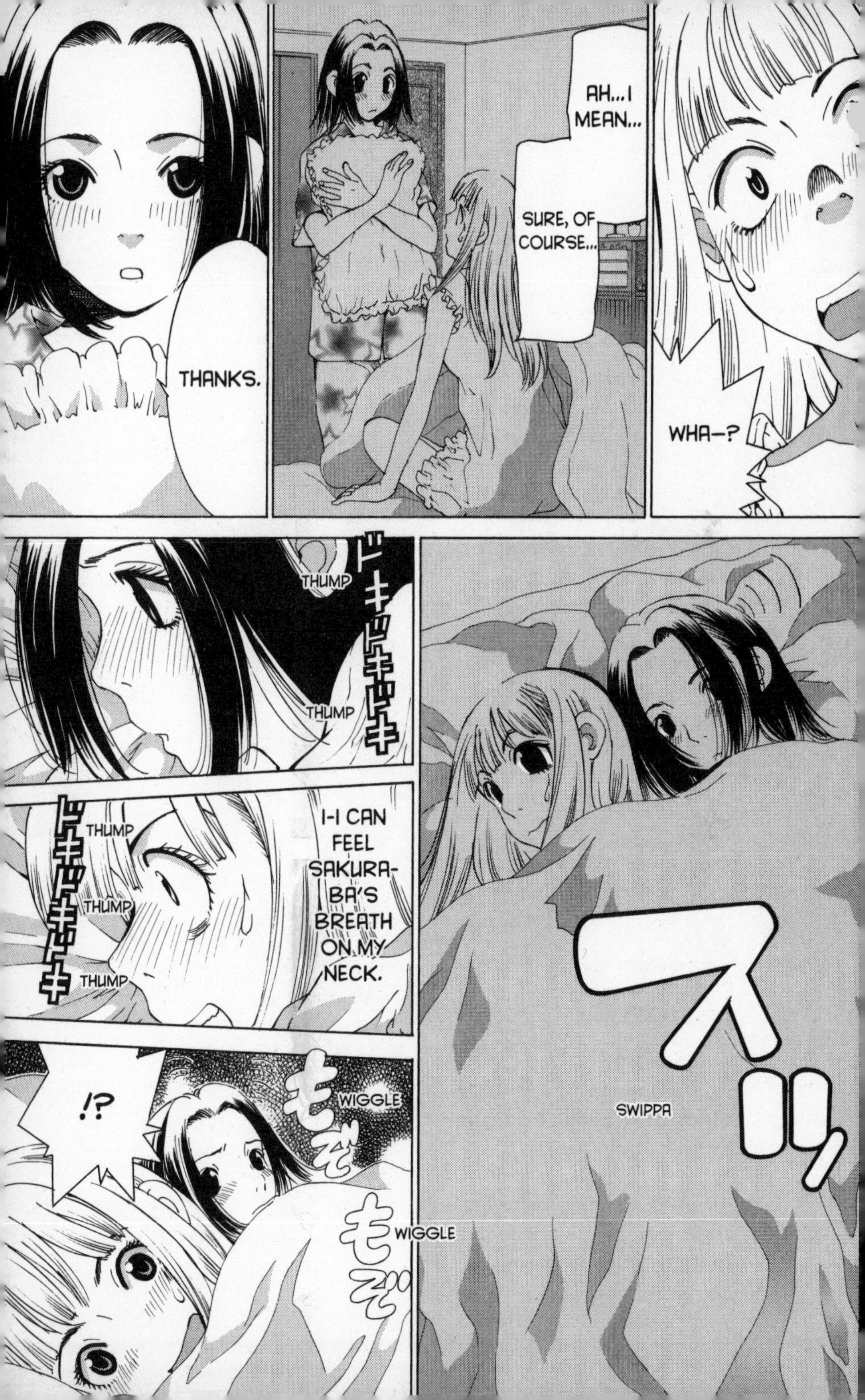

WHA-?
AH...I MEAN...
SURE, OF COURSE...
THANKS.
スッ
SWIPPA
ドキッドキッドキ
THUMP
THUMP
ドキドキドキドキ
THUMP
THUMP
THUMP
I-I CAN FEEL SAKURA-BA'S BREATH ON MY NECK.
!?
もぞ
WIGGLE
もぞ
WIGGLE

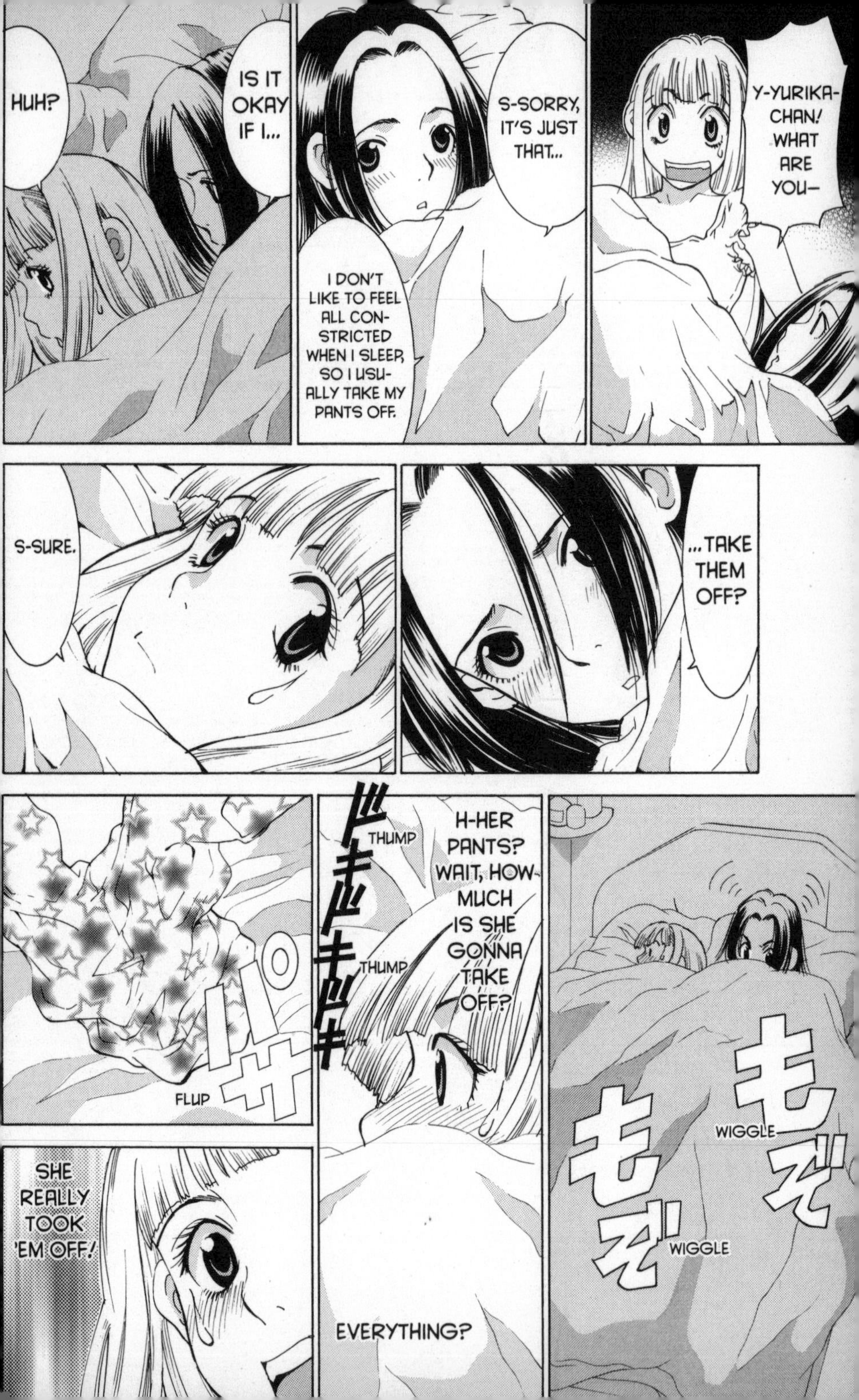
Y-YURIKA-CHAN! WHAT ARE YOU—
S-SORRY, IT'S JUST THAT...
I DON'T LIKE TO FEEL ALL CONSTRICTED WHEN I SLEEP, SO I USUALLY TAKE MY PANTS OFF.
IS IT OKAY IF I...
HUH?
...TAKE THEM OFF?
S-SURE.
もぞもぞ
WIGGLE
WIGGLE
THUMP
THUMP
H-HER PANTS? WAIT, HOW MUCH IS SHE GONNA TAKE OFF?
EVERYTHING?
FLUP
SHE REALLY TOOK 'EM OFF!

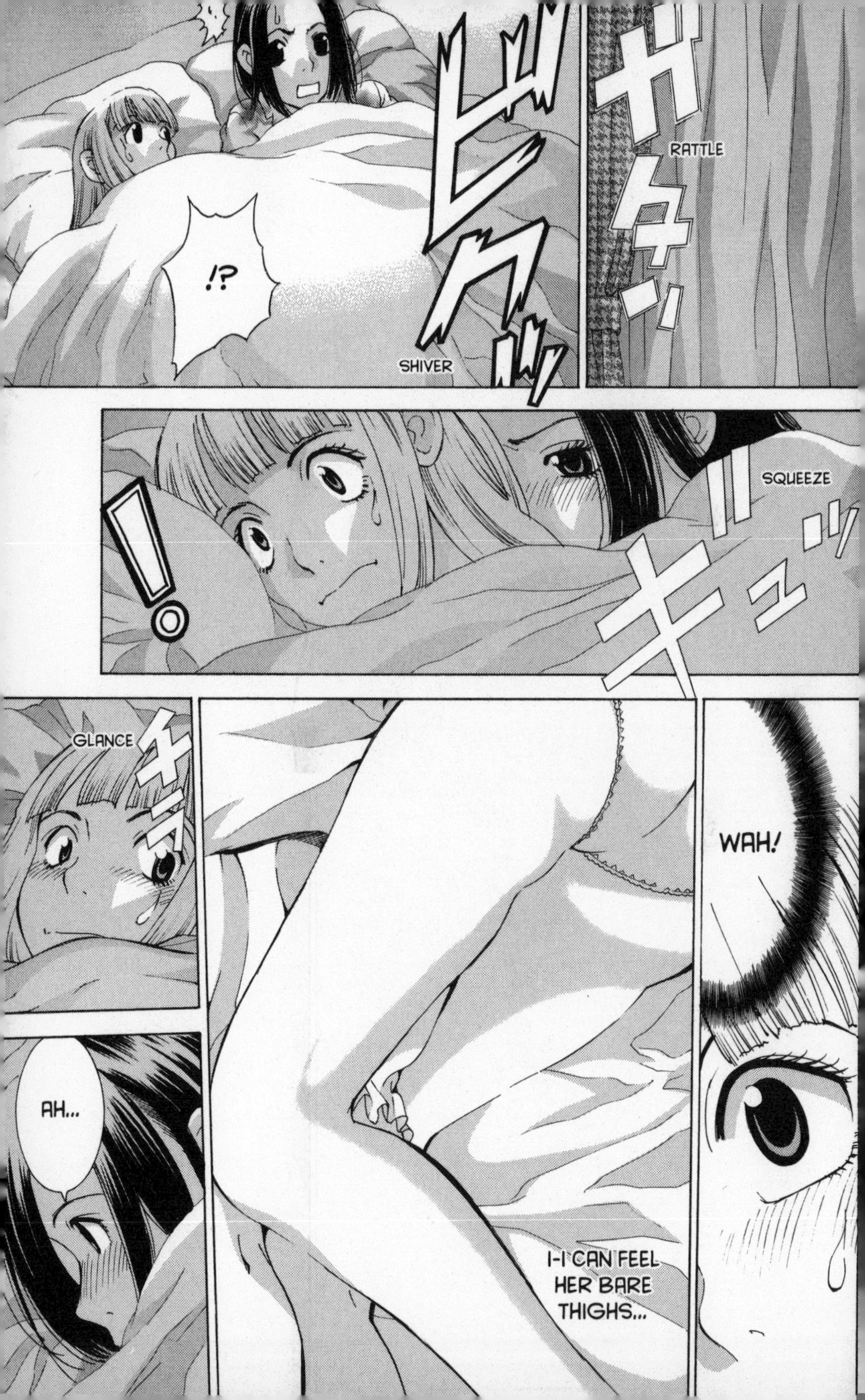
RATTLE
SHIVER
!?
SQUEEZE
WAH!
I-I CAN FEEL HER BARE THIGHS...
GLANCE
AH...

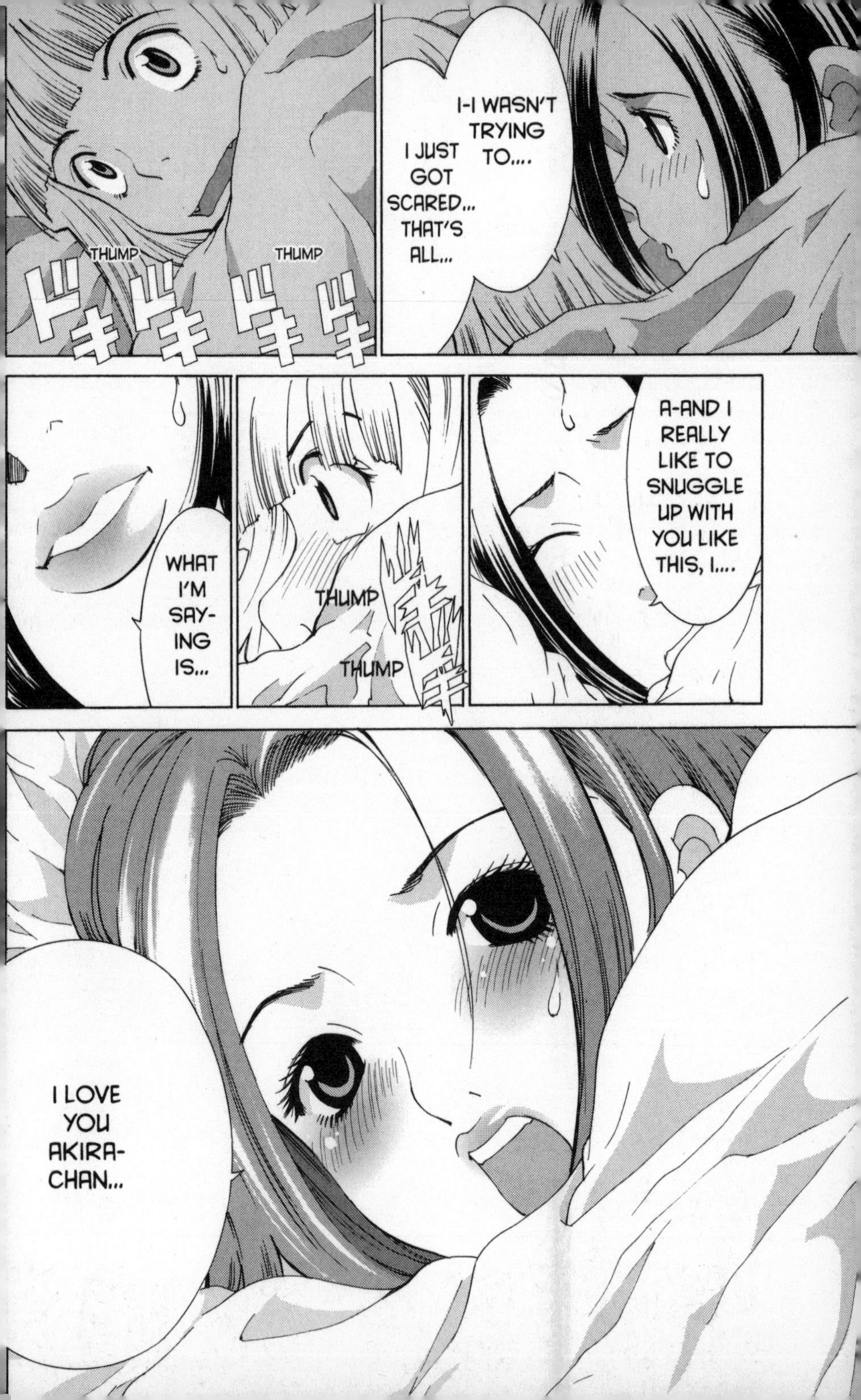
I-I WASN'T TRYING TO....
I JUST GOT SCARED... THAT'S ALL...
THUMP
THUMP
ドキドキドキドキ
A-AND I REALLY LIKE TO SNUGGLE UP WITH YOU LIKE THIS, I....
THUMP
THUMP
WHAT I'M SAY-ING IS...
I LOVE YOU AKIRA-CHAN...

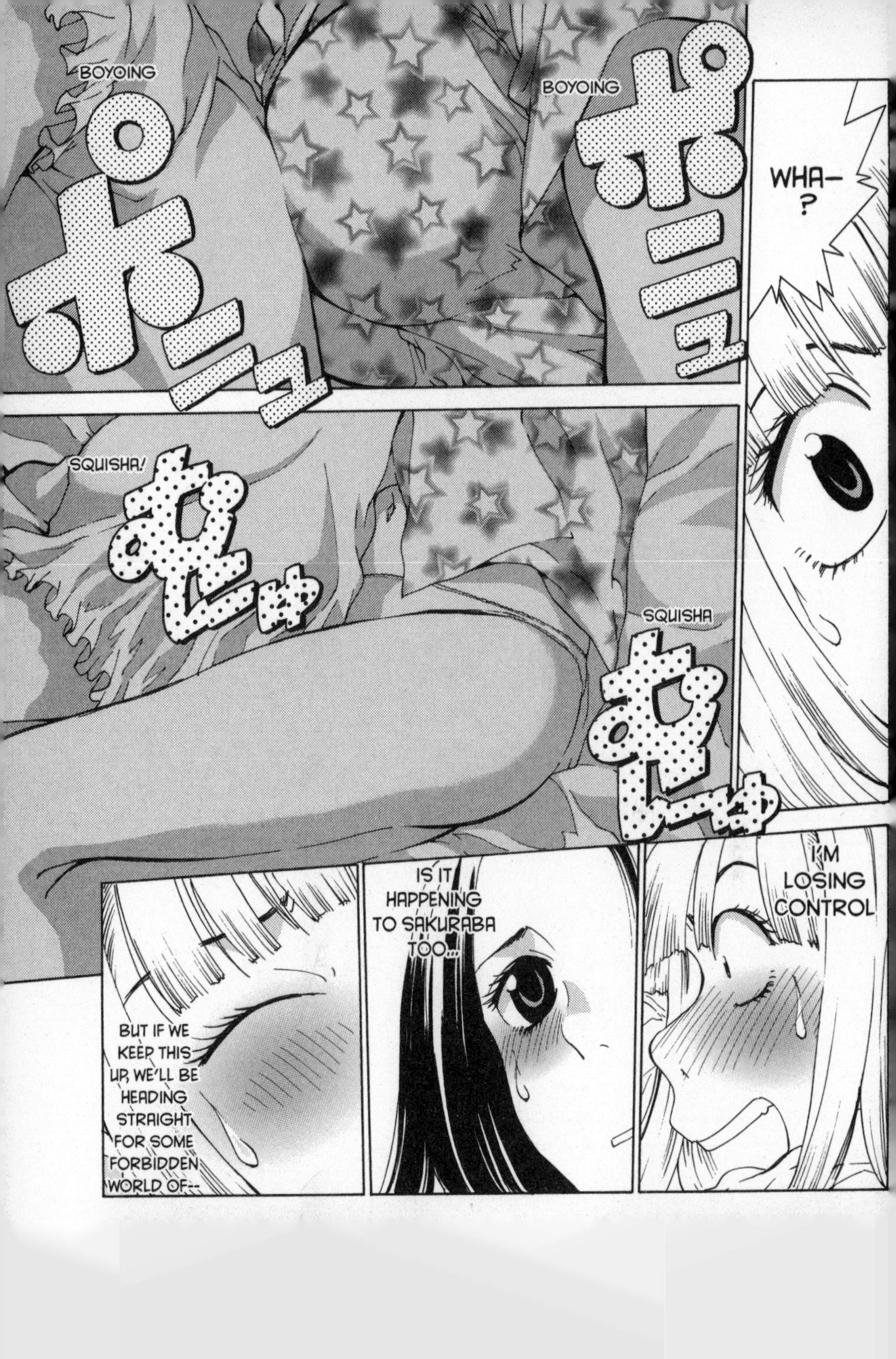
WHA—?
BOYOING
BOYOING
SQUISHA
SQUISHA!
I'M LOSING CONTROL
IS IT HAPPENING TO SAKURABA TOO...
BUT IF WE KEEP THIS UP, WE'LL BE HEADING STRAIGHT FOR SOME FORBIDDEN WORLD OF--

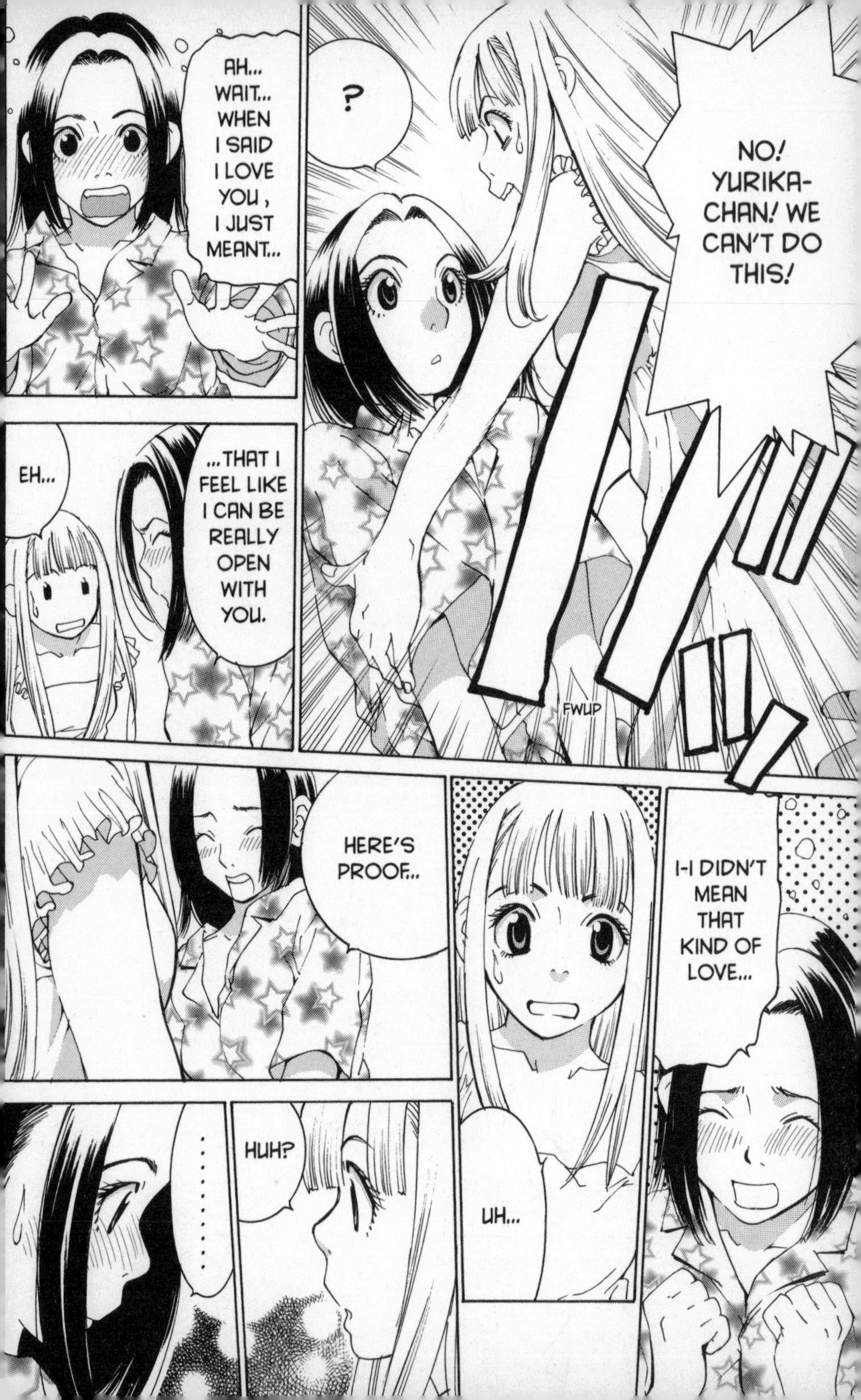
NO! YURIKA-CHAN! WE CAN'T DO THIS!
?
FWUP
AH... WAIT... WHEN I SAID I LOVE YOU, I JUST MEANT...
...THAT I FEEL LIKE I CAN BE REALLY OPEN WITH YOU.
EH...
I-I DIDN'T MEAN THAT KIND OF LOVE...
UH...
HERE'S PROOF...
HUH?
......

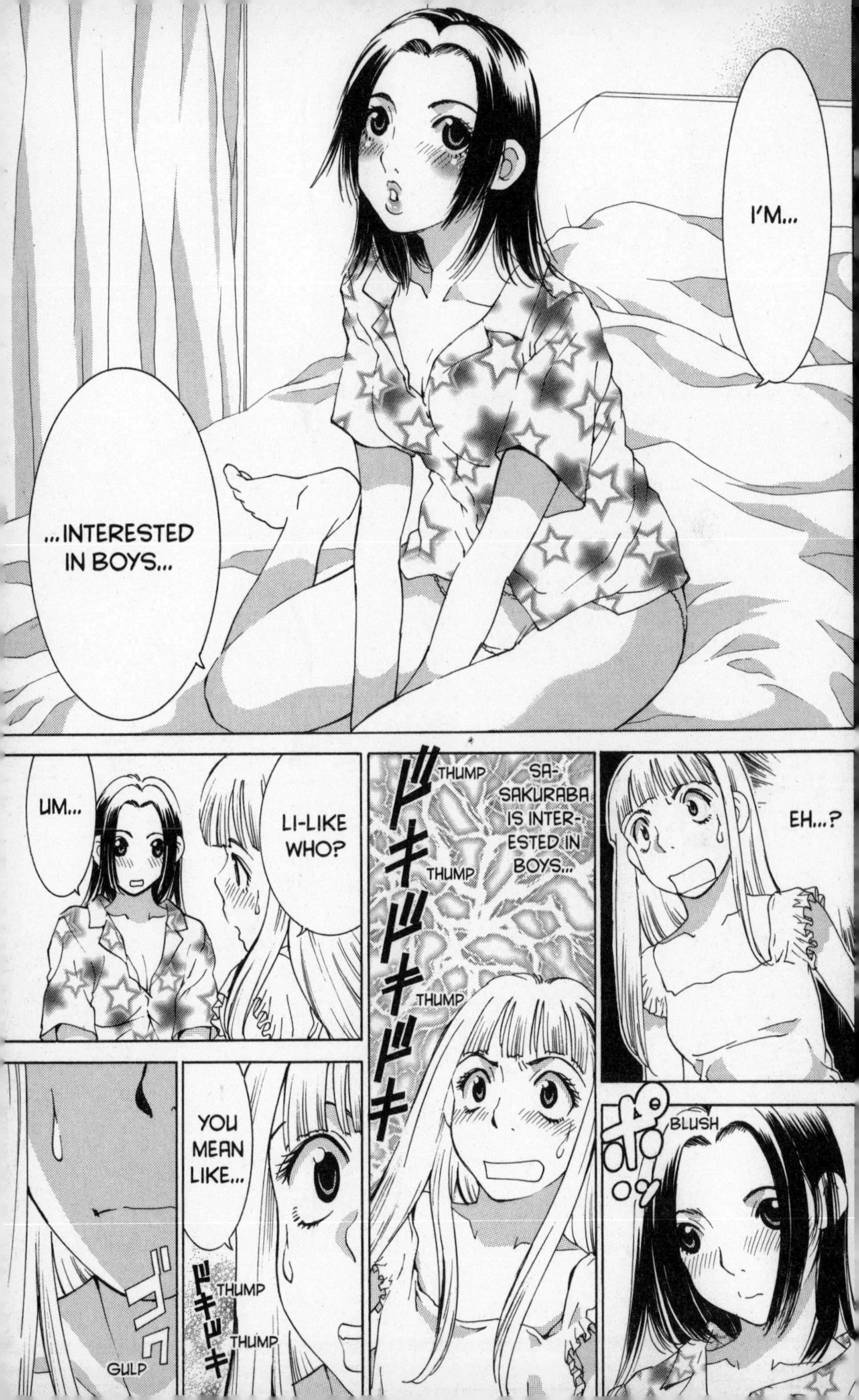
I'M...
...INTERESTED IN BOYS...
EH...?
BLUSH
THUMP
SA-SAKURABA IS INTER-ESTED IN BOYS...
THUMP
THUMP
LI-LIKE WHO?
UM...
YOU MEAN LIKE...
THUMP
THUMP
GULP

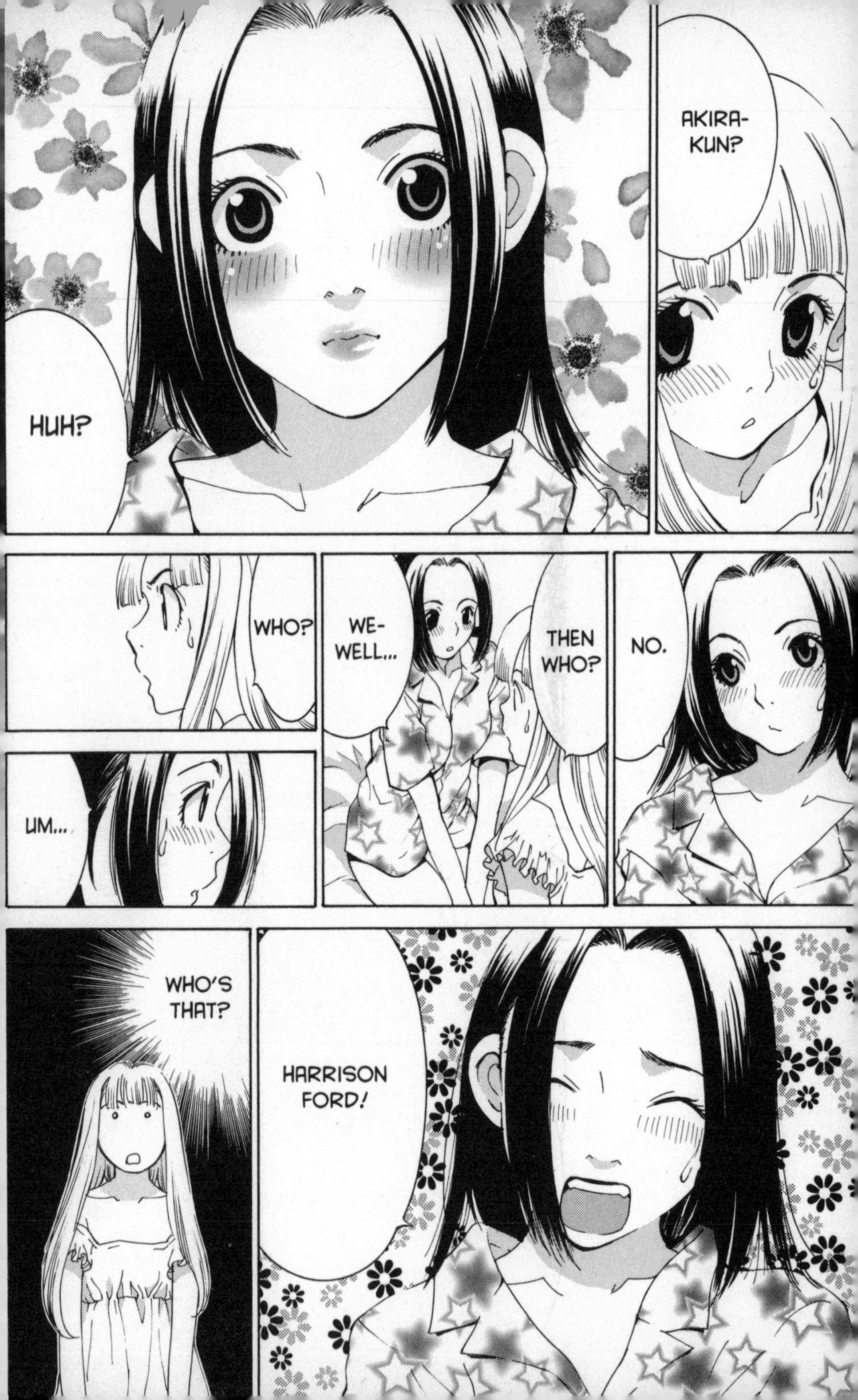
AKIRA-KUN?
HUH?
NO.
THEN WHO?
WE-WELL...
WHO?
UM...
HARRISON FORD!
WHO'S THAT?

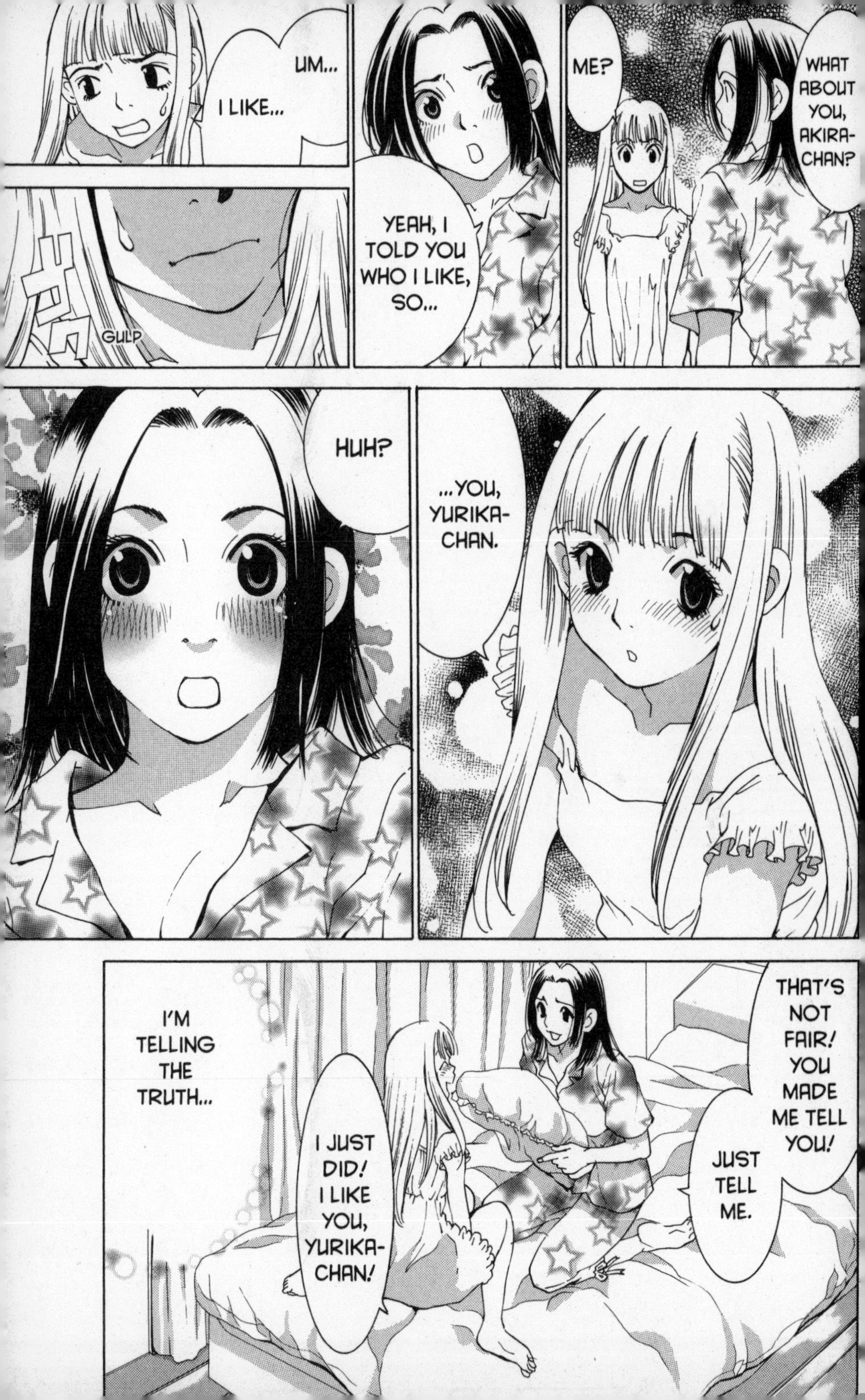

WHAT ABOUT YOU, AKIRA-CHAN?
ME?
YEAH, I TOLD YOU WHO I LIKE, SO...
UM...
I LIKE...
GULP
...YOU, YURIKA-CHAN.
HUH?
THAT'S NOT FAIR! YOU MADE ME TELL YOU!
JUST TELL ME.
I JUST DID! I LIKE YOU, YURIKA-CHAN!
I'M TELLING THE TRUTH...

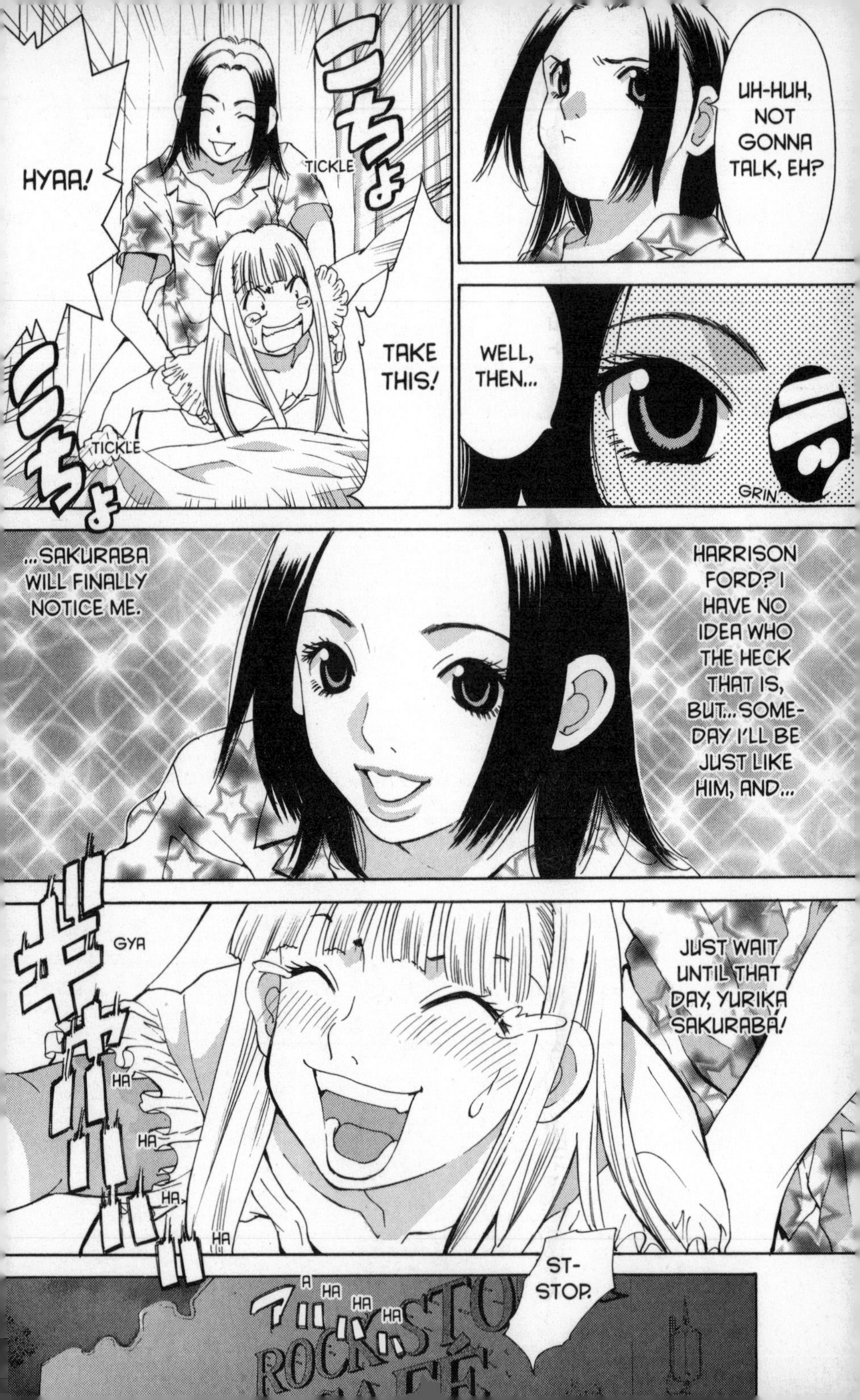
UH-HUH, NOT GONNA TALK, EH?
WELL, THEN...
GRIN
TAKE THIS!
こちょ
TICKLE
HYAA!
こちょ
TICKLE
HARRISON FORD? I HAVE NO IDEA WHO THE HECK THAT IS, BUT... SOMEDAY I'LL BE JUST LIKE HIM, AND...
...SAKURABA WILL FINALLY NOTICE ME.
JUST WAIT UNTIL THAT DAY, YURIKA SAKURABA!
GYA
HA
HA
HA
HA
ST-STOP.
A
HA
HA
HA

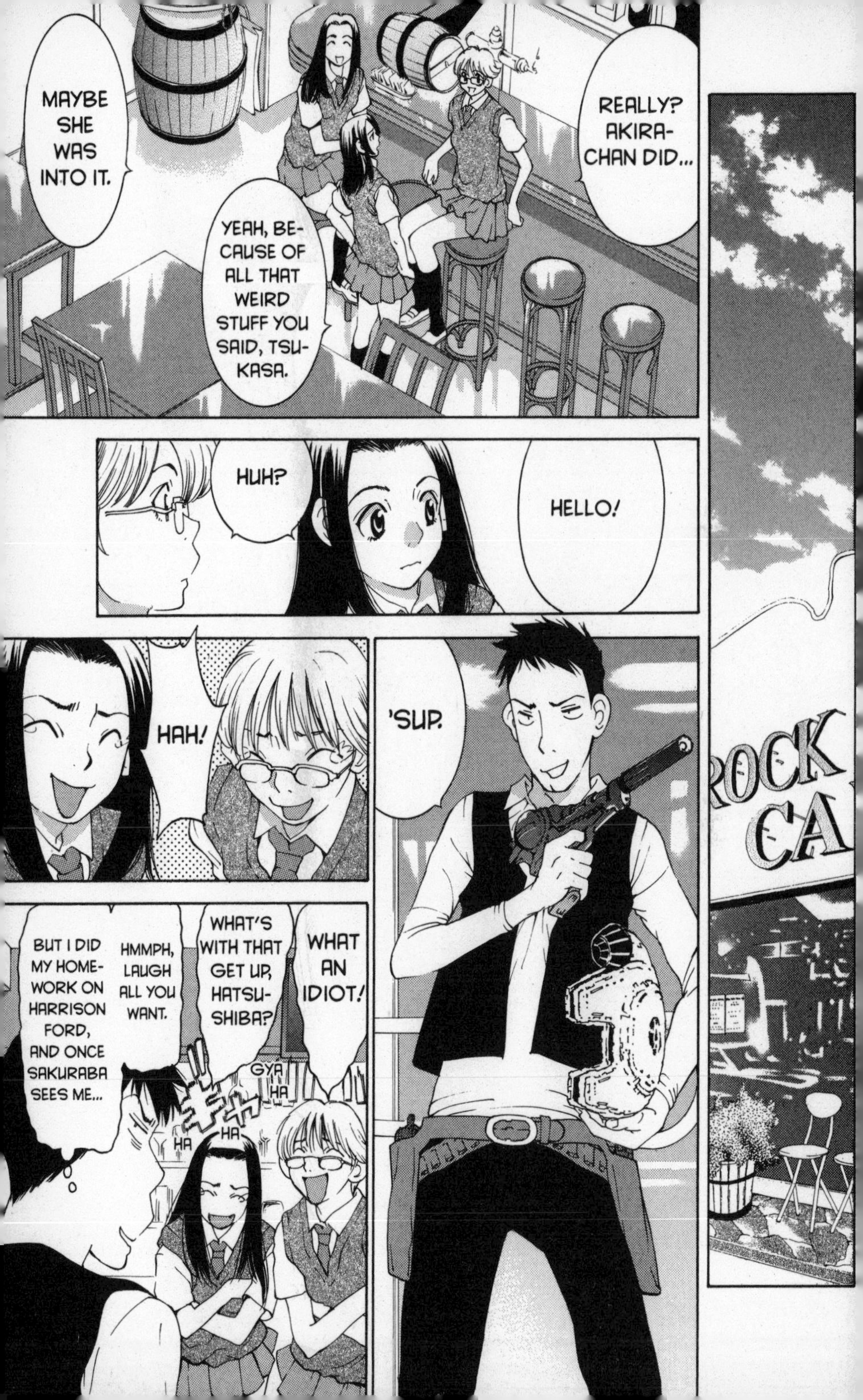
ROCK CA
REALLY? AKIRA-CHAN DID...
YEAH, BE-CAUSE OF ALL THAT WEIRD STUFF YOU SAID, TSU-KASA.
MAYBE SHE WAS INTO IT.
HELLO!
HUH?
'SUP.
HAH!
WHAT AN IDIOT!
WHAT'S WITH THAT GET UP, HATSU-SHIBA?
GYA HA
HA
HA
HMMPH, LAUGH ALL YOU WANT.
BUT I DID MY HOME-WORK ON HARRISON FORD, AND ONCE SAKURABA SEES ME...

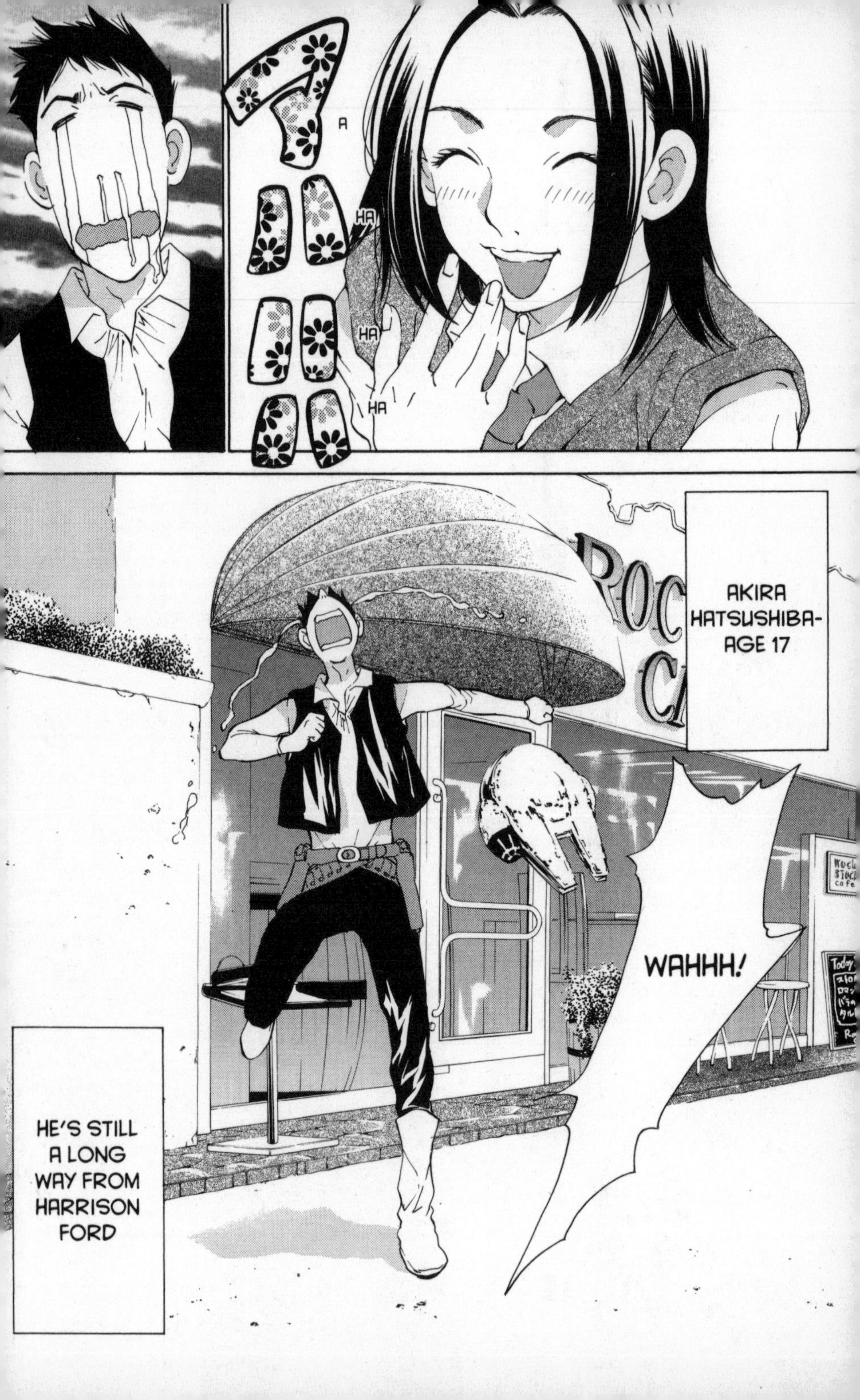
A
HA
HA
HA
AKIRA HATSUSHIBA-AGE 17
WAHHH!
HE'S STILL A LONG WAY FROM HARRISON FORD

Gacha Gacha

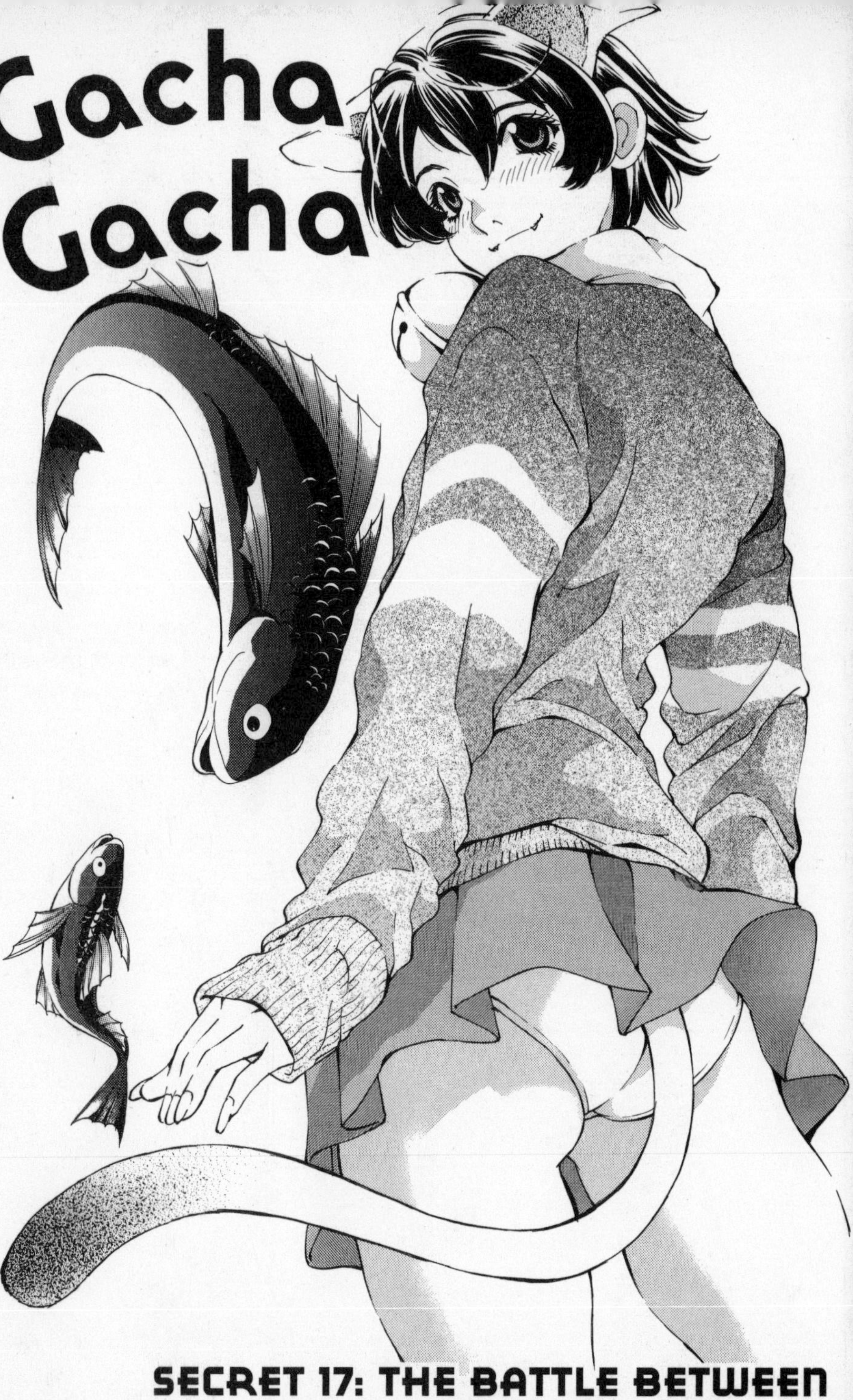

SECRET 17: THE BATTLE BETWEEN MAN AND WOMAN

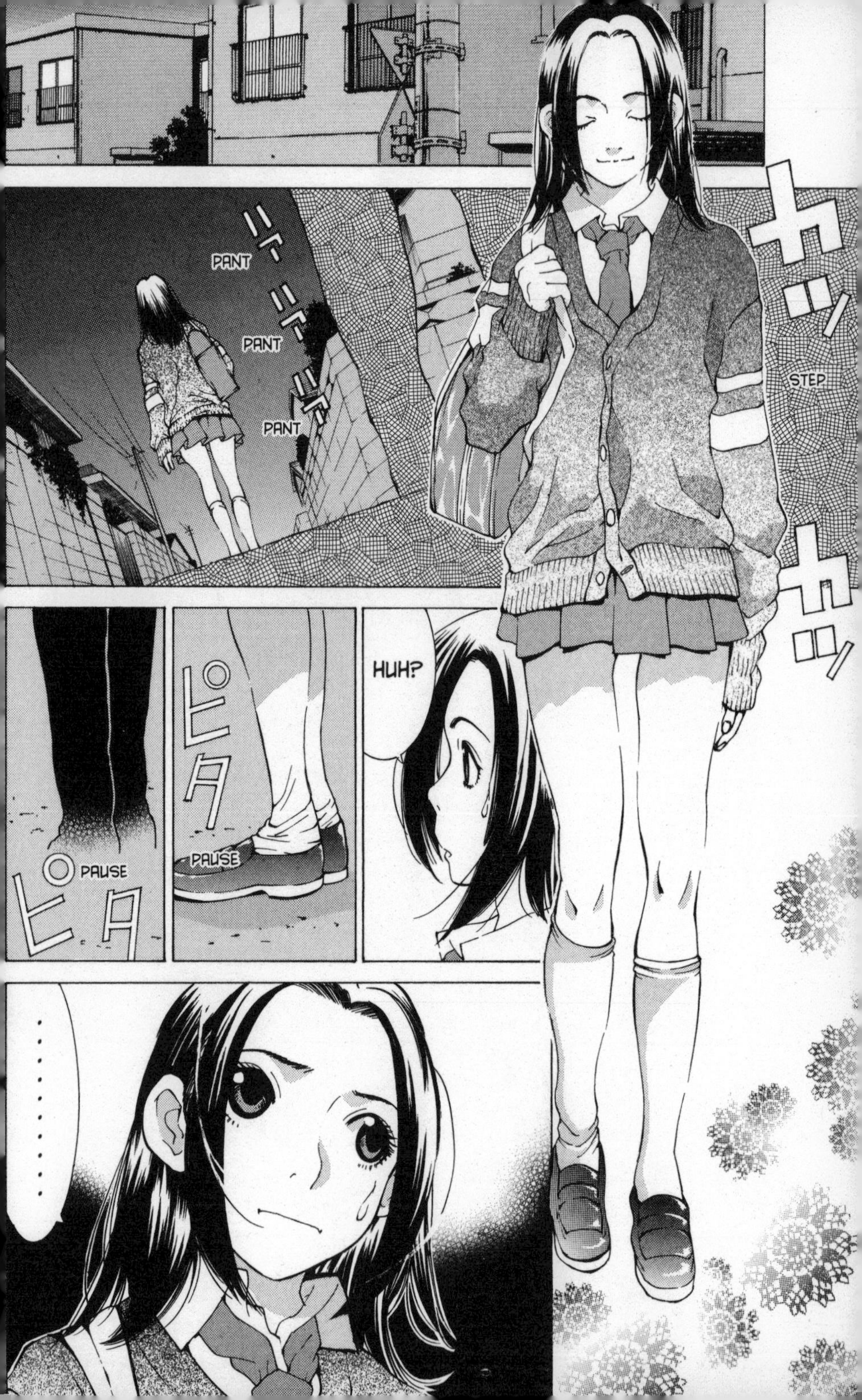
カッ
STEP
カッ
ハァ ハァ ハァ
PANT
PANT
PANT
HUH?
ピタ
PAUSE
ピタ
PAUSE
......

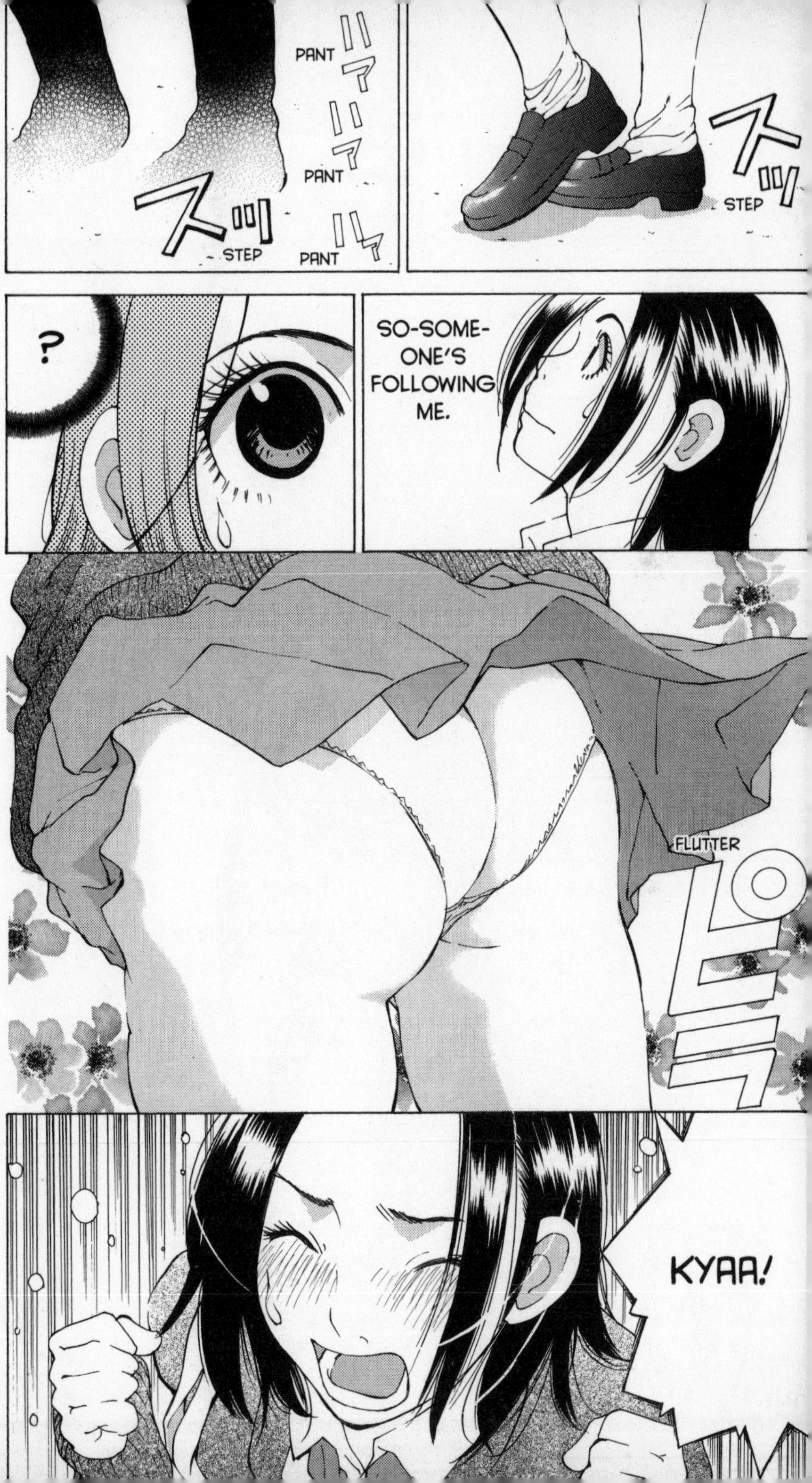
STEP
PANT
PANT
STEP
PANT
SO-SOME-ONE'S FOLLOWING ME.
?
FLUTTER
KYAA!

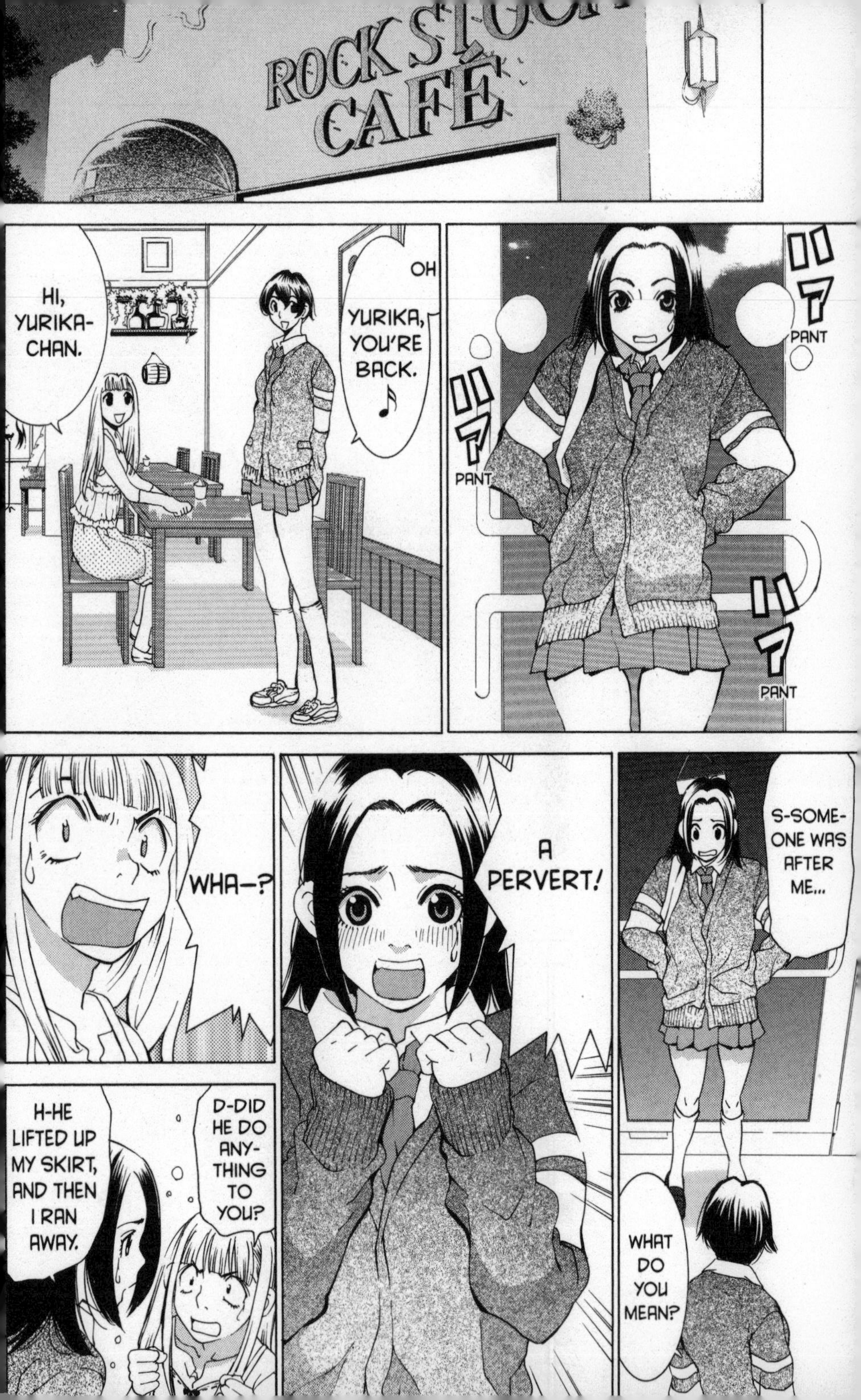
ROCK
CAFÉ
ハァ
PANT
ハァ
PANT
ハァ
PANT
OH
YURIKA, YOU'RE BACK. ♪
HI, YURIKA-CHAN.
S-SOMEONE WAS AFTER ME...
WHAT DO YOU MEAN?
A PERVERT!
WHA-?
D-DID HE DO ANYTHING TO YOU?
H-HE LIFTED UP MY SKIRT, AND THEN I RAN AWAY.

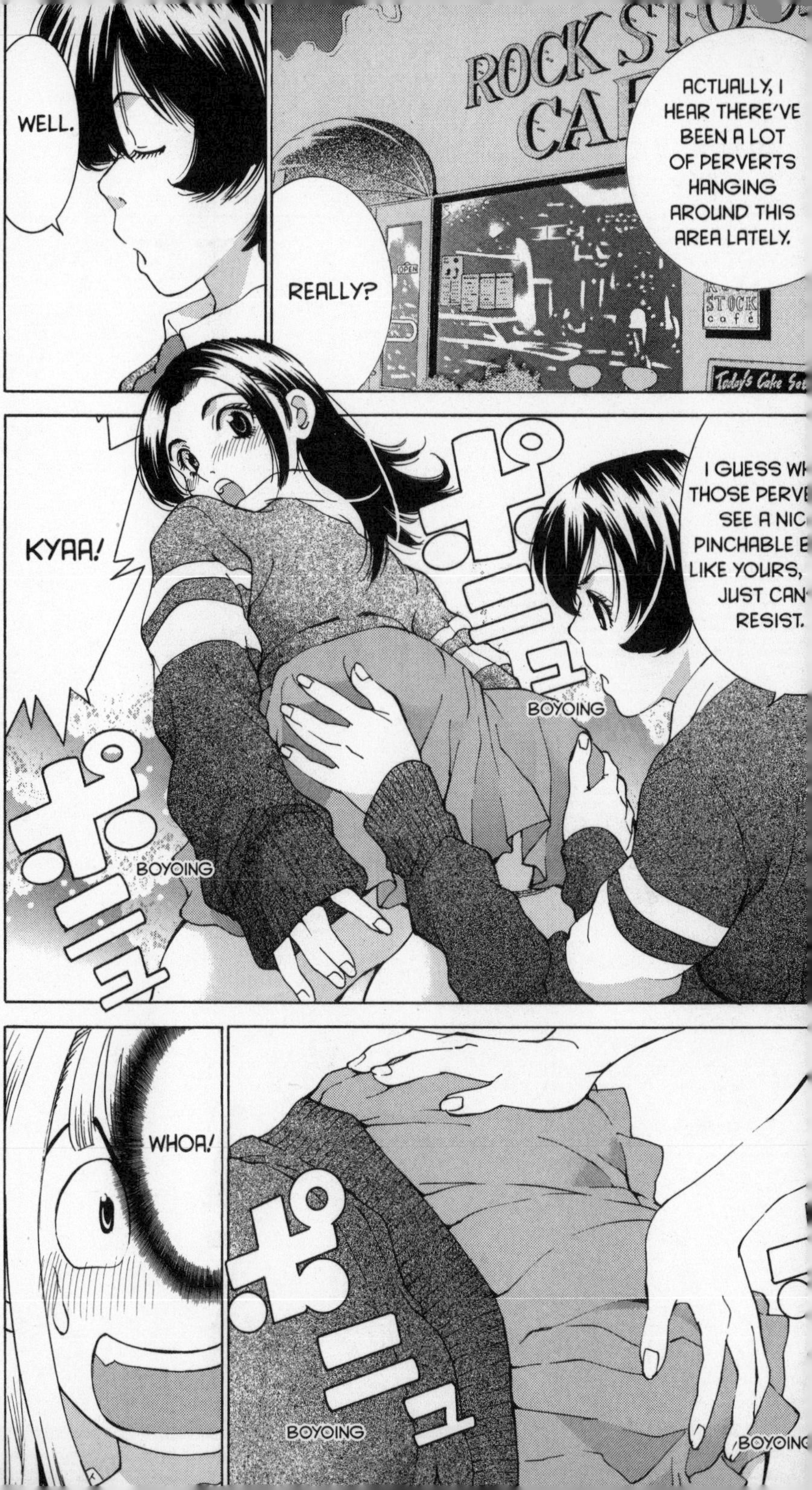
ACTUALLY, I HEAR THERE'VE BEEN A LOT OF PERVERTS HANGING AROUND THIS AREA LATELY.
ROCK STO CA
REALLY?
WELL.
I GUESS WH THOSE PERVE SEE A NIC PINCHABLE B LIKE YOURS, JUST CAN RESIST.
KYAA!
BOYOING
BOYOING
BOYOING
WHOA!
BOYOING

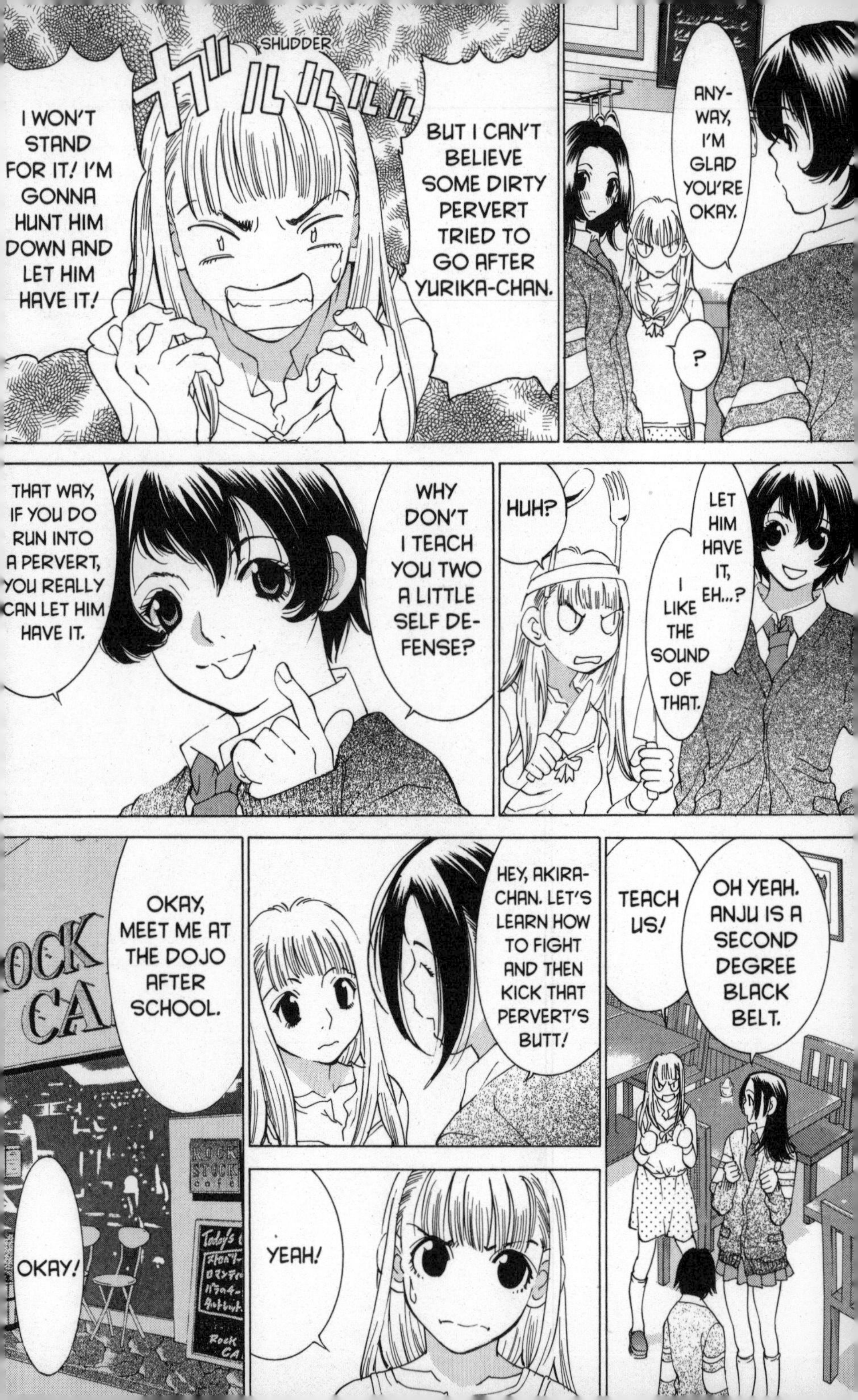
ANY-WAY, I'M GLAD YOU'RE OKAY.
?
SHUDDER
BUT I CAN'T BELIEVE SOME DIRTY PERVERT TRIED TO GO AFTER YURIKA-CHAN.
I WON'T STAND FOR IT! I'M GONNA HUNT HIM DOWN AND LET HIM HAVE IT!
LET HIM HAVE IT, EH...?
I LIKE THE SOUND OF THAT.
HUH?
WHY DON'T I TEACH YOU TWO A LITTLE SELF DE-FENSE?
THAT WAY, IF YOU DO RUN INTO A PERVERT, YOU REALLY CAN LET HIM HAVE IT.
OH YEAH. ANJU IS A SECOND DEGREE BLACK BELT.
TEACH US!
HEY, AKIRA-CHAN. LET'S LEARN HOW TO FIGHT AND THEN KICK THAT PERVERT'S BUTT!
YEAH!
OKAY, MEET ME AT THE DOJO AFTER SCHOOL.
OKAY!

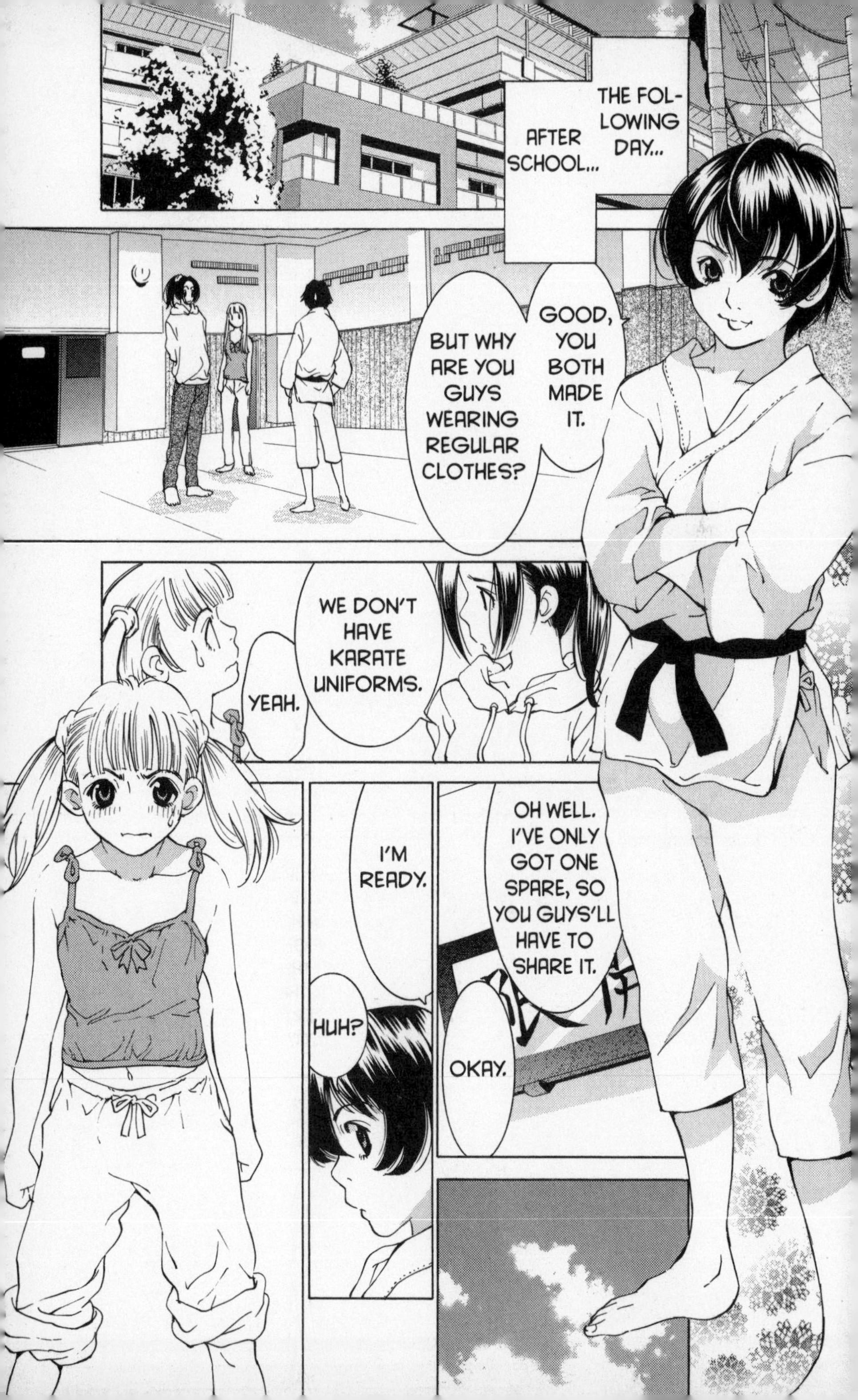
THE FOL-LOWING DAY...
AFTER SCHOOL...
GOOD, YOU BOTH MADE IT.
BUT WHY ARE YOU GUYS WEARING REGULAR CLOTHES?
WE DON'T HAVE KARATE UNIFORMS.
YEAH.
OH WELL. I'VE ONLY GOT ONE SPARE, SO YOU GUYS'LL HAVE TO SHARE IT.
OKAY.
I'M READY.
HUH?

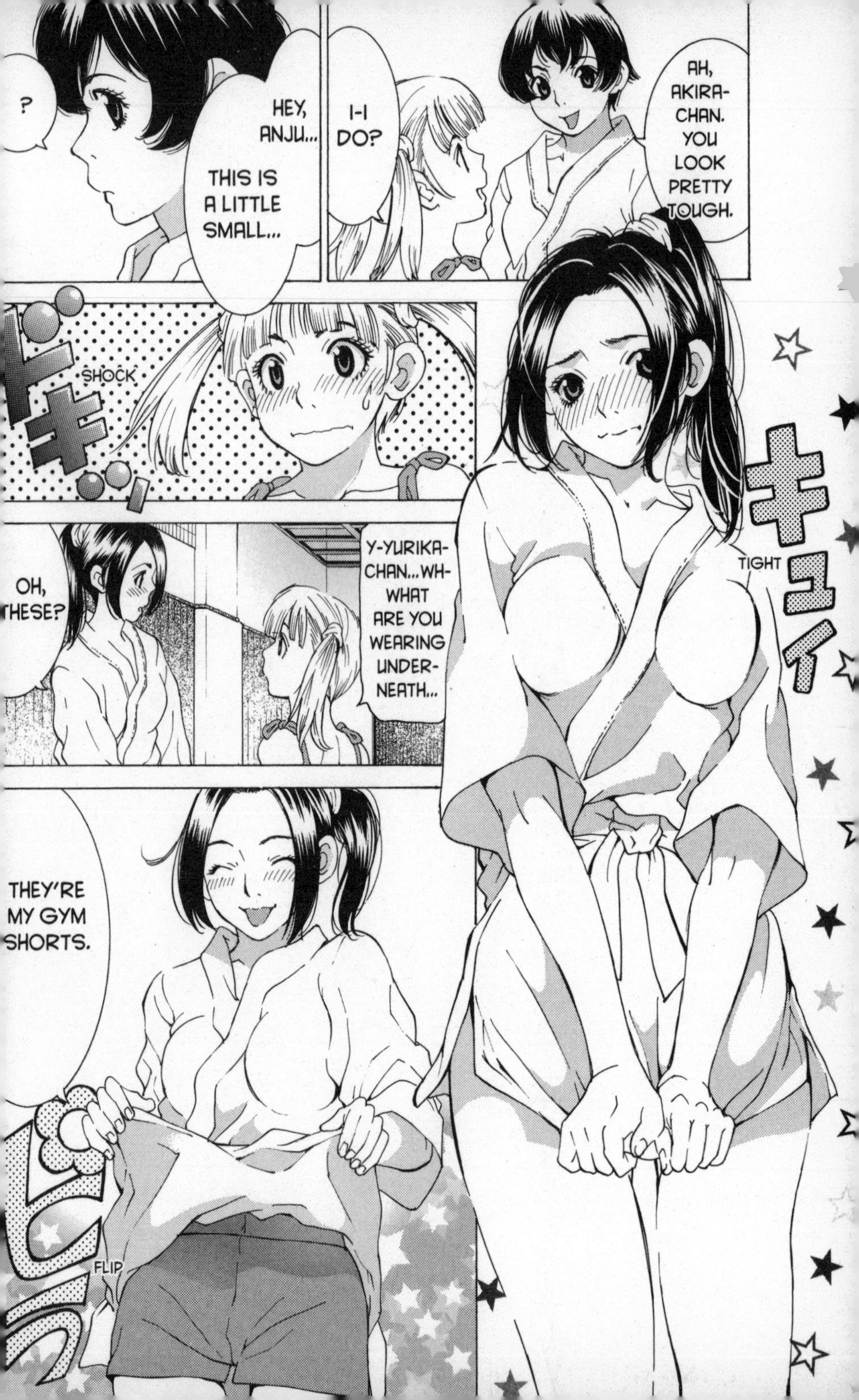
AH, AKIRA-CHAN. YOU LOOK PRETTY TOUGH.
I-I DO?
HEY, ANJU...
THIS IS A LITTLE SMALL...
?
TIGHT
SHOCK
Y-YURIKA-CHAN...WH-WHAT ARE YOU WEARING UNDERNEATH...
OH, THESE?
THEY'RE MY GYM SHORTS.
FLIP

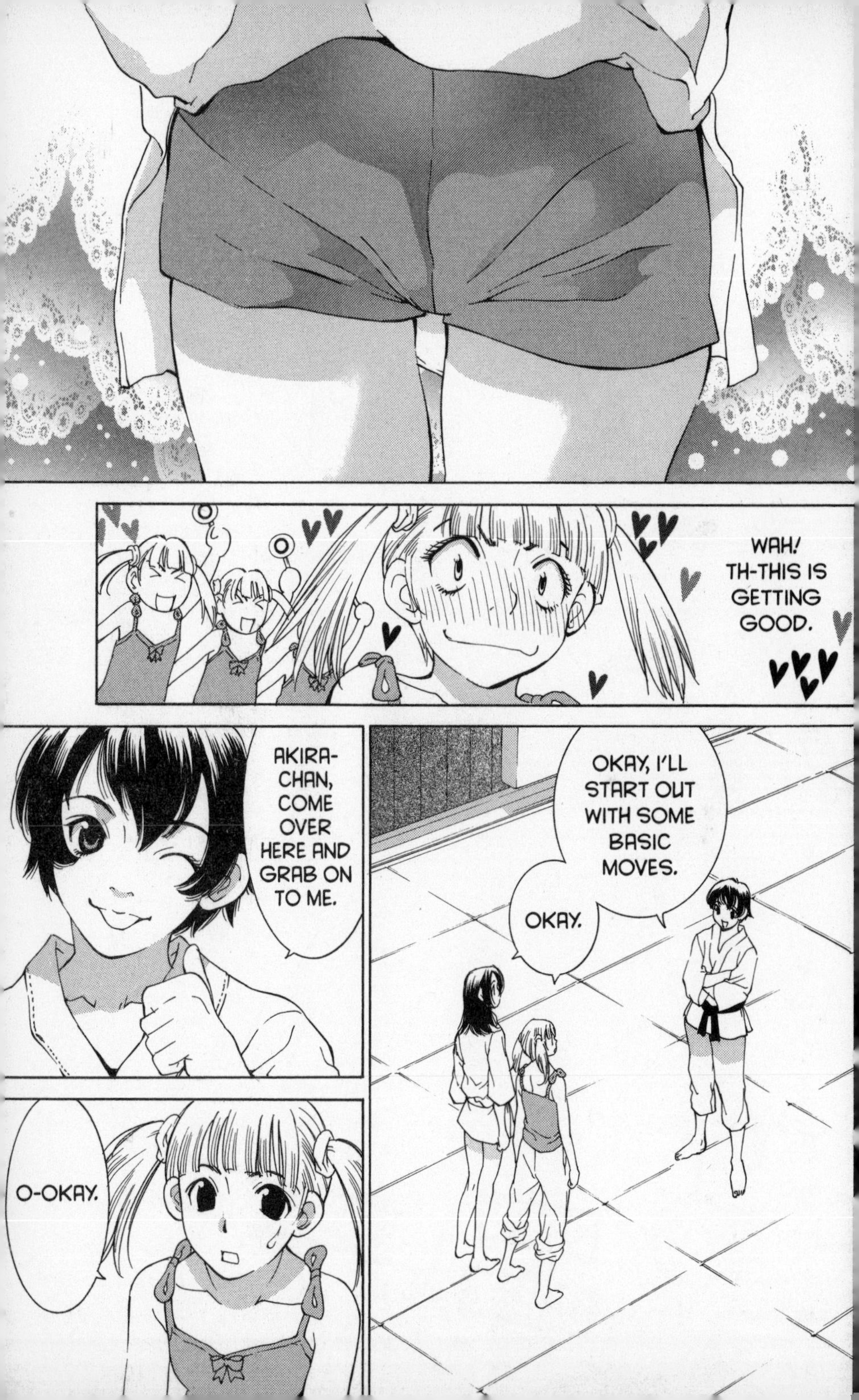
WAH! TH-THIS IS GETTING GOOD.
OKAY, I'LL START OUT WITH SOME BASIC MOVES.
OKAY.
AKIRA-CHAN, COME OVER HERE AND GRAB ON TO ME.
O-OKAY.

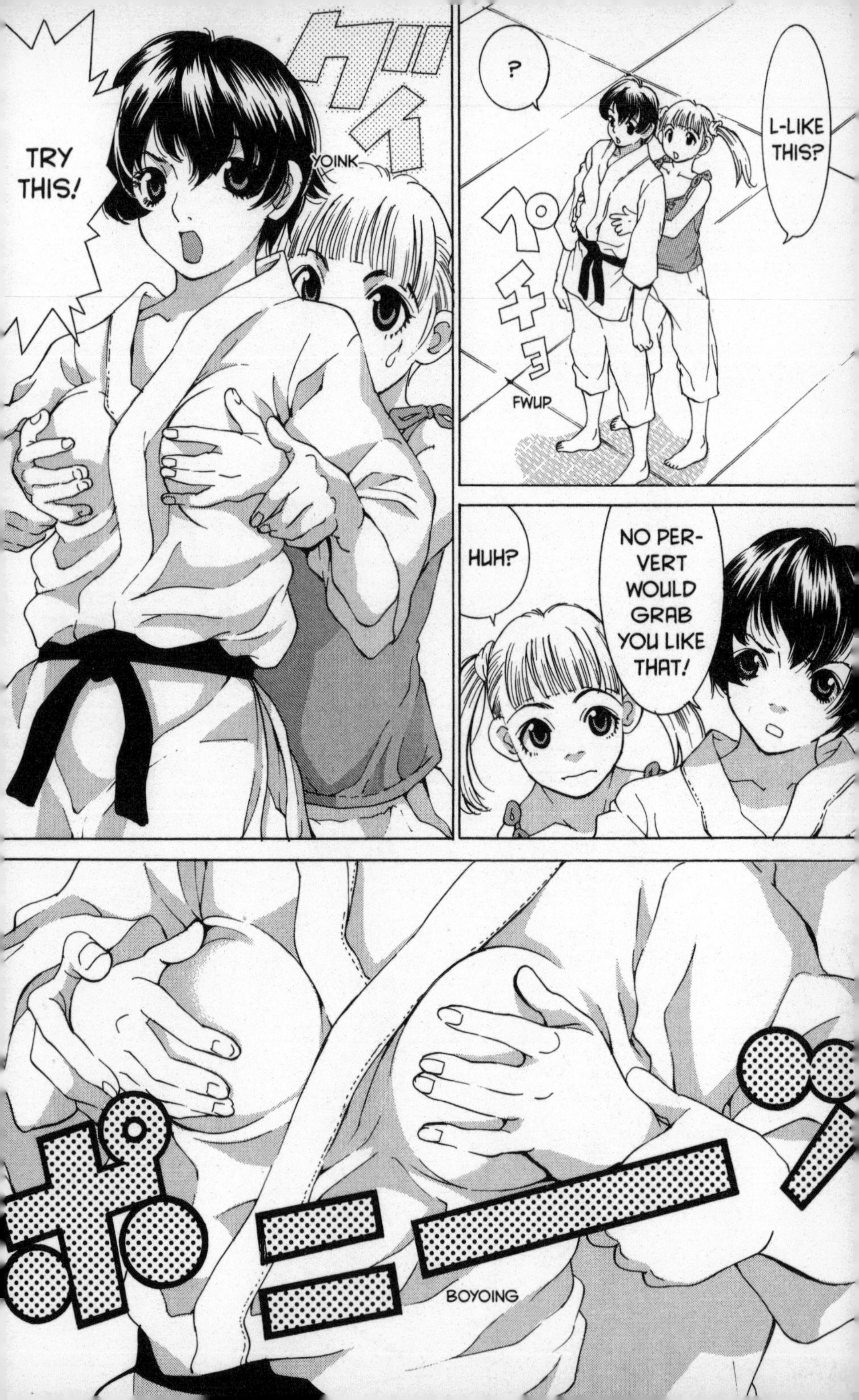
L-LIKE THIS?
?
FWUP
NO PER-VERT WOULD GRAB YOU LIKE THAT!
HUH?
YOINK
TRY THIS!
BOYOING

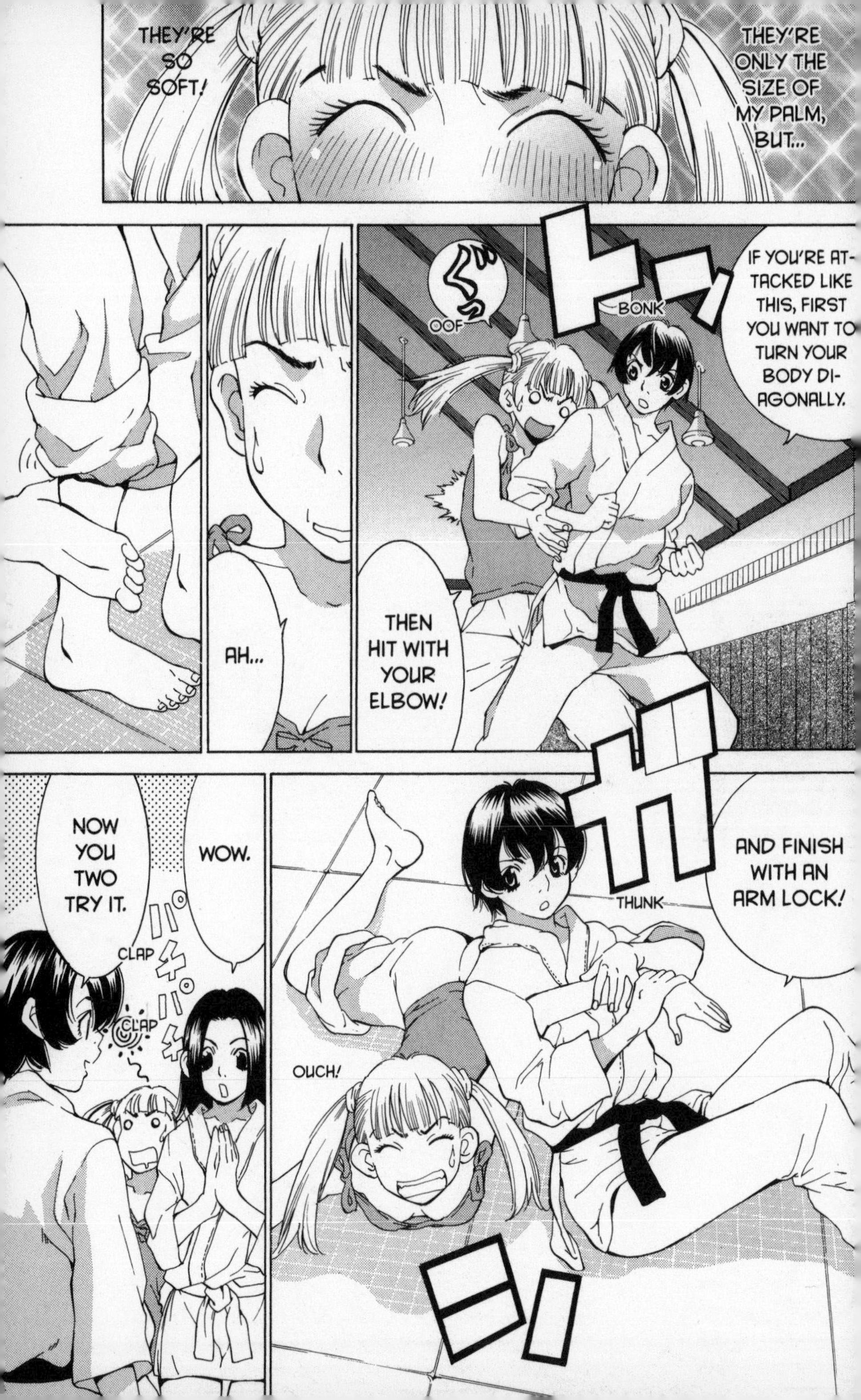
THEY'RE ONLY THE SIZE OF MY PALM, BUT...
THEY'RE SO SOFT!
IF YOU'RE ATTACKED LIKE THIS, FIRST YOU WANT TO TURN YOUR BODY DIAGONALLY.
BONK
OOF
THEN HIT WITH YOUR ELBOW!
AH...
AND FINISH WITH AN ARM LOCK!
THUNK
OUCH!
WOW.
NOW YOU TWO TRY IT.
CLAP
CLAP

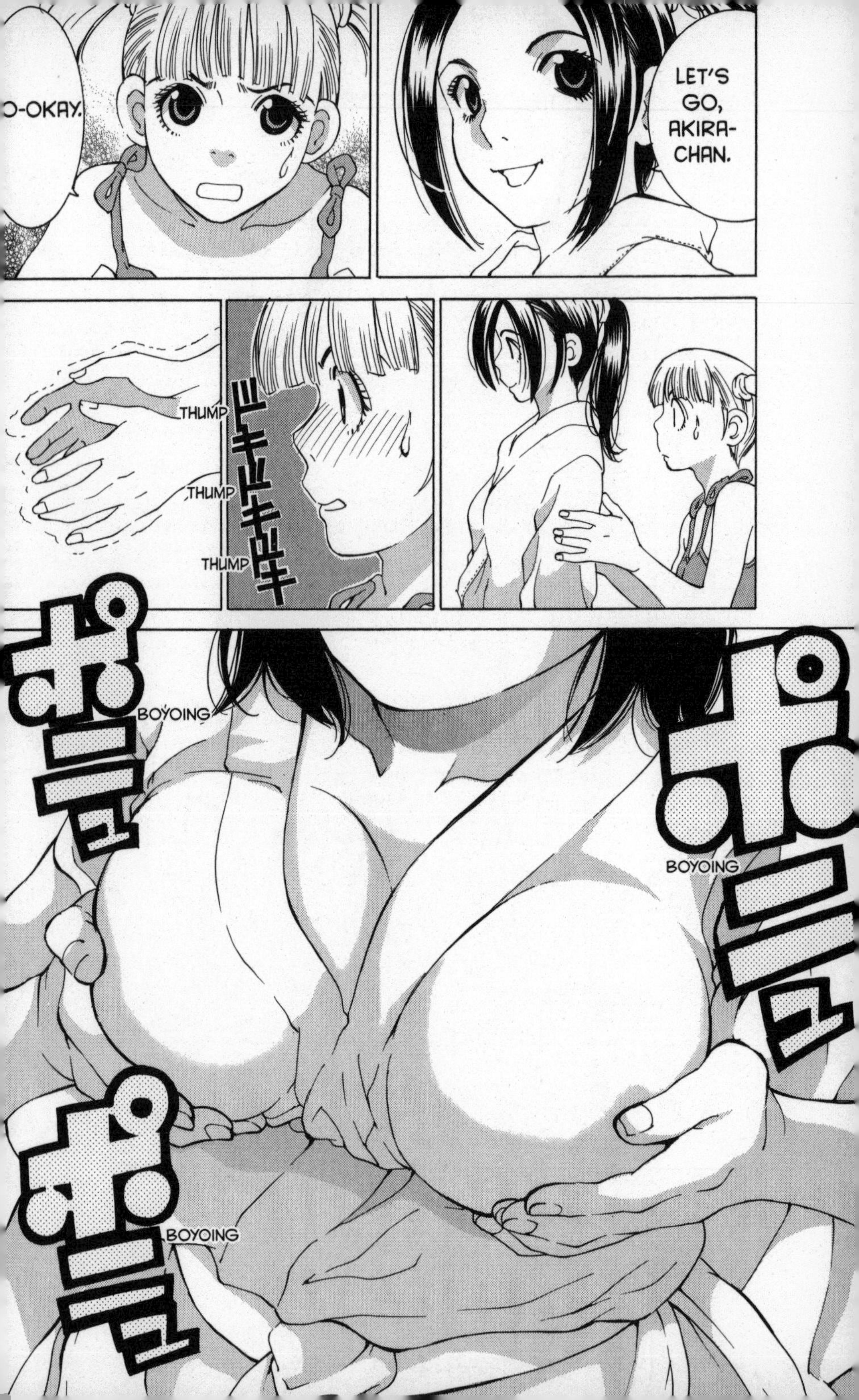
LET'S GO, AKIRA-CHAN.
O-OKAY.
THUMP
THUMP
THUMP
BOYOING
BOYOING
BOYOING

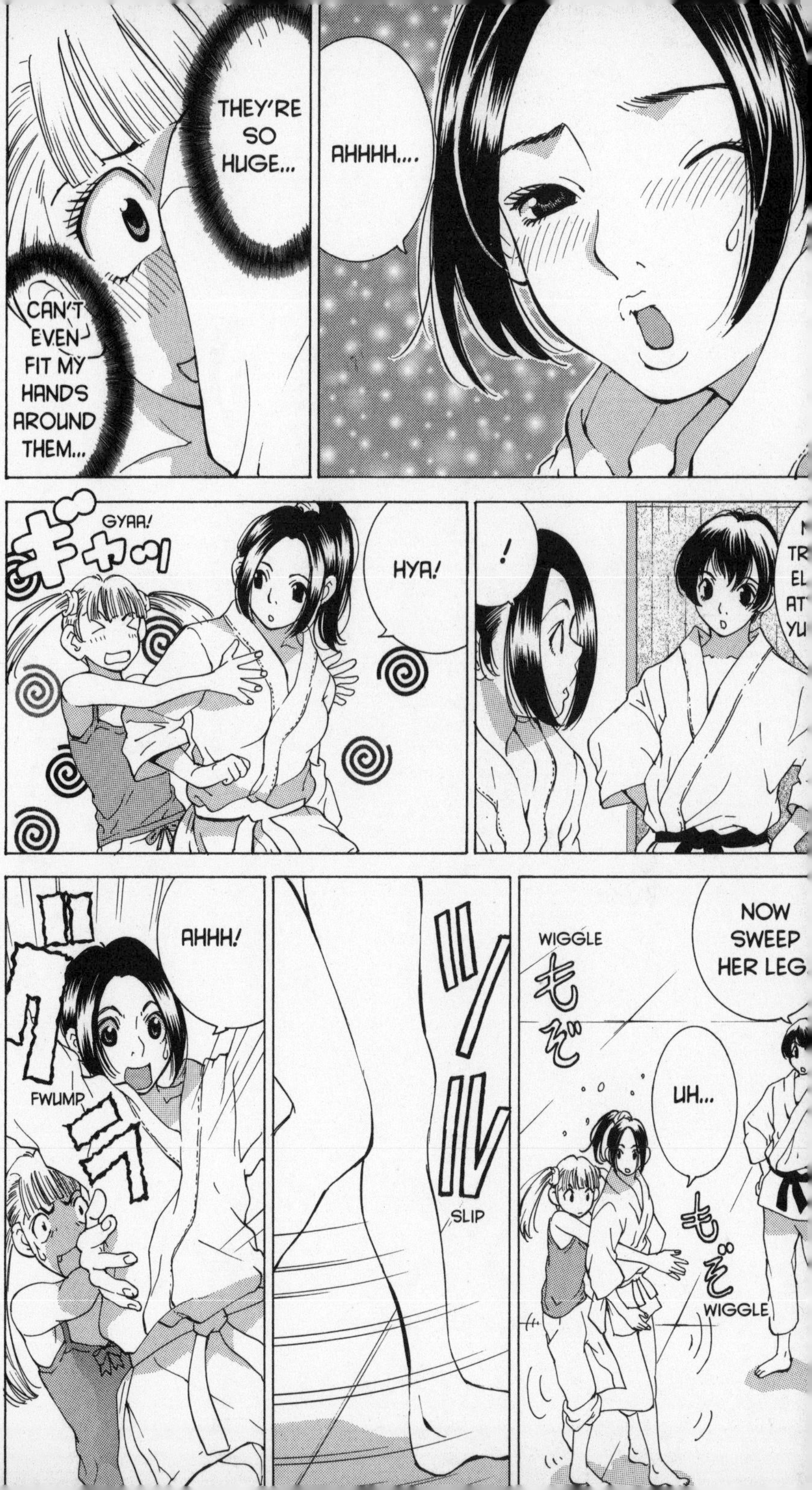
AHHHH....
THEY'RE SO HUGE...
CAN'T EVEN FIT MY HANDS AROUND THEM...
!
HYA!
GYAA!
NOW SWEEP HER LEG.
WIGGLE
もぞ
UH...
もぞ
WIGGLE
SLIP
AHHH!
FWUMP

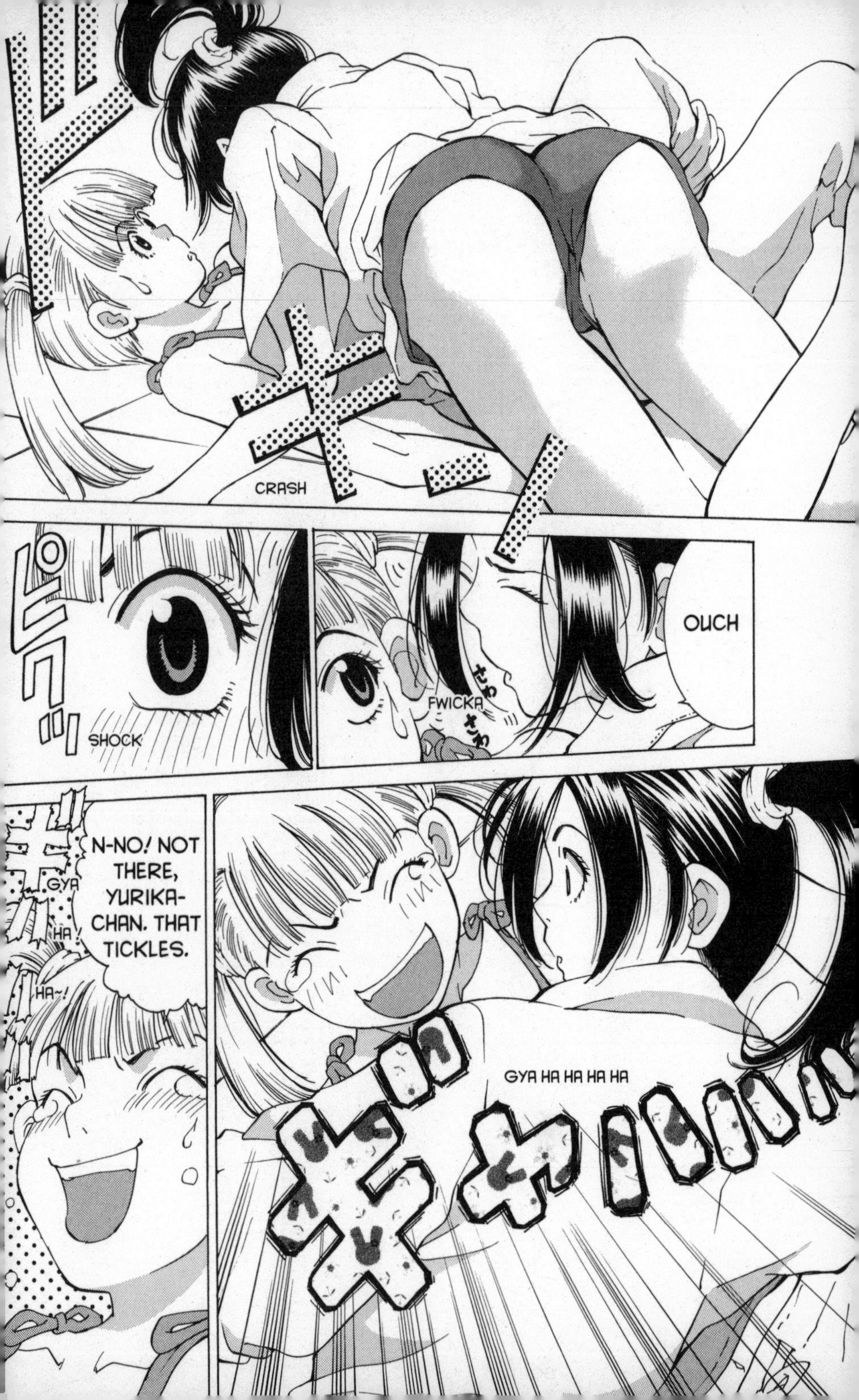
CRASH
OUCH
FWICKA
SHOCK
GYA HA HA HA HA
N-NO! NOT THERE, YURIKA-CHAN. THAT TICKLES.
GYA
HA!
HA~!

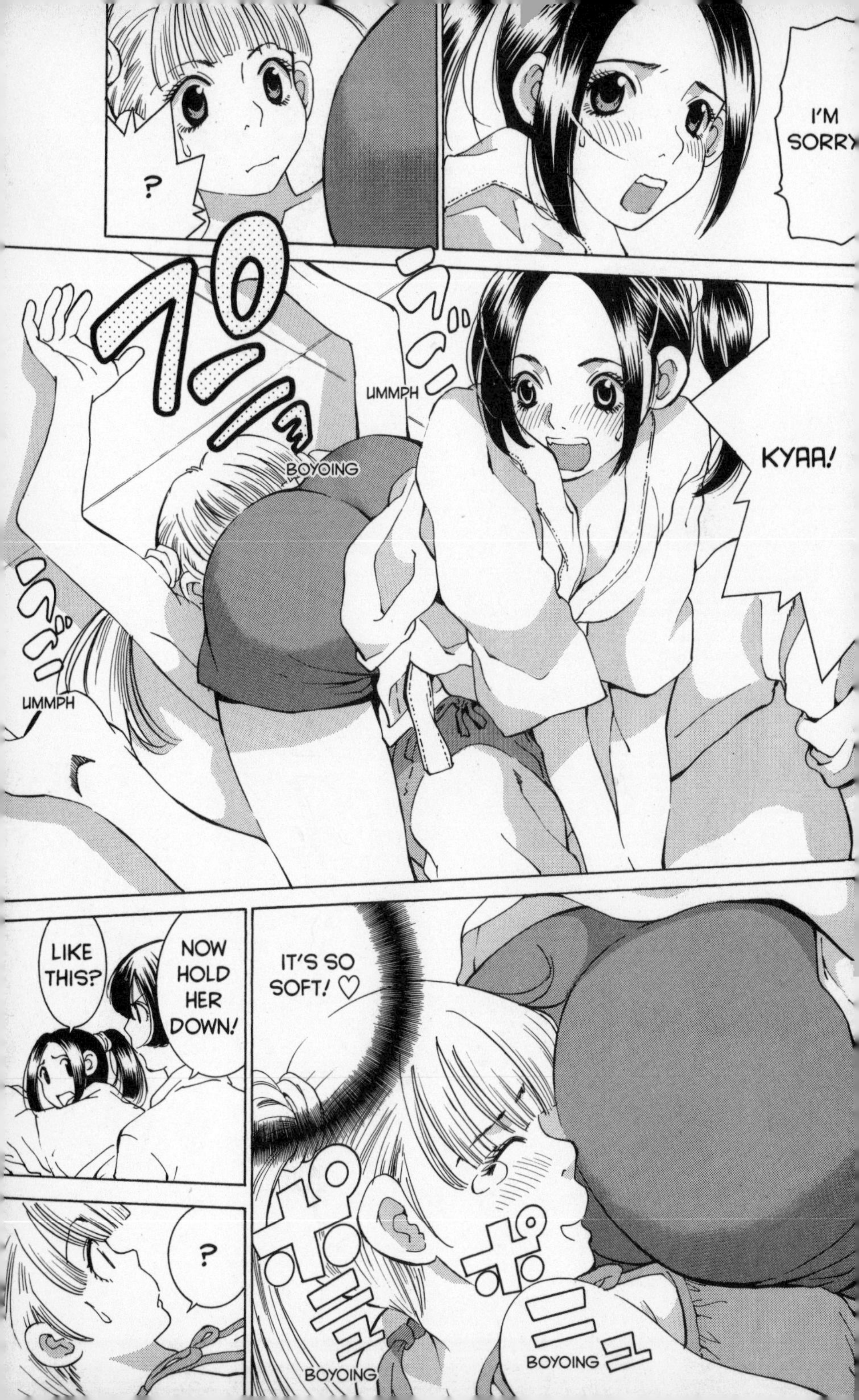
I'M SORRY
?
KYAA!
UMMPH
BOYOING
UMMPH
IT'S SO SOFT! ♡
BOYOING
BOYOING
NOW HOLD HER DOWN!
LIKE THIS?
?

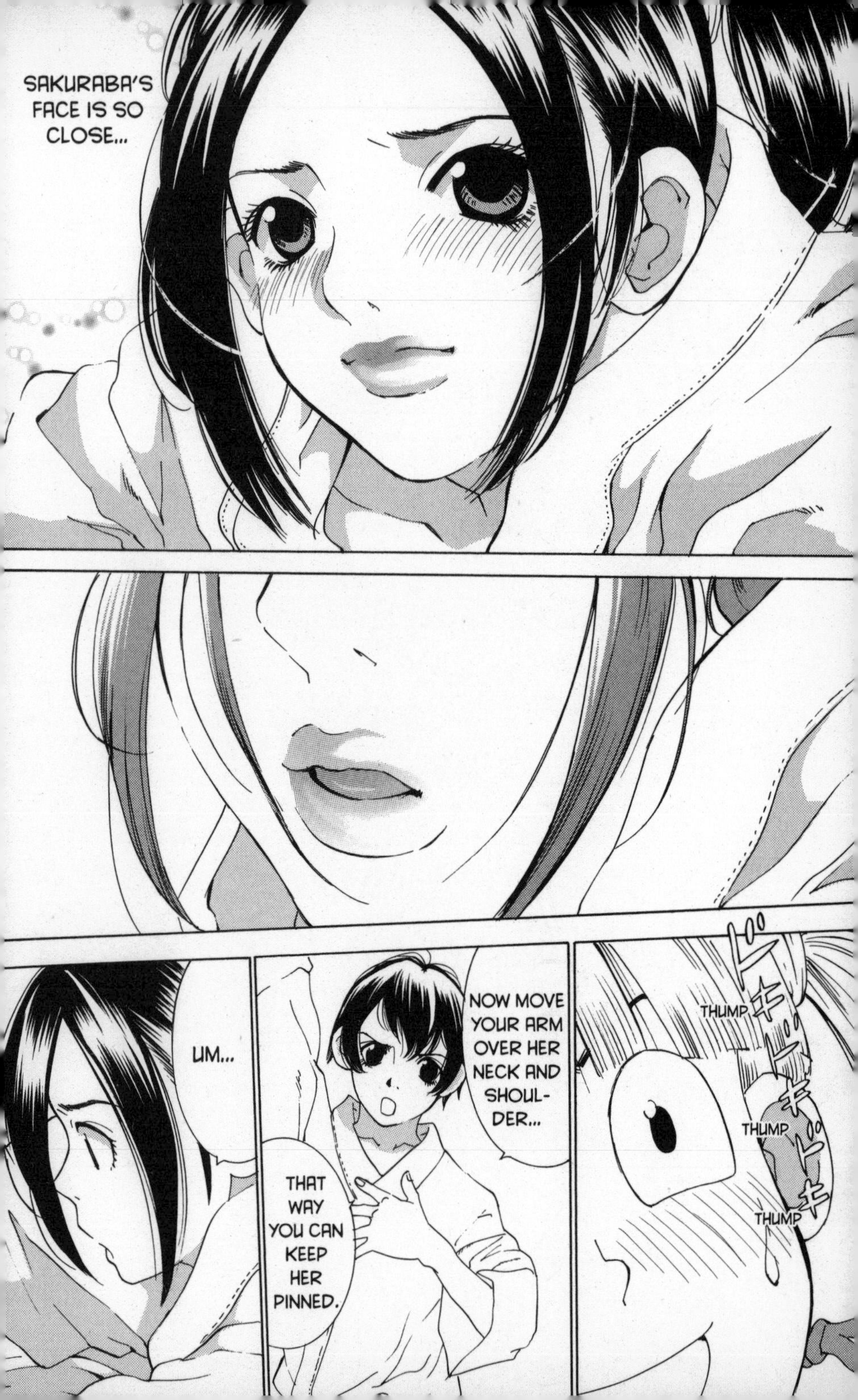
SAKURABA'S FACE IS SO CLOSE...
THUMP
THUMP
THUMP
NOW MOVE YOUR ARM OVER HER NECK AND SHOUL-DER...
THAT WAY YOU CAN KEEP HER PINNED.
UM...

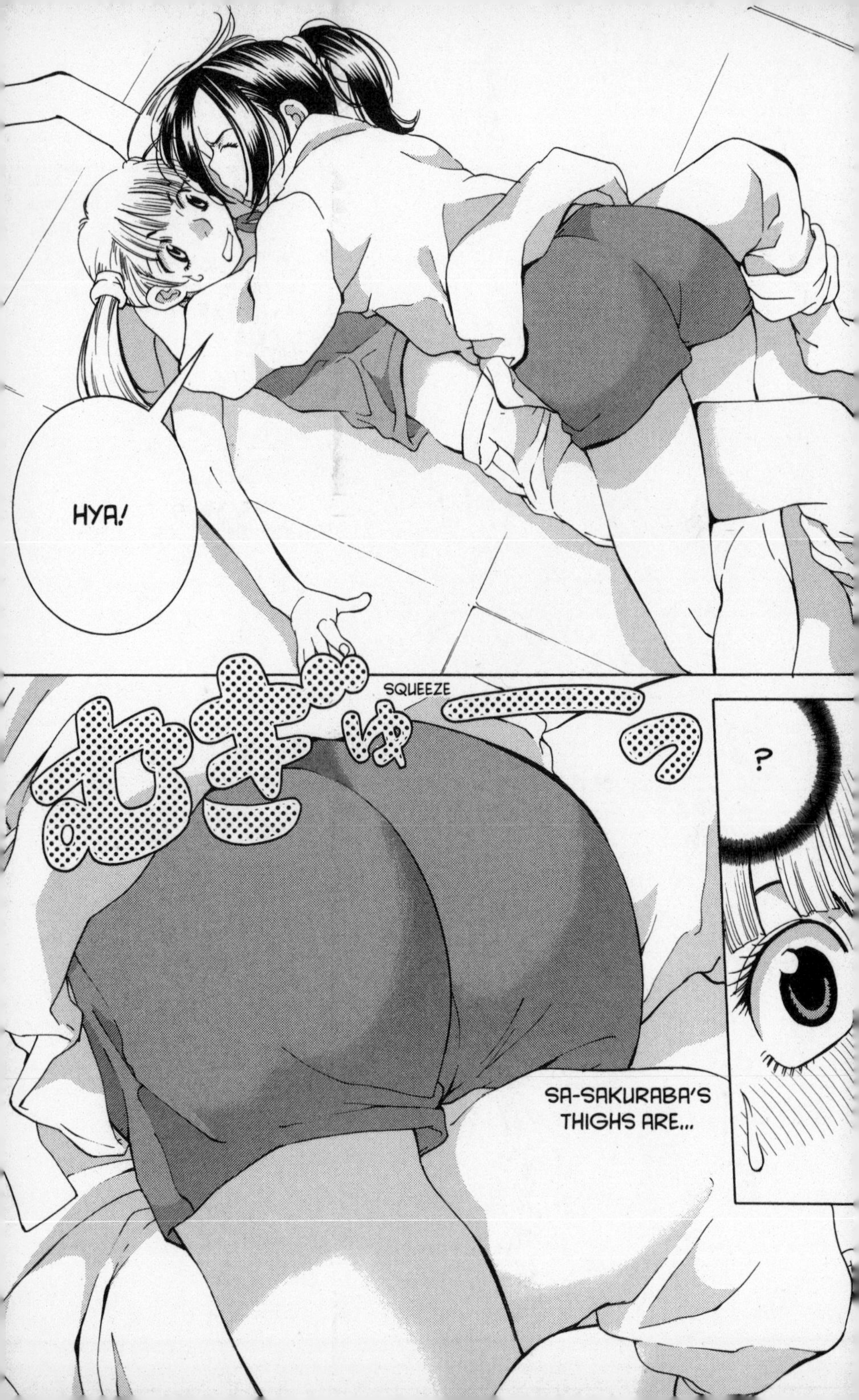
HYA!
?
むぎゅーっ
SQUEEZE
SA-SAKURABA'S THIGHS ARE...

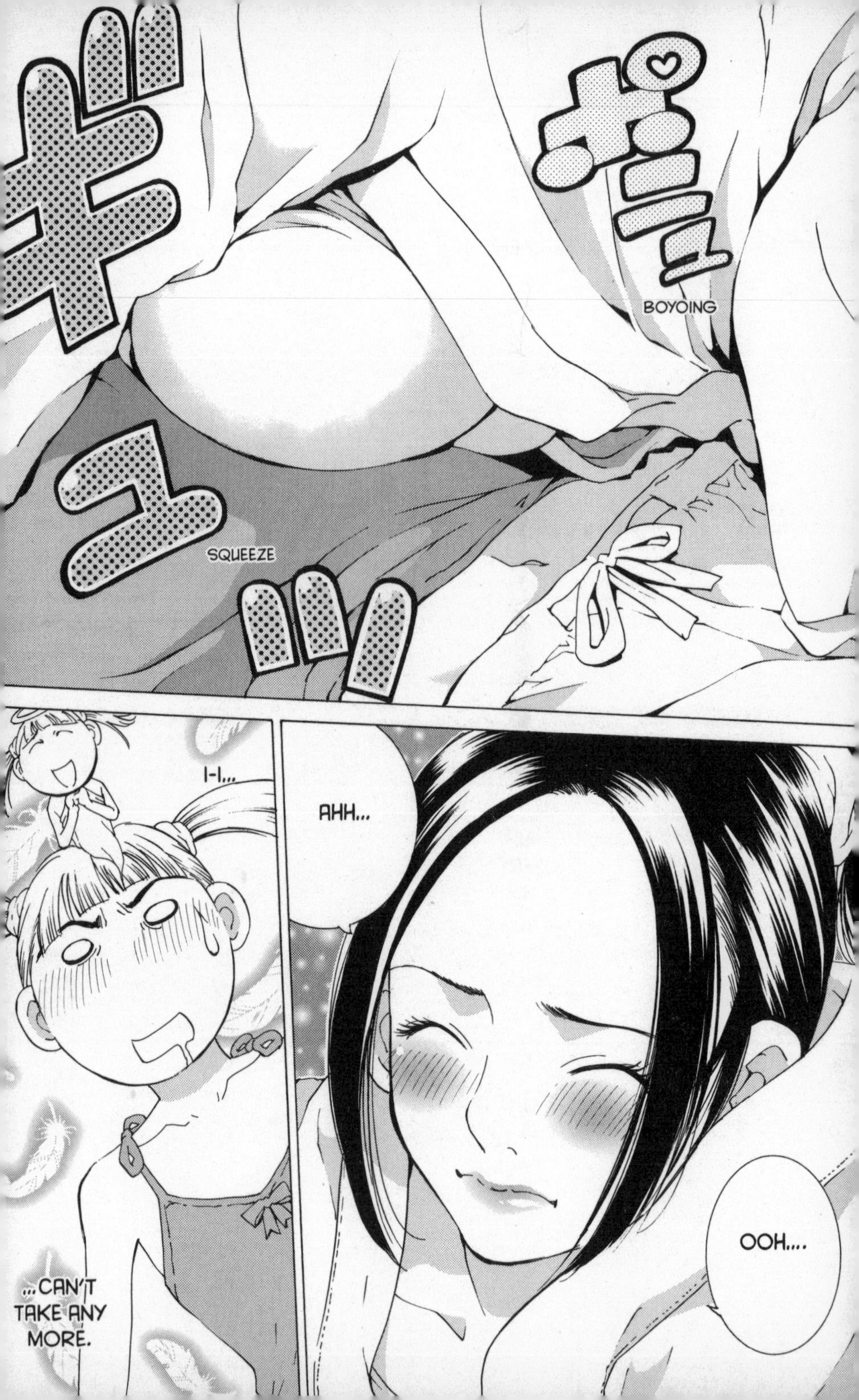
ポニュ
BOYOING
ギュッ
SQUEEZE
AHH...
OOH....
I-I...
...CAN'T TAKE ANY MORE.

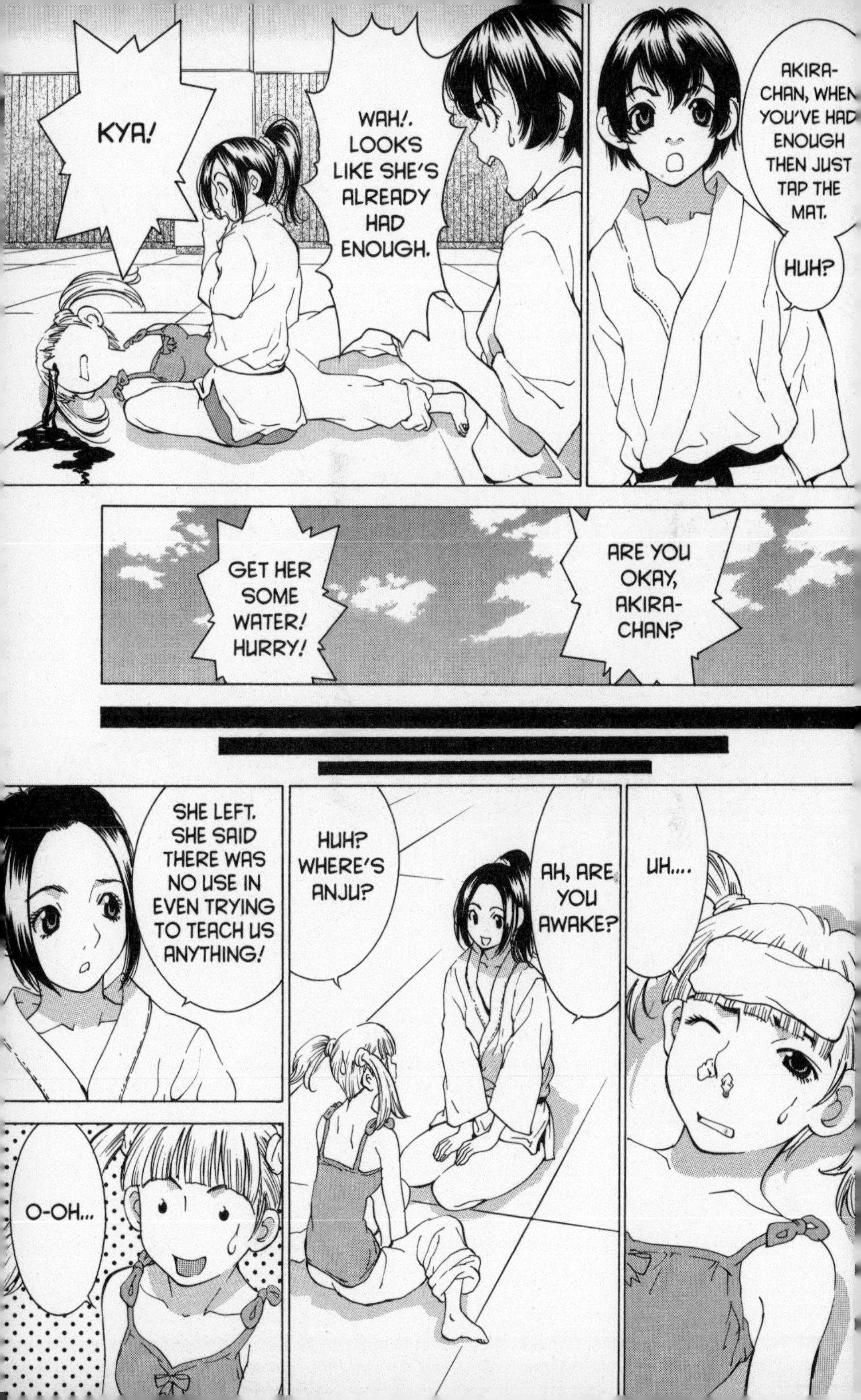
AKIRA-CHAN, WHEN YOU'VE HAD ENOUGH THEN JUST TAP THE MAT.
HUH?
WAH!. LOOKS LIKE SHE'S ALREADY HAD ENOUGH.
KYA!
ARE YOU OKAY, AKIRA-CHAN?
GET HER SOME WATER! HURRY!
UH....
AH, ARE YOU AWAKE?
HUH? WHERE'S ANJU?
SHE LEFT. SHE SAID THERE WAS NO USE IN EVEN TRYING TO TEACH US ANYTHING!
O-OH...

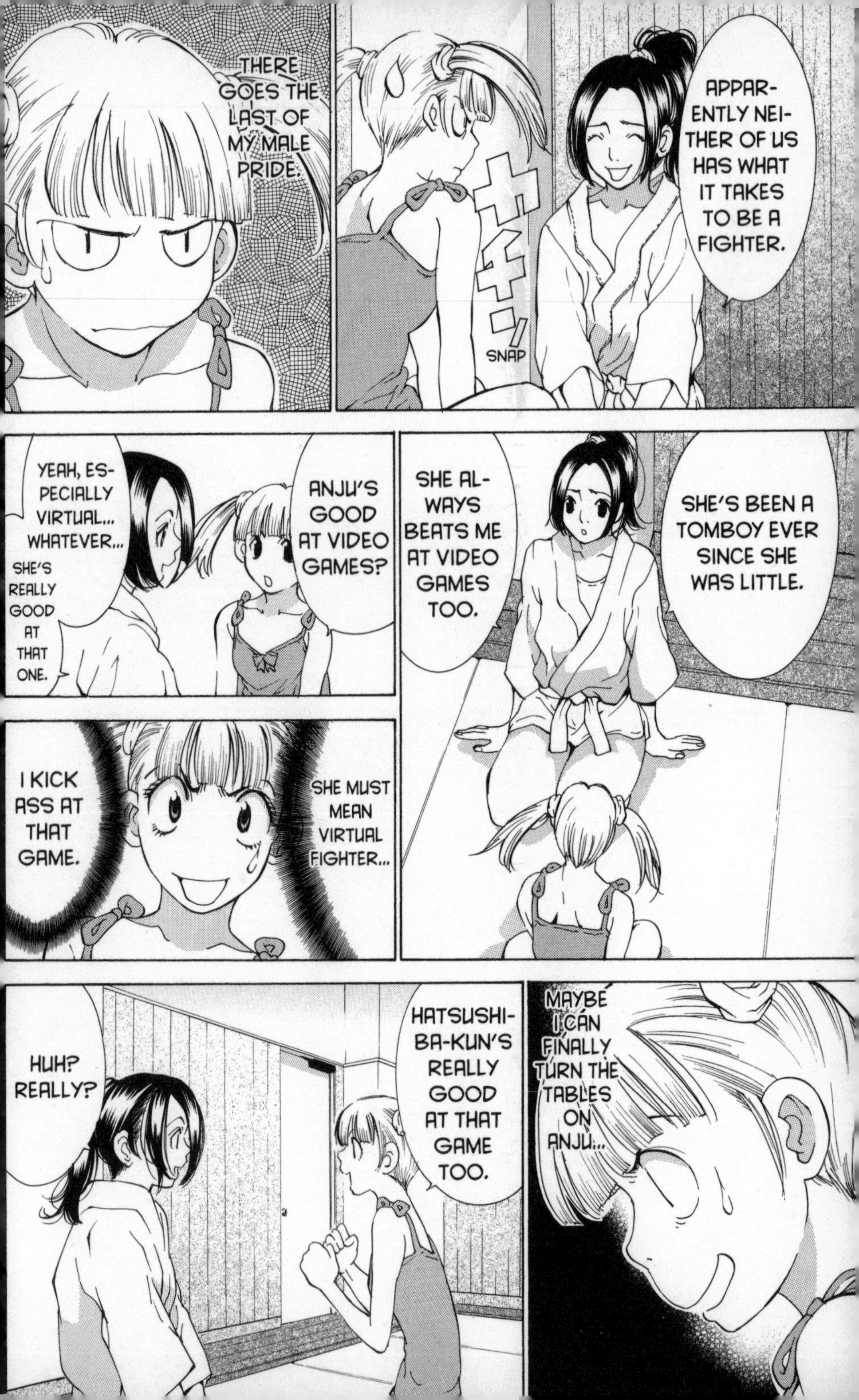
APPARENTLY NEITHER OF US HAS WHAT IT TAKES TO BE A FIGHTER.
SNAP
THERE GOES THE LAST OF MY MALE PRIDE.
SHE'S BEEN A TOMBOY EVER SINCE SHE WAS LITTLE.
SHE ALWAYS BEATS ME AT VIDEO GAMES TOO.
ANJU'S GOOD AT VIDEO GAMES?
YEAH, ESPECIALLY VIRTUAL... WHATEVER...
SHE'S REALLY GOOD AT THAT ONE.
SHE MUST MEAN VIRTUAL FIGHTER...
I KICK ASS AT THAT GAME.
MAYBE I CAN FINALLY TURN THE TABLES ON ANJU...
HATSUSHIBA-KUN'S REALLY GOOD AT THAT GAME TOO.
HUH? REALLY?

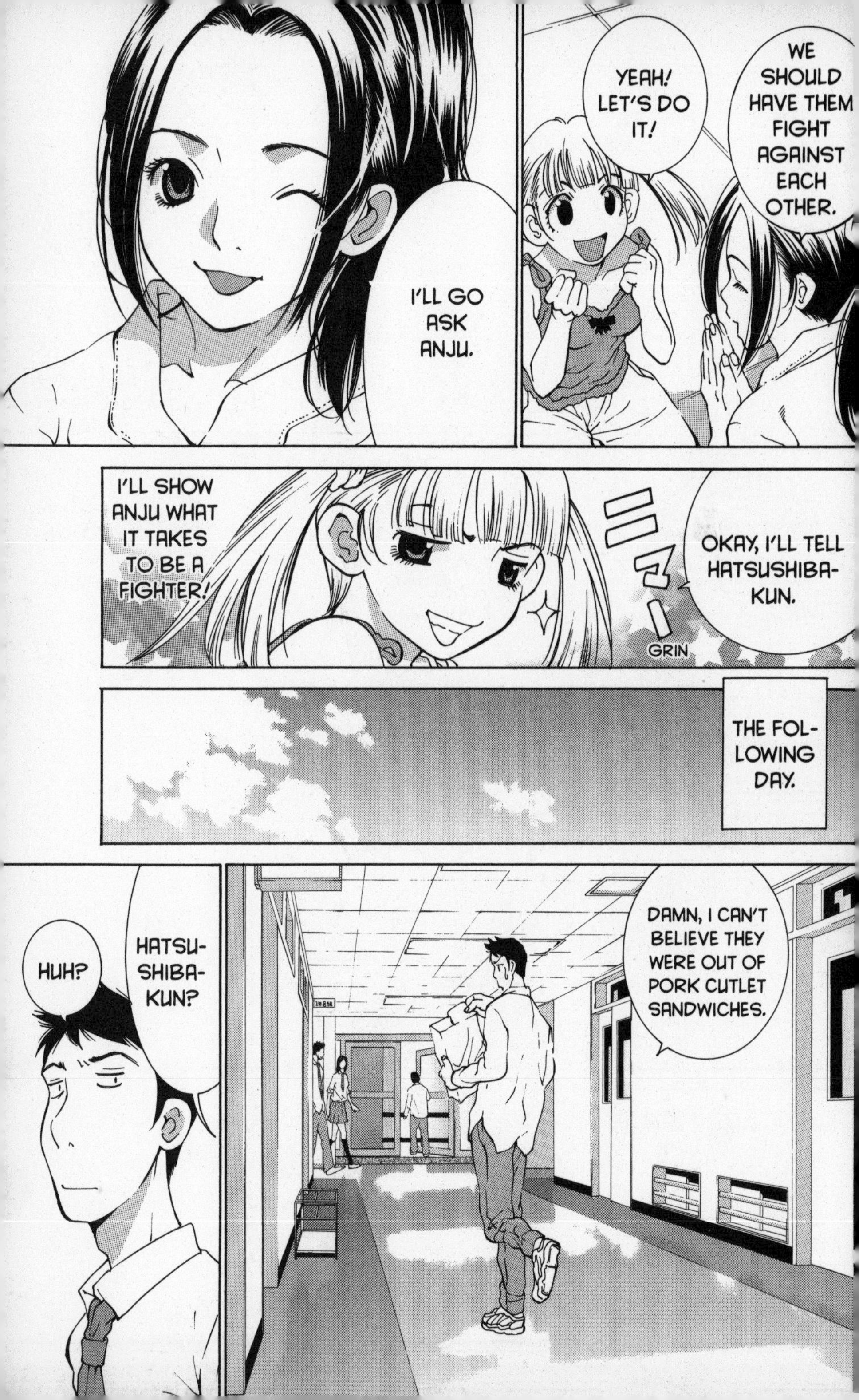
WE SHOULD HAVE THEM FIGHT AGAINST EACH OTHER.
YEAH! LET'S DO IT!
I'LL GO ASK ANJU.
OKAY, I'LL TELL HATSUSHIBA-KUN.
GRIN
I'LL SHOW ANJU WHAT IT TAKES TO BE A FIGHTER!
THE FOL-LOWING DAY.
DAMN, I CAN'T BELIEVE THEY WERE OUT OF PORK CUTLET SANDWICHES.
HATSU-SHIBA-KUN?
HUH?

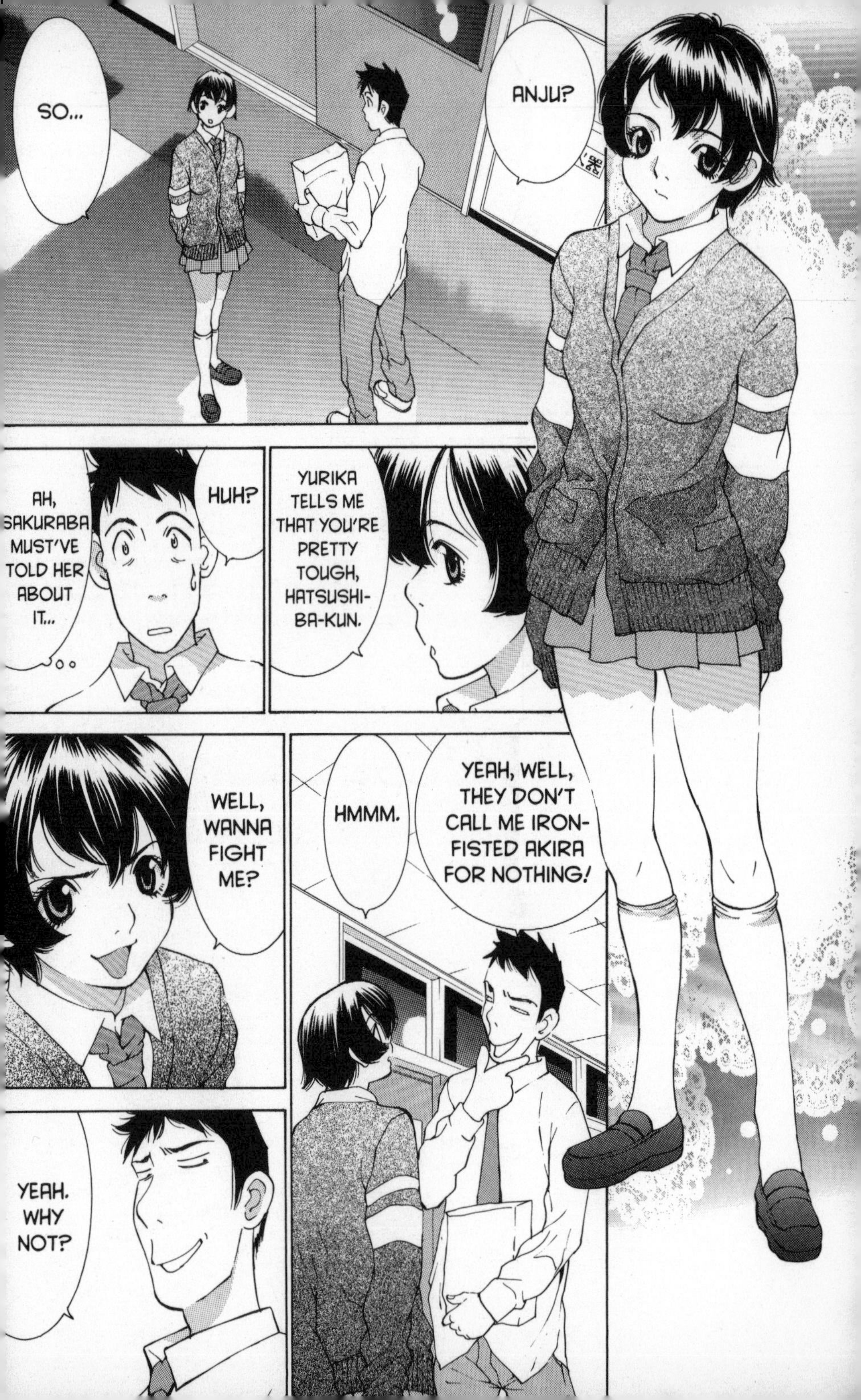
ANJU?
SO...
YURIKA TELLS ME THAT YOU'RE PRETTY TOUGH, HATSUSHIBA-KUN.
HUH?
AH, SAKURABA MUST'VE TOLD HER ABOUT IT...
YEAH, WELL, THEY DON'T CALL ME IRON-FISTED AKIRA FOR NOTHING!
HMMM.
WELL, WANNA FIGHT ME?
YEAH. WHY NOT?

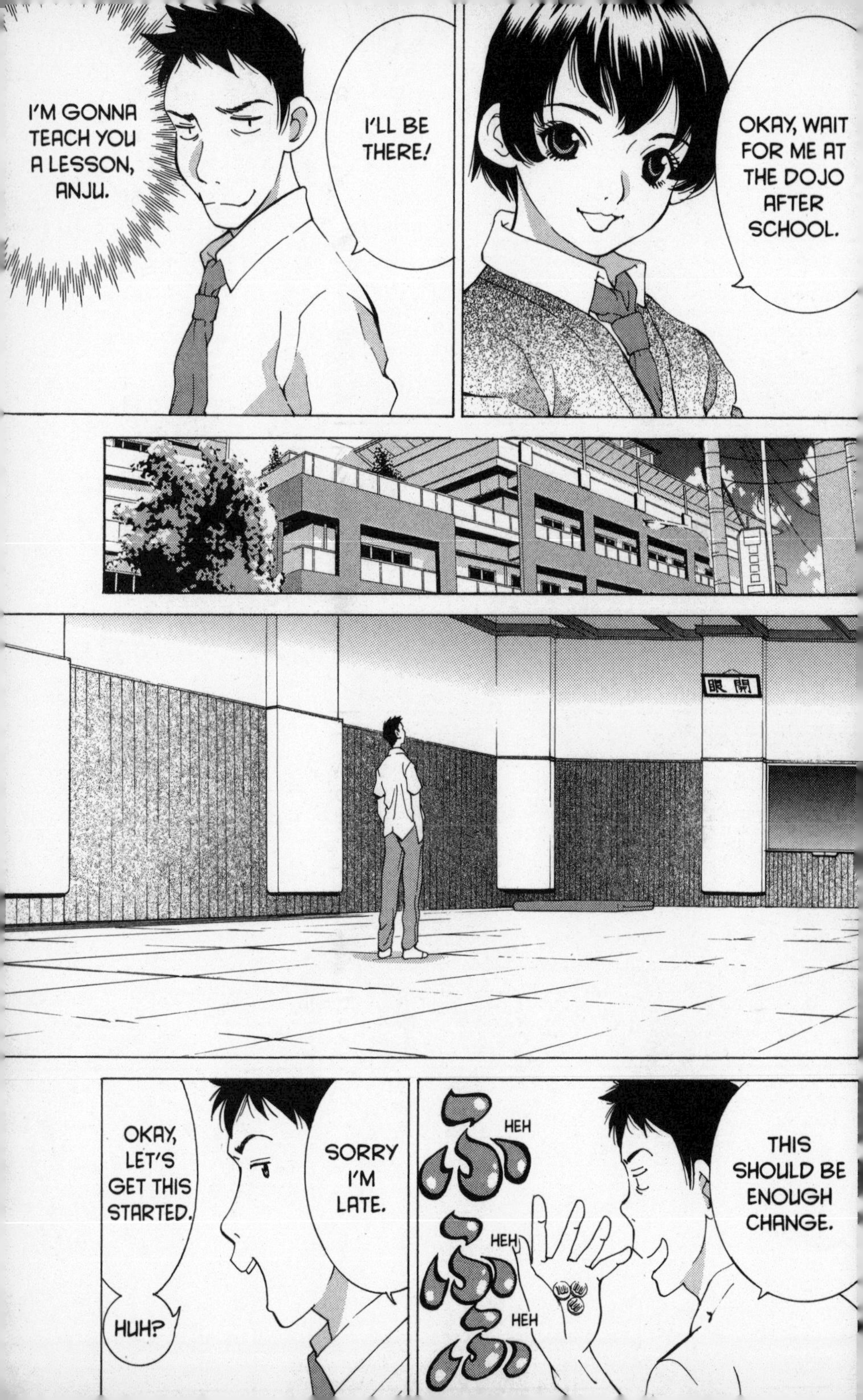
OKAY, WAIT FOR ME AT THE DOJO AFTER SCHOOL.
I'LL BE THERE!
I'M GONNA TEACH YOU A LESSON, ANJU.
THIS SHOULD BE ENOUGH CHANGE.
HEH
HEH
HEH
SORRY I'M LATE.
OKAY, LET'S GET THIS STARTED.
HUH?

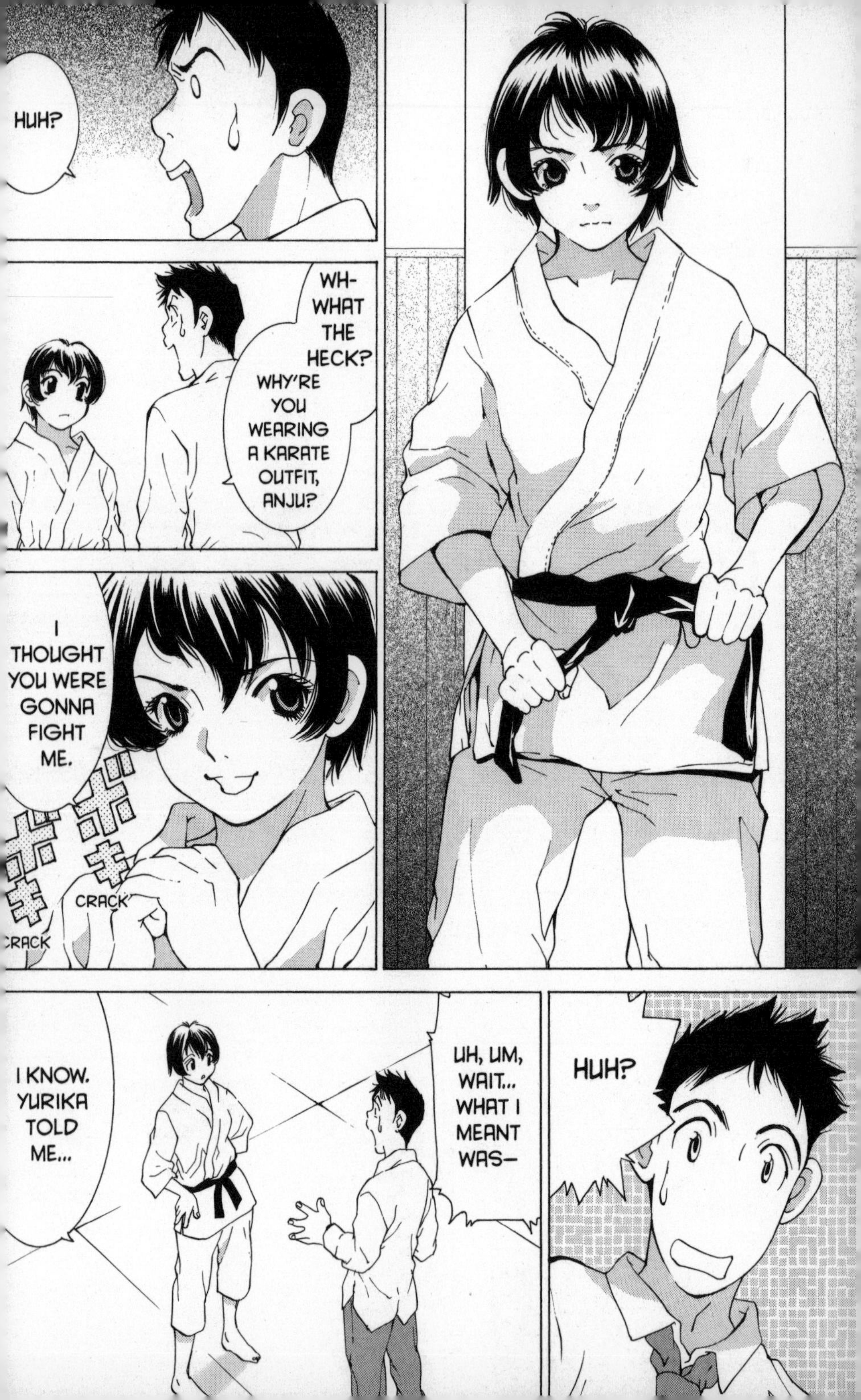
HUH?
WH- WHAT THE HECK?
WHY'RE YOU WEARING A KARATE OUTFIT, ANJU?
I THOUGHT YOU WERE GONNA FIGHT ME.
CRACK
CRACK
HUH?
UH, UM, WAIT... WHAT I MEANT WAS—
I KNOW. YURIKA TOLD ME...

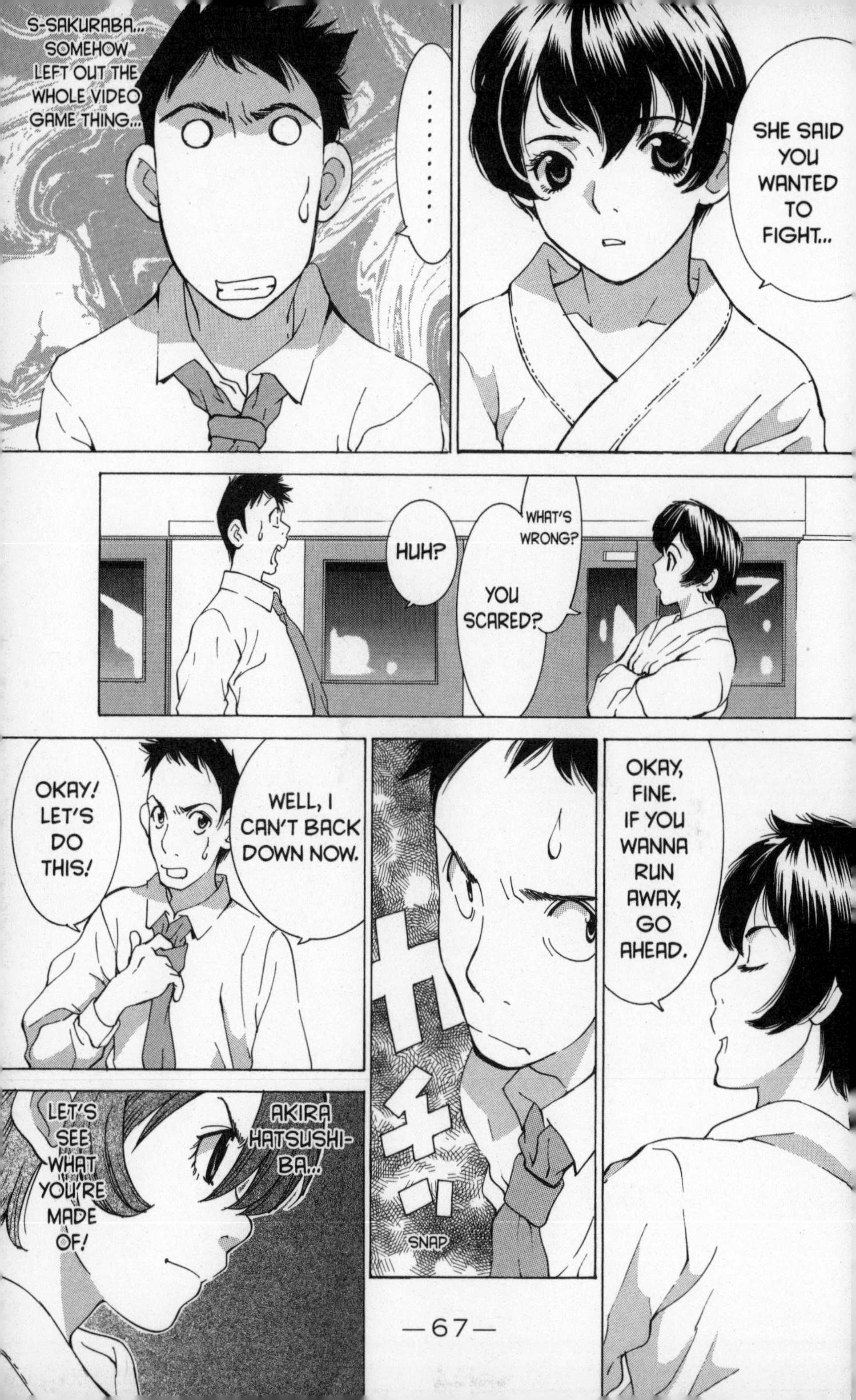
SHE SAID YOU WANTED TO FIGHT...
......
S-SAKURABA... SOMEHOW LEFT OUT THE WHOLE VIDEO GAME THING...
WHAT'S WRONG?
YOU SCARED?
HUH?
OKAY, FINE. IF YOU WANNA RUN AWAY, GO AHEAD.
SNAP
WELL, I CAN'T BACK DOWN NOW.
OKAY! LET'S DO THIS!
AKIRA HATSUSHIBA...
LET'S SEE WHAT YOU'RE MADE OF!

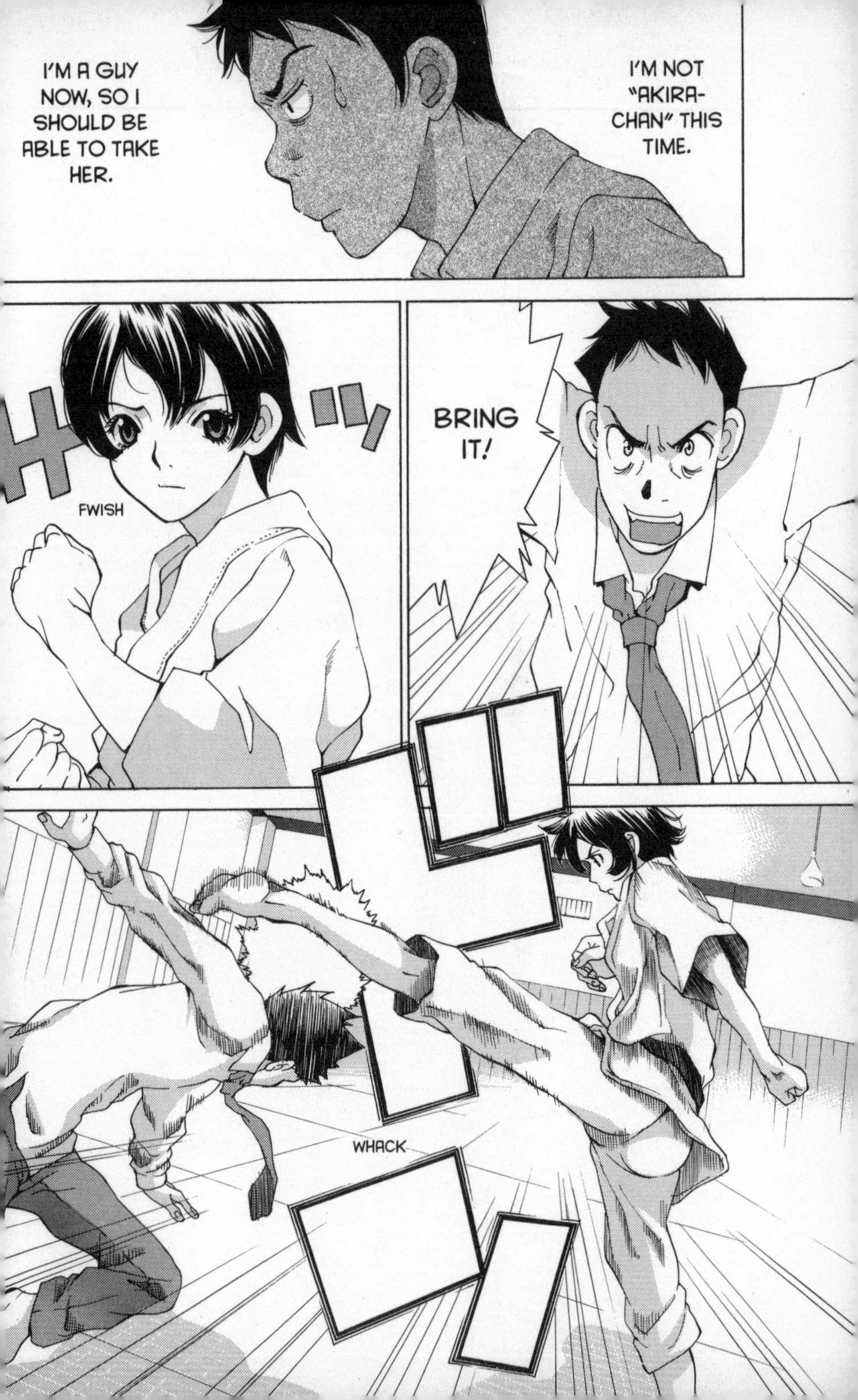
I'M NOT "AKIRA-CHAN" THIS TIME.
I'M A GUY NOW, SO I SHOULD BE ABLE TO TAKE HER.
BRING IT!
FWISH
WHACK

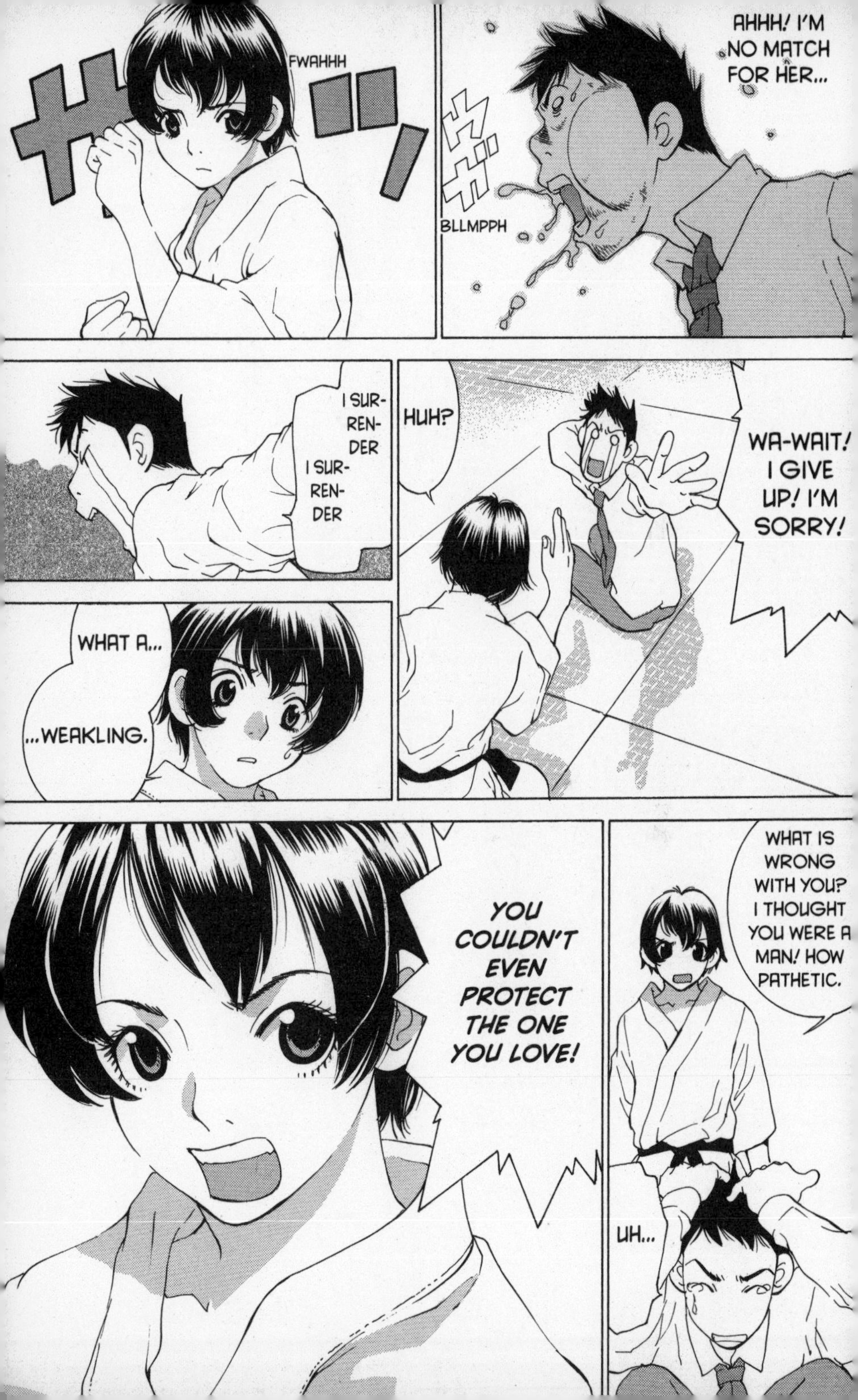

AHHH! I'M NO MATCH FOR HER...
BLLMPPH
FWAHHH
WA-WAIT! I GIVE UP! I'M SORRY!
HUH?
I SUR-REN-DER I SUR-REN-DER
WHAT A...
...WEAKLING.
WHAT IS WRONG WITH YOU? I THOUGHT YOU WERE A MAN! HOW PATHETIC.
UH...
YOU COULDN'T EVEN PROTECT THE ONE YOU LOVE!

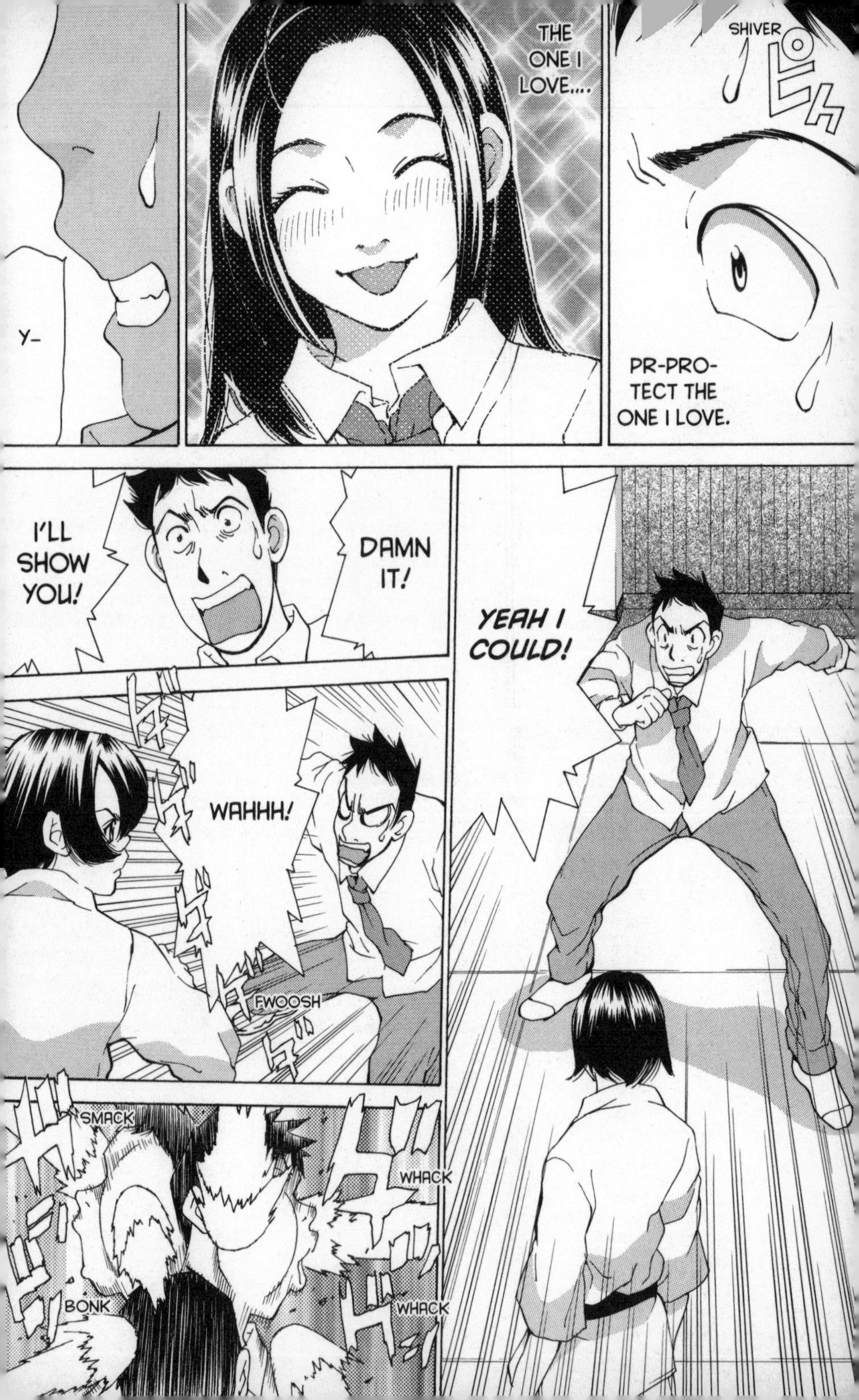
SHIVER
PR-PROTECT THE ONE I LOVE.
THE ONE I LOVE....
Y-
YEAH I COULD!
DAMN IT!
I'LL SHOW YOU!
WAHHH!
FWOOSH
SMACK
WHACK
WHACK
BONK

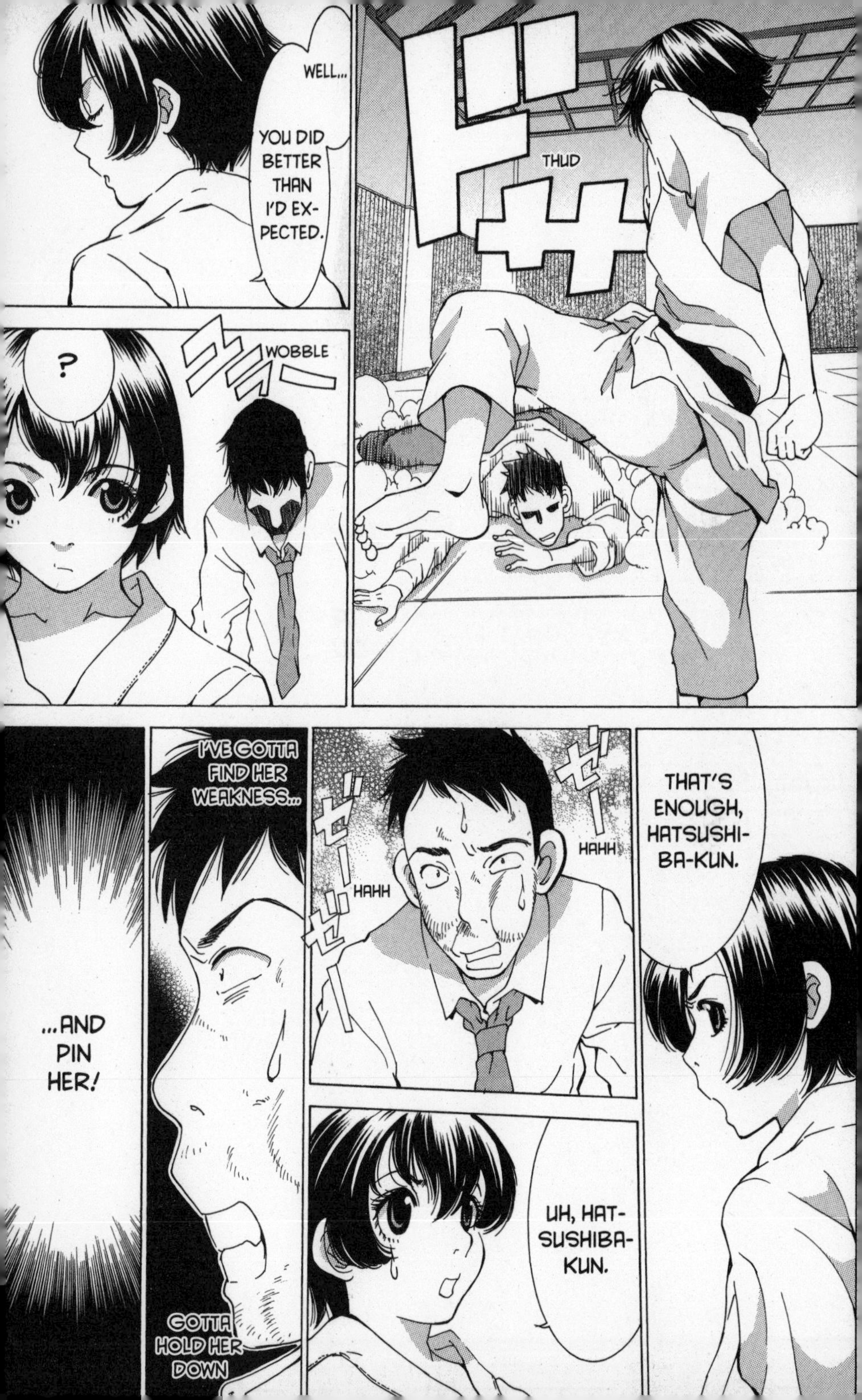
ドサ
THUD
WELL...
YOU DID BETTER THAN I'D EX-PECTED.
?
WOBBLE
THAT'S ENOUGH, HATSUSHI-BA-KUN.
HAHH
HAHH
UH, HAT-SUSHIBA-KUN.
I'VE GOTTA FIND HER WEAKNESS...
GOTTA HOLD HER DOWN
...AND PIN HER!

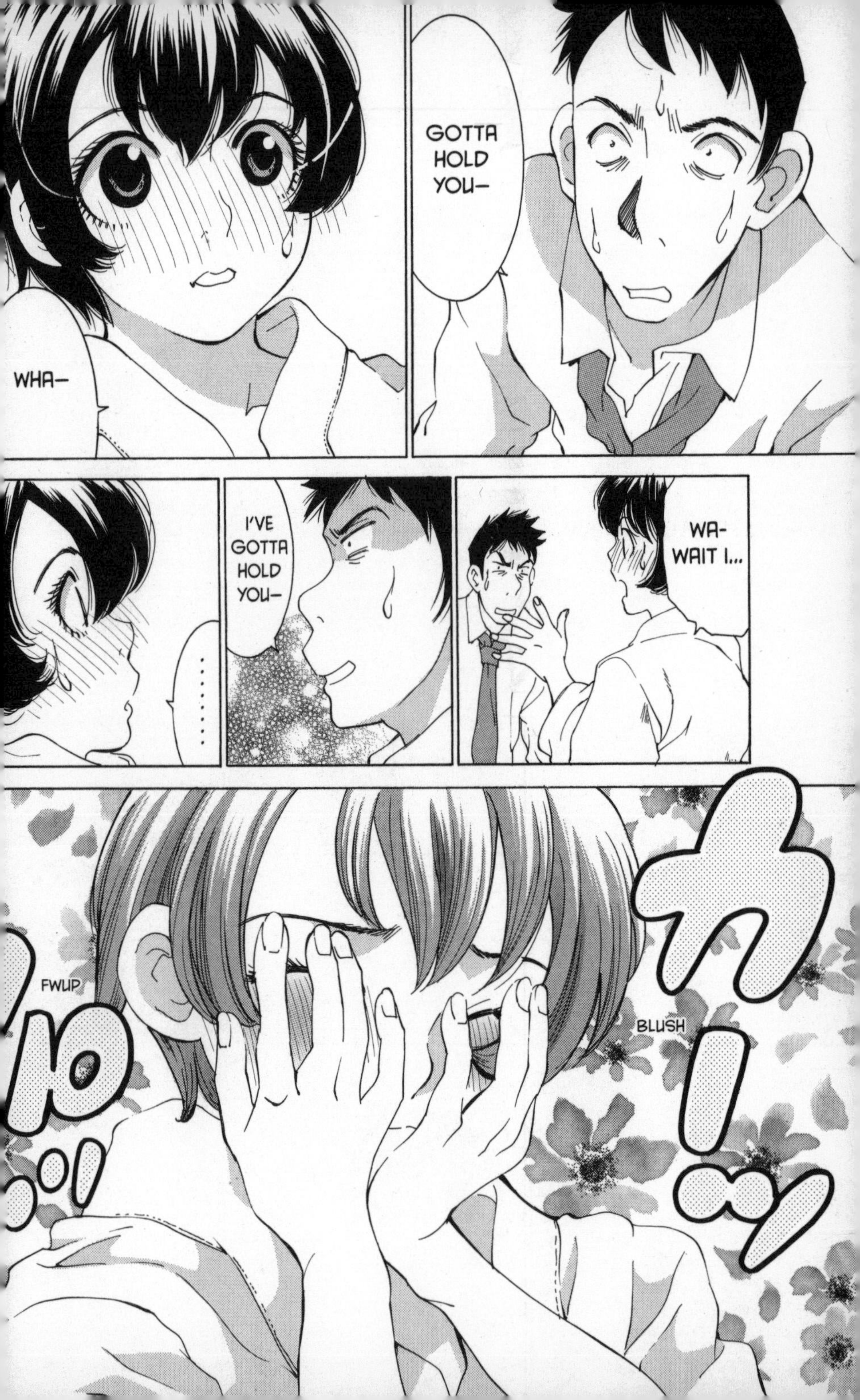
GOTTA HOLD YOU—
WHA—
WA- WAIT I...
I'VE GOTTA HOLD YOU—
......
BLUSH
FWUP

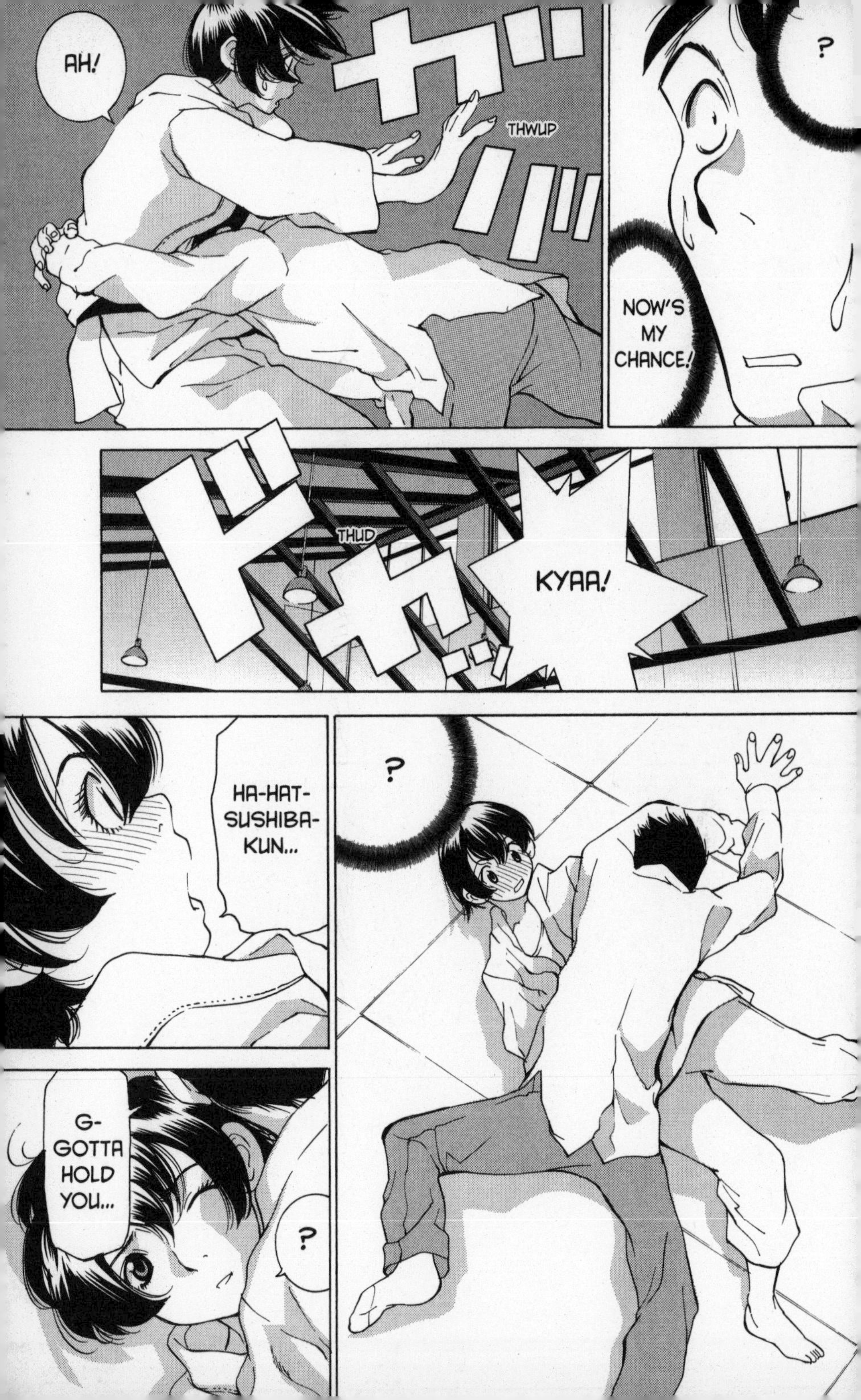
?
NOW'S MY CHANCE!
AH!
THWUP
KYAA!
THUD
?
HA-HAT-SUSHIBA-KUN...
G-GOTTA HOLD YOU...
?

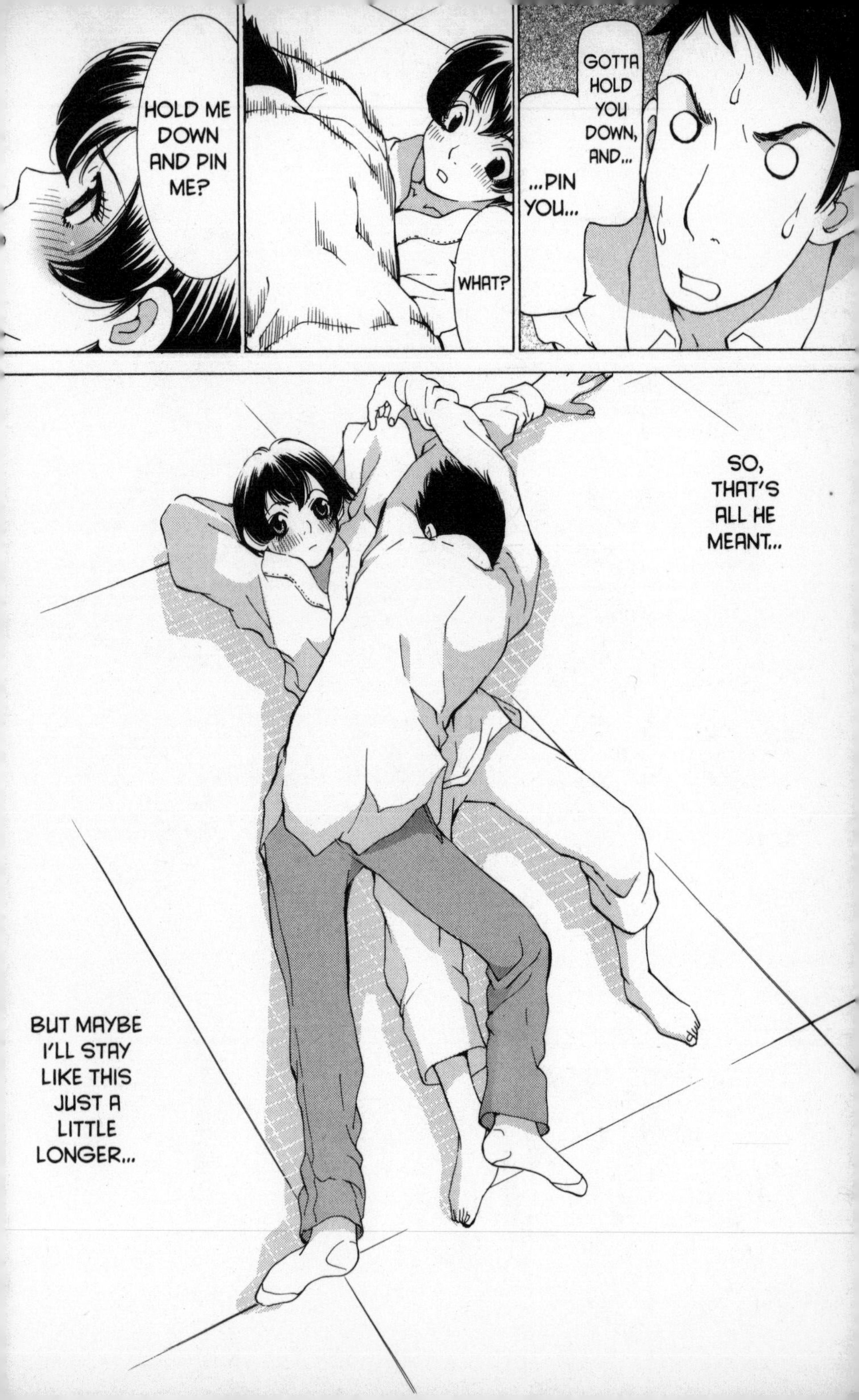
GOTTA HOLD YOU DOWN, AND...
...PIN YOU...
WHAT?
HOLD ME DOWN AND PIN ME?
SO, THAT'S ALL HE MEANT...
BUT MAYBE I'LL STAY LIKE THIS JUST A LITTLE LONGER...

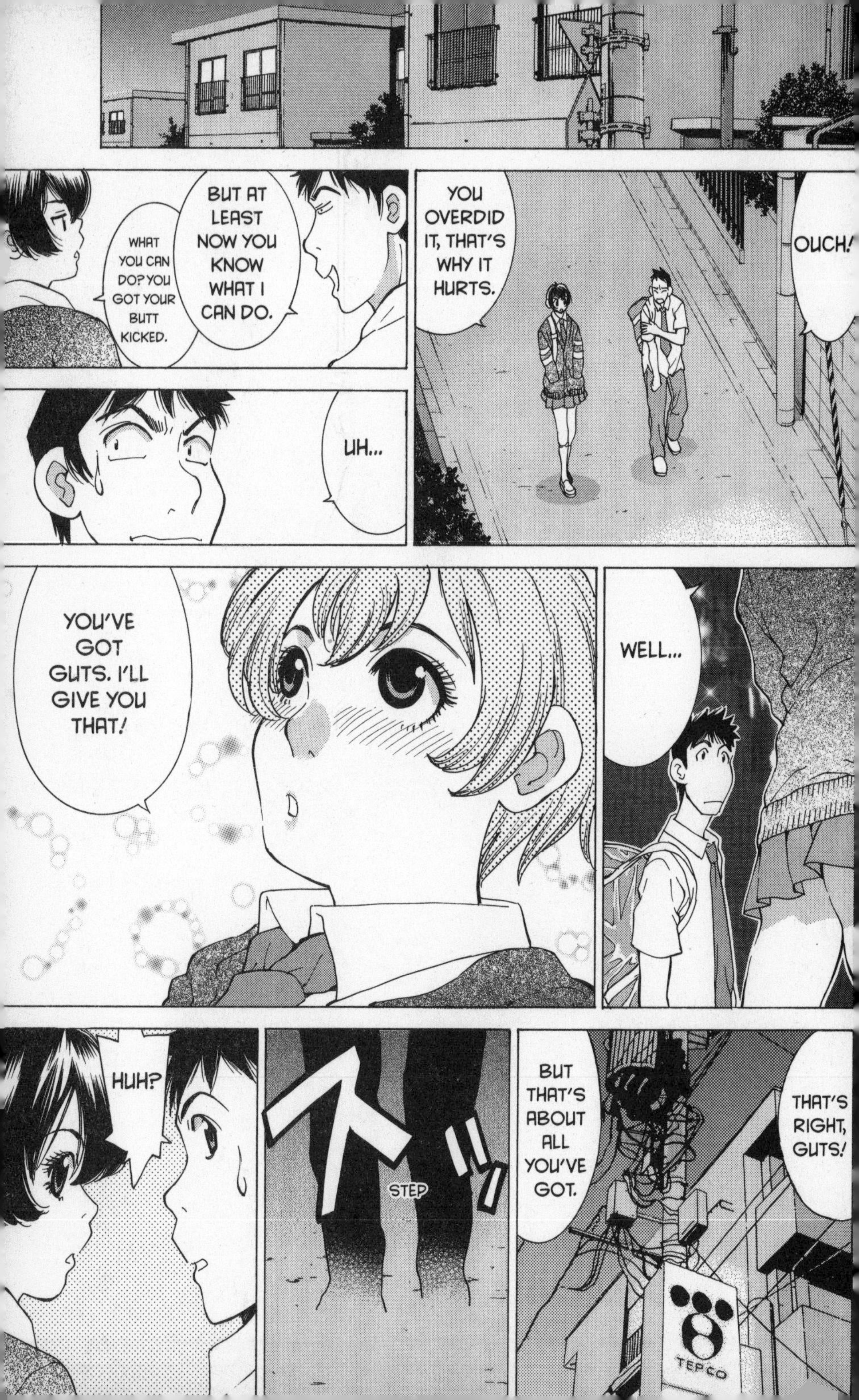
OUCH!
YOU OVERDID IT, THAT'S WHY IT HURTS.
BUT AT LEAST NOW YOU KNOW WHAT I CAN DO.
WHAT YOU CAN DO? YOU GOT YOUR BUTT KICKED.
UH...
WELL...
YOU'VE GOT GUTS. I'LL GIVE YOU THAT!
THAT'S RIGHT, GUTS!
BUT THAT'S ABOUT ALL YOU'VE GOT.
TEPCO
STEP
HUH?

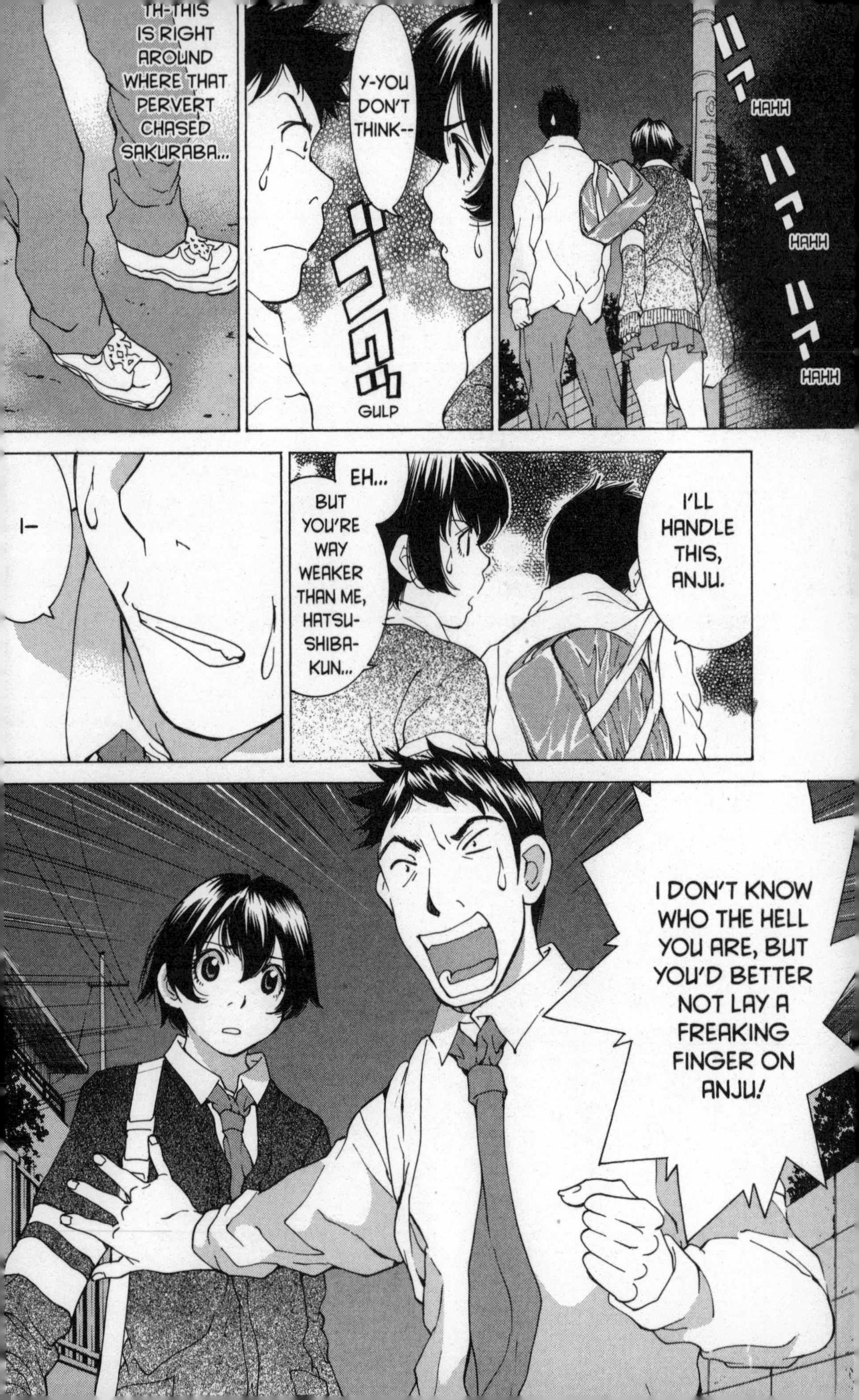
HAHH
HAHH
HAHH
Y-YOU DON'T THINK--
GULP
TH-THIS IS RIGHT AROUND WHERE THAT PERVERT CHASED SAKURABA...
I'LL HANDLE THIS, ANJU.
EH... BUT YOU'RE WAY WEAKER THAN ME, HATSUSHIBA-KUN...
I—
I DON'T KNOW WHO THE HELL YOU ARE, BUT YOU'D BETTER NOT LAY A FREAKING FINGER ON ANJU!

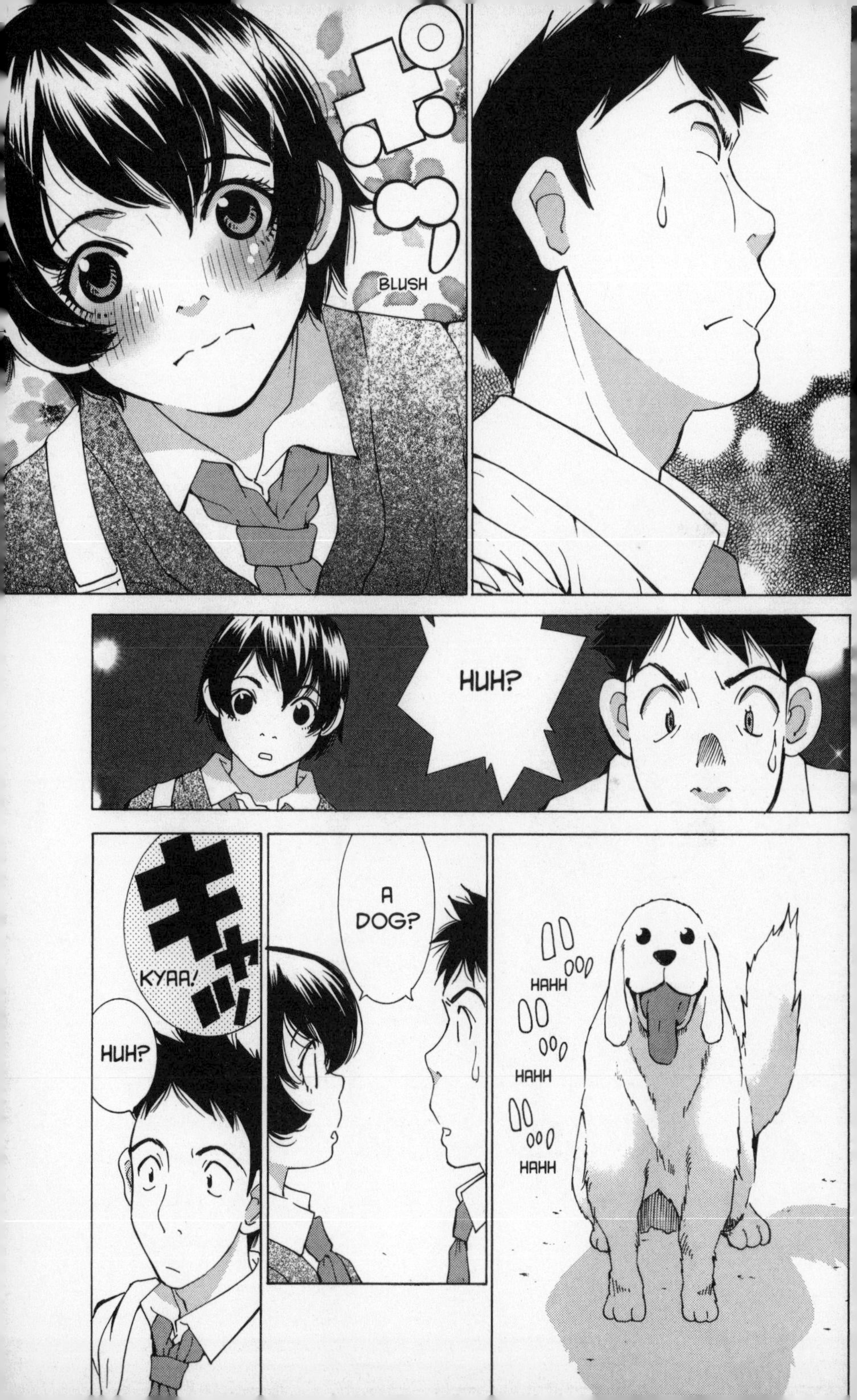
BLUSH
HUH?
HAHH
HAHH
HAHH
A DOG?
KYAA!
HUH?

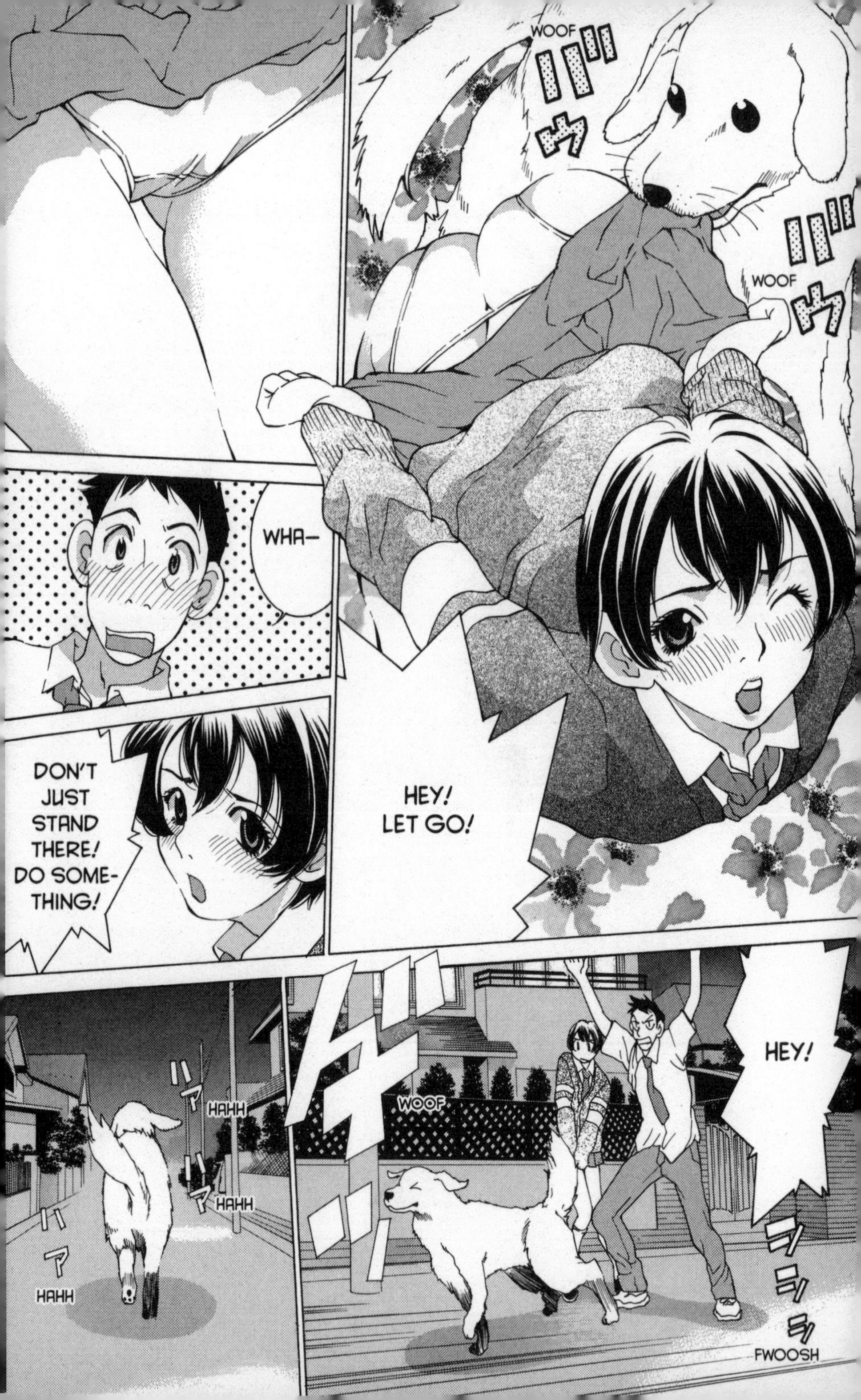
WOOF
WOOF
HEY! LET GO!
WHA—
DON'T JUST STAND THERE! DO SOME-THING!
HEY!
WOOF
FWOOSH
HAHH
HAHH
HAHH

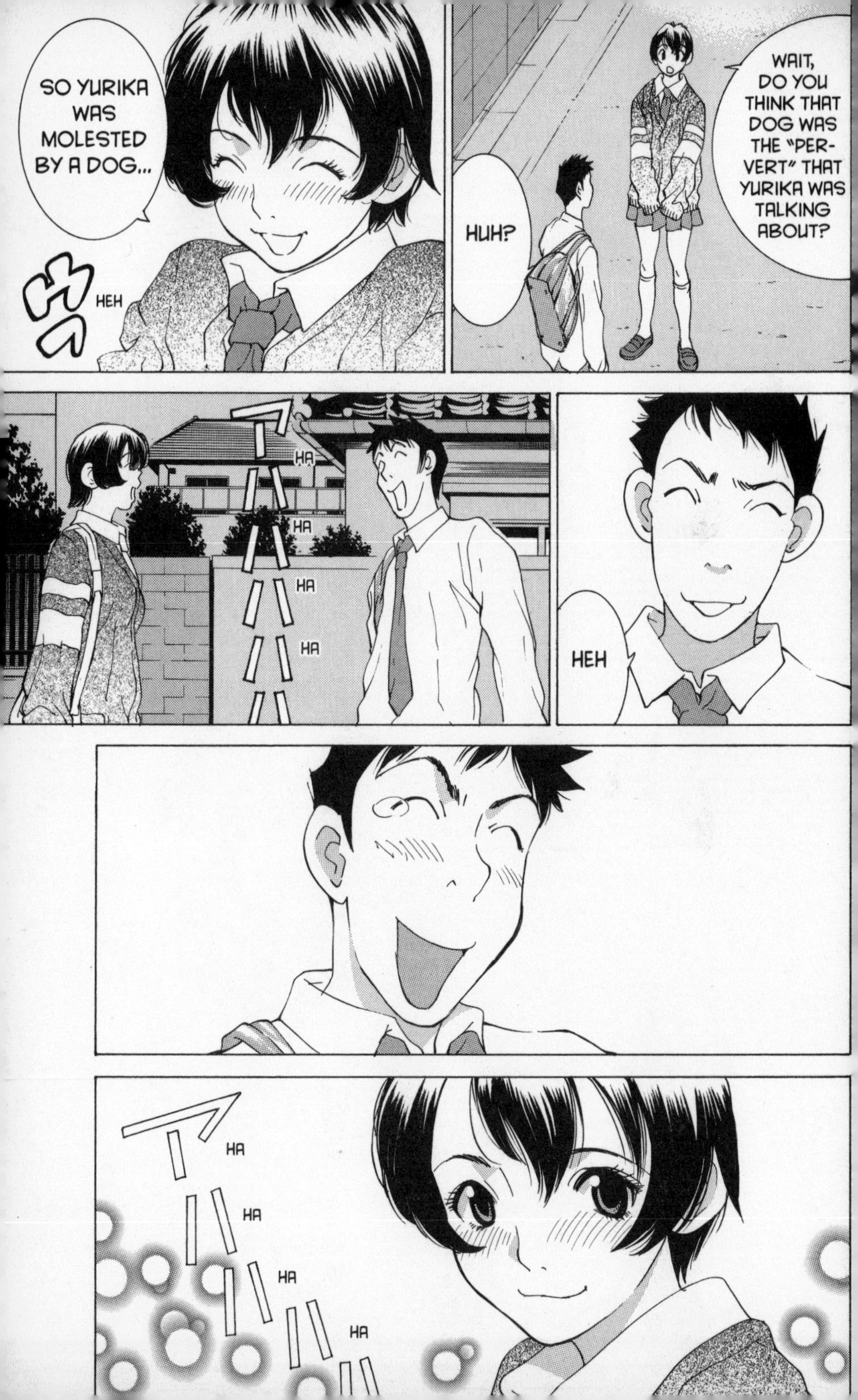
WAIT, DO YOU THINK THAT DOG WAS THE "PER-VERT" THAT YURIKA WAS TALKING ABOUT?
HUH?
SO YURIKA WAS MOLESTED BY A DOG...
HEH
HEH
HA
HA
HA
HA
HA
HA
HA
HA

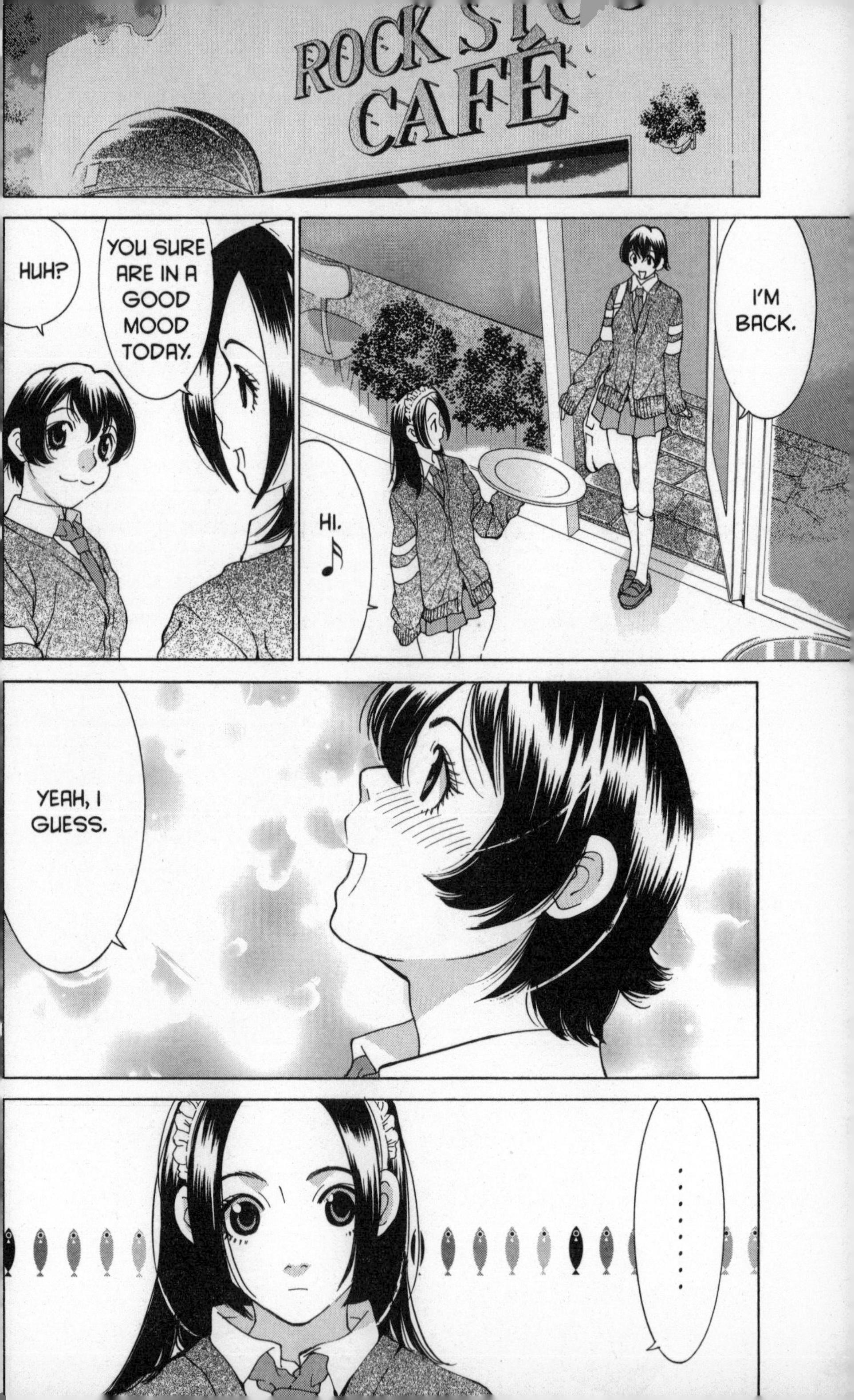
ROCK ST
CAFÉ
I'M BACK.
HI. ♪
YOU SURE ARE IN A GOOD MOOD TODAY.
HUH?
YEAH, I GUESS.
....

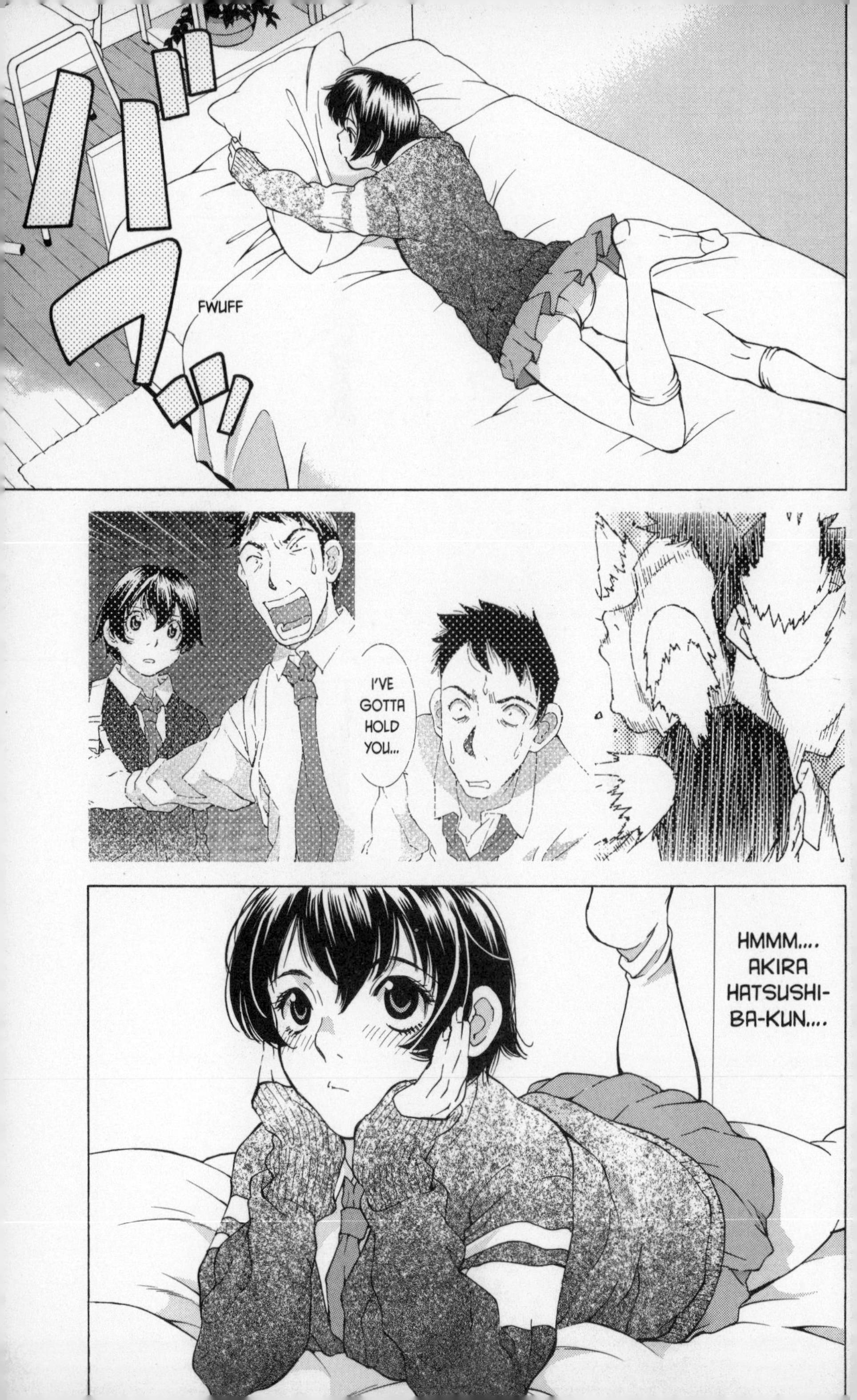
FWUFF
I'VE GOTTA HOLD YOU...
HMMM.... AKIRA HATSUSHIBA-KUN....

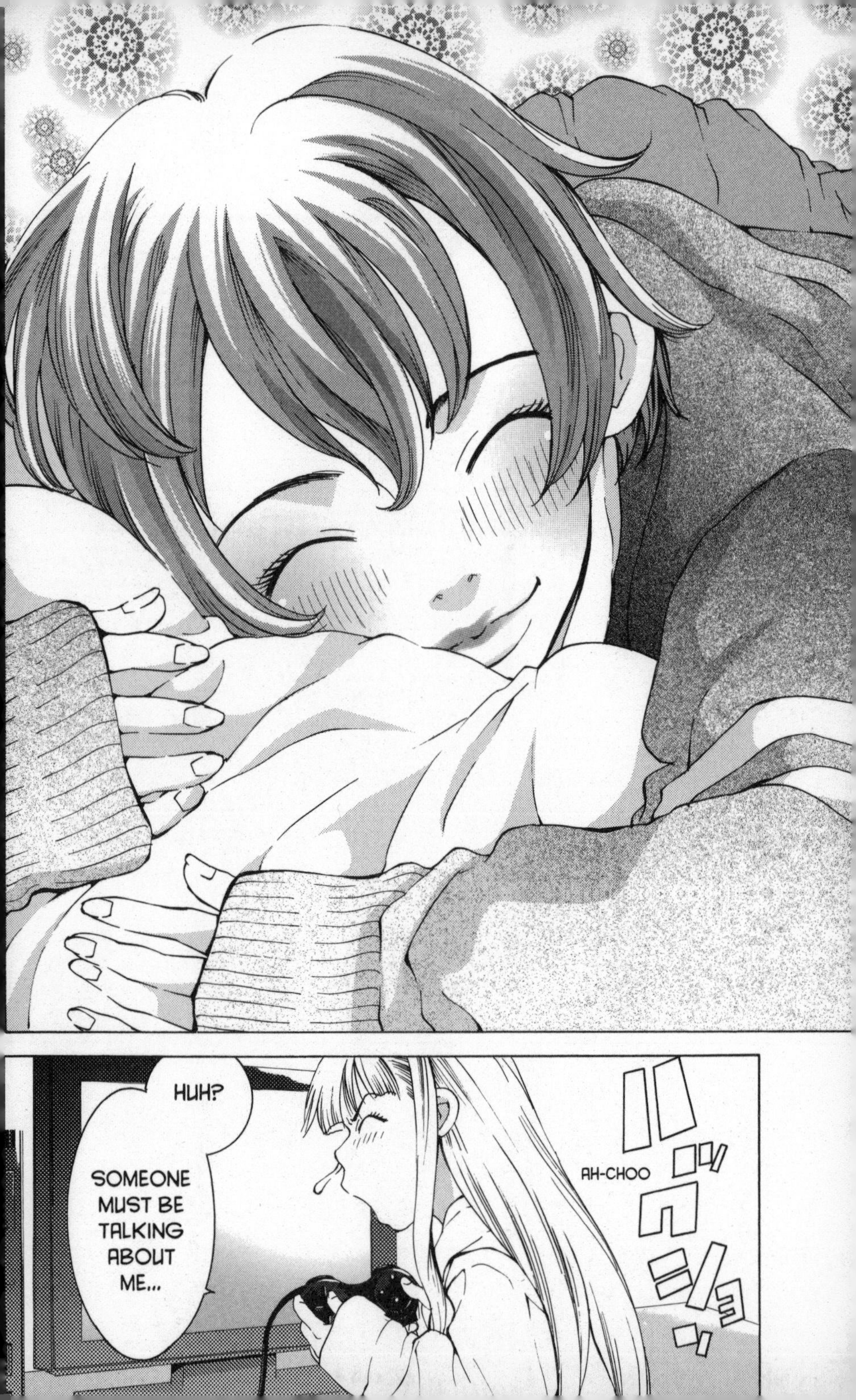
AH-CHOO
HUH?
SOMEONE MUST BE TALKING ABOUT ME...

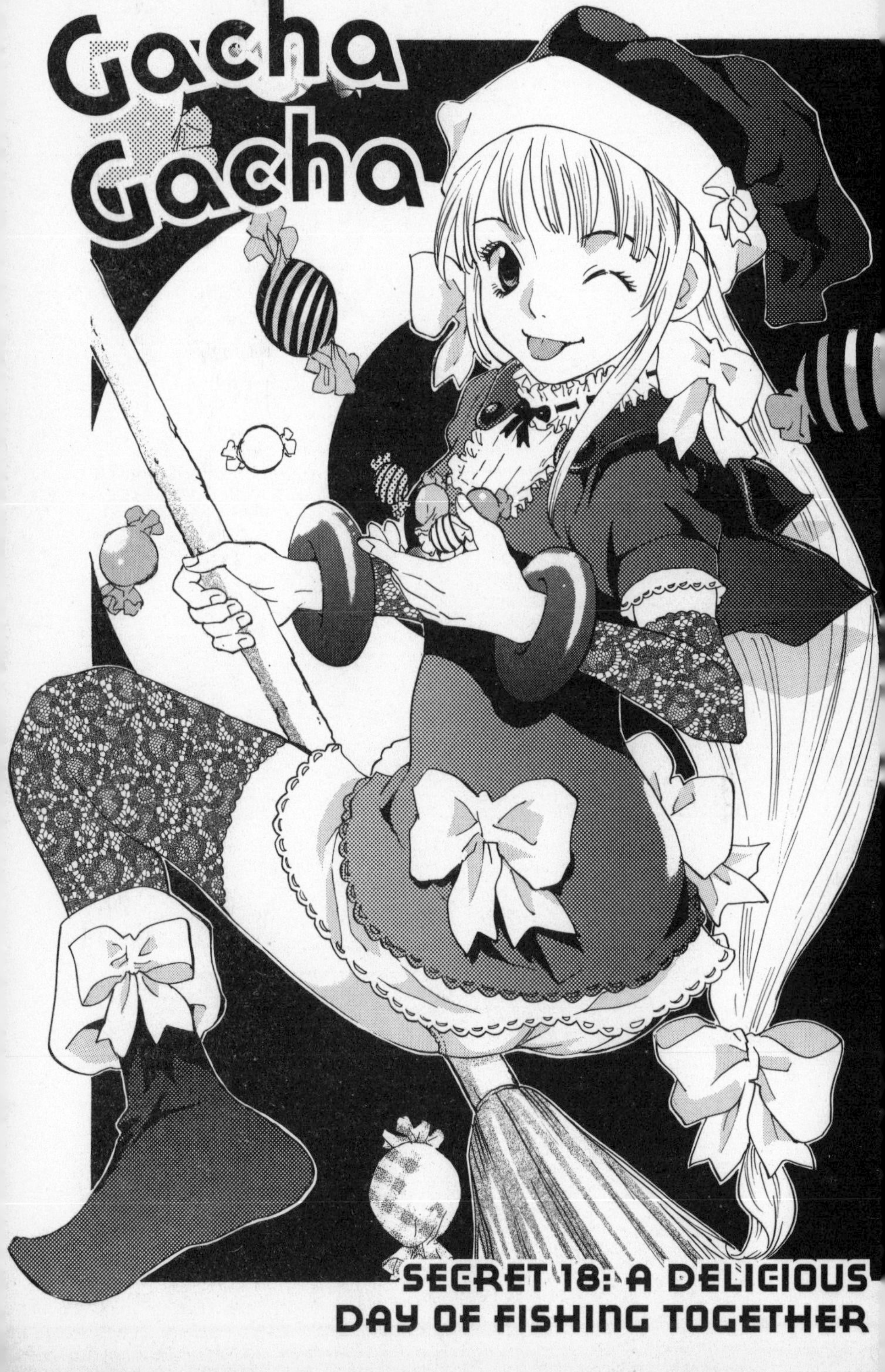
Gacha Gacha
SECRET 18: A DELICIOUS DAY OF FISHING TOGETHER

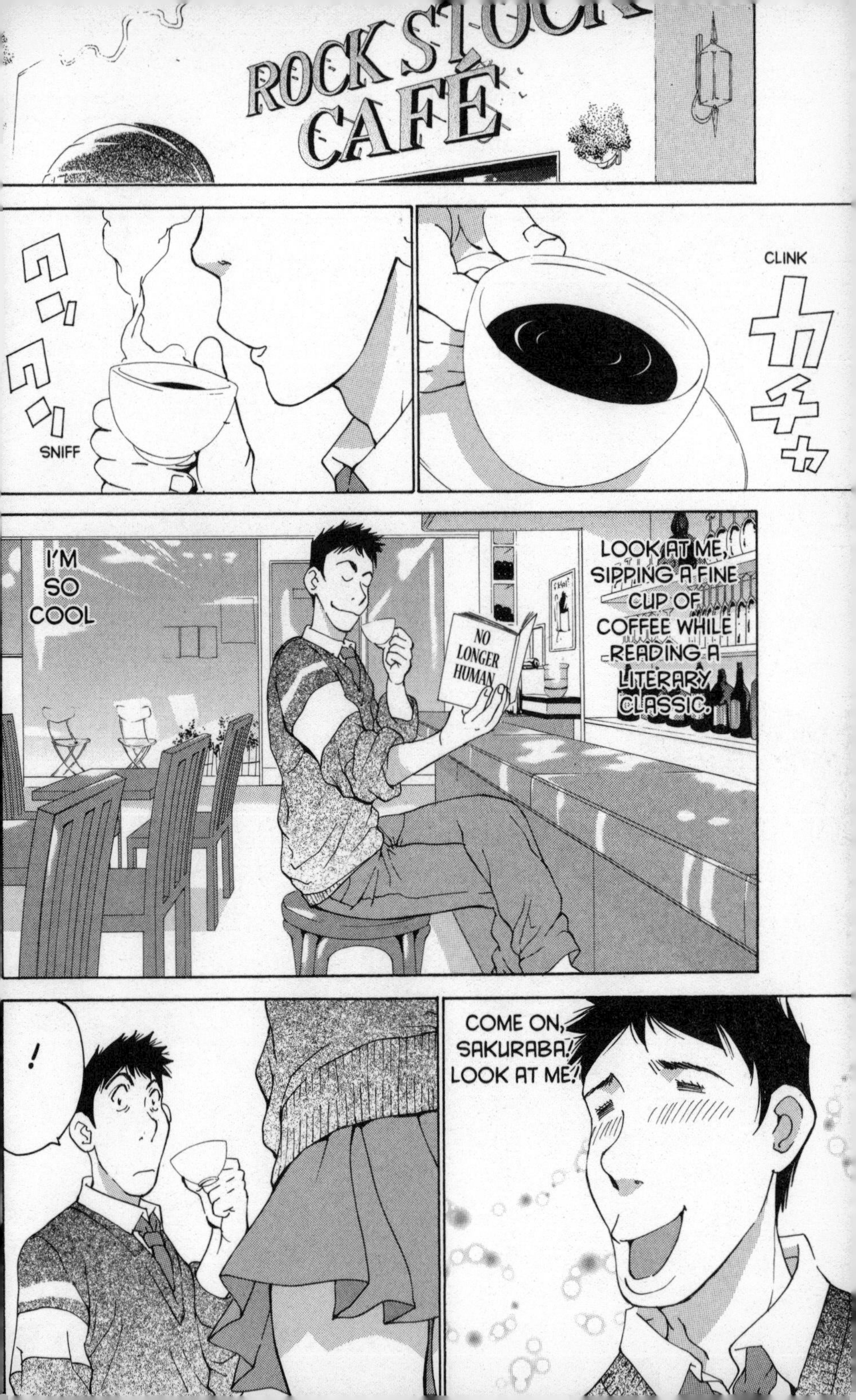
ROCK STOC
CAFÉ
CLINK
カチャ
クンクン
SNIFF
LOOK AT ME, SIPPING A FINE CUP OF COFFEE WHILE READING A LITERARY CLASSIC.
NO LONGER HUMAN
I'M SO COOL
COME ON, SAKURABA! LOOK AT ME!
!

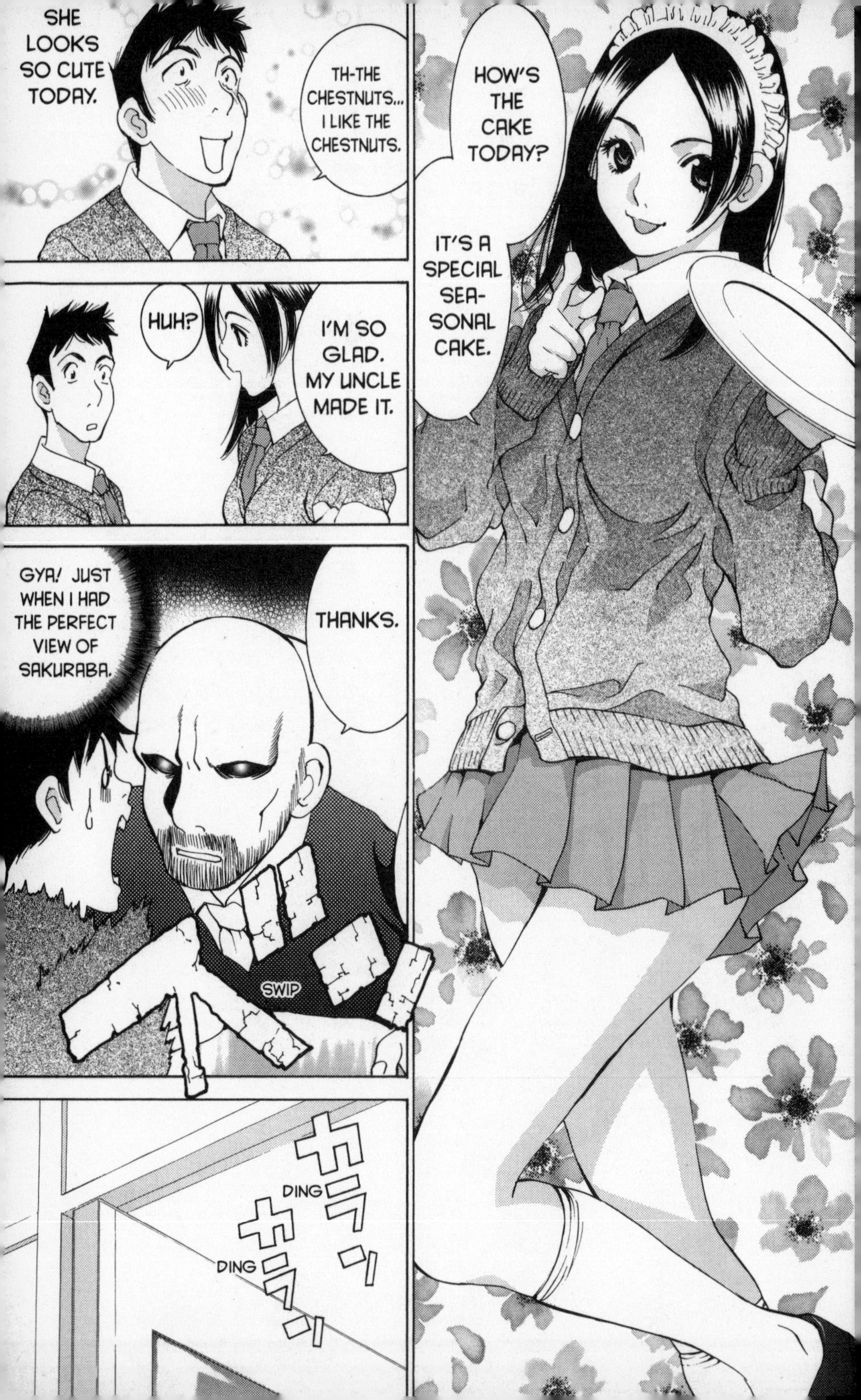
HOW'S THE CAKE TODAY?
IT'S A SPECIAL SEA-SONAL CAKE.
TH-THE CHESTNUTS... I LIKE THE CHESTNUTS.
SHE LOOKS SO CUTE TODAY.
I'M SO GLAD. MY UNCLE MADE IT.
HUH?
THANKS.
GYA! JUST WHEN I HAD THE PERFECT VIEW OF SAKURABA.
SWIP
DING
DING

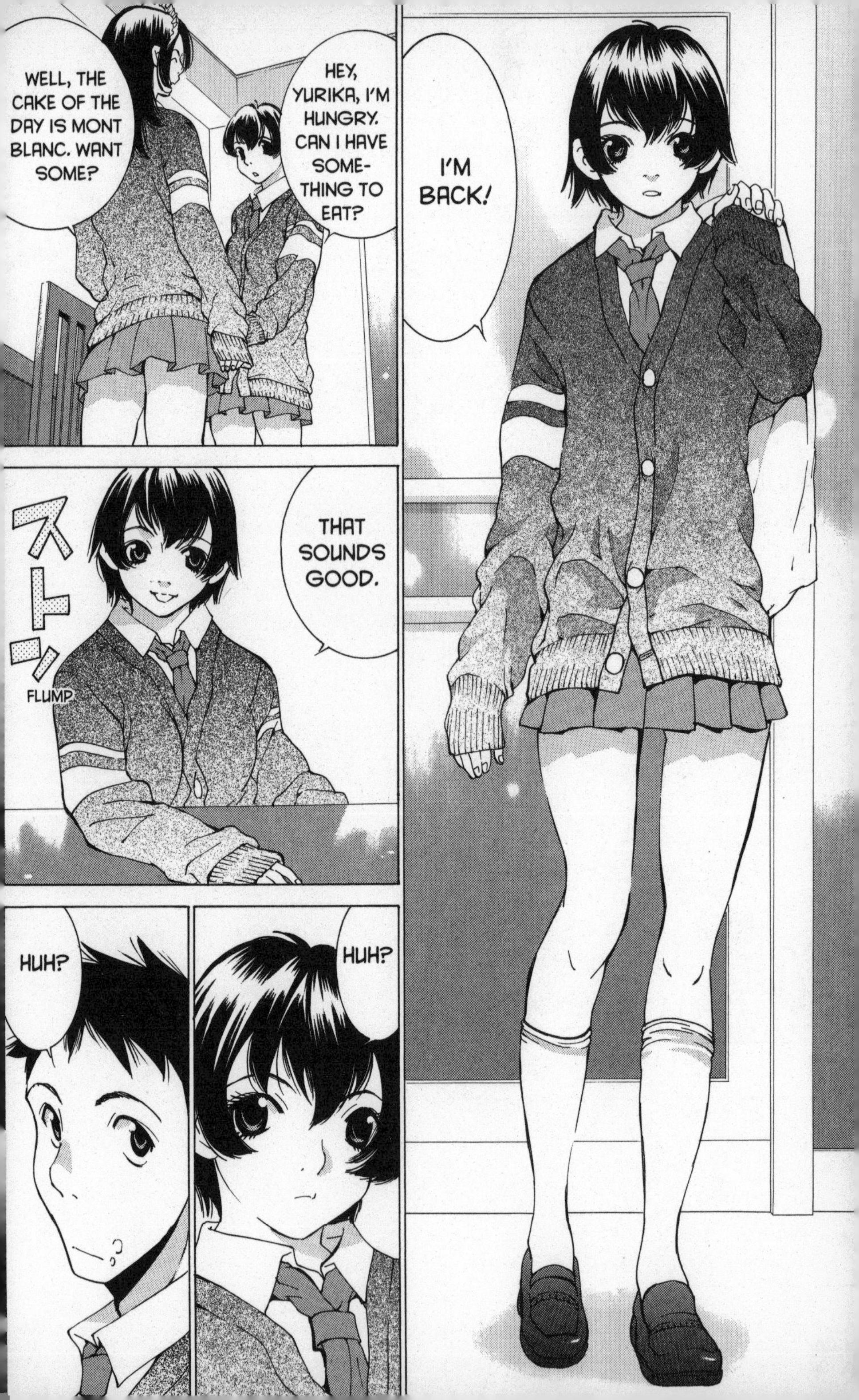
I'M BACK!
HEY, YURIKA, I'M HUNGRY. CAN I HAVE SOMETHING TO EAT?
WELL, THE CAKE OF THE DAY IS MONT BLANC. WANT SOME?
THAT SOUNDS GOOD.
ストッ
FLUMP
HUH?
HUH?

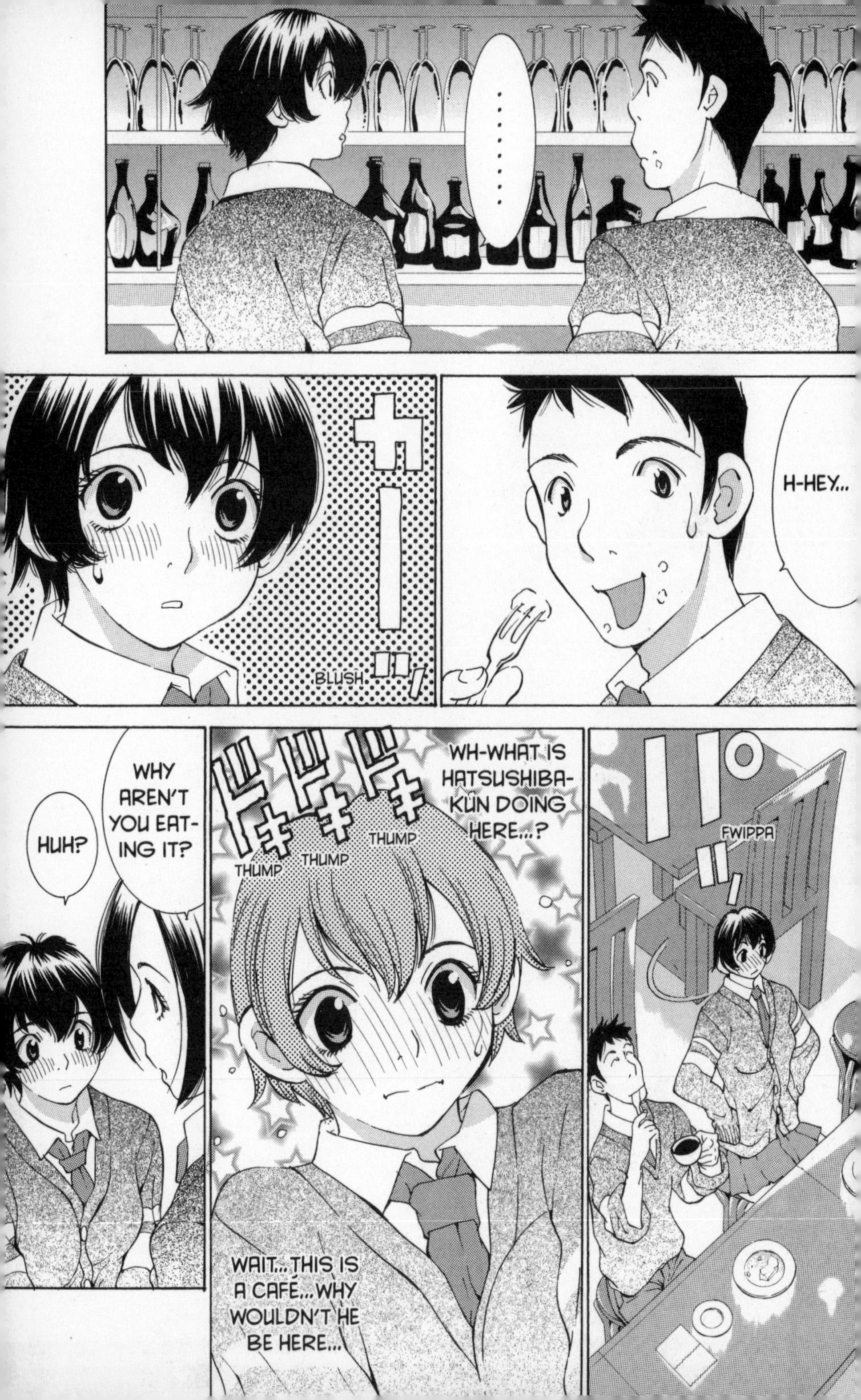
......
H-HEY...
BLUSH
FWIPPA
WH-WHAT IS HATSUSHIBA-KUN DOING HERE...?
THUMP THUMP THUMP
WAIT... THIS IS A CAFÉ... WHY WOULDN'T HE BE HERE...
WHY AREN'T YOU EAT-ING IT?
HUH?

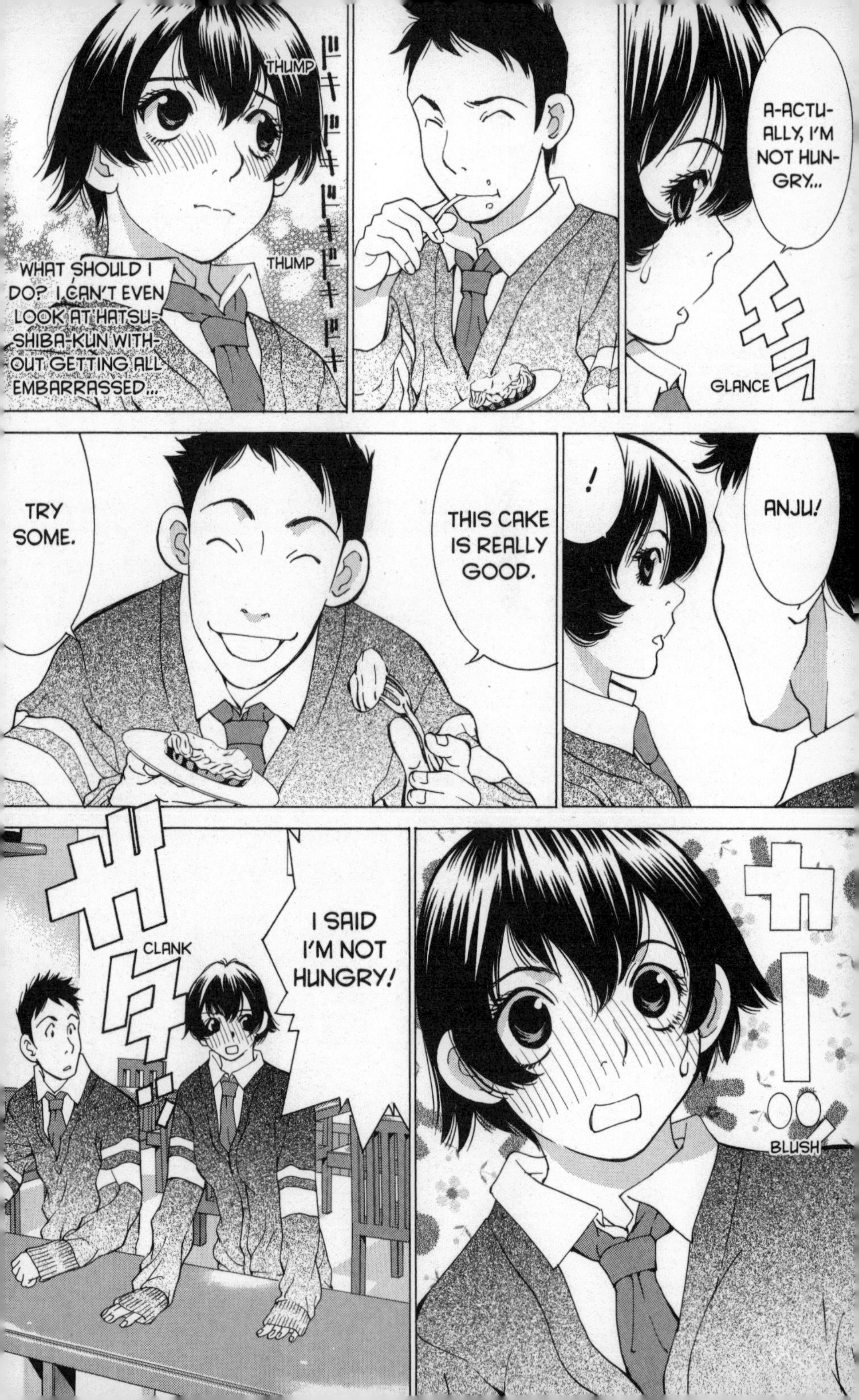
A-ACTU-ALLY, I'M NOT HUN-GRY...
GLANCE
THUMP
THUMP
WHAT SHOULD I DO? I CAN'T EVEN LOOK AT HATSU-SHIBA-KUN WITH-OUT GETTING ALL EMBARRASSED...
ANJU!
!
THIS CAKE IS REALLY GOOD.
TRY SOME.
BLUSH
I SAID I'M NOT HUNGRY!
CLANK

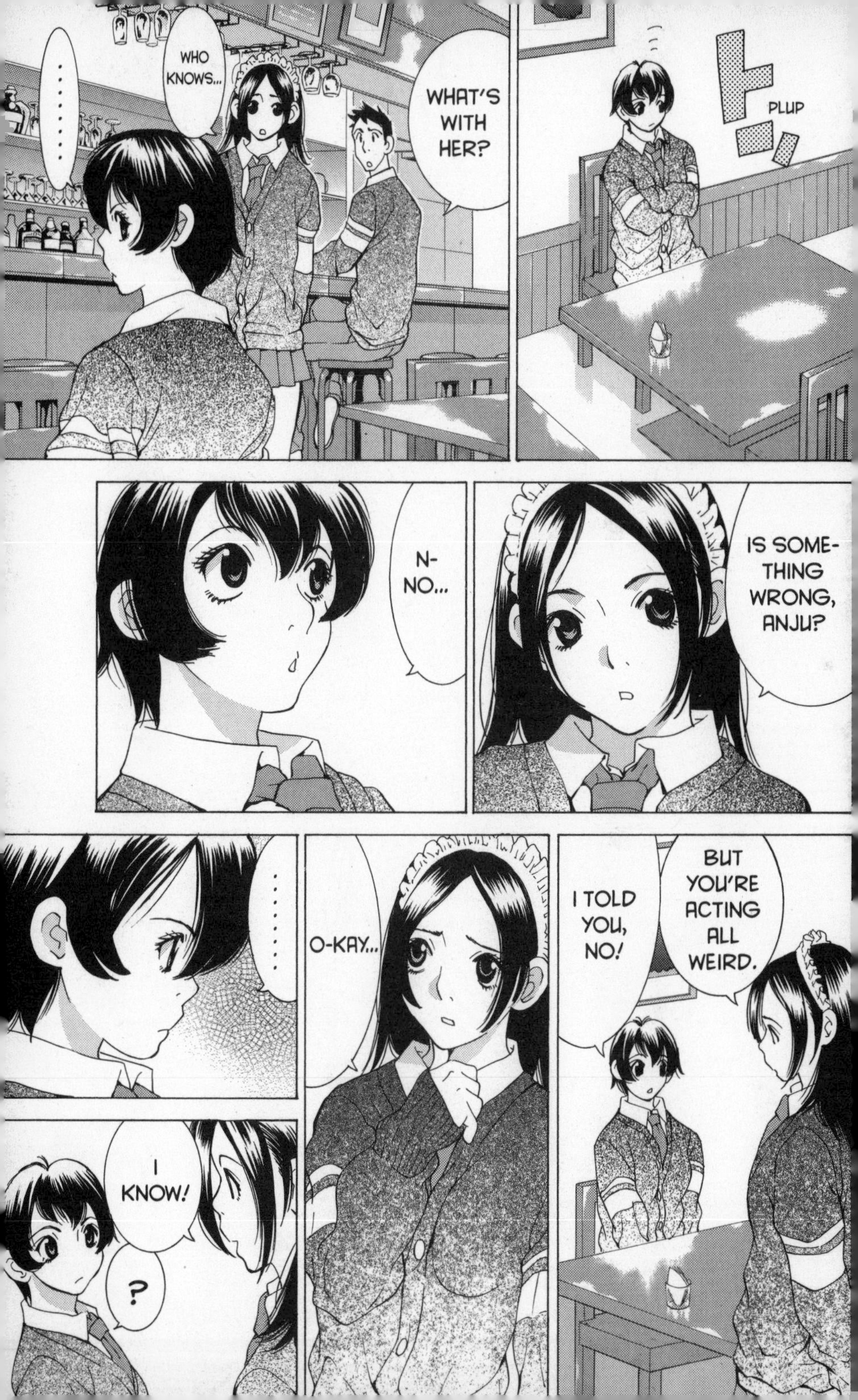
PLUP
WHAT'S WITH HER?
WHO KNOWS...
......
IS SOME-THING WRONG, ANJU?
N-NO...
BUT YOU'RE ACTING ALL WEIRD.
I TOLD YOU, NO!
O-KAY...
......
I KNOW!
?

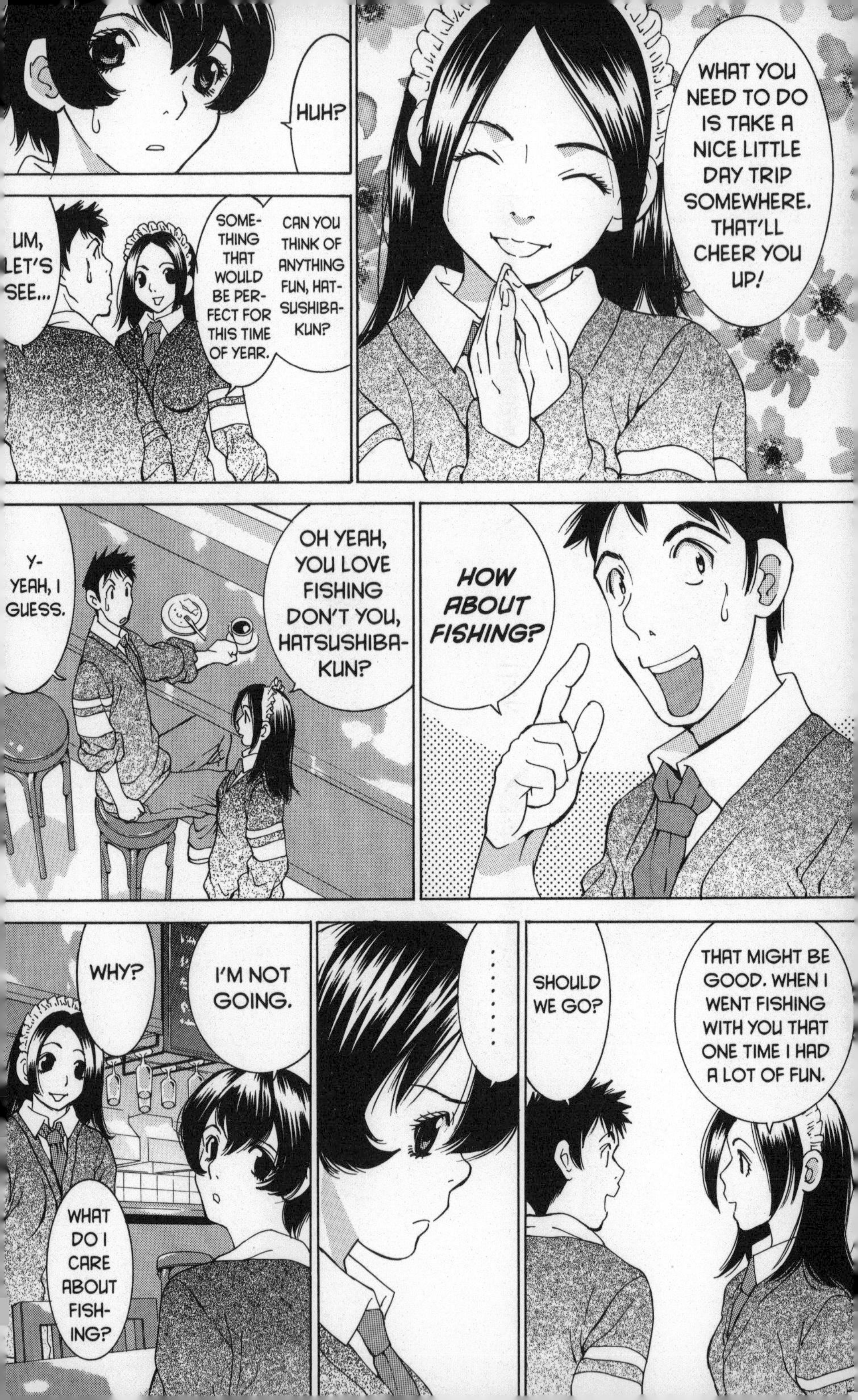
WHAT YOU NEED TO DO IS TAKE A NICE LITTLE DAY TRIP SOMEWHERE. THAT'LL CHEER YOU UP!
HUH?
CAN YOU THINK OF ANYTHING FUN, HATSUSHIBA-KUN?
SOMETHING THAT WOULD BE PERFECT FOR THIS TIME OF YEAR.
UM, LET'S SEE...
HOW ABOUT FISHING?
OH YEAH, YOU LOVE FISHING DON'T YOU, HATSUSHIBA-KUN?
Y-YEAH, I GUESS.
THAT MIGHT BE GOOD. WHEN I WENT FISHING WITH YOU THAT ONE TIME I HAD A LOT OF FUN.
SHOULD WE GO?
....
I'M NOT GOING.
WHY?
WHAT DO I CARE ABOUT FISHING?

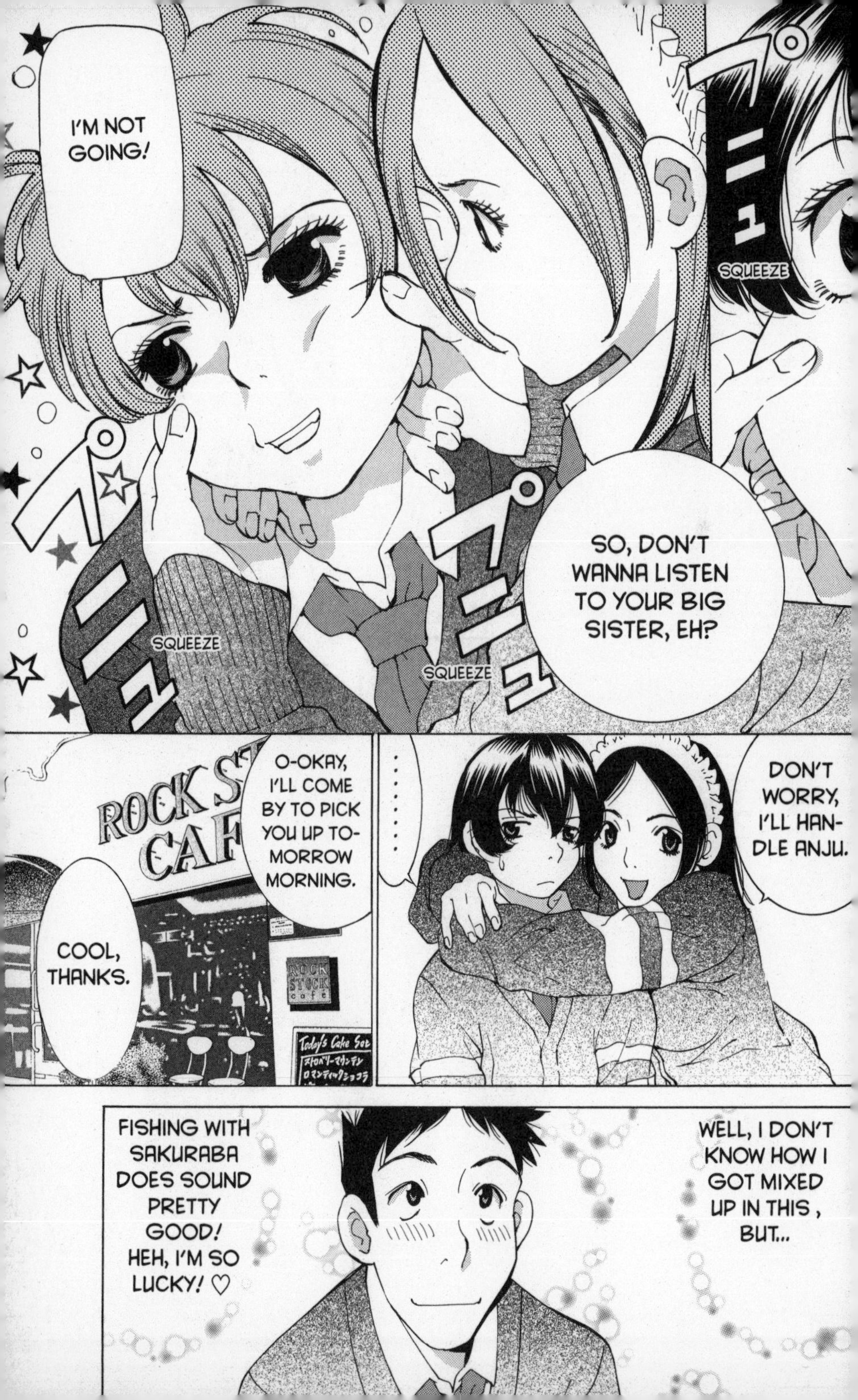
I'M NOT GOING!
SQUEEZE
SQUEEZE
SQUEEZE
SO, DON'T WANNA LISTEN TO YOUR BIG SISTER, EH?
DON'T WORRY, I'LL HANDLE ANJU.
......
O-OKAY, I'LL COME BY TO PICK YOU UP TOMORROW MORNING.
COOL, THANKS.
ROCK STOCK cafe
WELL, I DON'T KNOW HOW I GOT MIXED UP IN THIS , BUT...
FISHING WITH SAKURABA DOES SOUND PRETTY GOOD! HEH, I'M SO LUCKY! ♡

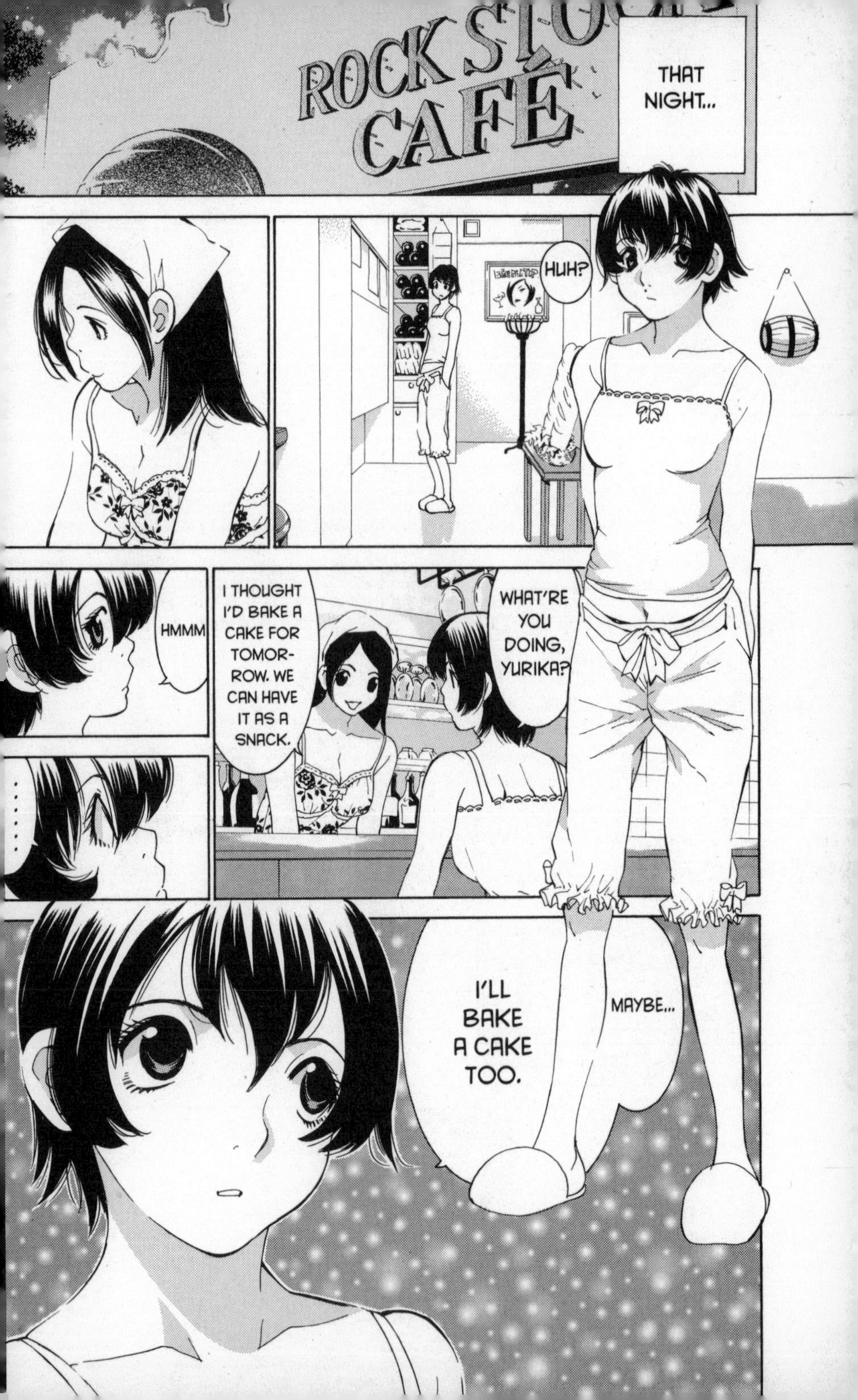
THAT NIGHT...
HUH?
WHAT'RE YOU DOING, YURIKA?
I THOUGHT I'D BAKE A CAKE FOR TOMOR-ROW. WE CAN HAVE IT AS A SNACK.
HMMM
......
MAYBE...
I'LL BAKE A CAKE TOO.

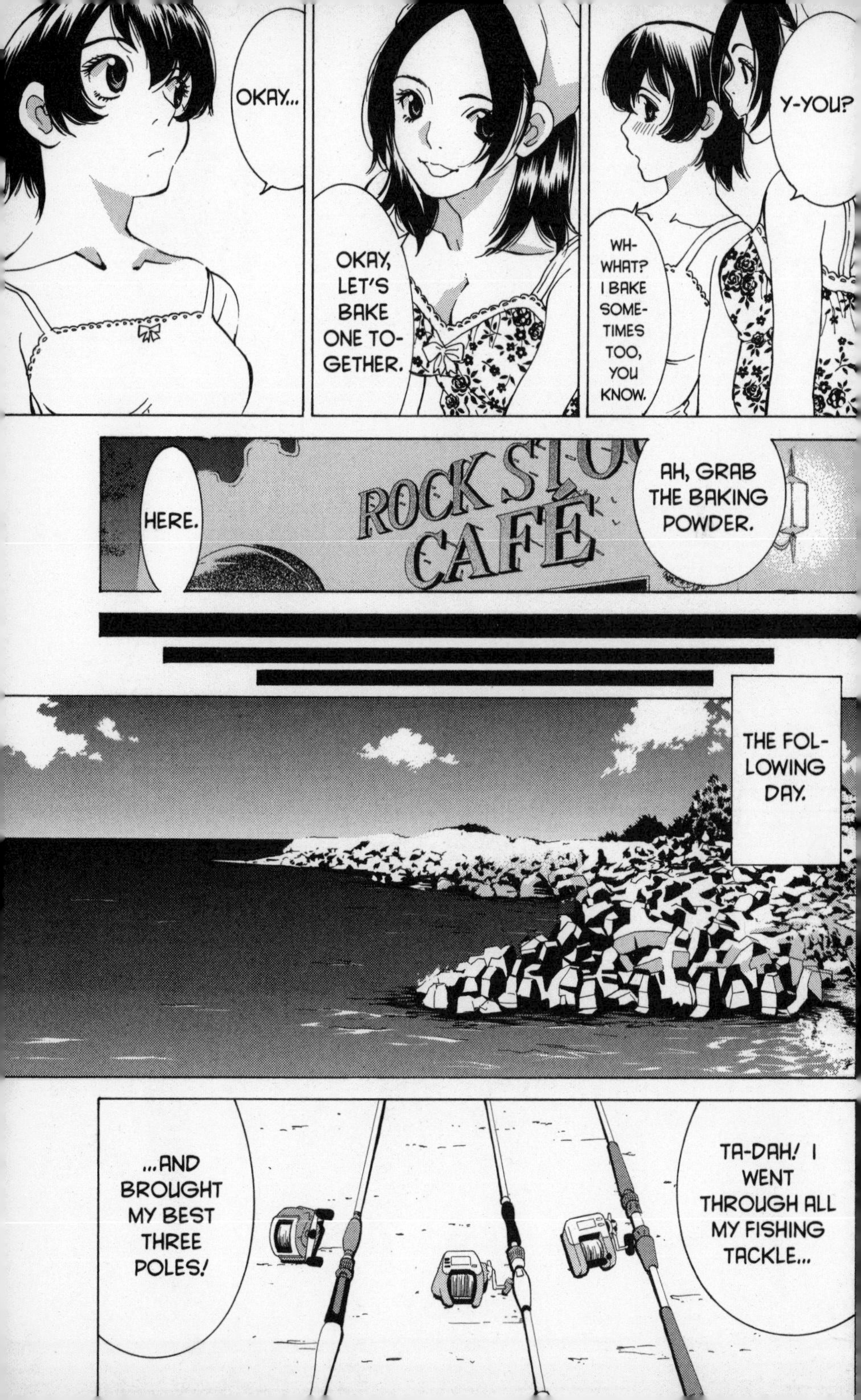
Y-YOU?
WH-WHAT? I BAKE SOMETIMES TOO, YOU KNOW.
OKAY, LET'S BAKE ONE TOGETHER.
OKAY...
AH, GRAB THE BAKING POWDER.
ROCK STO
CAFÉ
HERE.
THE FOLLOWING DAY.
TA-DAH! I WENT THROUGH ALL MY FISHING TACKLE...
...AND BROUGHT MY BEST THREE POLES!

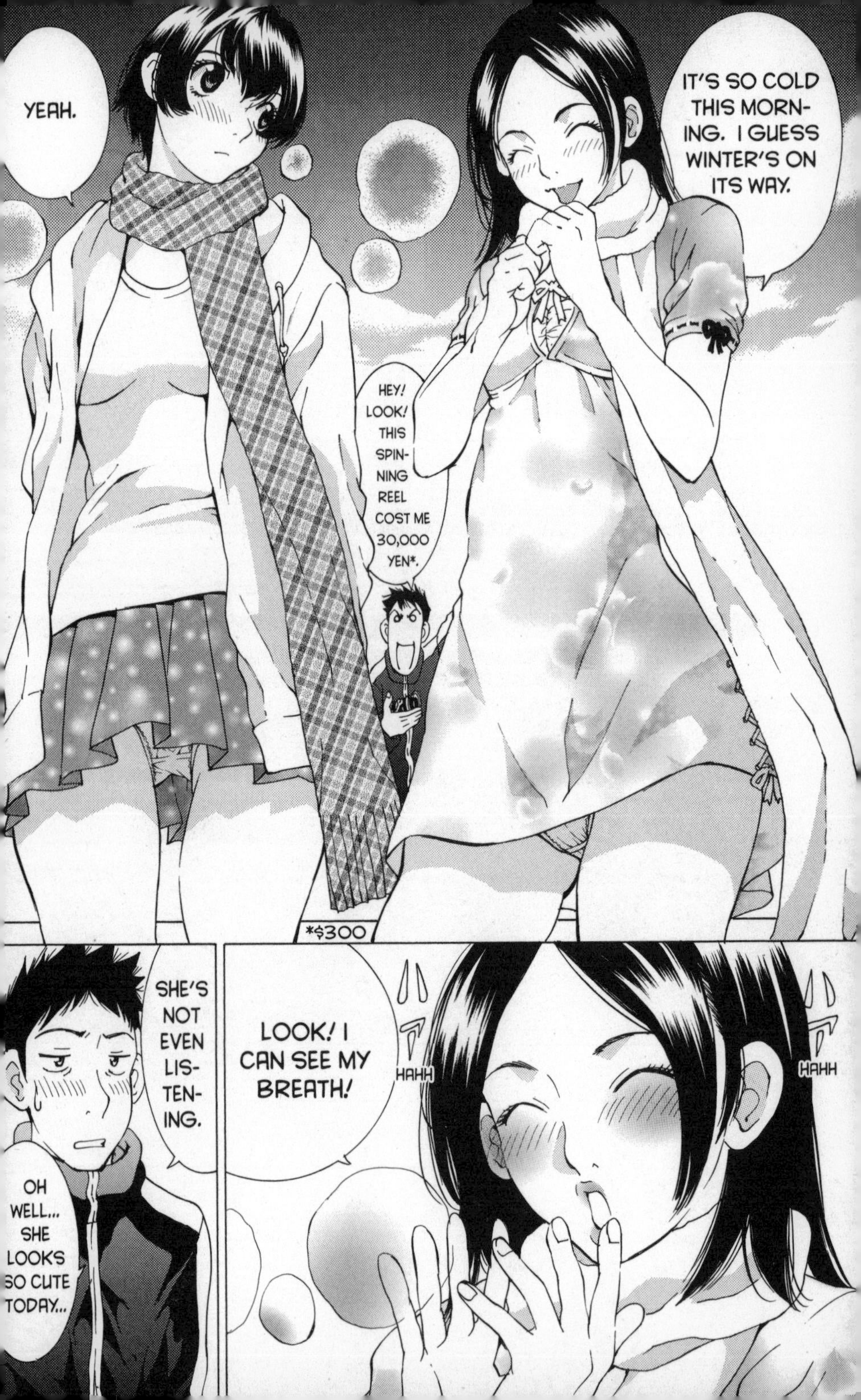
IT'S SO COLD THIS MORNING. I GUESS WINTER'S ON ITS WAY.
YEAH.
HEY! LOOK! THIS SPINNING REEL COST ME 30,000 YEN*.
*$300
LOOK! I CAN SEE MY BREATH!
HAHH
HAHH
SHE'S NOT EVEN LISTENING.
OH WELL... SHE LOOKS SO CUTE TODAY...

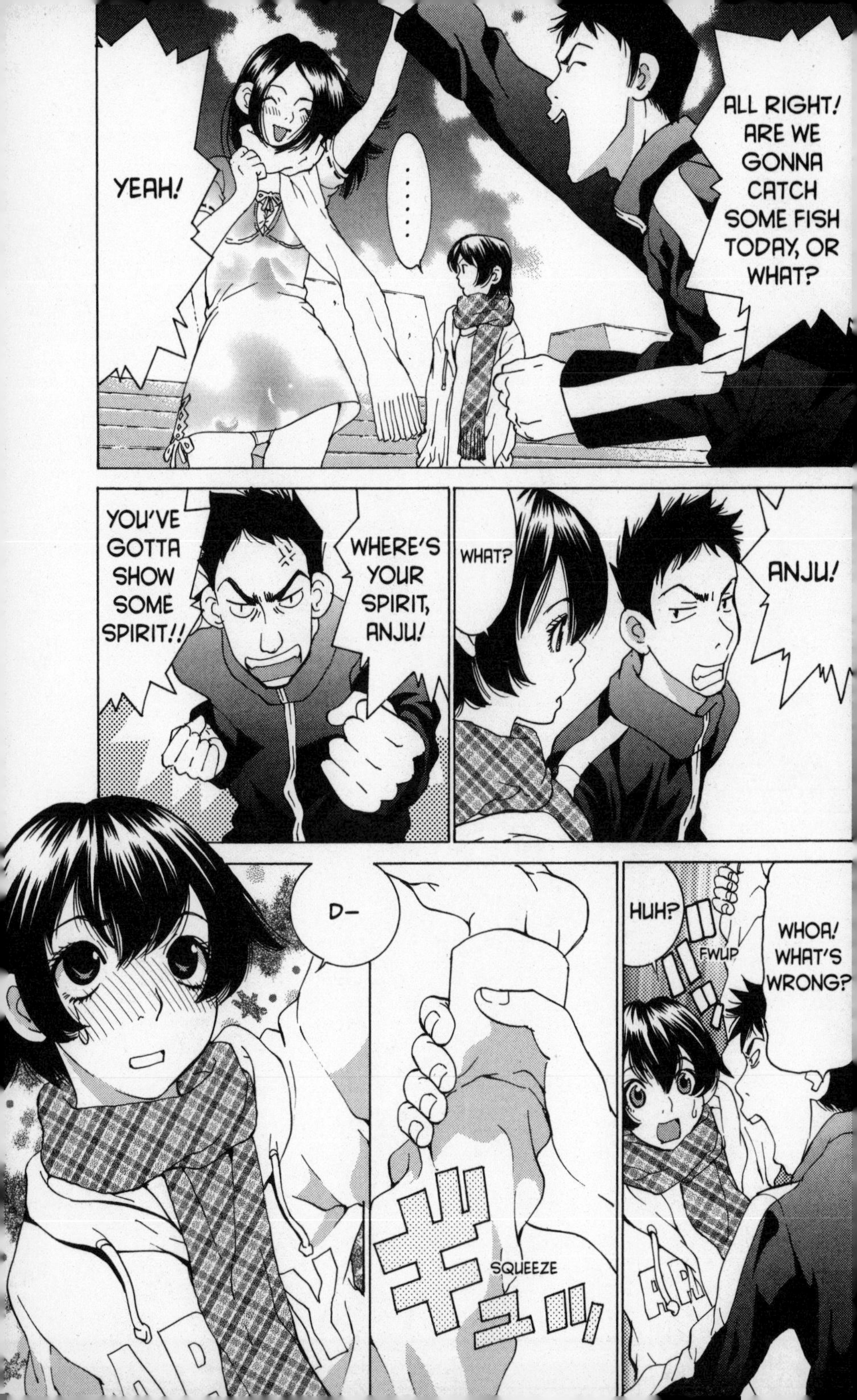
ALL RIGHT! ARE WE GONNA CATCH SOME FISH TODAY, OR WHAT?
YEAH!
......
ANJU!
WHAT?
WHERE'S YOUR SPIRIT, ANJU!
YOU'VE GOTTA SHOW SOME SPIRIT!!
WHOA! WHAT'S WRONG?
HUH?
FWUP
SQUEEZE
D–

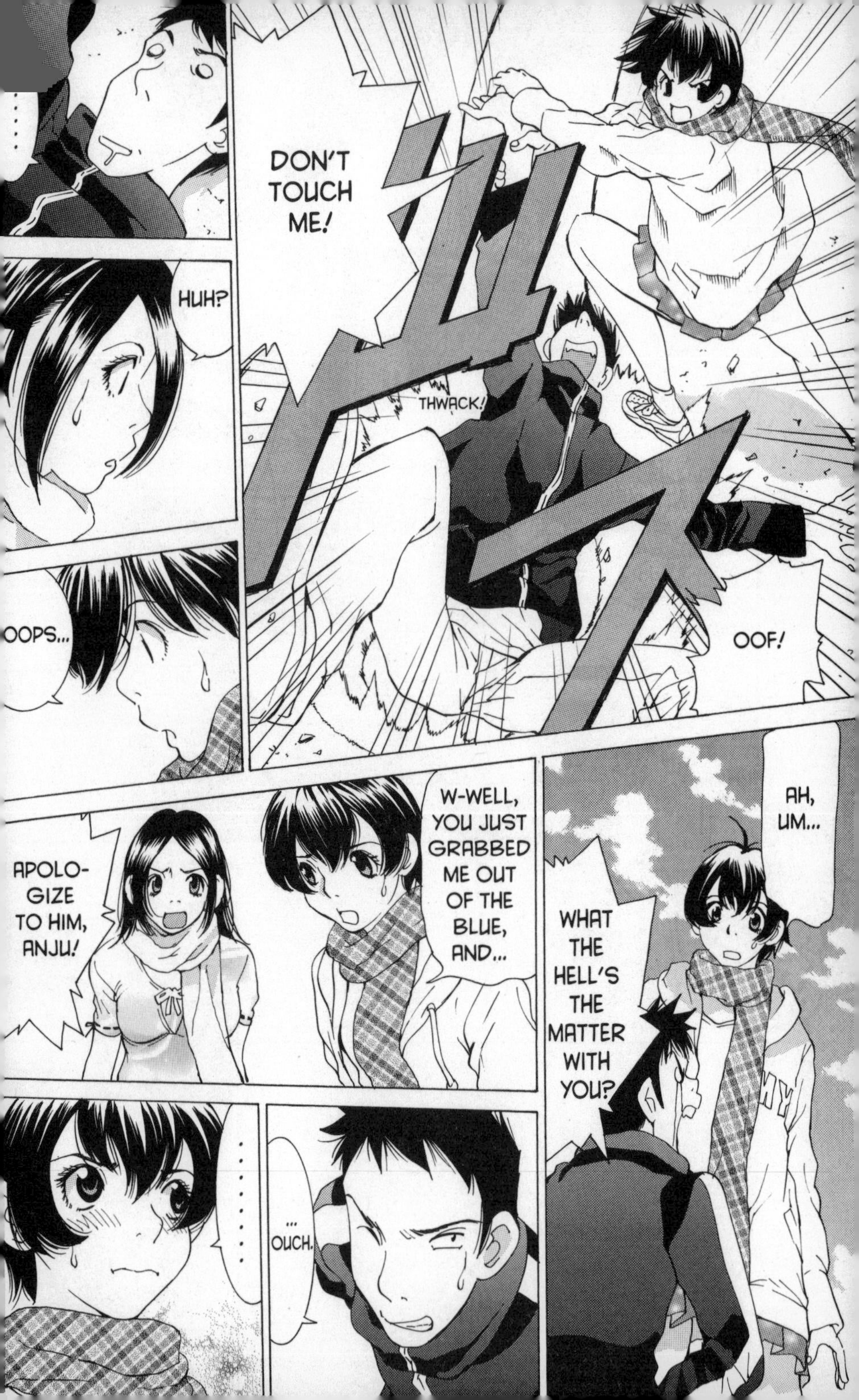
DON'T TOUCH ME!
THWACK!
OOF!
......
HUH?
OOPS...
AH, UM...
WHAT THE HELL'S THE MATTER WITH YOU?
W-WELL, YOU JUST GRABBED ME OUT OF THE BLUE, AND...
APOLO-GIZE TO HIM, ANJU!
... OUCH.
......

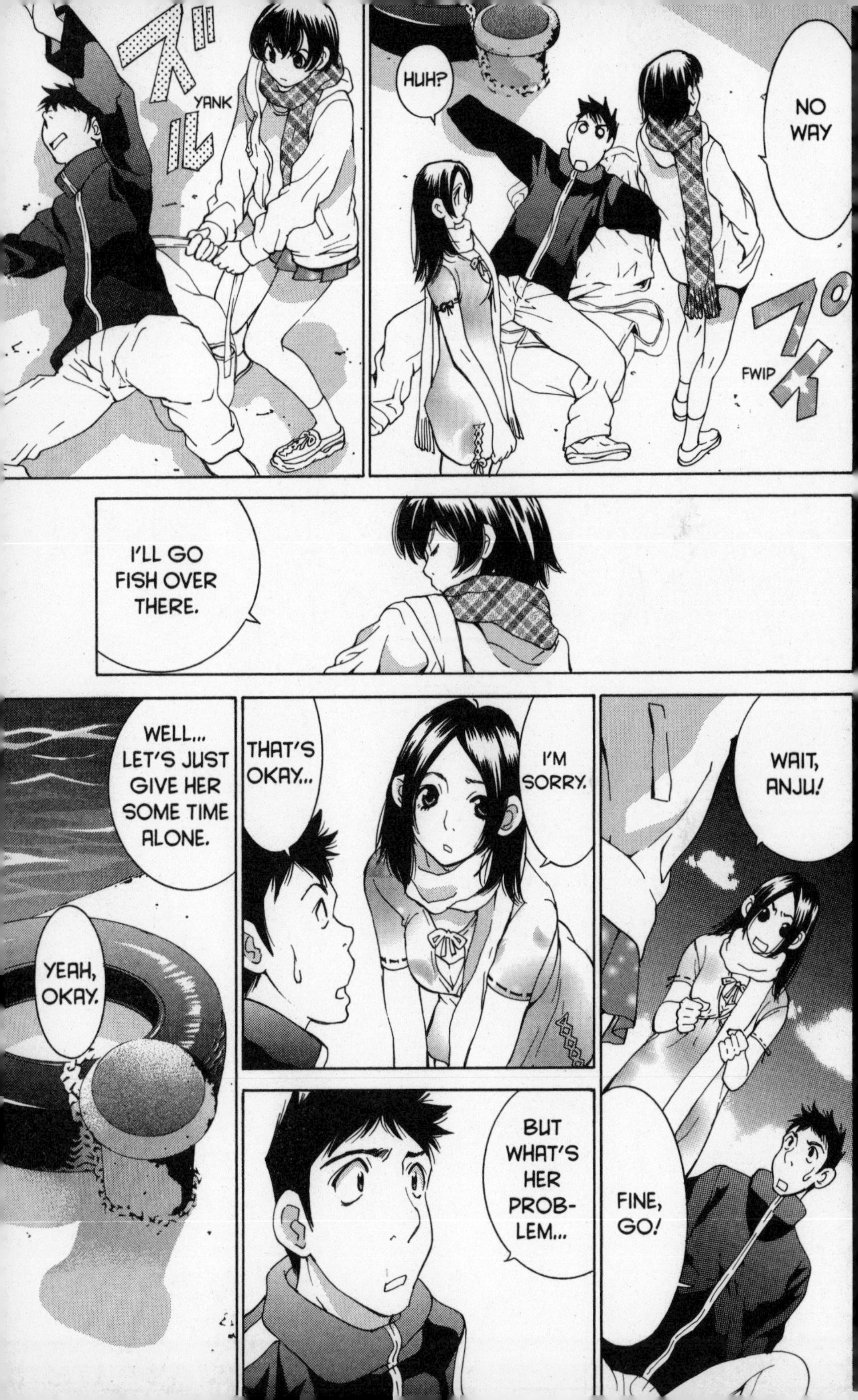
NO WAY
HUH?
FWIP
YANK
I'LL GO FISH OVER THERE.
WAIT, ANJU!
FINE, GO!
I'M SORRY.
THAT'S OKAY...
BUT WHAT'S HER PROB-LEM...
WELL... LET'S JUST GIVE HER SOME TIME ALONE.
YEAH, OKAY.

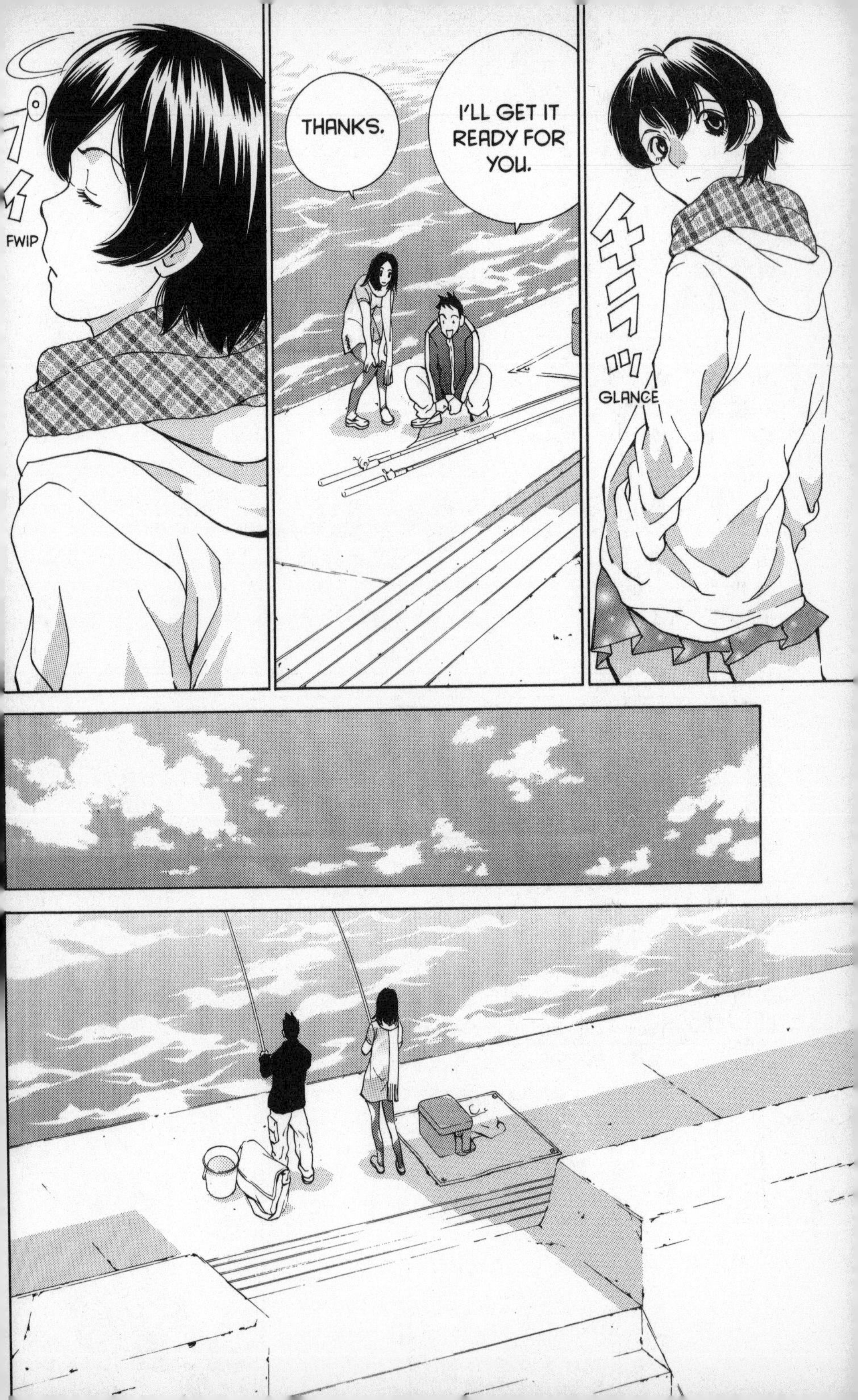
チラッ
GLANCE
I'LL GET IT READY FOR YOU.
THANKS.
プイ
FWIP

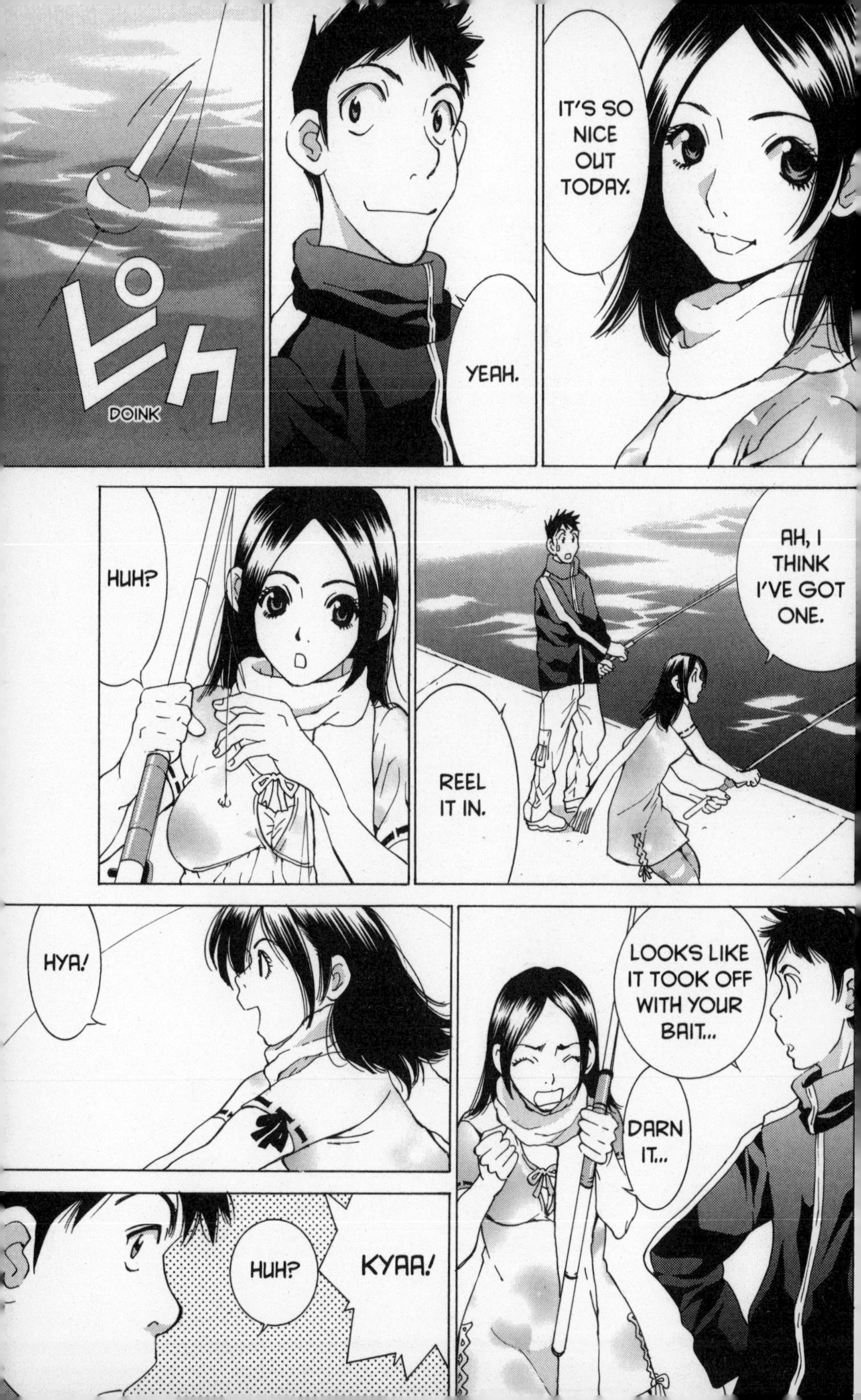
IT'S SO NICE OUT TODAY.
YEAH.
ピクン
DOINK
AH, I THINK I'VE GOT ONE.
REEL IT IN.
HUH?
LOOKS LIKE IT TOOK OFF WITH YOUR BAIT...
DARN IT...
HYA!
KYAA!
HUH?

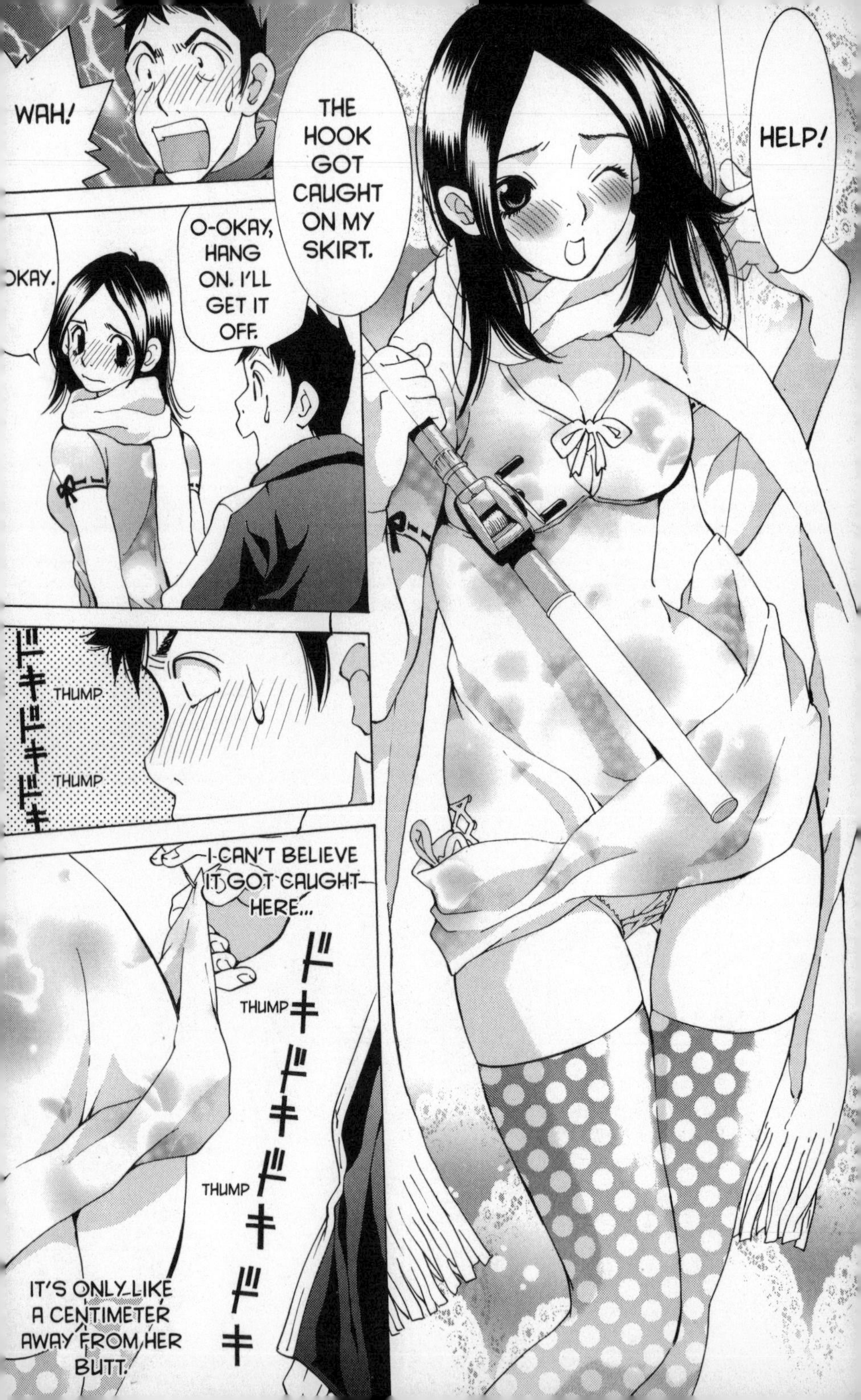
HELP!
THE HOOK GOT CAUGHT ON MY SKIRT.
WAH!
O-OKAY, HANG ON. I'LL GET IT OFF.
OKAY.
ドキ THUMP
ドキ THUMP
ドキ
I CAN'T BELIEVE IT GOT CAUGHT HERE...
ドキ THUMP
ドキ THUMP
ドキ
ドキ
IT'S ONLY LIKE A CENTIMETER AWAY FROM HER BUTT.

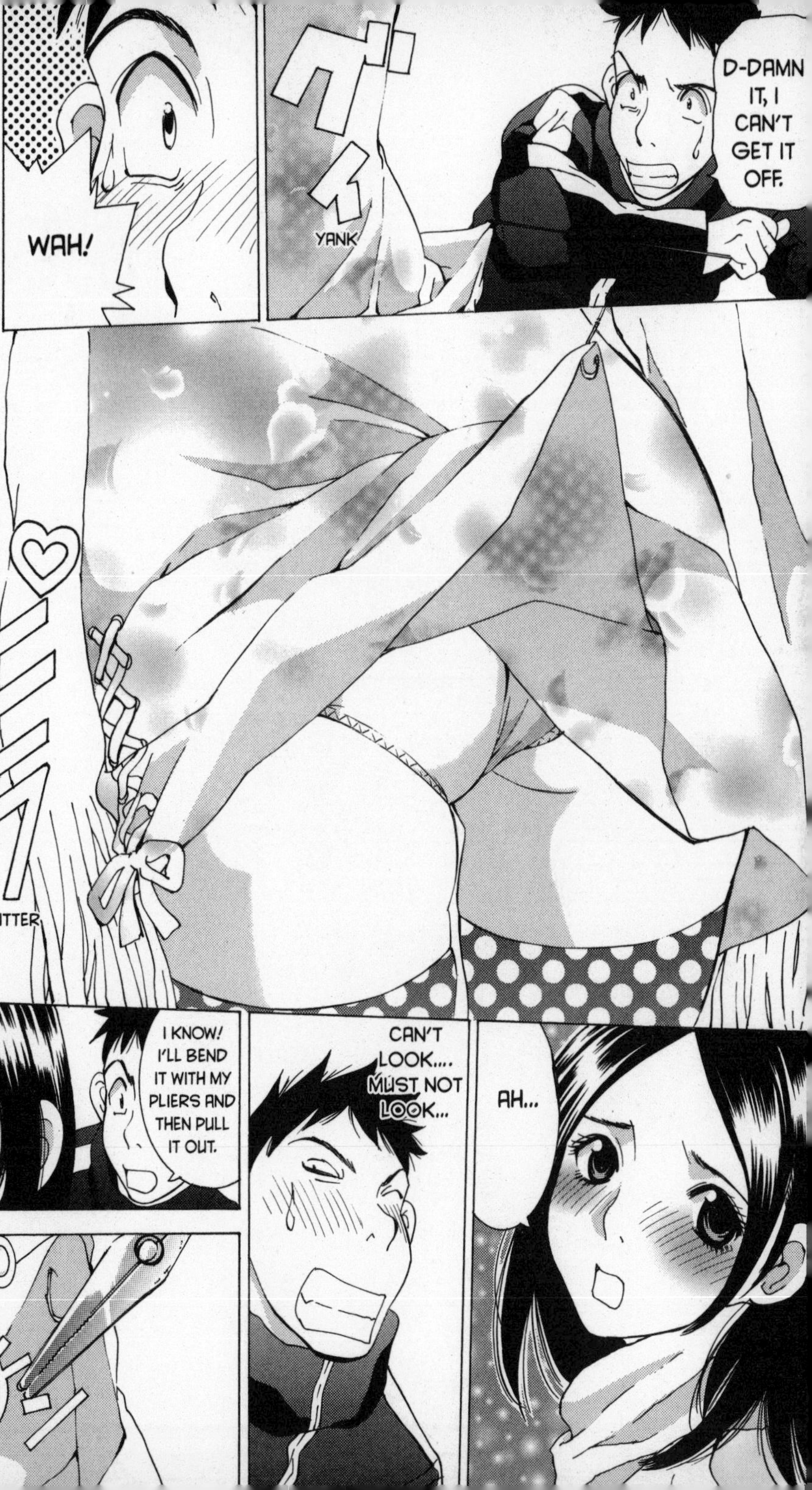
D-DAMN IT, I CAN'T GET IT OFF.
YANK
WAH!
FLUTTER
AH...
CAN'T LOOK.... MUST NOT LOOK...
I KNOW! I'LL BEND IT WITH MY PLIERS AND THEN PULL IT OUT.
HUH?
CLINK

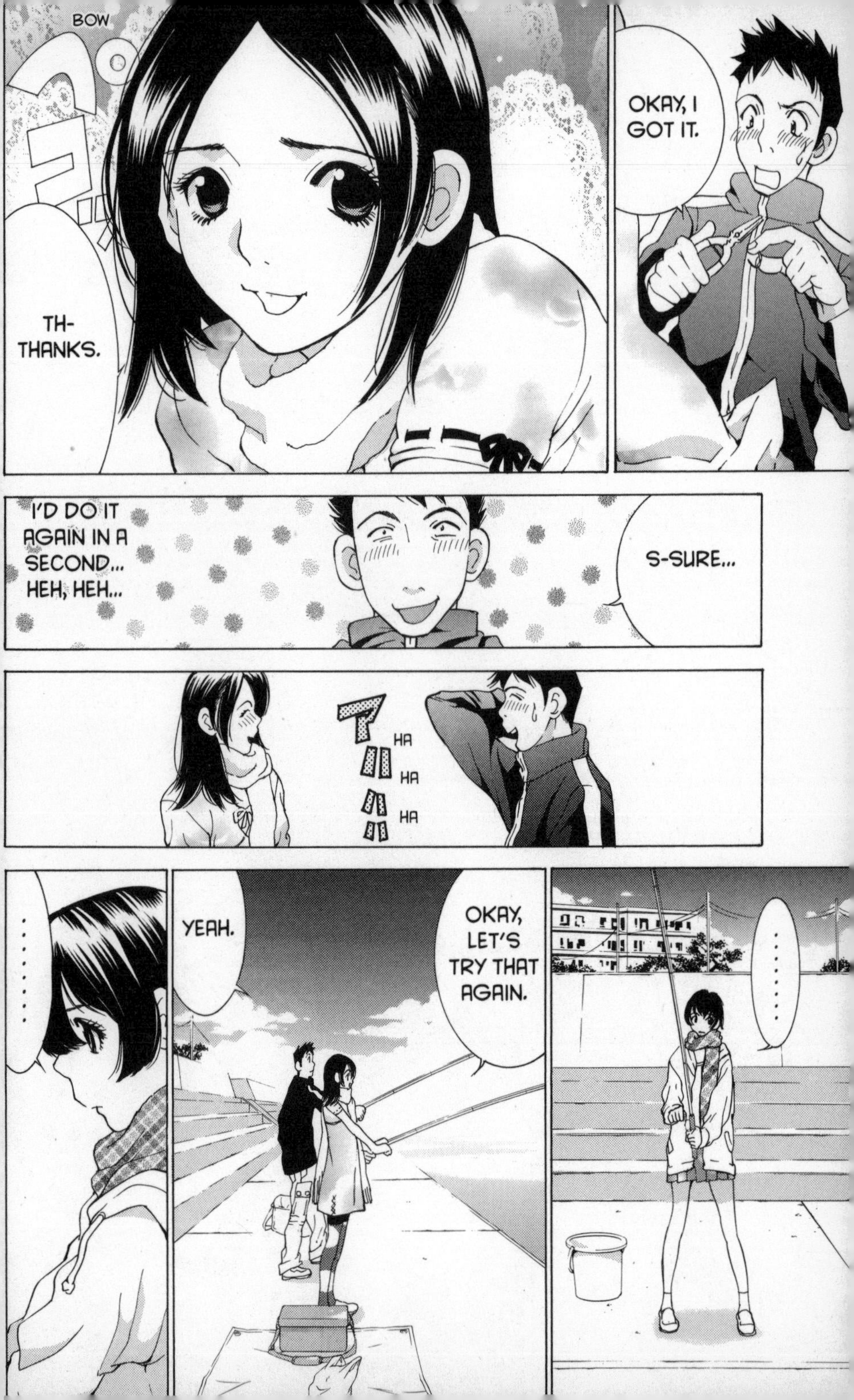
OKAY, I GOT IT.
BOW
TH- THANKS.
S-SURE...
I'D DO IT AGAIN IN A SECOND... HEH, HEH...
HA HA HA
....
OKAY, LET'S TRY THAT AGAIN.
YEAH.
....

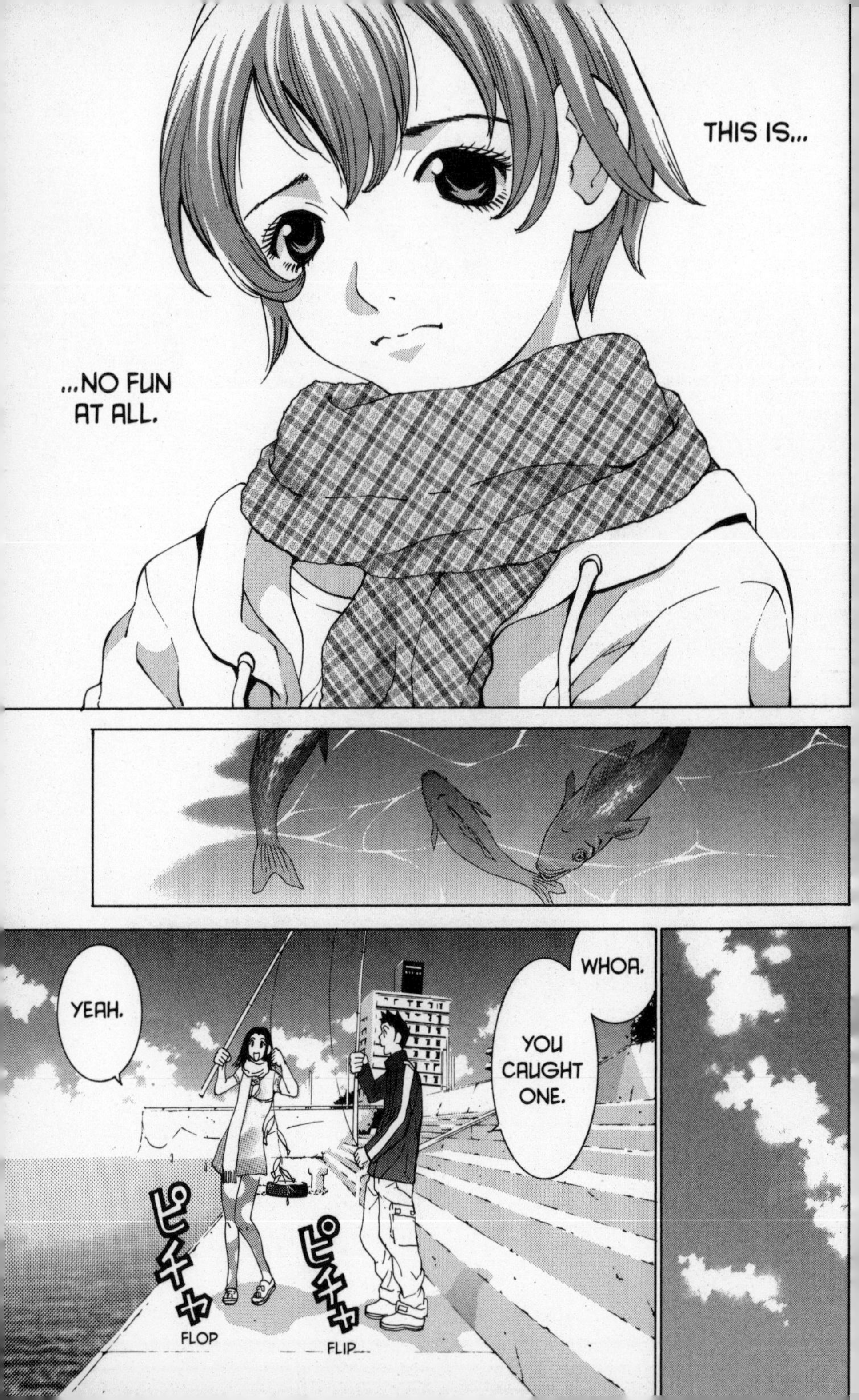
THIS IS...
...NO FUN AT ALL.
WHOA.
YOU CAUGHT ONE.
YEAH.
ピチャ
FLIP
ピチャ
FLOP

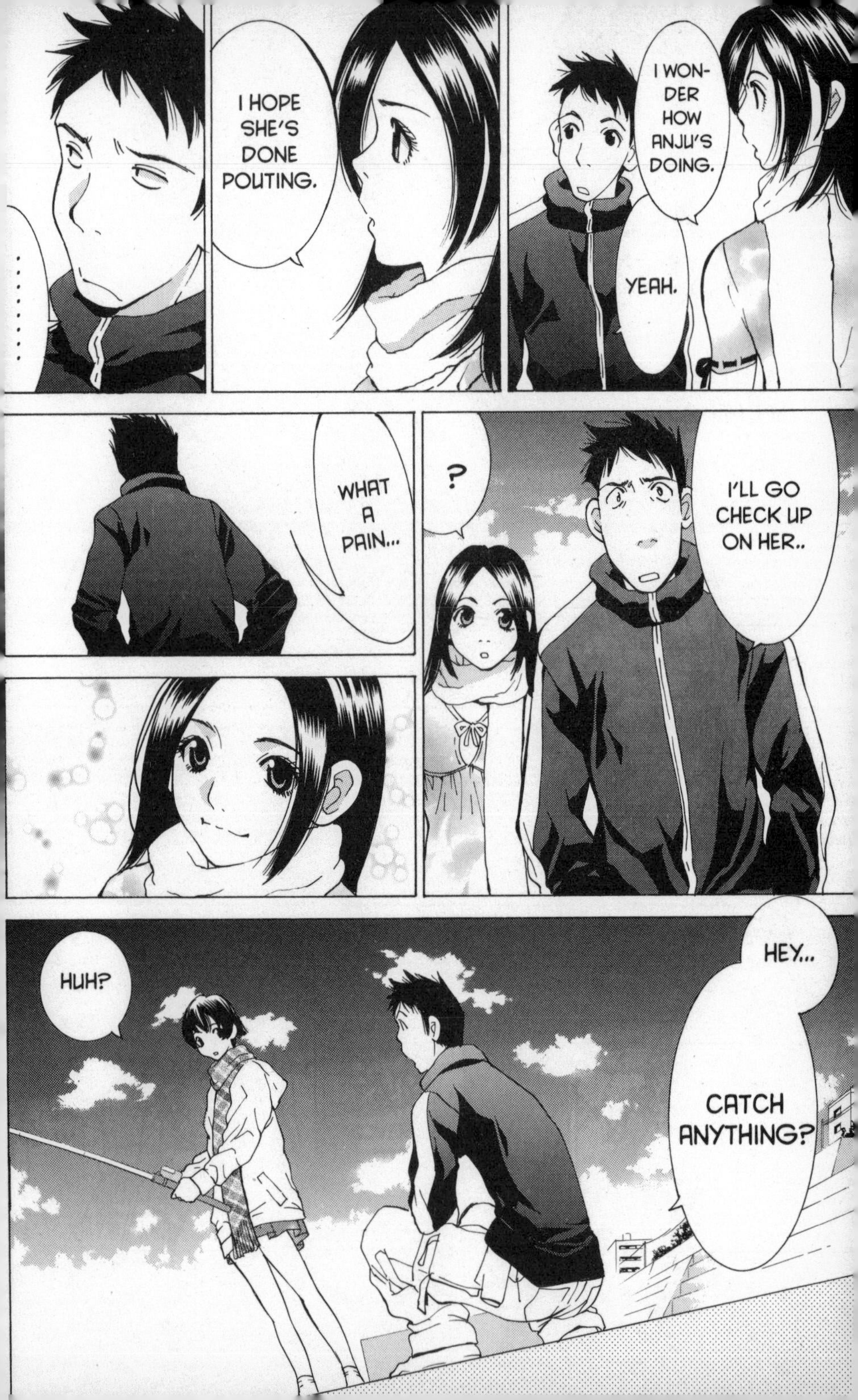
I WON-DER HOW ANJU'S DOING.
YEAH.
I HOPE SHE'S DONE POUTING.
......
I'LL GO CHECK UP ON HER..
?
WHAT A PAIN...
HEY...
CATCH ANYTHING?
HUH?

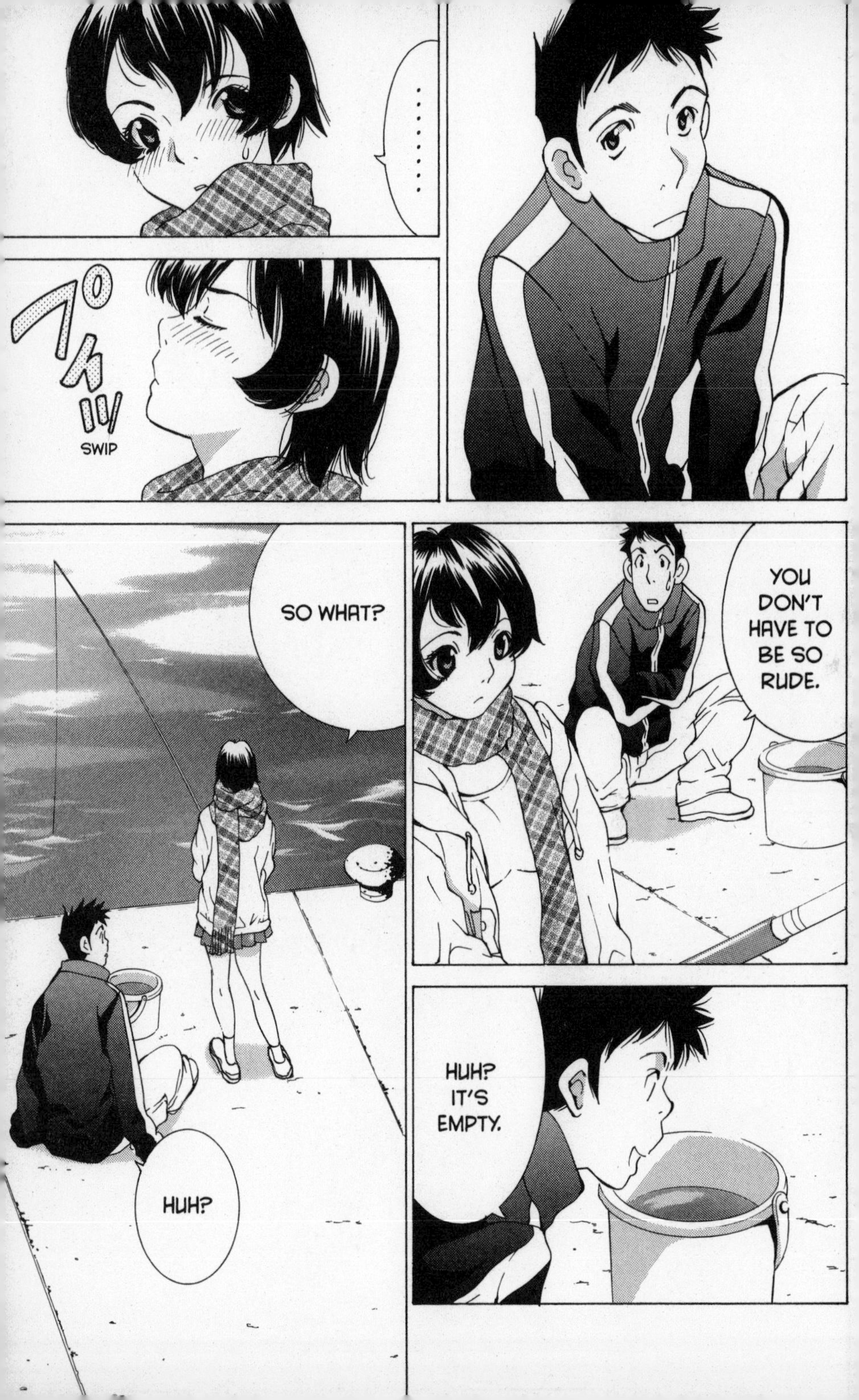
......
ぷんッ
SWIP
YOU DON'T HAVE TO BE SO RUDE.
HUH? IT'S EMPTY.
SO WHAT?
HUH?

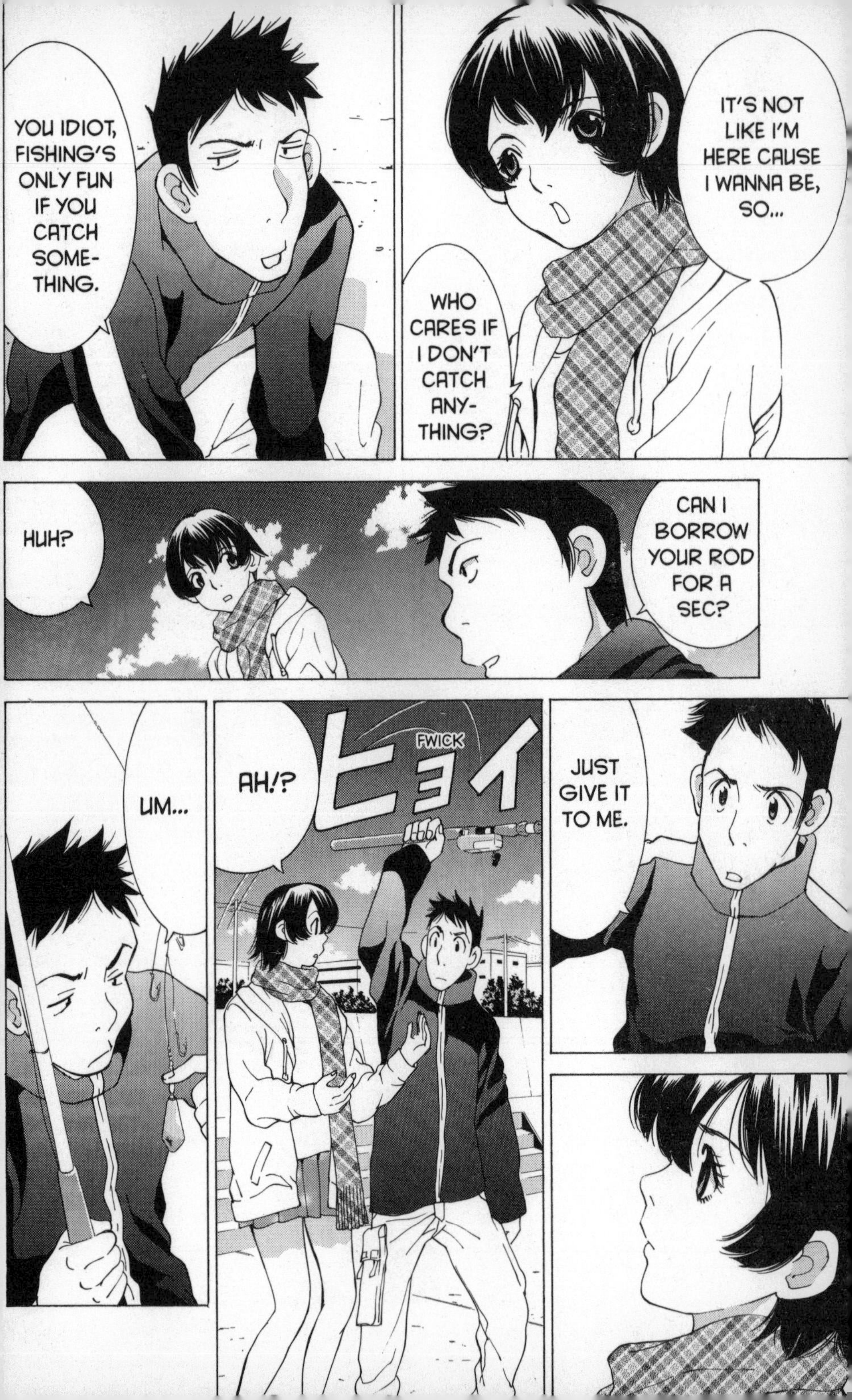
IT'S NOT LIKE I'M HERE CAUSE I WANNA BE, SO...
WHO CARES IF I DON'T CATCH ANYTHING?
YOU IDIOT, FISHING'S ONLY FUN IF YOU CATCH SOMETHING.
CAN I BORROW YOUR ROD FOR A SEC?
HUH?
JUST GIVE IT TO ME.
ヒョイ
FWICK
AH!?
UM...

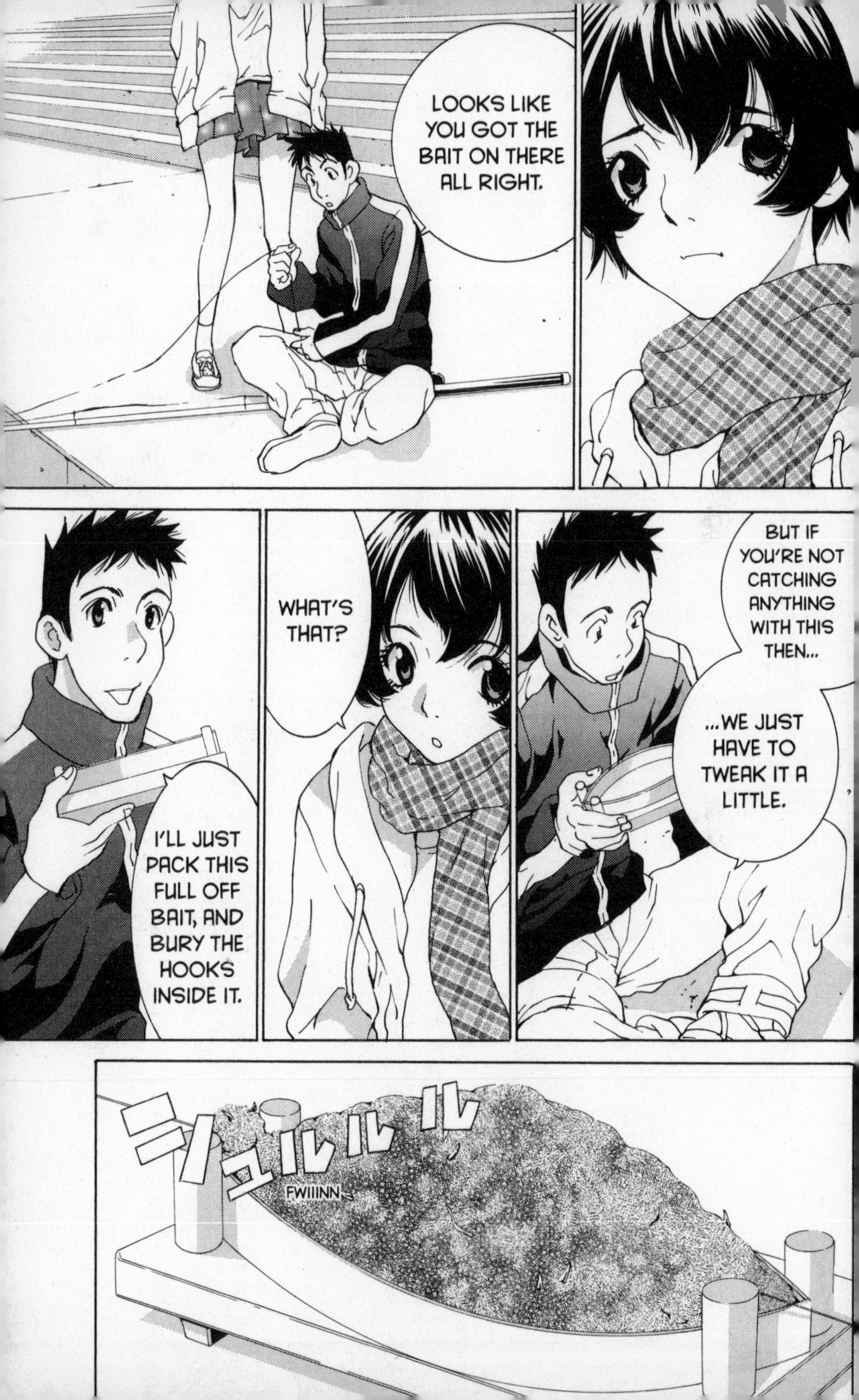
LOOKS LIKE YOU GOT THE BAIT ON THERE ALL RIGHT.
BUT IF YOU'RE NOT CATCHING ANYTHING WITH THIS THEN...
...WE JUST HAVE TO TWEAK IT A LITTLE.
WHAT'S THAT?
I'LL JUST PACK THIS FULL OFF BAIT, AND BURY THE HOOKS INSIDE IT.
FWIIINN

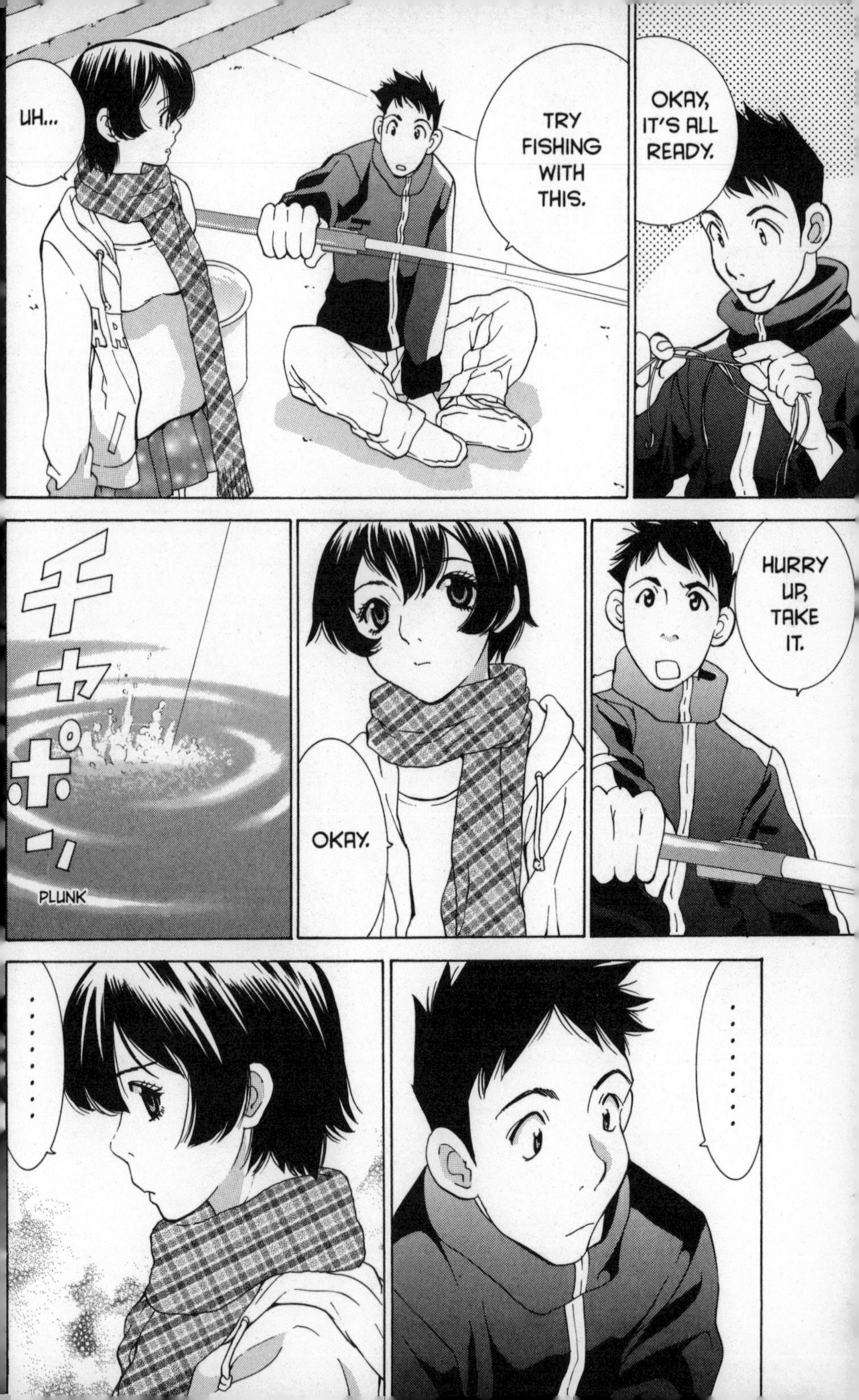
OKAY, IT'S ALL READY.
TRY FISHING WITH THIS.
UH...
HURRY UP, TAKE IT.
OKAY.
チャポーン
PLUNK
......
......

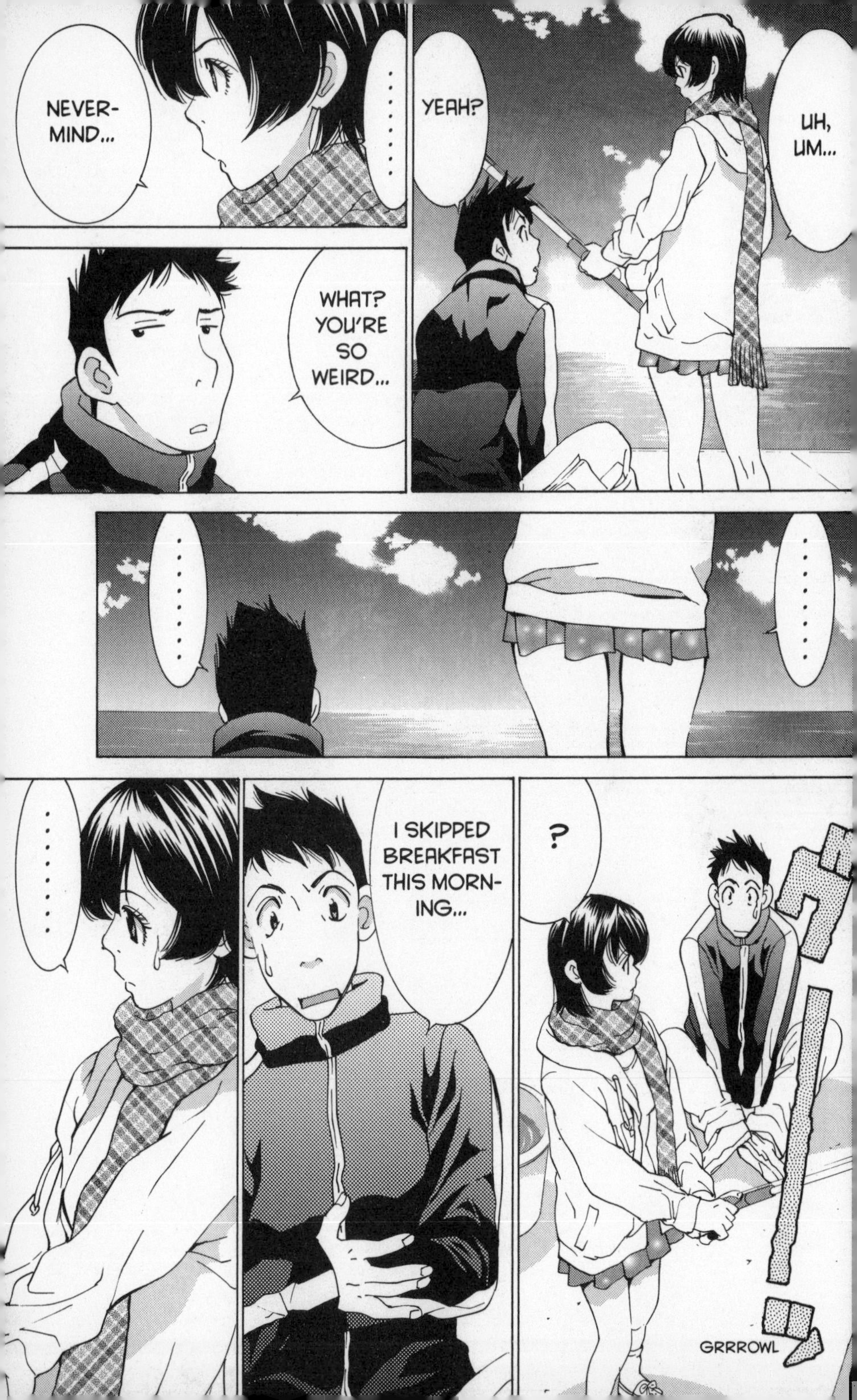
UH, UM...
YEAH?
......
NEVER-MIND...
WHAT? YOU'RE SO WEIRD...
......
......
?
GRRROWL
I SKIPPED BREAKFAST THIS MORNING...
......

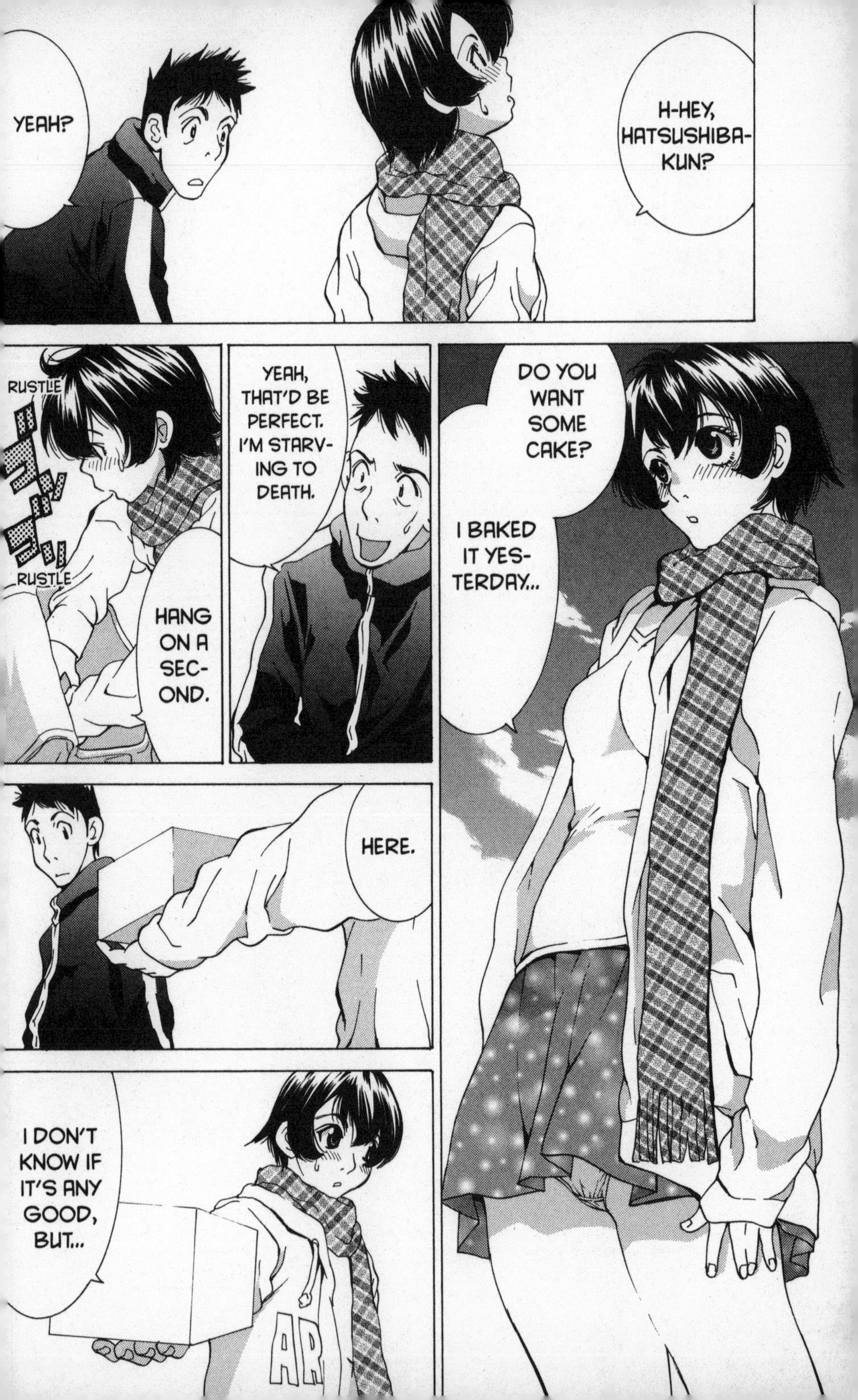
H-HEY, HATSUSHIBA-KUN?
YEAH?
DO YOU WANT SOME CAKE?
I BAKED IT YESTERDAY...
YEAH, THAT'D BE PERFECT. I'M STARVING TO DEATH.
RUSTLE
RUSTLE
HANG ON A SECOND.
HERE.
I DON'T KNOW IF IT'S ANY GOOD, BUT...

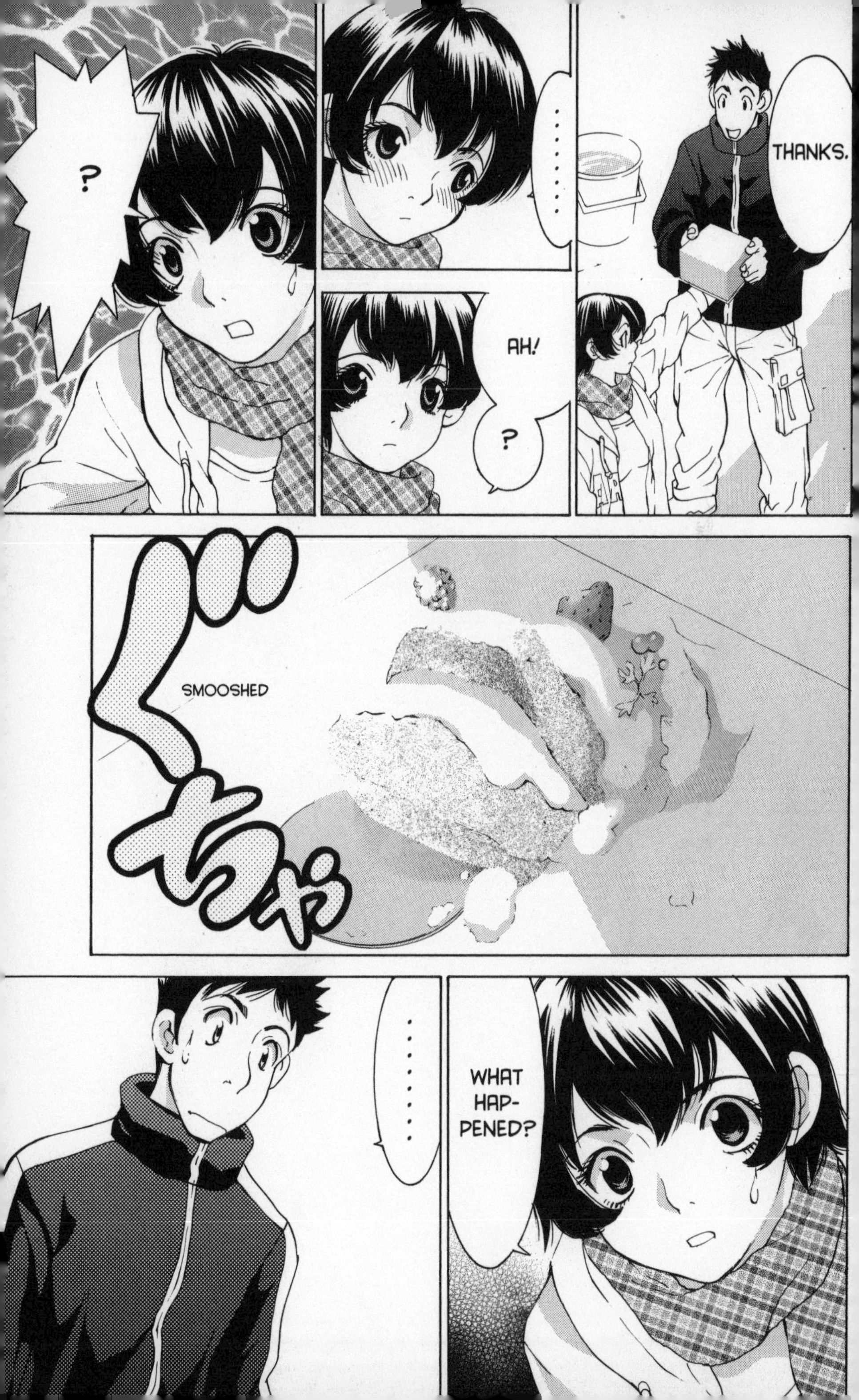
THANKS.
……
AH!
?
?
ぐちゃ
SMOOSHED
WHAT HAP-PENED?
……

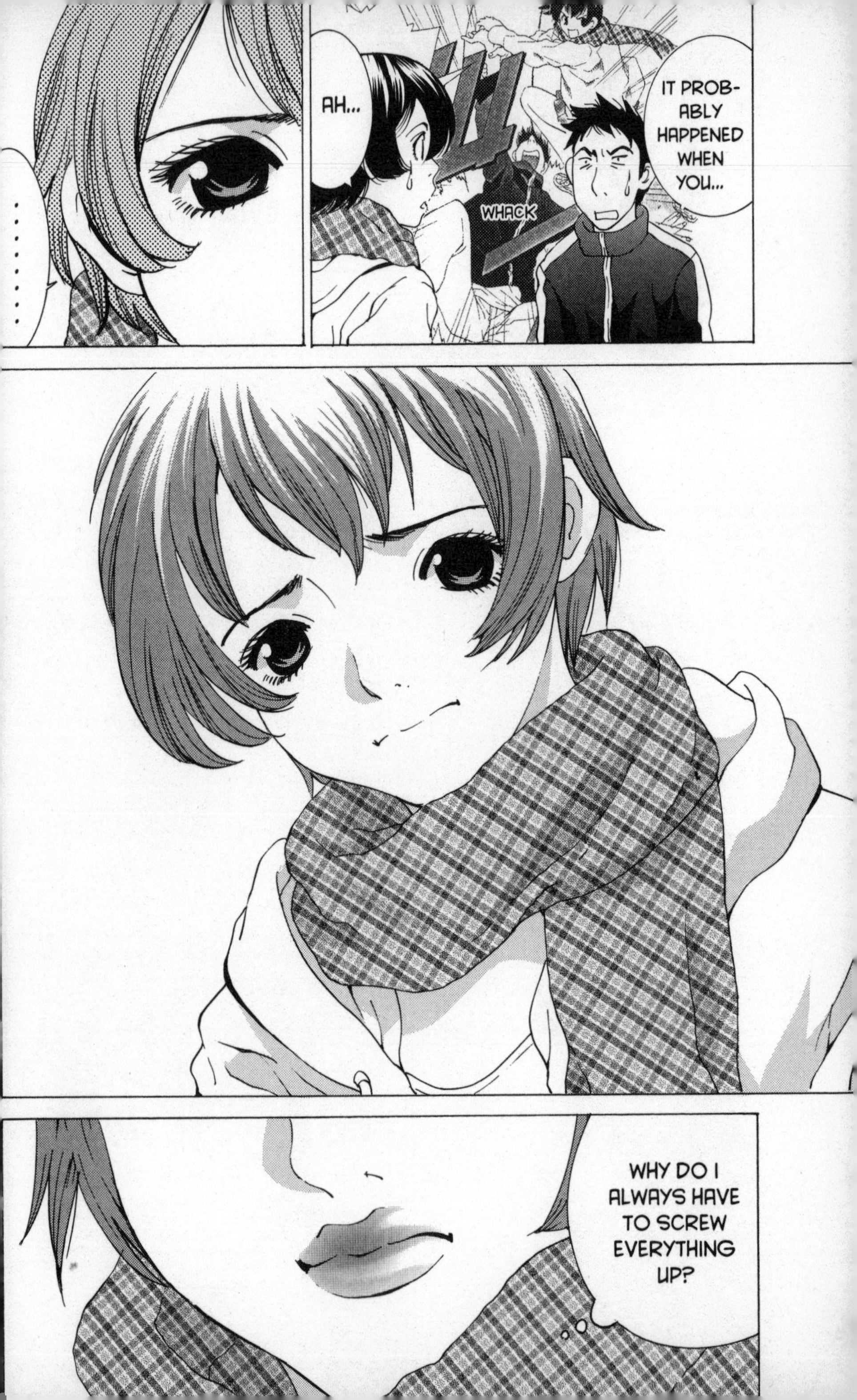
IT PROB-ABLY HAPPENED WHEN YOU...
AH...
WHACK
......
WHY DO I ALWAYS HAVE TO SCREW EVERYTHING UP?

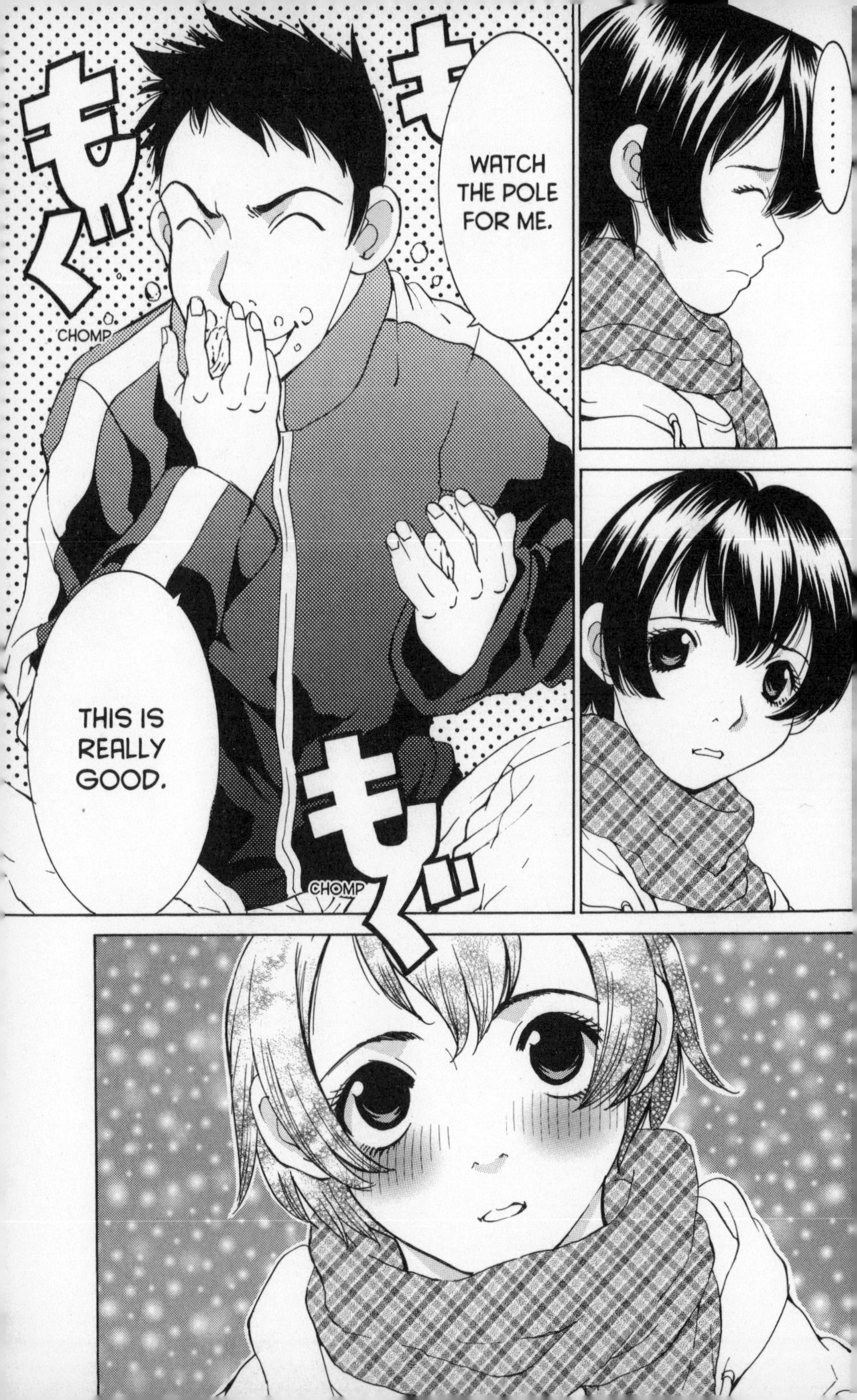
……
WATCH THE POLE FOR ME.
もぐ
CHOMP
THIS IS REALLY GOOD.
もぐ
CHOMP

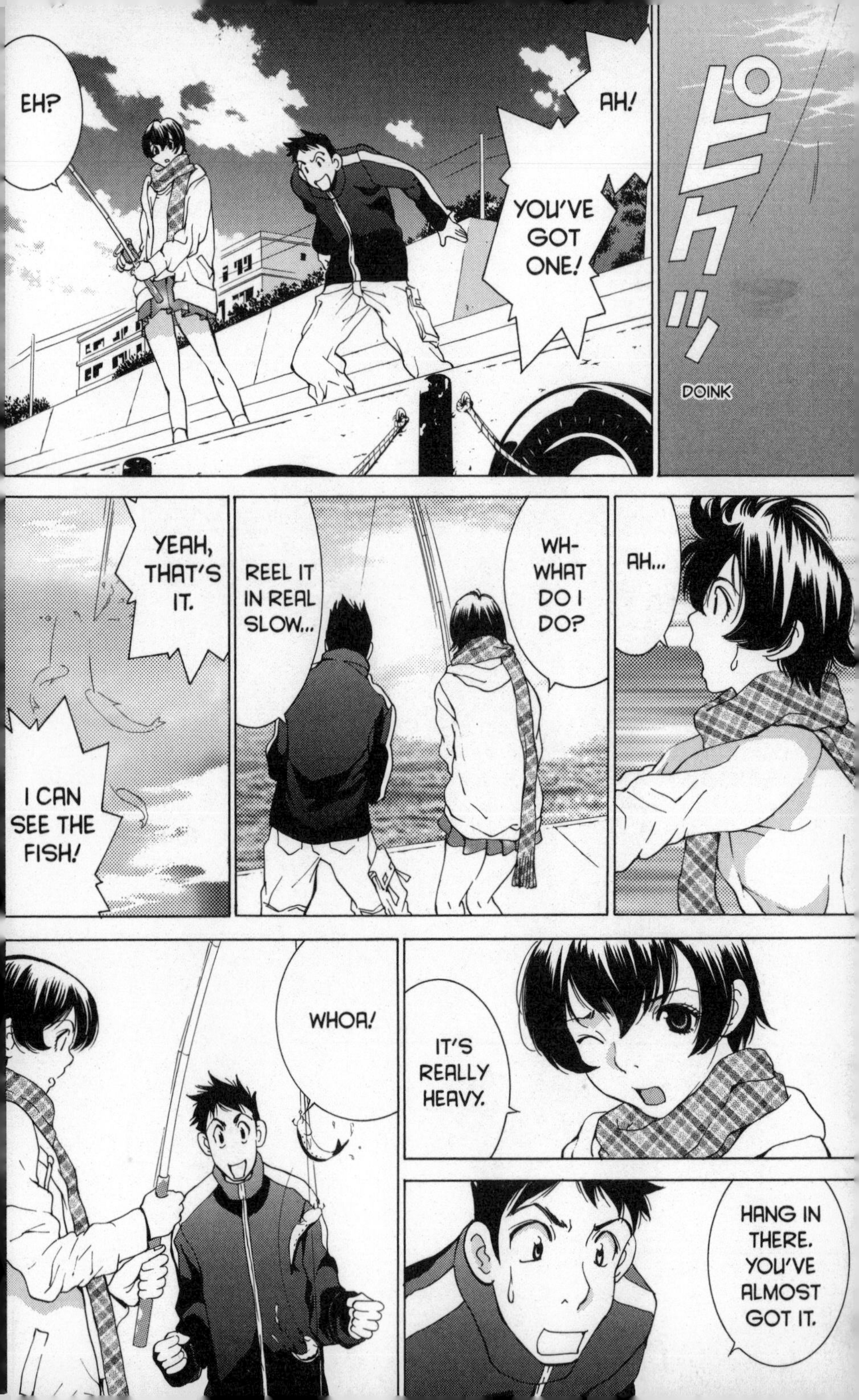
ピクッ
DOINK
AH!
YOU'VE GOT ONE!
EH?
AH...
WH-WHAT DO I DO?
REEL IT IN REAL SLOW...
YEAH, THAT'S IT.
I CAN SEE THE FISH!
IT'S REALLY HEAVY.
HANG IN THERE. YOU'VE ALMOST GOT IT.
WHOA!

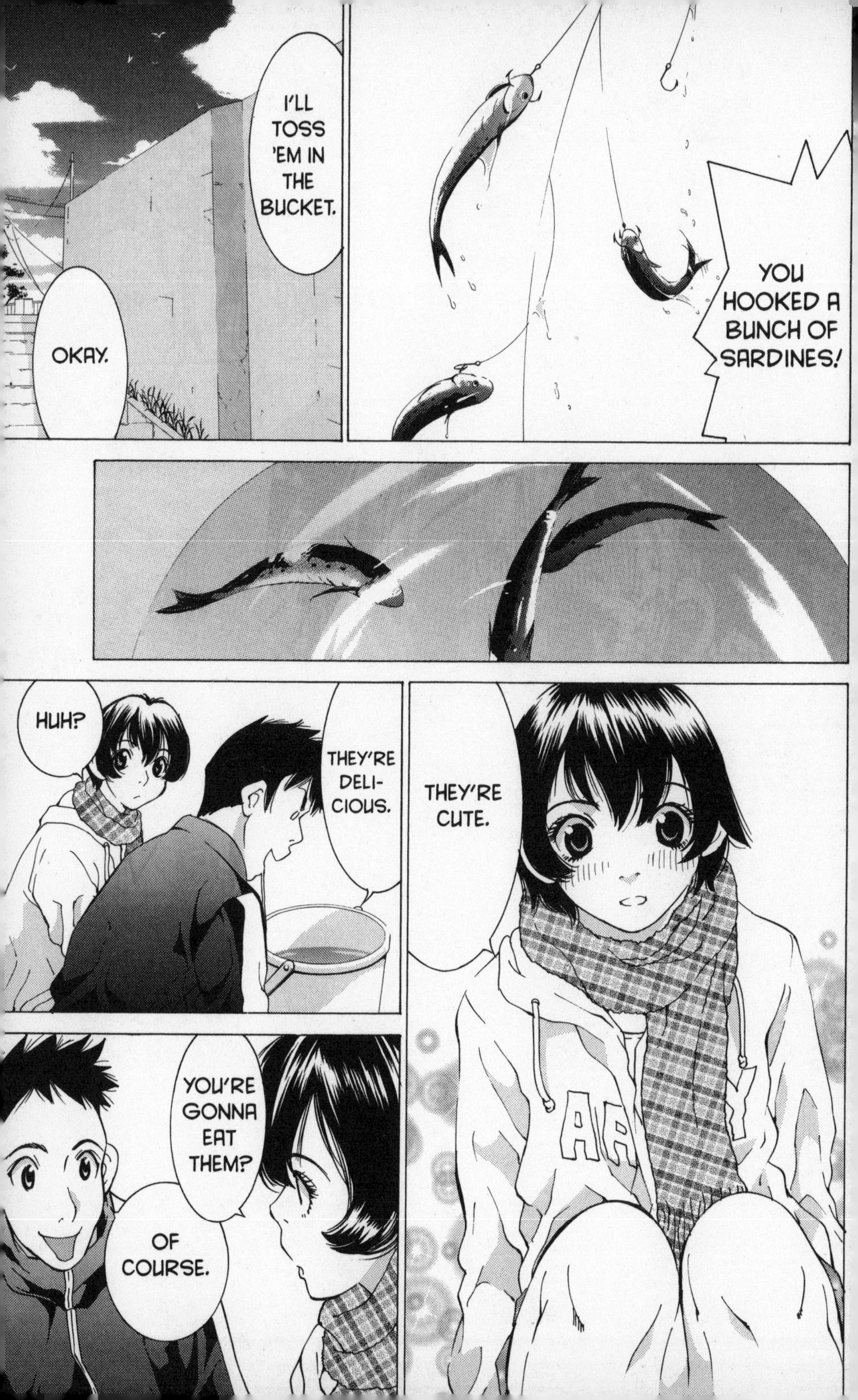
YOU HOOKED A BUNCH OF SARDINES!
I'LL TOSS 'EM IN THE BUCKET.
OKAY.
THEY'RE CUTE.
THEY'RE DELI-CIOUS.
HUH?
YOU'RE GONNA EAT THEM?
OF COURSE.

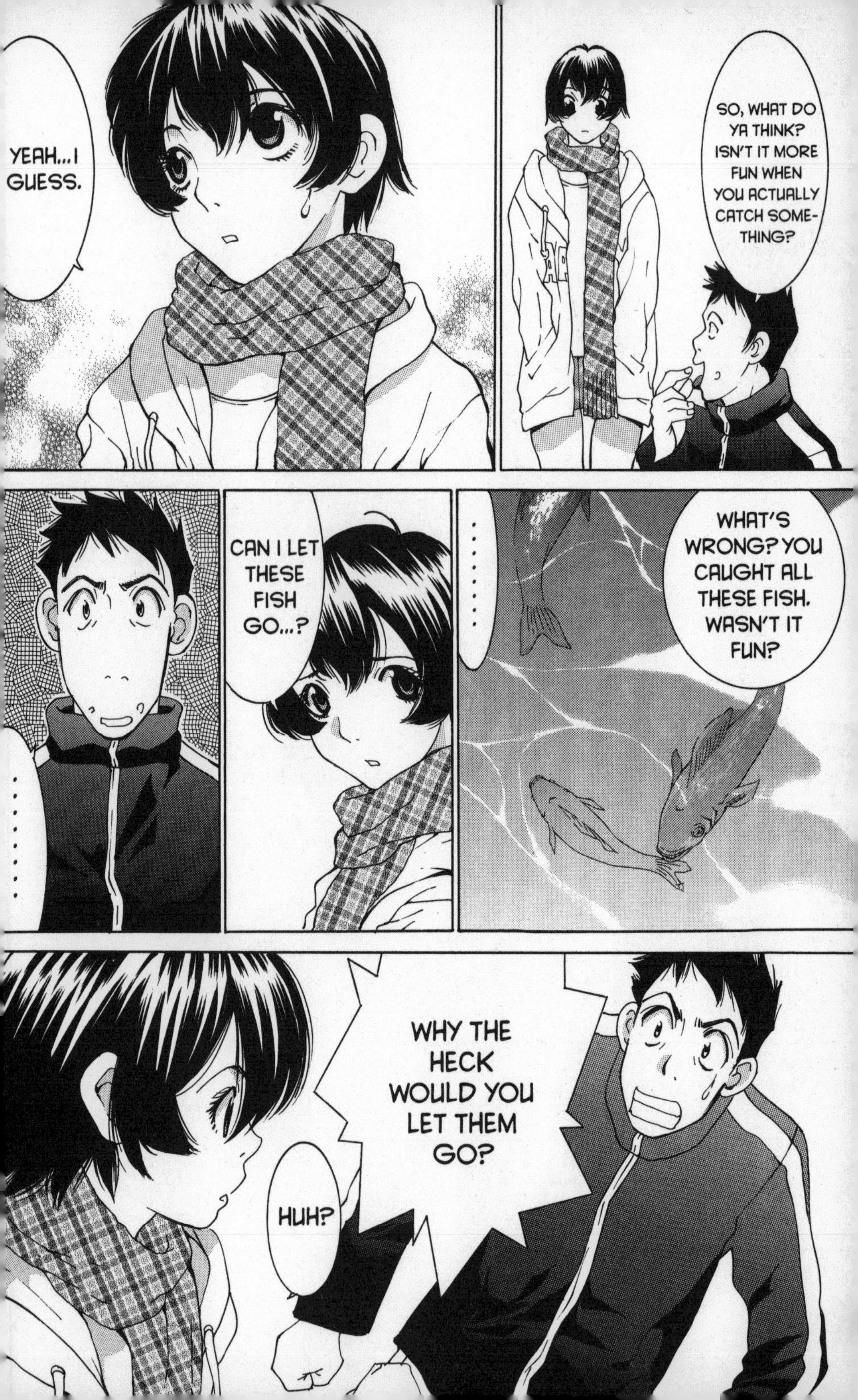
SO, WHAT DO YA THINK? ISN'T IT MORE FUN WHEN YOU ACTUALLY CATCH SOME-THING?
YEAH...I GUESS.
WHAT'S WRONG? YOU CAUGHT ALL THESE FISH. WASN'T IT FUN?
......
CAN I LET THESE FISH GO...?
......
WHY THE HECK WOULD YOU LET THEM GO?
HUH?

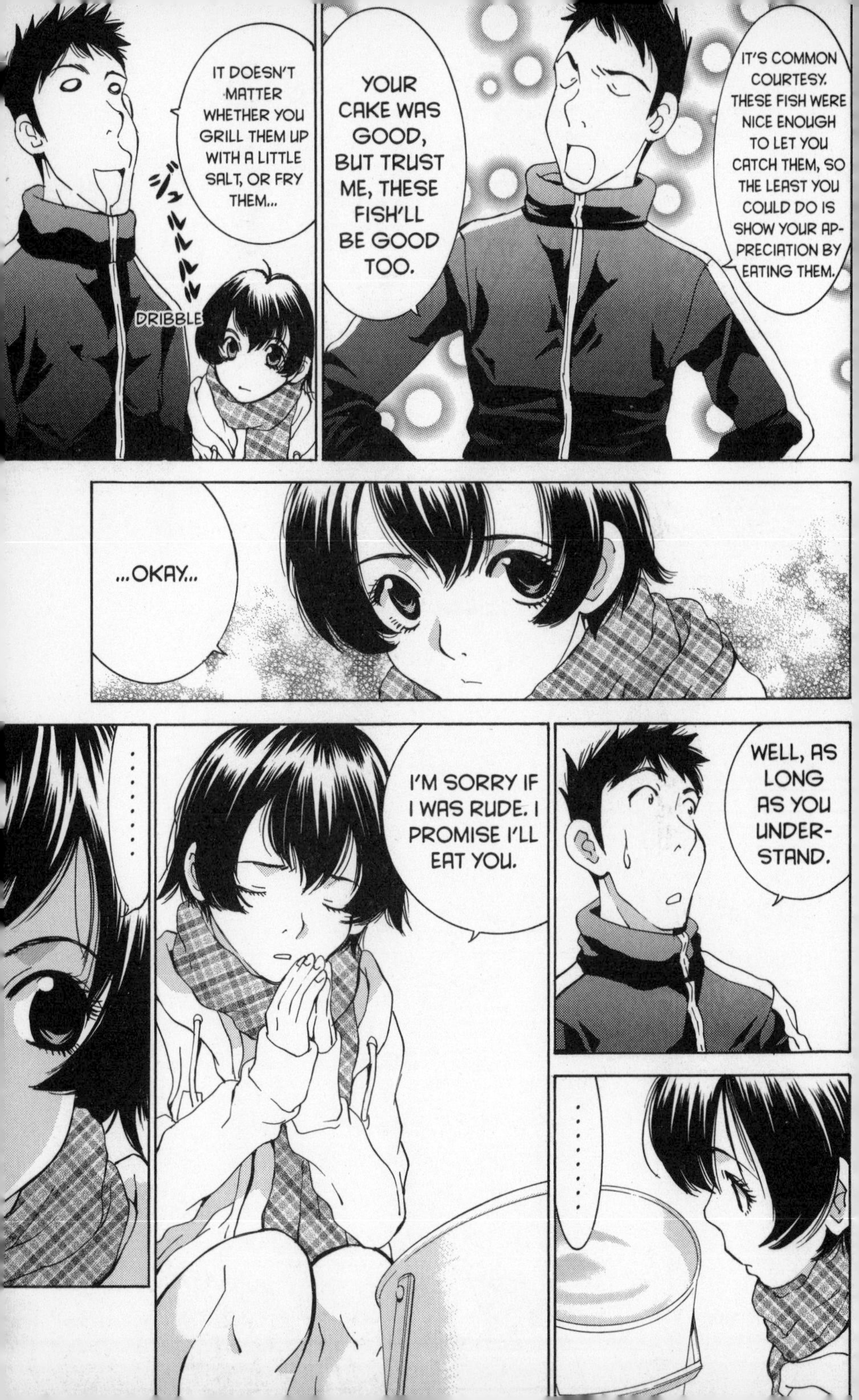
IT'S COMMON COURTESY. THESE FISH WERE NICE ENOUGH TO LET YOU CATCH THEM, SO THE LEAST YOU COULD DO IS SHOW YOUR APPRECIATION BY EATING THEM.
YOUR CAKE WAS GOOD, BUT TRUST ME, THESE FISH'LL BE GOOD TOO.
IT DOESN'T MATTER WHETHER YOU GRILL THEM UP WITH A LITTLE SALT, OR FRY THEM...
ジュルルルル
DRIBBLE
...OKAY...
WELL, AS LONG AS YOU UNDERSTAND.
......
I'M SORRY IF I WAS RUDE. I PROMISE I'LL EAT YOU.
......

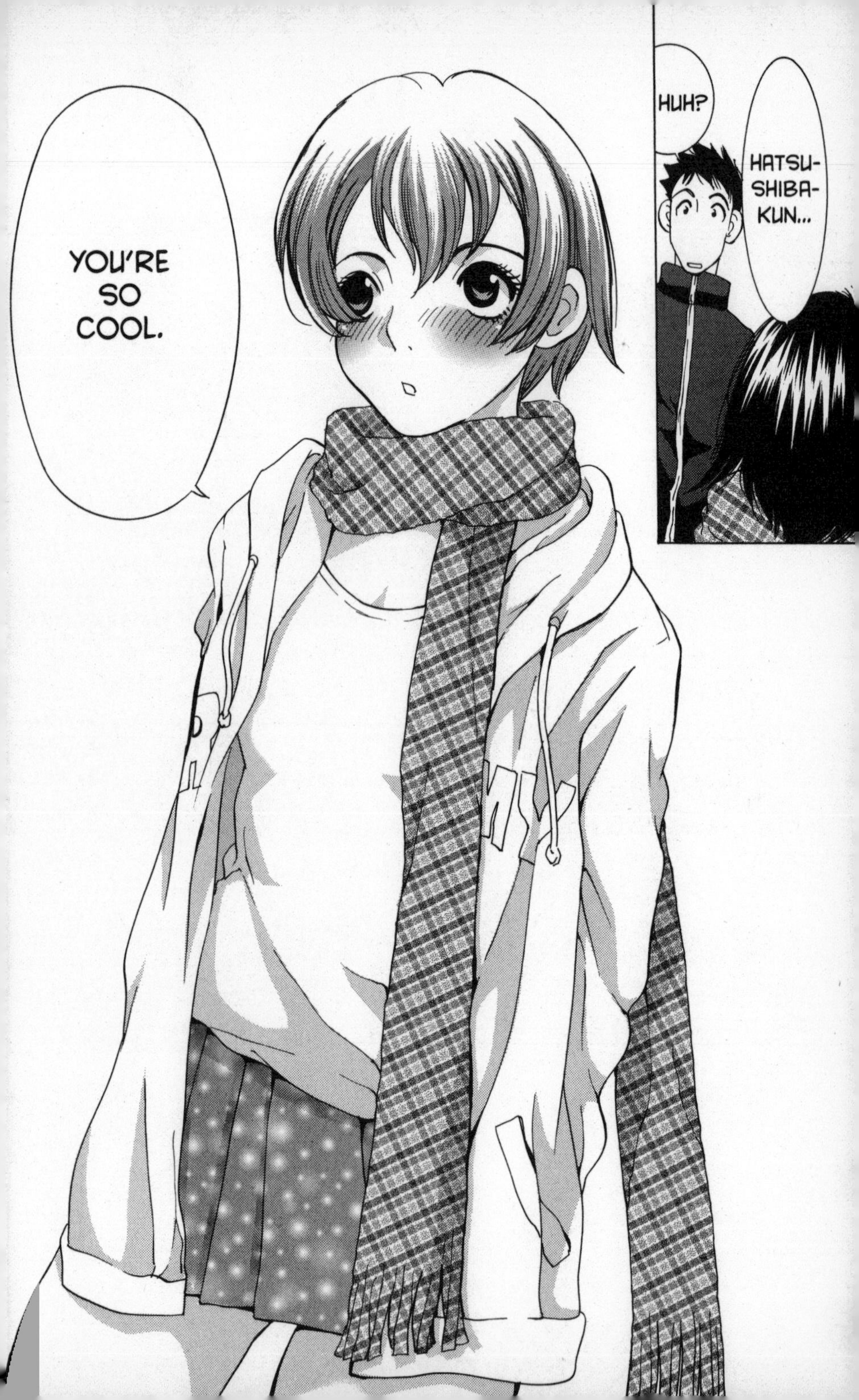
HATSU-SHIBA-KUN...
HUH?
YOU'RE SO COOL.

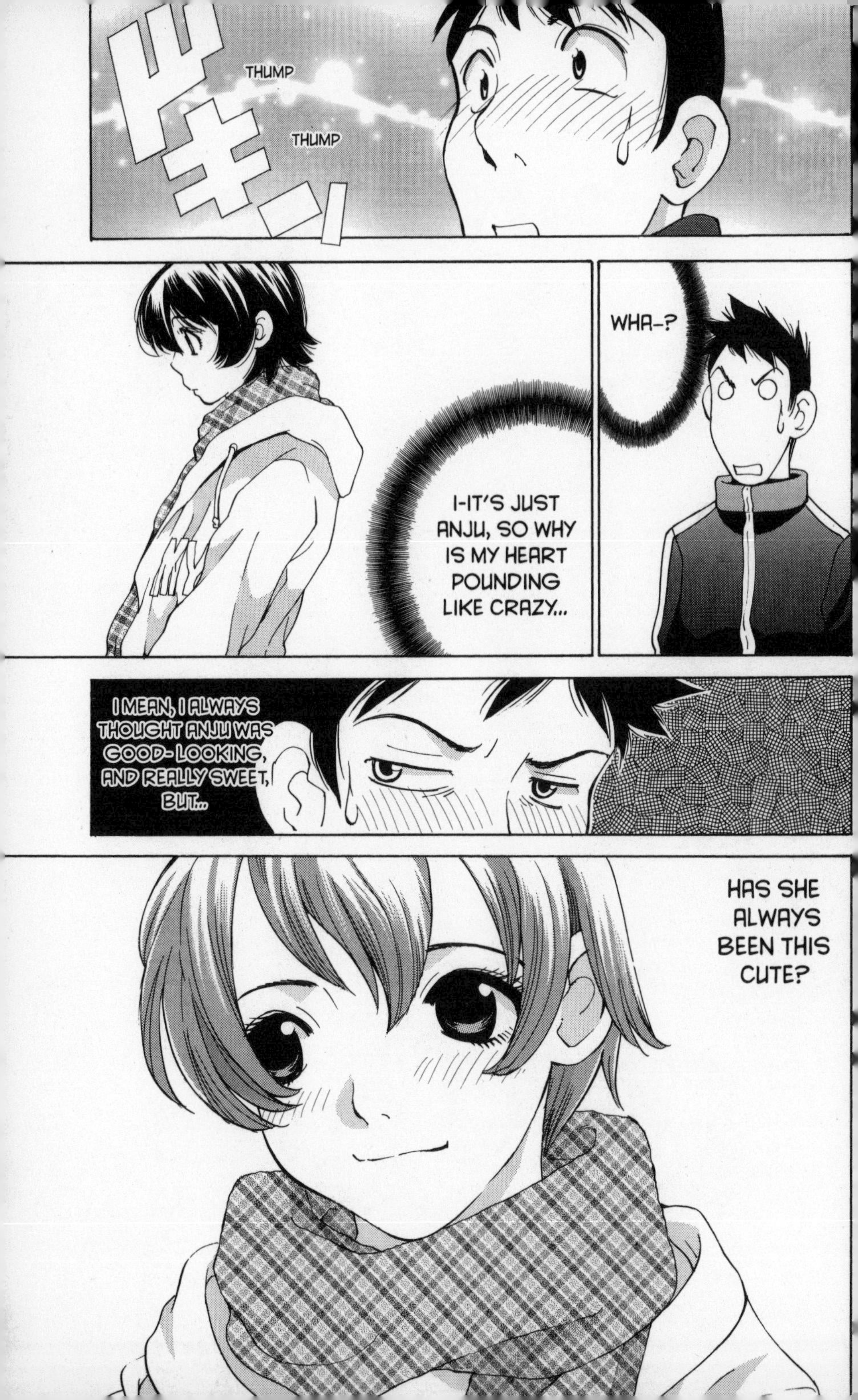
THUMP
THUMP
WHA-?
I-IT'S JUST ANJU, SO WHY IS MY HEART POUNDING LIKE CRAZY...
I MEAN, I ALWAYS THOUGHT ANJU WAS GOOD-LOOKING, AND REALLY SWEET, BUT...
HAS SHE ALWAYS BEEN THIS CUTE?

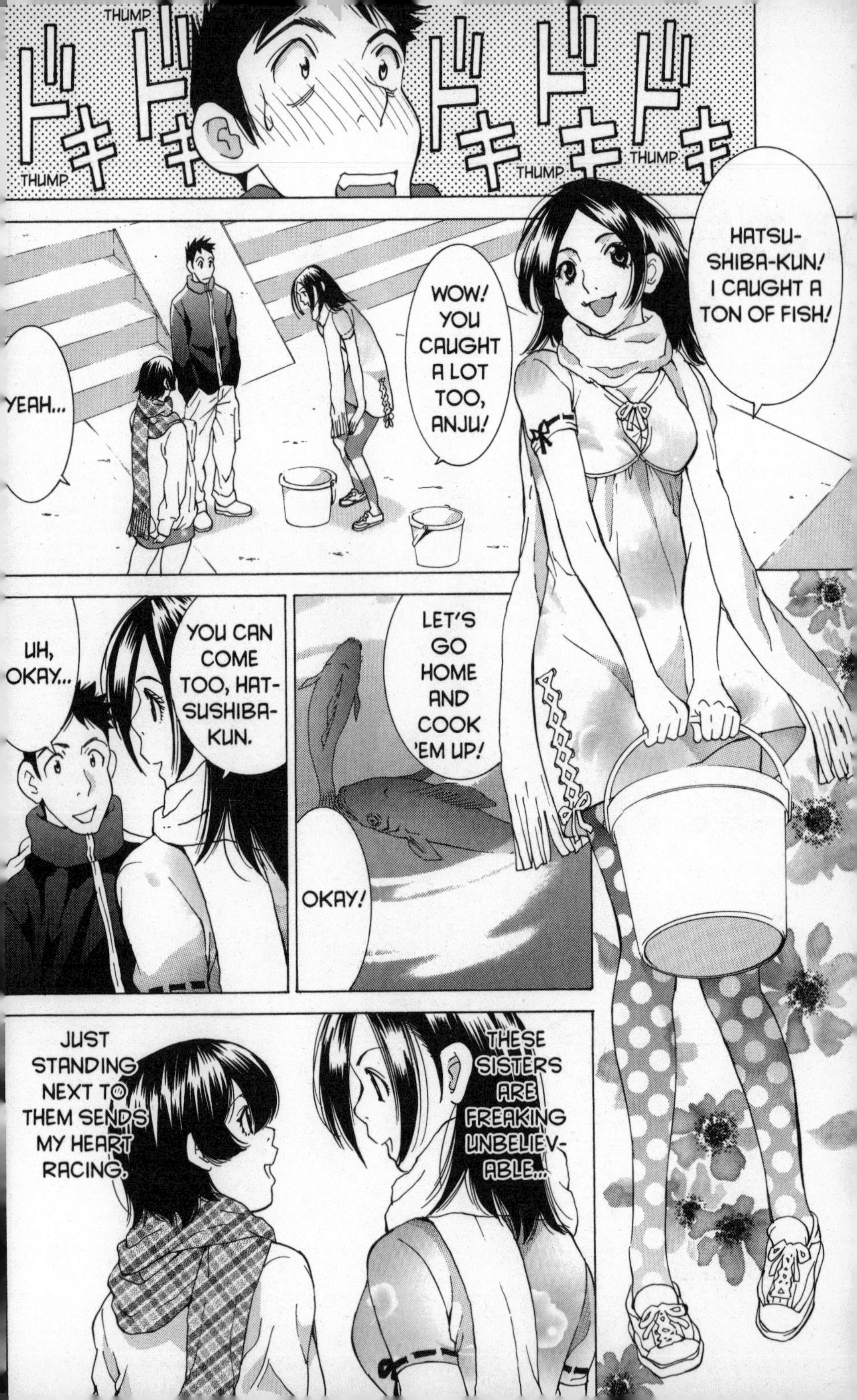

ドキ THUMP
ドキ THUMP
ドキ THUMP
ドキ THUMP
HATSU-SHIBA-KUN! I CAUGHT A TON OF FISH!
WOW! YOU CAUGHT A LOT TOO, ANJU!
YEAH...
LET'S GO HOME AND COOK 'EM UP!
OKAY!
YOU CAN COME TOO, HAT-SUSHIBA-KUN.
UH, OKAY...
THESE SISTERS ARE FREAKING UNBELIEV-ABLE...
JUST STANDING NEXT TO THEM SENDS MY HEART RACING.

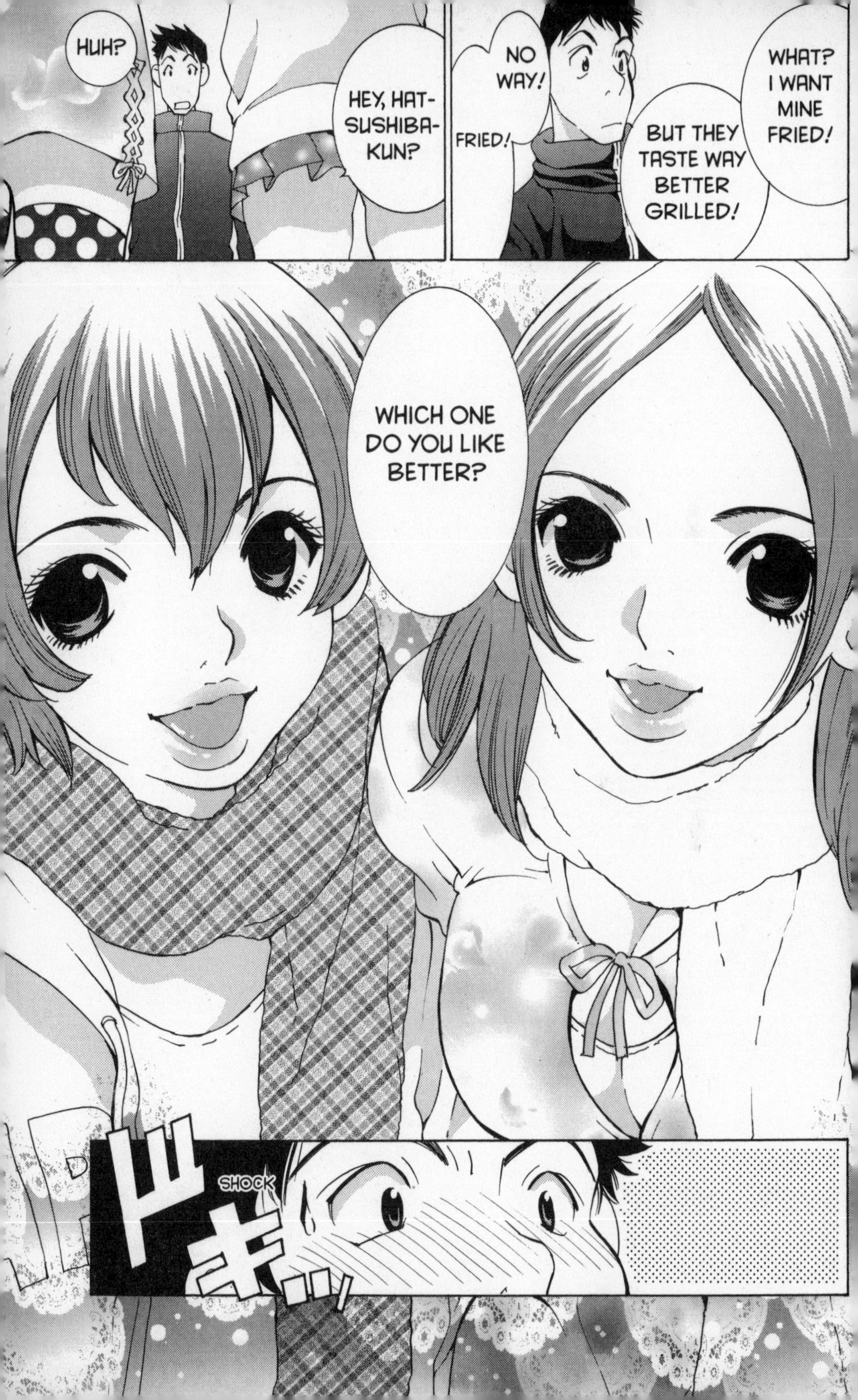
WHAT? I WANT MINE FRIED!
NO WAY!
BUT THEY TASTE WAY BETTER GRILLED!
FRIED!
HEY, HAT-SUSHIBA-KUN?
HUH?
WHICH ONE DO YOU LIKE BETTER?
SHOCK

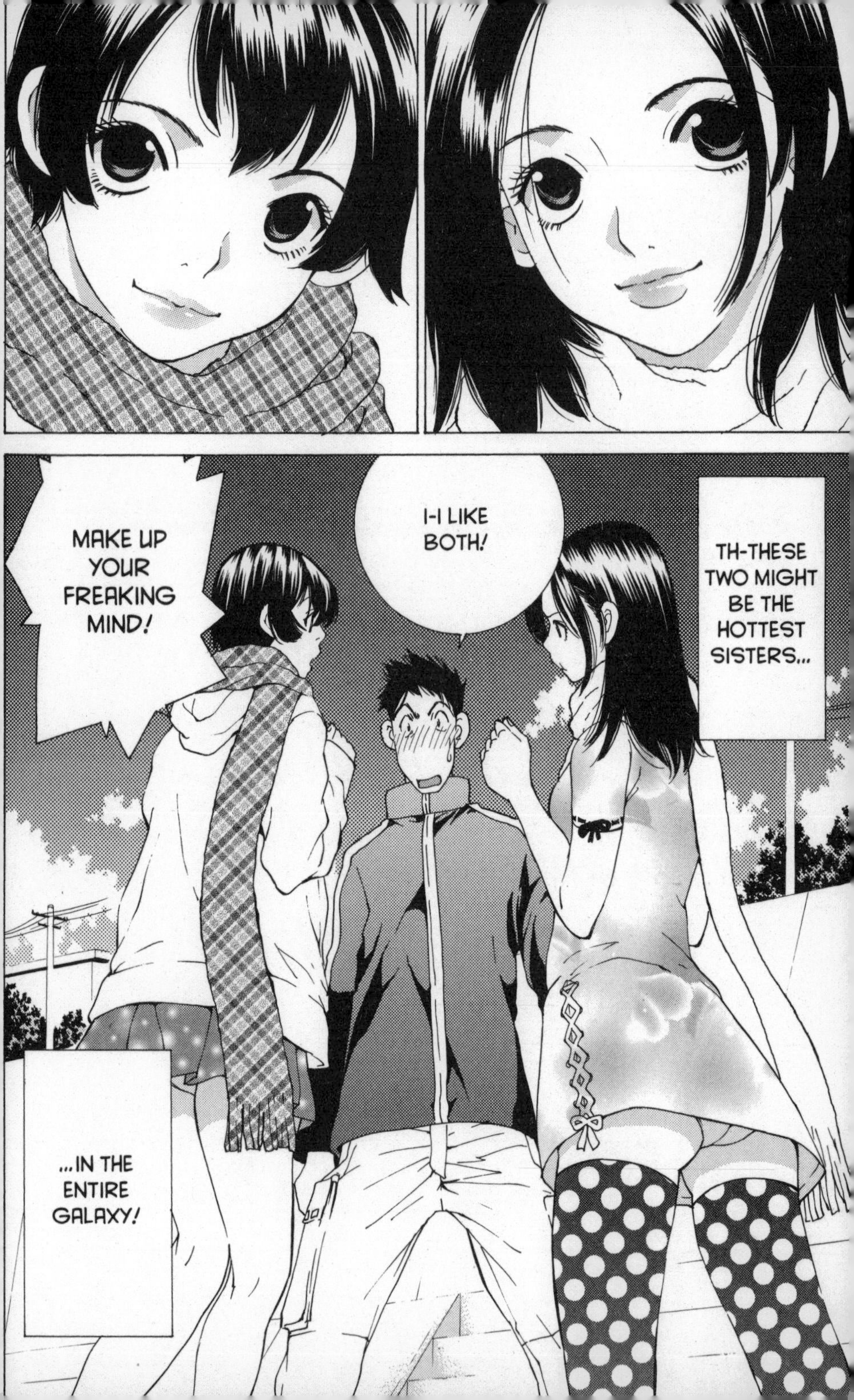
TH-THESE TWO MIGHT BE THE HOTTEST SISTERS...
I-I LIKE BOTH!
MAKE UP YOUR FREAKING MIND!
...IN THE ENTIRE GALAXY!

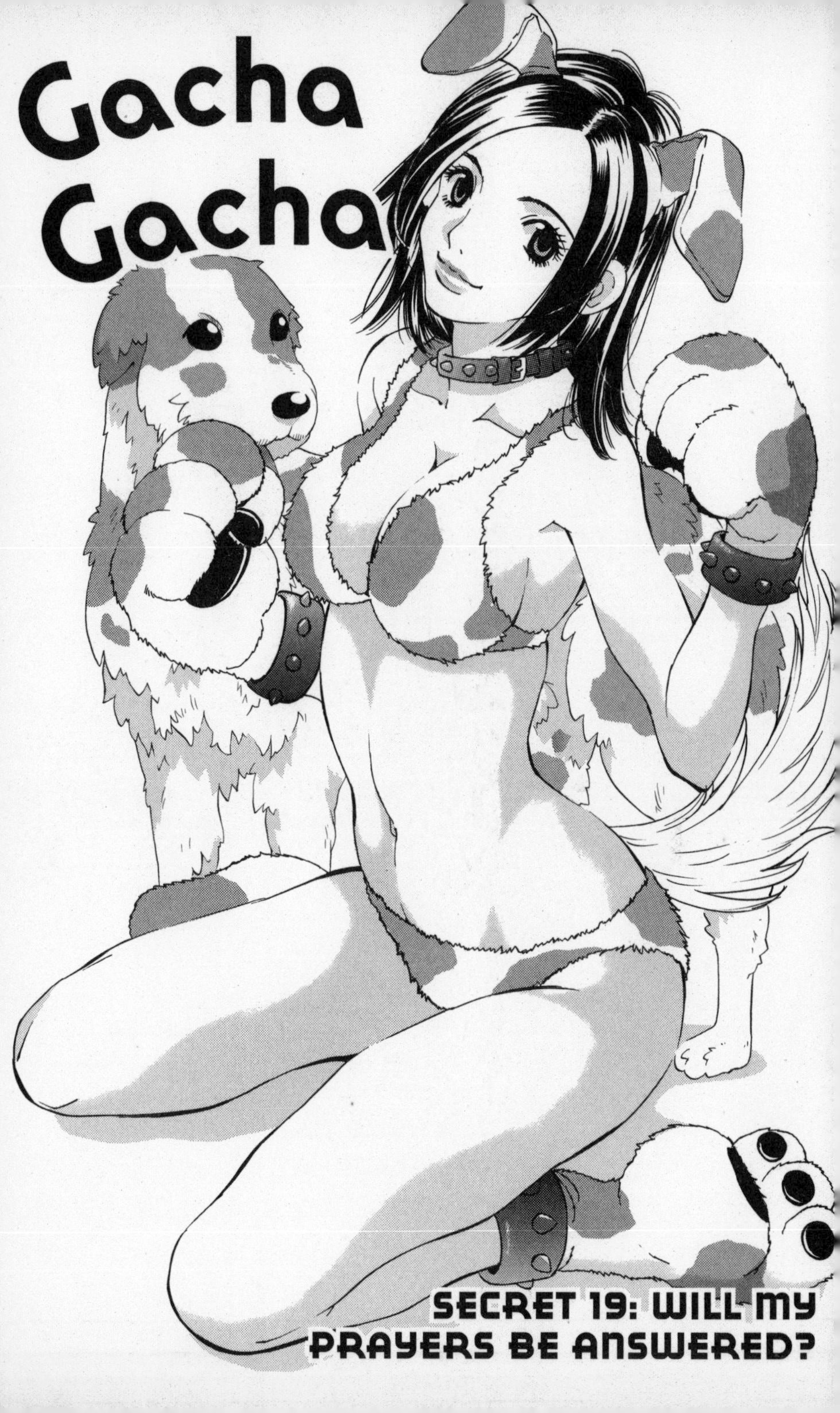
Gacha
Gacha
SECRET 19: WILL MY
PRAYERS BE ANSWERED?

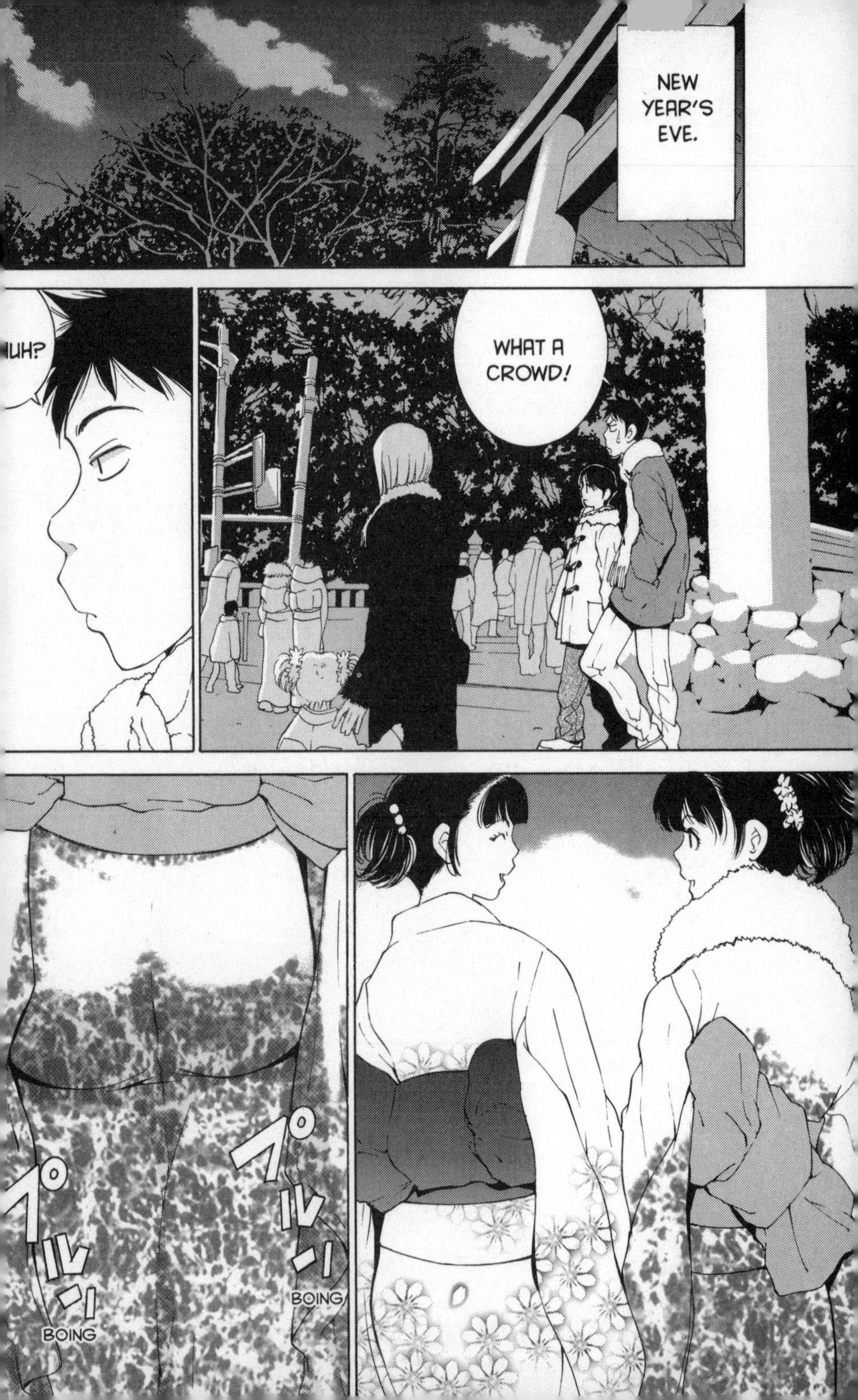
NEW YEAR'S EVE.
WHAT A CROWD!
HUH?
BOING
BOING

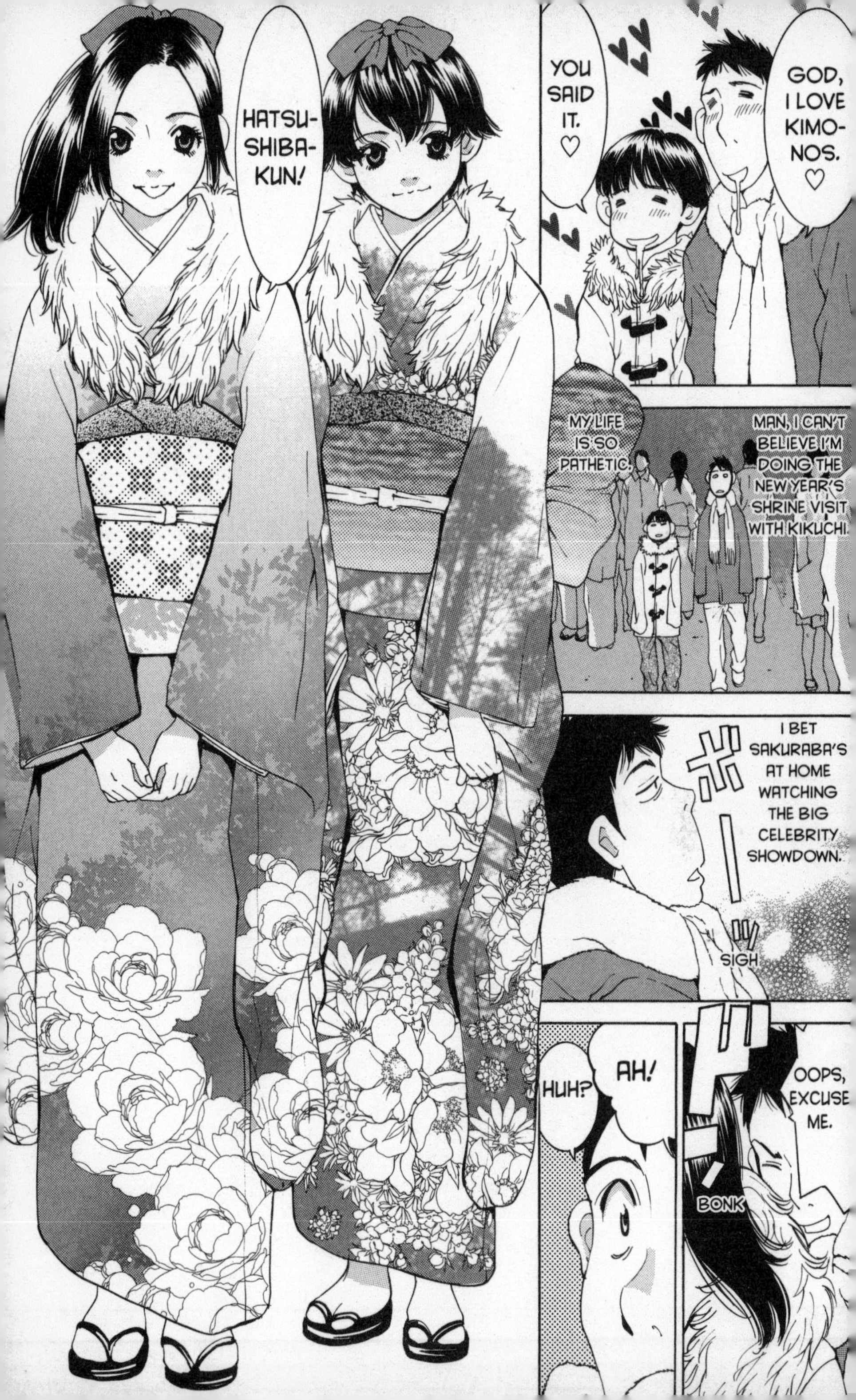
GOD, I LOVE KIMO-NOS. ♡
YOU SAID IT. ♡
MAN, I CAN'T BELIEVE I'M DOING THE NEW YEAR'S SHRINE VISIT WITH KIKUCHI.
MY LIFE IS SO PATHETIC.
I BET SAKURABA'S AT HOME WATCHING THE BIG CELEBRITY SHOWDOWN.
SIGH
OOPS, EXCUSE ME.
BONK
AH!
HUH?
HATSU-SHIBA-KUN!

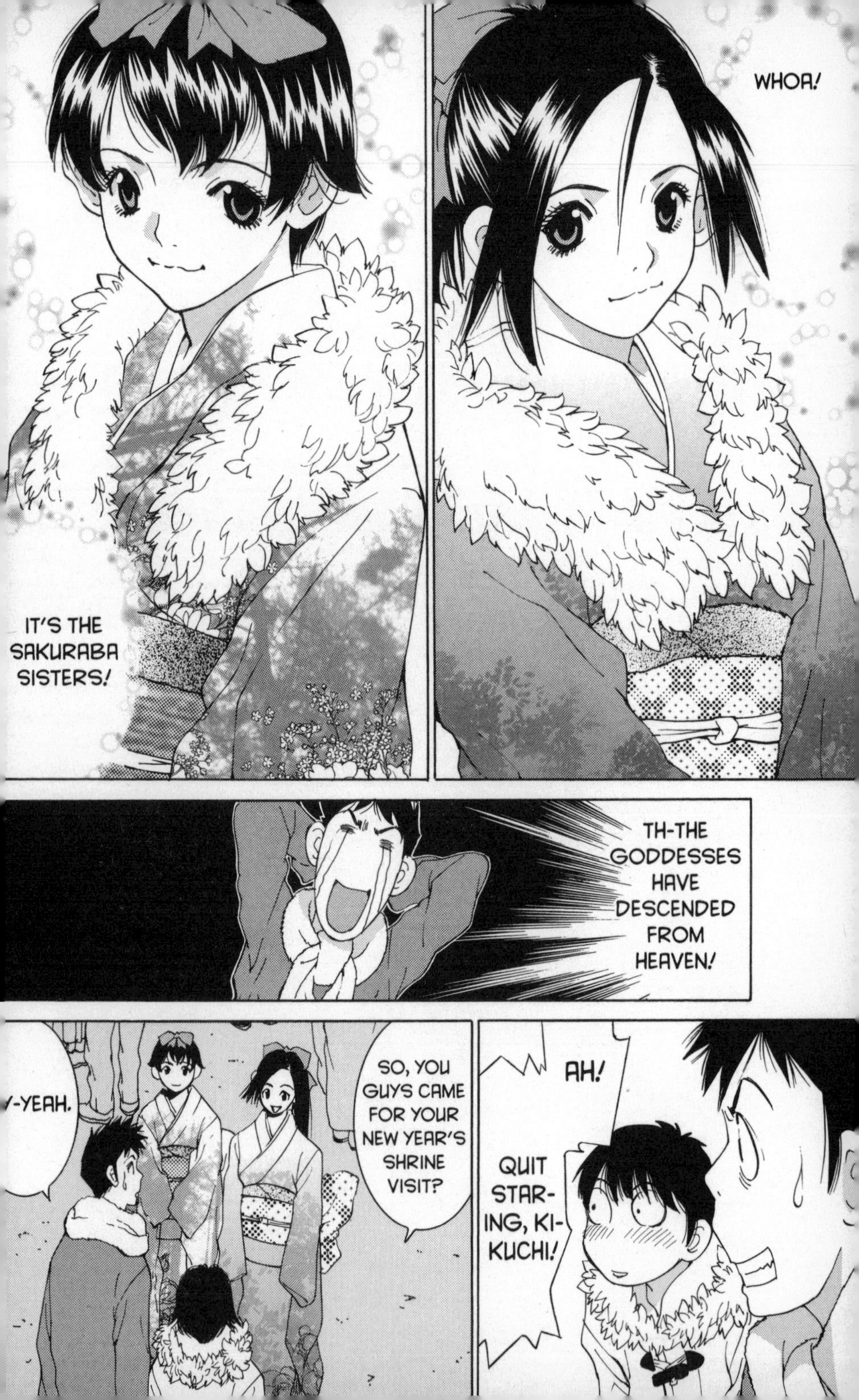
WHOA!
IT'S THE SAKURABA SISTERS!
TH-THE GODDESSES HAVE DESCENDED FROM HEAVEN!
AH!
QUIT STAR-ING, KI-KUCHI!
SO, YOU GUYS CAME FOR YOUR NEW YEAR'S SHRINE VISIT?
-YEAH.

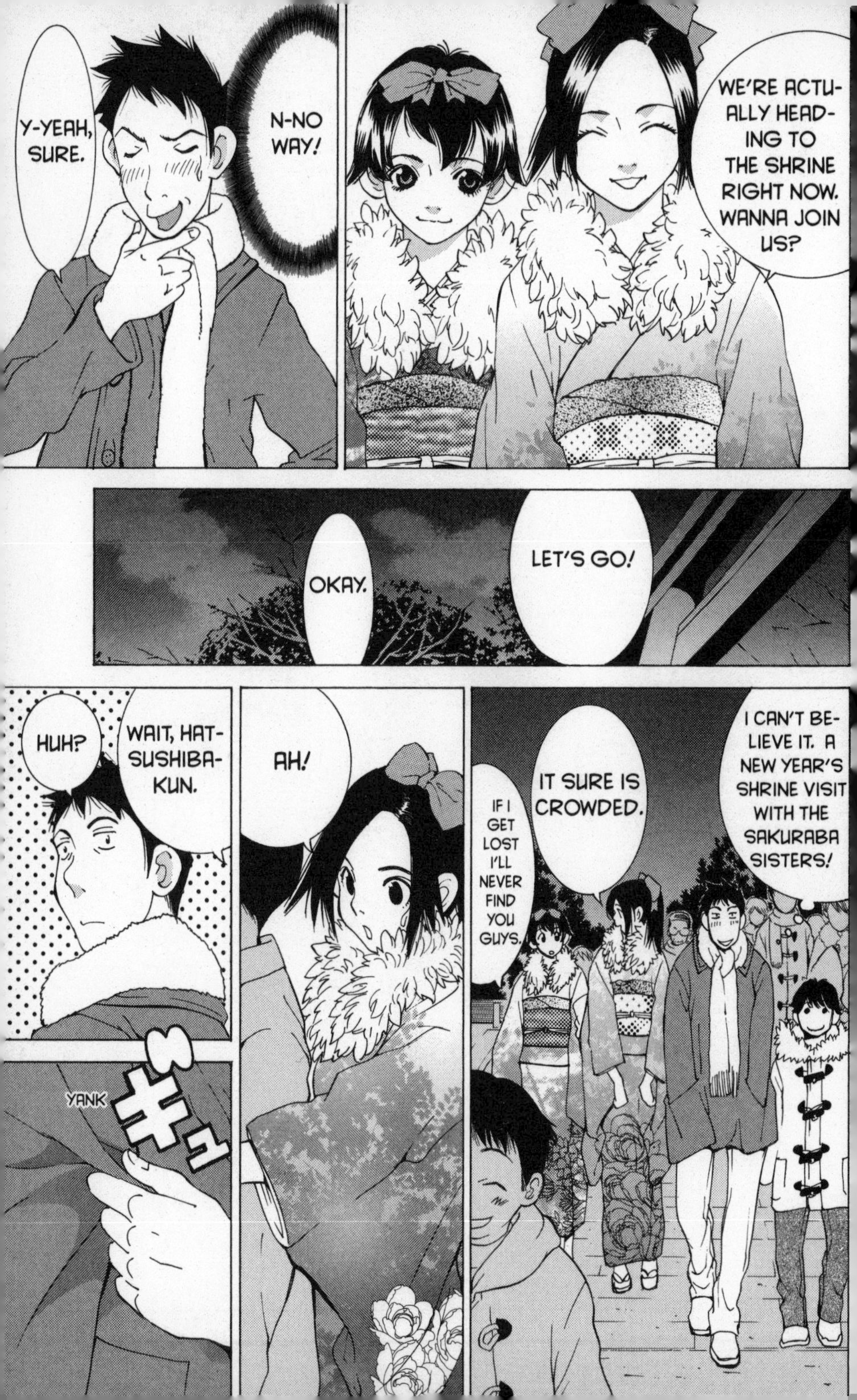
WE'RE ACTU-ALLY HEAD-ING TO THE SHRINE RIGHT NOW. WANNA JOIN US?
N-NO WAY!
Y-YEAH, SURE.
LET'S GO!
OKAY.
I CAN'T BE-LIEVE IT. A NEW YEAR'S SHRINE VISIT WITH THE SAKURABA SISTERS!
IT SURE IS CROWDED.
IF I GET LOST I'LL NEVER FIND YOU GUYS.
AH!
WAIT, HAT-SUSHIBA-KUN.
HUH?
YANK

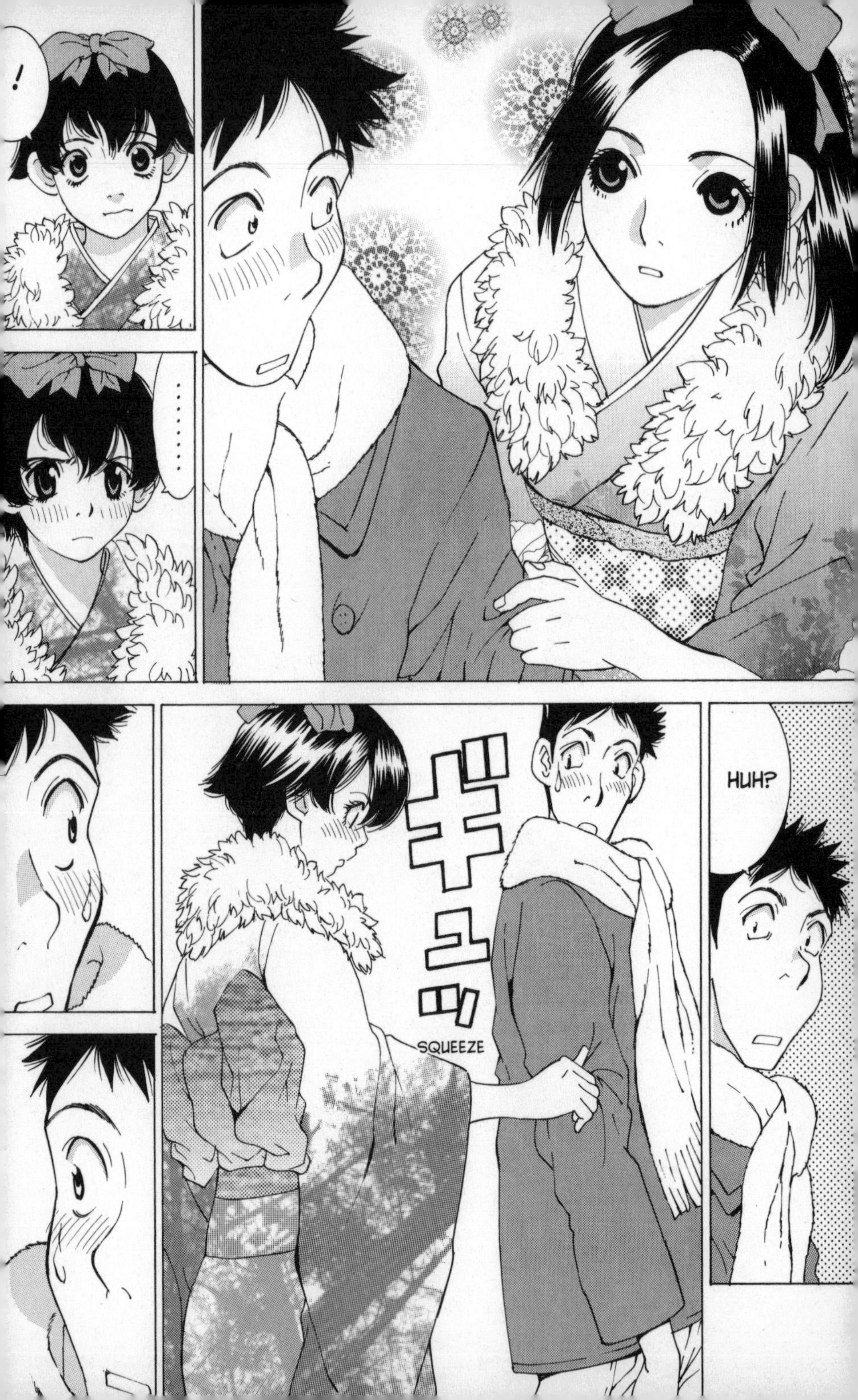
!
......
HUH?
ギュッ
SQUEEZE

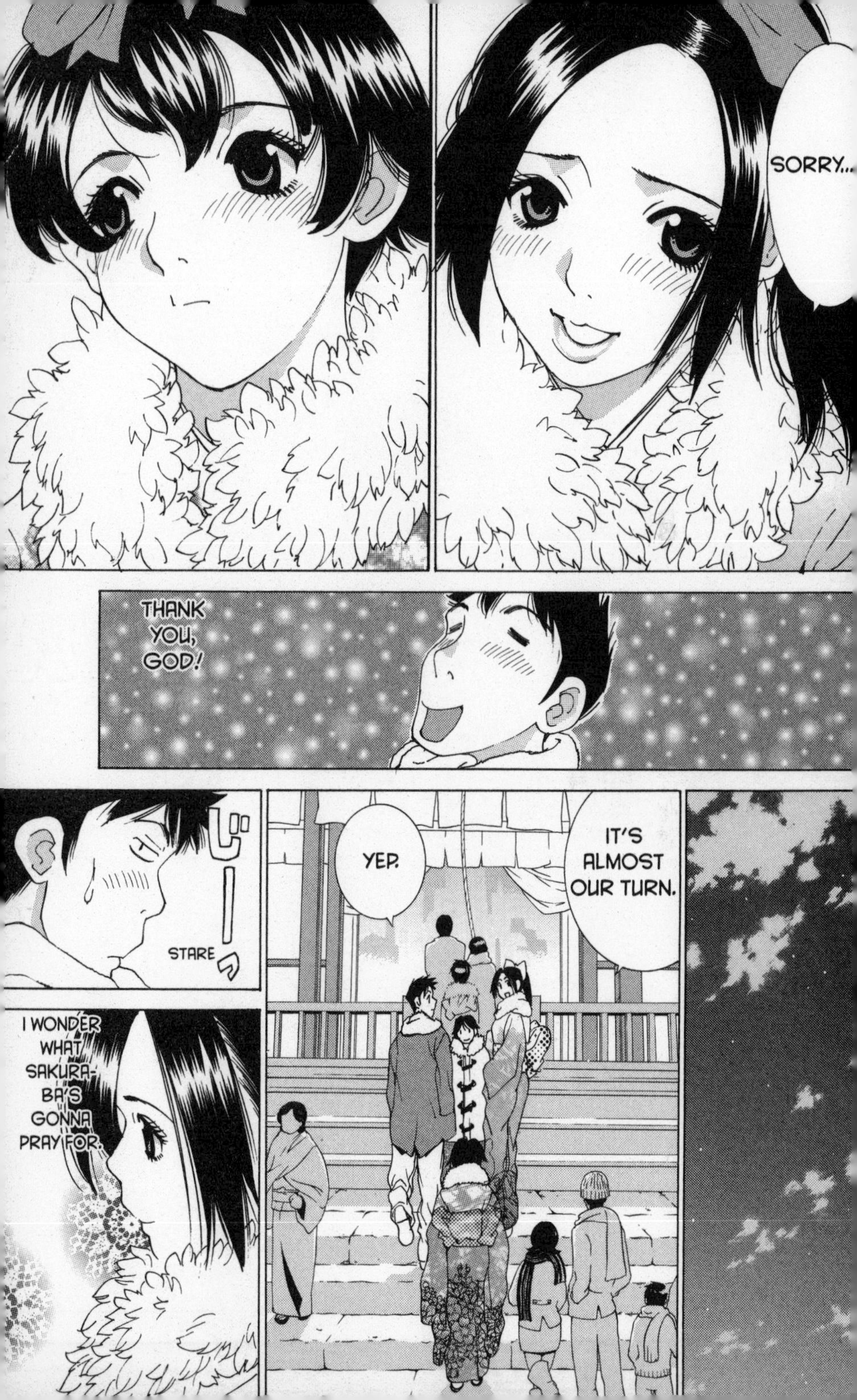
SORRY...
THANK YOU, GOD!
IT'S ALMOST OUR TURN.
YEP.
じーッ
STARE
I WONDER WHAT SAKURA-BA'S GONNA PRAY FOR.

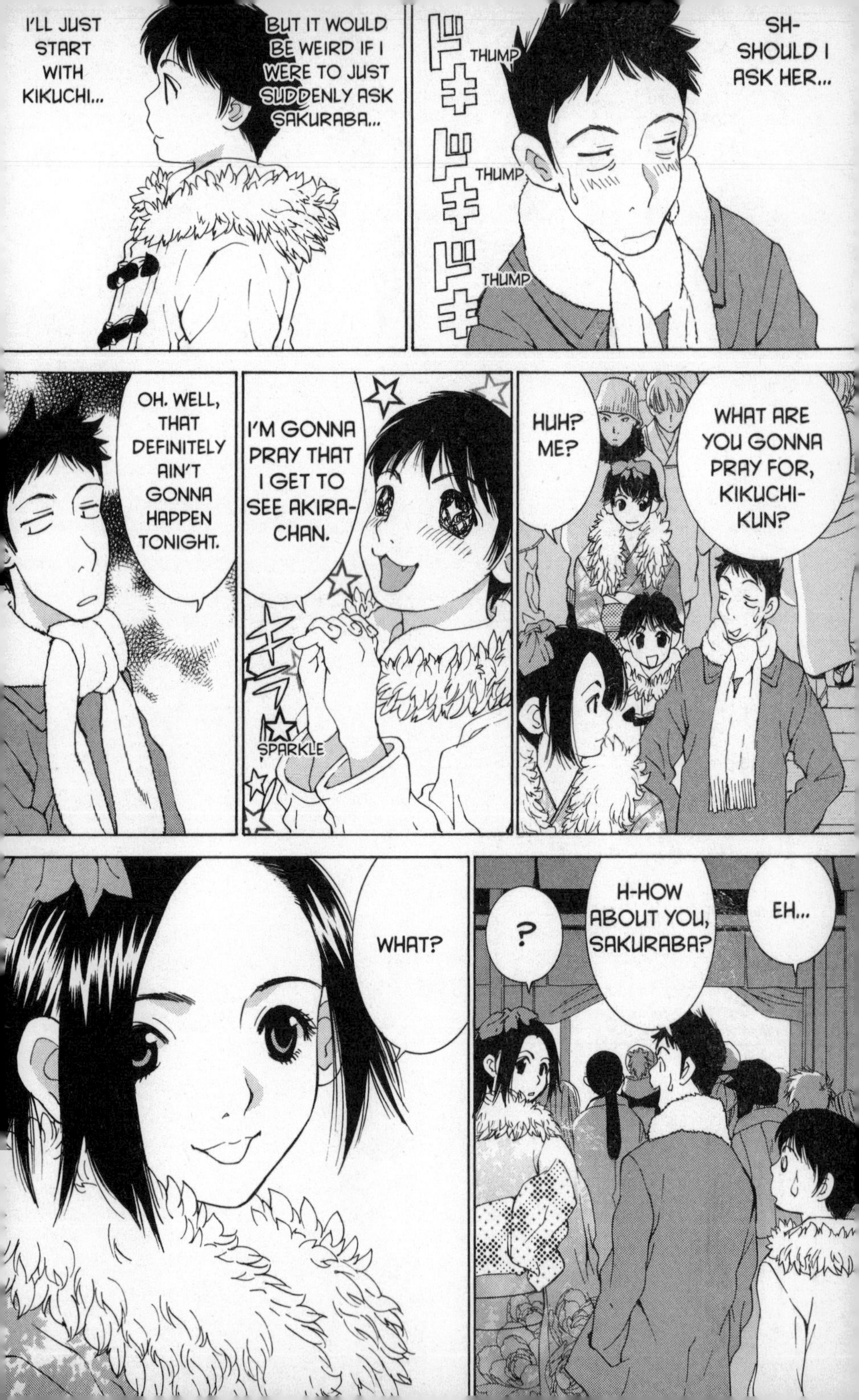
SH- SHOULD I ASK HER...
ドキドキドキ
THUMP
THUMP
THUMP
BUT IT WOULD BE WEIRD IF I WERE TO JUST SUDDENLY ASK SAKURABA...
I'LL JUST START WITH KIKUCHI...
WHAT ARE YOU GONNA PRAY FOR, KIKUCHI-KUN?
HUH? ME?
I'M GONNA PRAY THAT I GET TO SEE AKIRA-CHAN.
SPARKLE
OH. WELL, THAT DEFINITELY AIN'T GONNA HAPPEN TONIGHT.
EH...
H-HOW ABOUT YOU, SAKURABA?
?
WHAT?

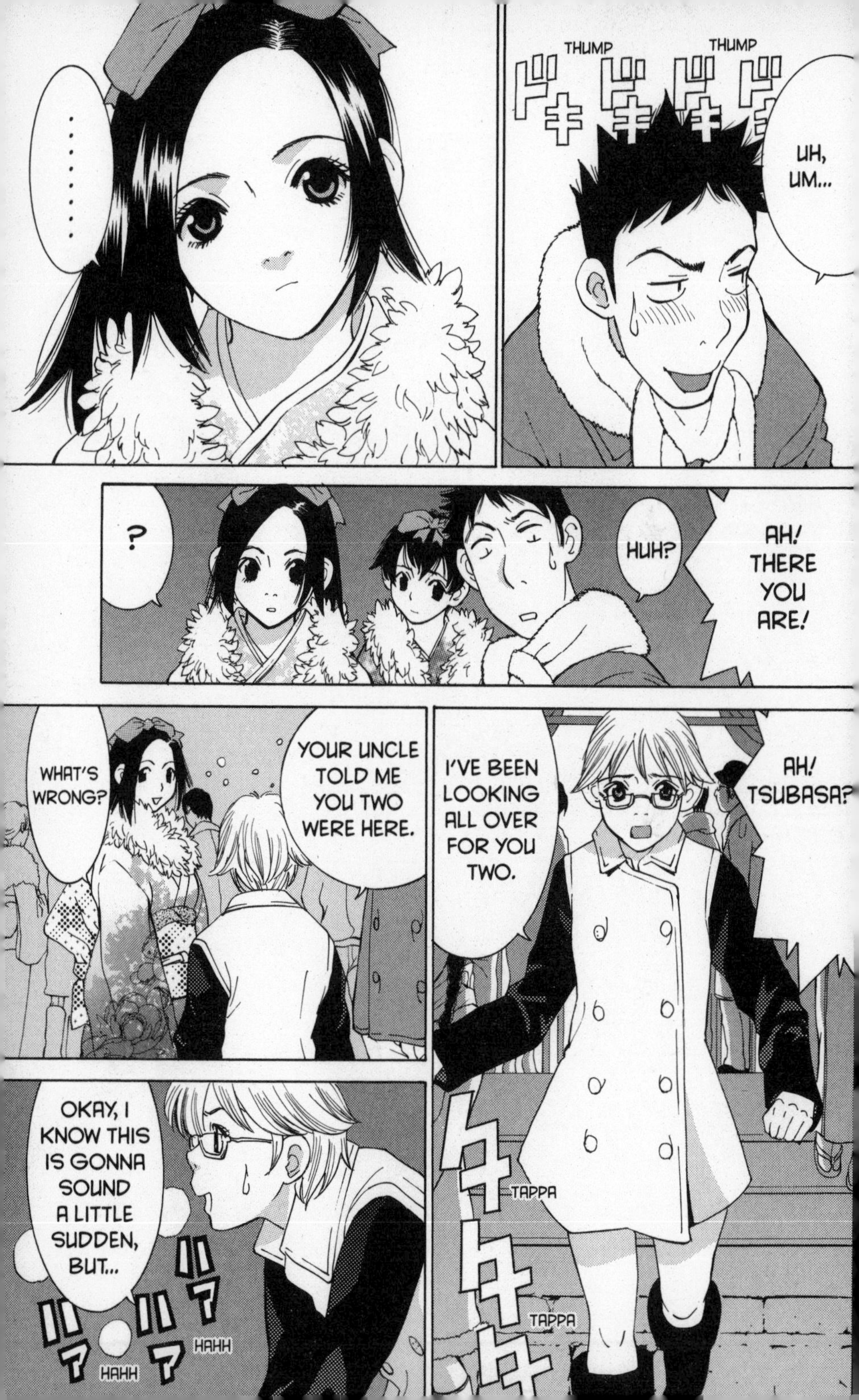
THUMP
THUMP
UH, UM...
......
AH! THERE YOU ARE!
HUH?
?
AH! TSUBASA?
I'VE BEEN LOOKING ALL OVER FOR YOU TWO.
TAPPA
TAPPA
YOUR UNCLE TOLD ME YOU TWO WERE HERE.
WHAT'S WRONG?
OKAY, I KNOW THIS IS GONNA SOUND A LITTLE SUDDEN, BUT...
HAHH
HAHH

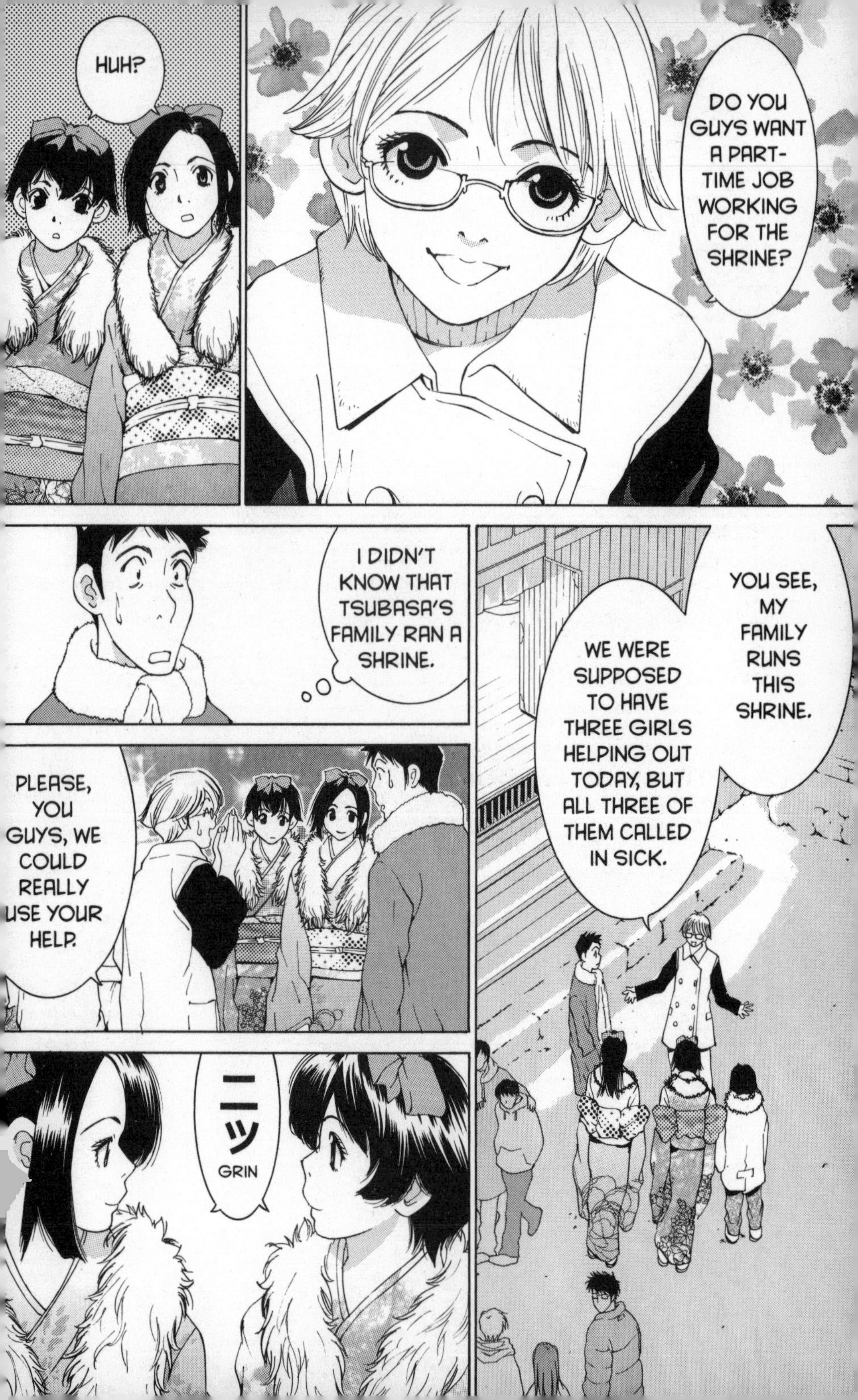
DO YOU GUYS WANT A PART-TIME JOB WORKING FOR THE SHRINE?
HUH?
YOU SEE, MY FAMILY RUNS THIS SHRINE.
WE WERE SUPPOSED TO HAVE THREE GIRLS HELPING OUT TODAY, BUT ALL THREE OF THEM CALLED IN SICK.
I DIDN'T KNOW THAT TSUBASA'S FAMILY RAN A SHRINE.
PLEASE, YOU GUYS, WE COULD REALLY USE YOUR HELP.
ニッ
GRIN

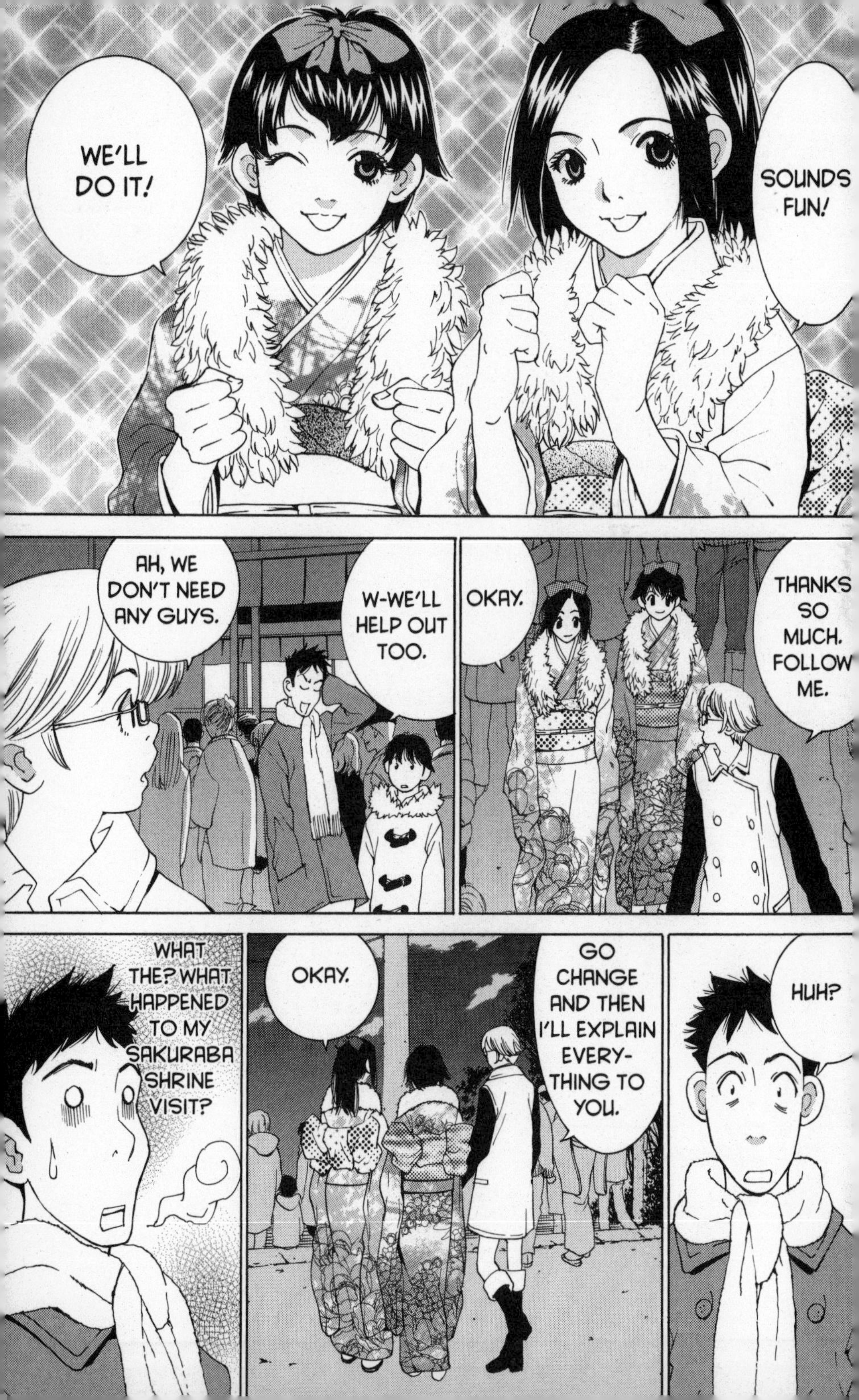
SOUNDS FUN!
WE'LL DO IT!
THANKS SO MUCH. FOLLOW ME.
OKAY.
W-WE'LL HELP OUT TOO.
AH, WE DON'T NEED ANY GUYS.
HUH?
GO CHANGE AND THEN I'LL EXPLAIN EVERY-THING TO YOU.
OKAY.
WHAT THE? WHAT HAPPENED TO MY SAKURABA SHRINE VISIT?

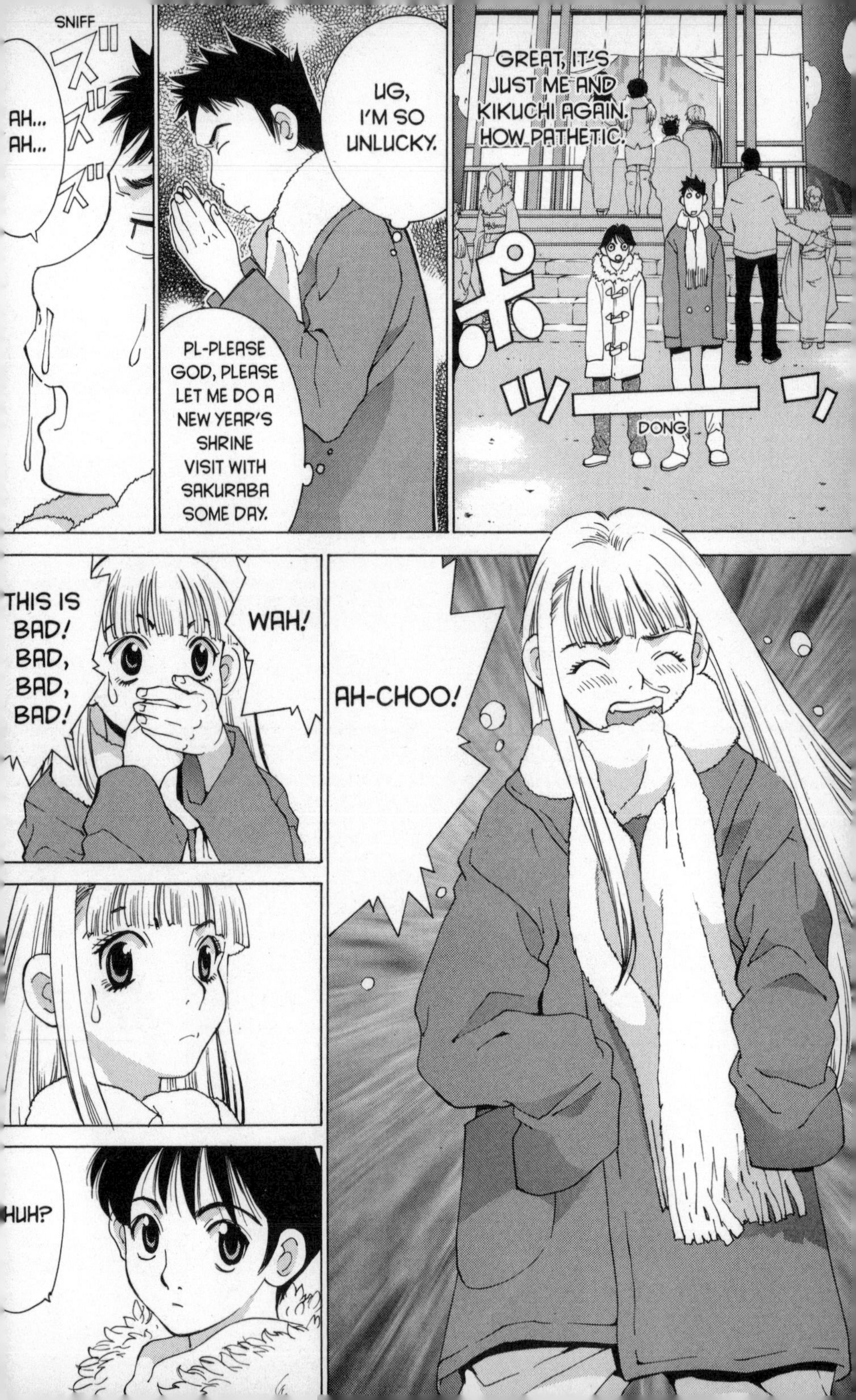
GREAT, IT'S JUST ME AND KIKUCHI AGAIN. HOW PATHETIC.
DONG
UG, I'M SO UNLUCKY.
PL-PLEASE GOD, PLEASE LET ME DO A NEW YEAR'S SHRINE VISIT WITH SAKURABA SOME DAY.
SNIFF
AH... AH...
AH-CHOO!
WAH!
THIS IS BAD! BAD, BAD, BAD!
HUH?

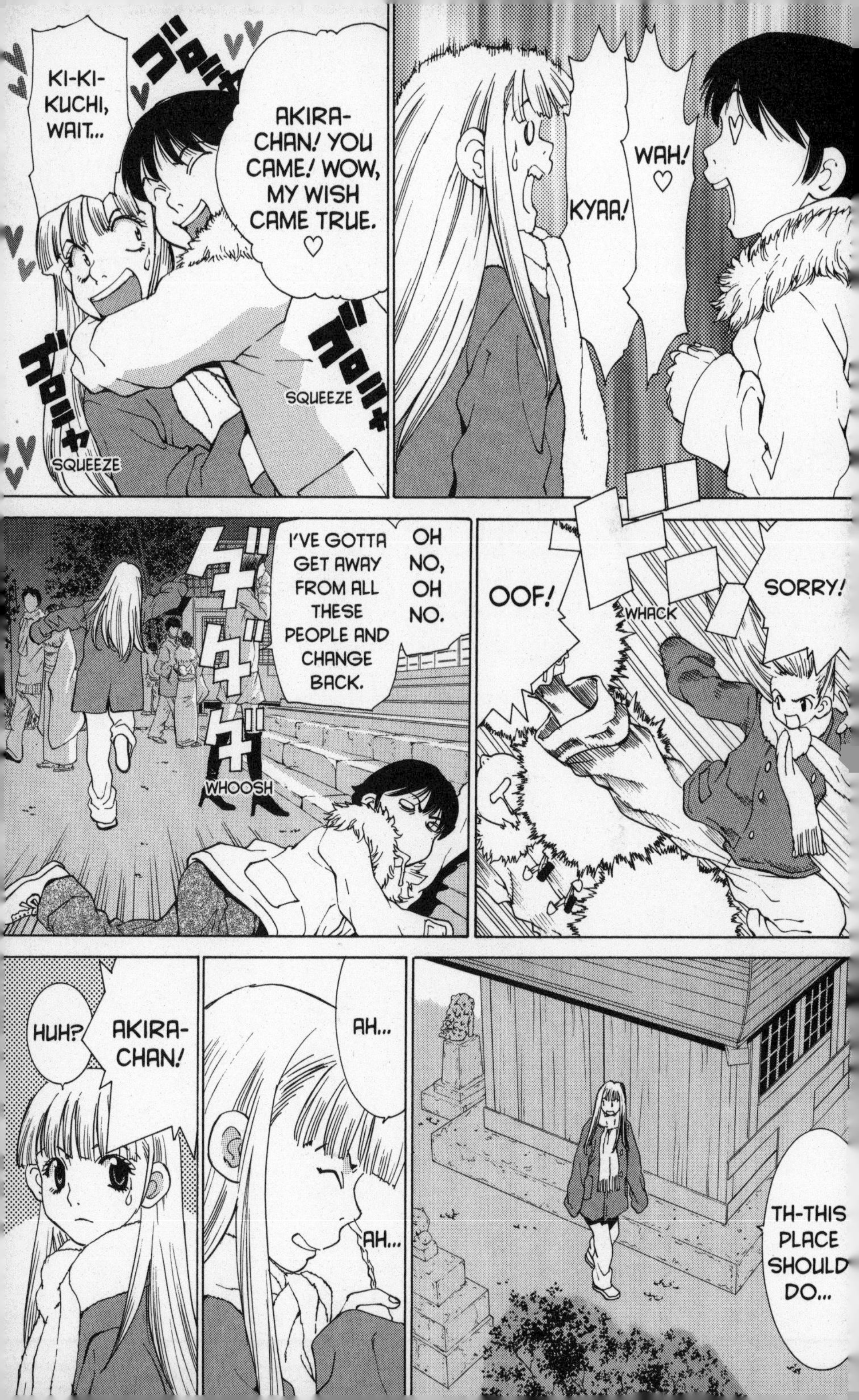

WAH! ♡
KYAA!
AKIRA-CHAN! YOU CAME! WOW, MY WISH CAME TRUE. ♡
KI-KI-KUCHI, WAIT...
SQUEEZE
SQUEEZE
SORRY!
WHACK
OOF!
OH NO, OH NO.
I'VE GOTTA GET AWAY FROM ALL THESE PEOPLE AND CHANGE BACK.
WHOOSH
TH-THIS PLACE SHOULD DO...
AH...
AH...
AKIRA-CHAN!
HUH?

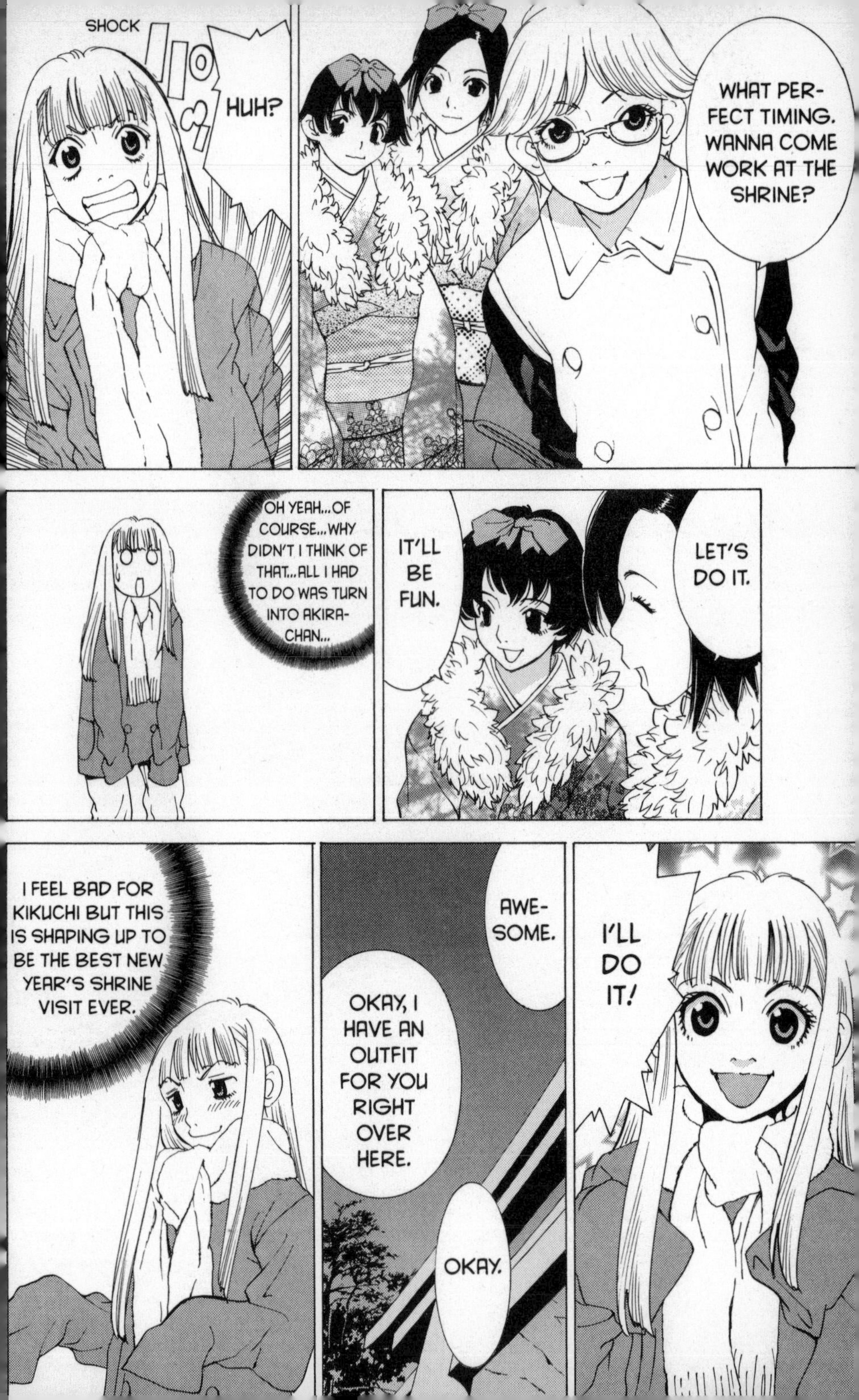
WHAT PER-FECT TIMING. WANNA COME WORK AT THE SHRINE?
SHOCK
HUH?
LET'S DO IT.
IT'LL BE FUN.
OH YEAH...OF COURSE...WHY DIDN'T I THINK OF THAT...ALL I HAD TO DO WAS TURN INTO AKIRA-CHAN...
I'LL DO IT!
AWE-SOME.
OKAY, I HAVE AN OUTFIT FOR YOU RIGHT OVER HERE.
OKAY.
I FEEL BAD FOR KIKUCHI BUT THIS IS SHAPING UP TO BE THE BEST NEW YEAR'S SHRINE VISIT EVER.

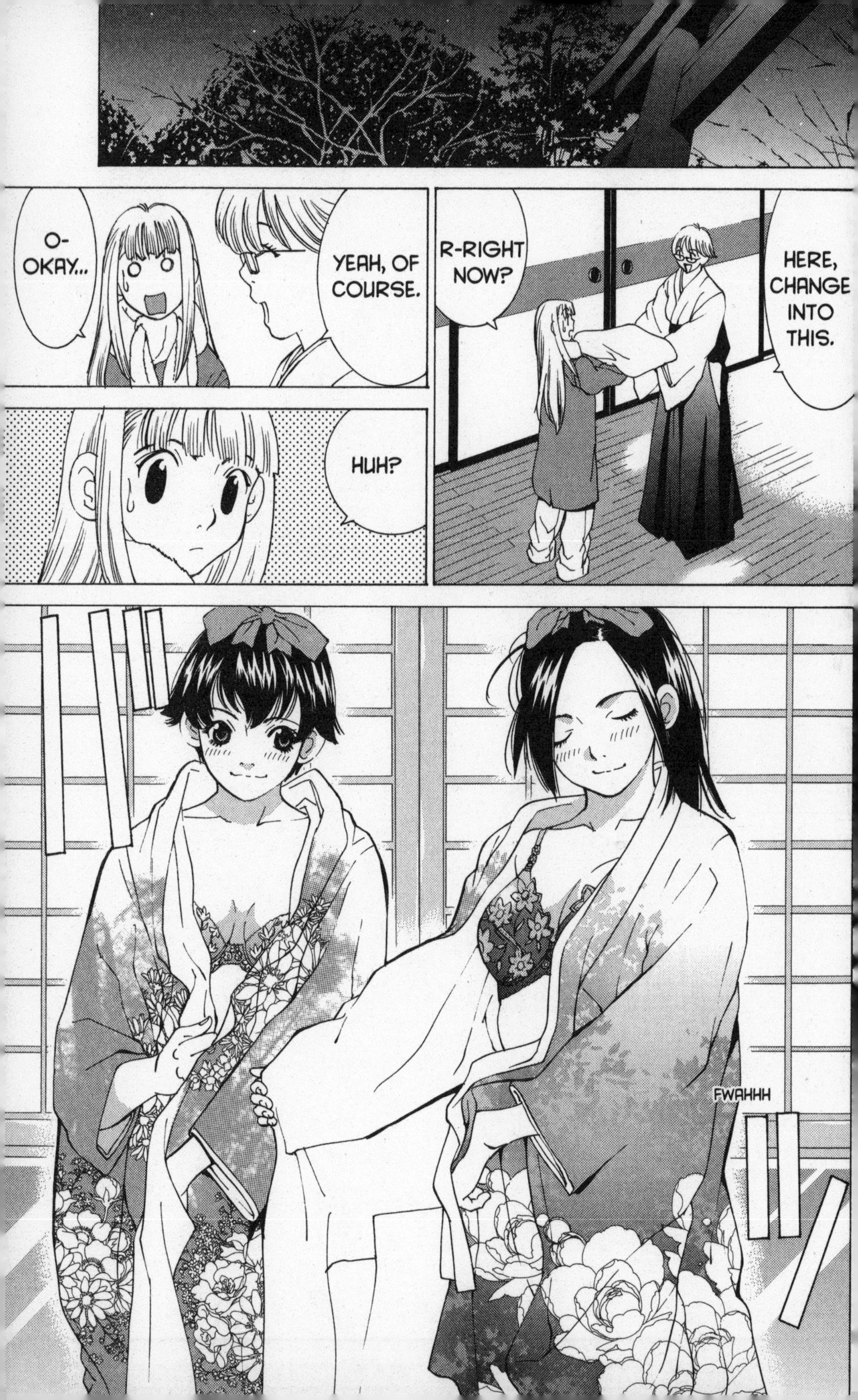
HERE, CHANGE INTO THIS.
R-RIGHT NOW?
YEAH, OF COURSE.
O-OKAY...
HUH?
FWAHHH

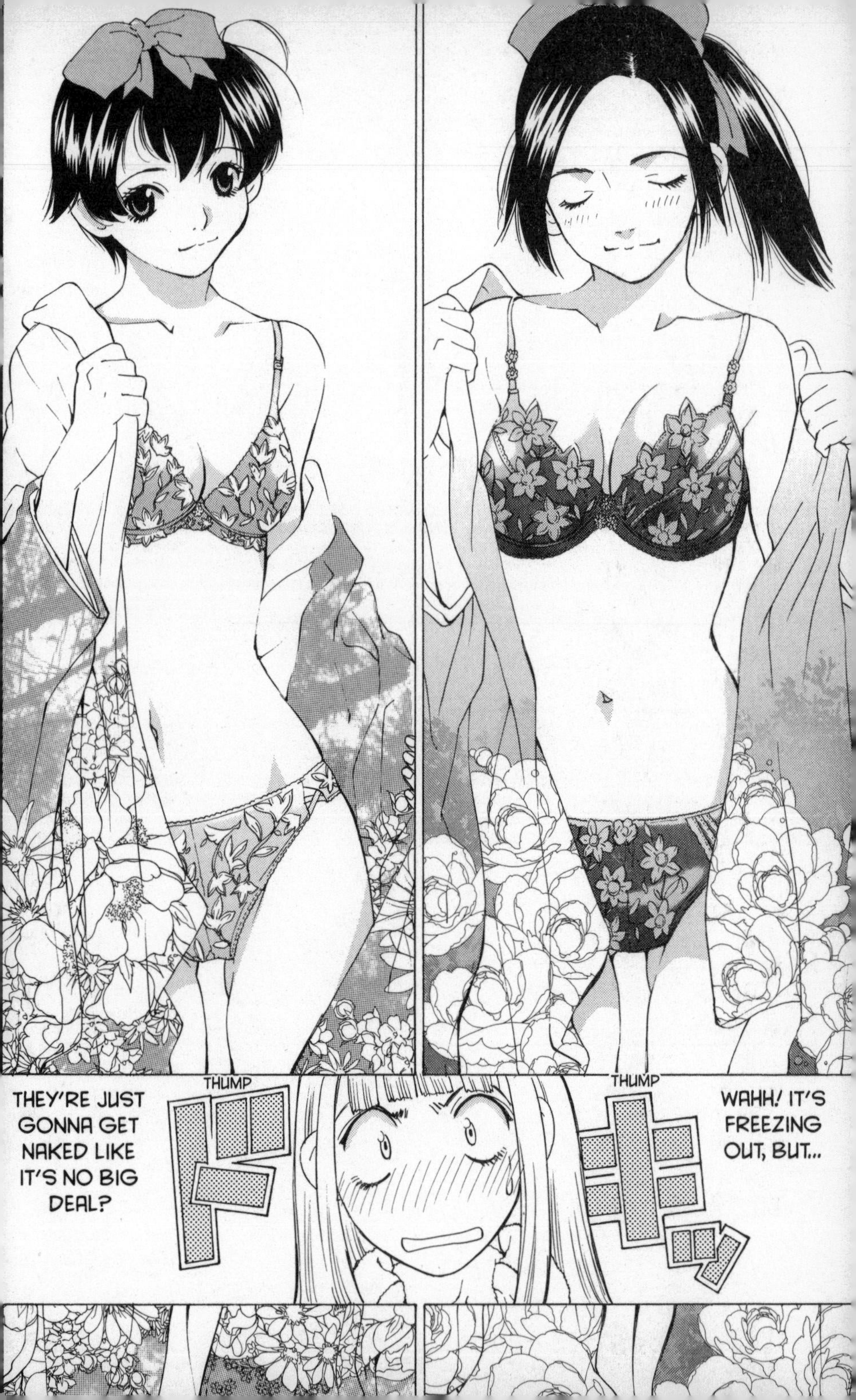
WAHH! IT'S FREEZING OUT, BUT...
THUMP
THUMP
THEY'RE JUST GONNA GET NAKED LIKE IT'S NO BIG DEAL?

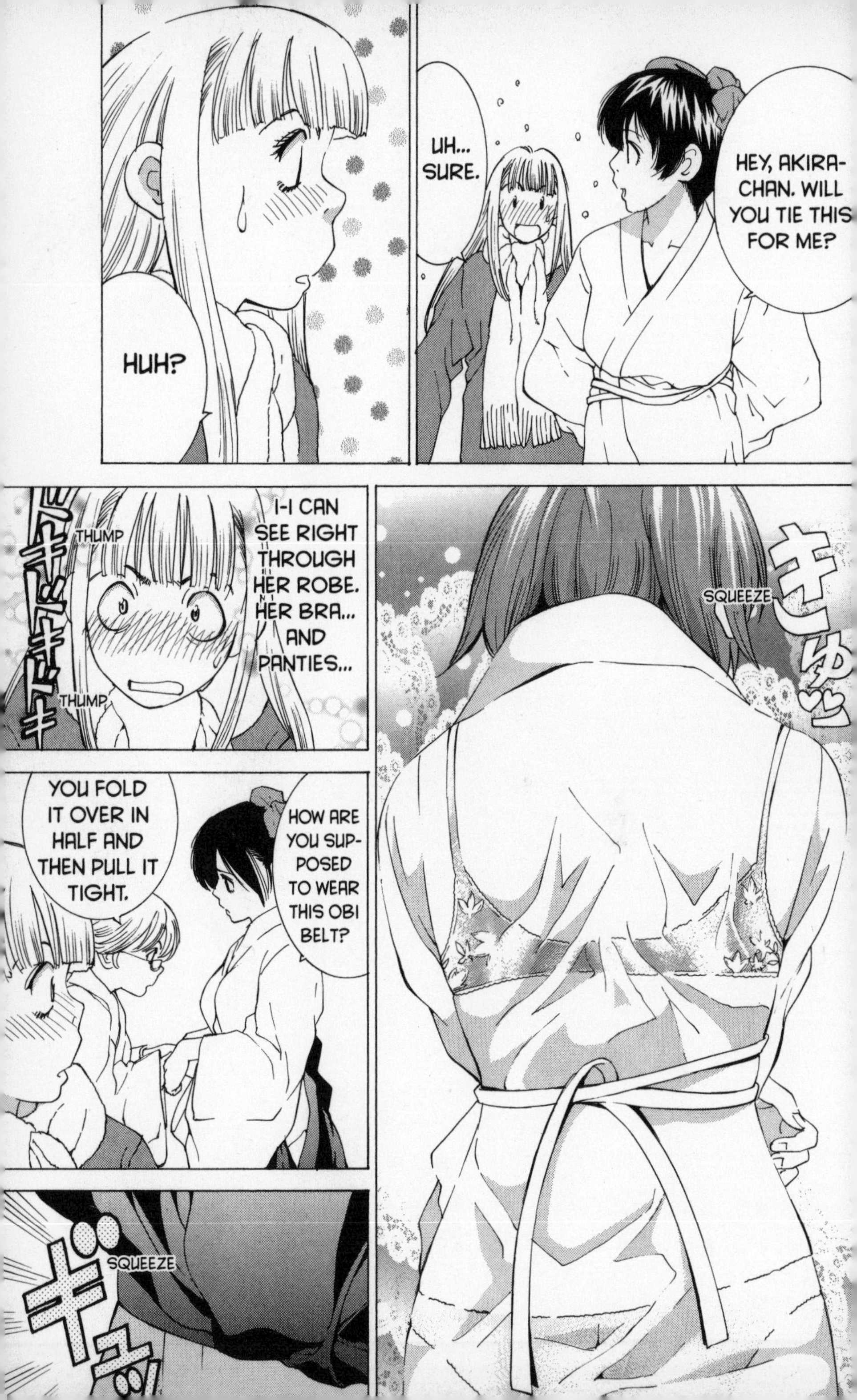
HEY, AKIRA-CHAN. WILL YOU TIE THIS FOR ME?
UH... SURE.
HUH?
SQUEEZE
THUMP
THUMP
I-I CAN SEE RIGHT THROUGH HER ROBE. HER BRA... AND PANTIES...
HOW ARE YOU SUP-POSED TO WEAR THIS OBI BELT?
YOU FOLD IT OVER IN HALF AND THEN PULL IT TIGHT.
SQUEEZE

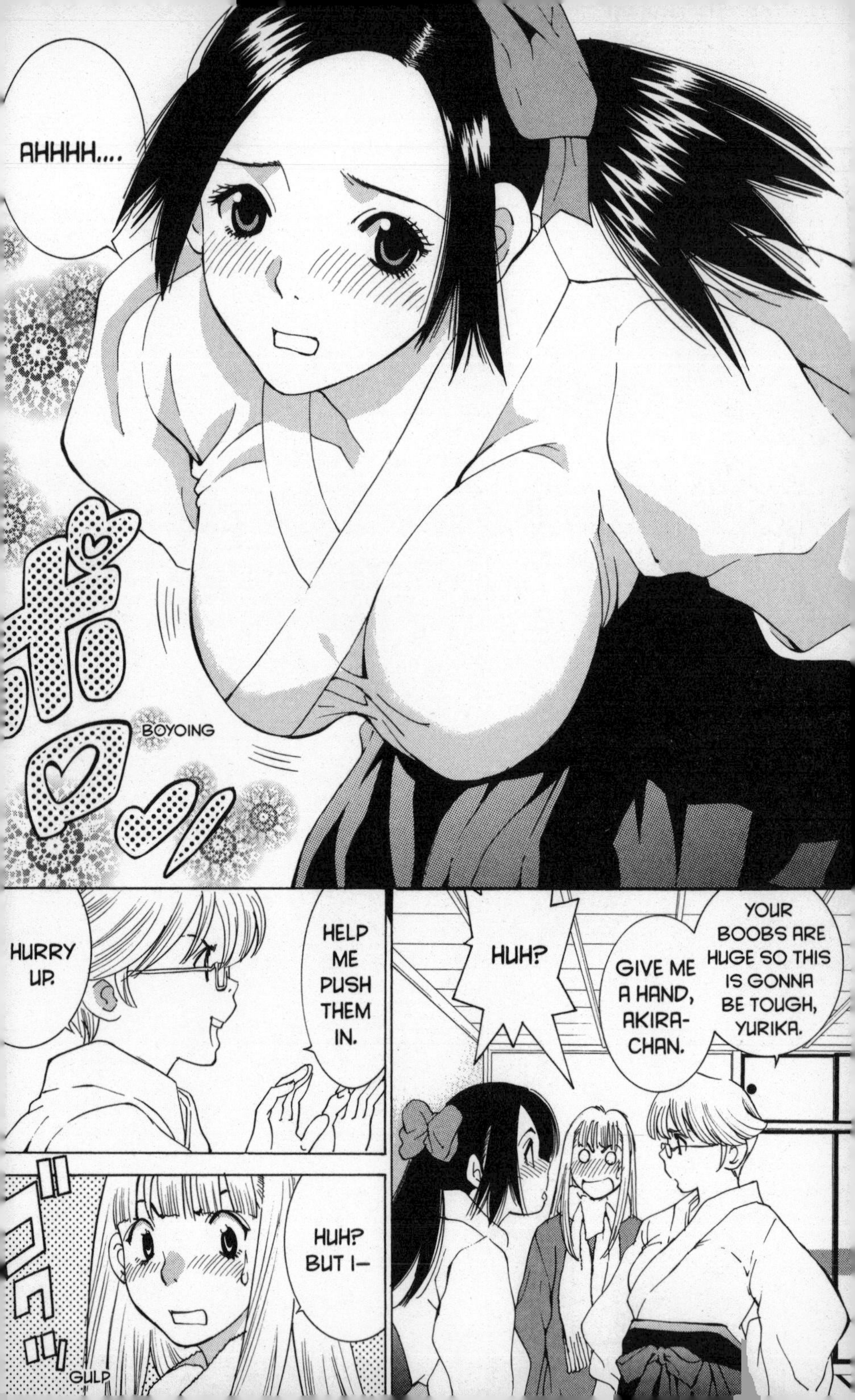
AHHHH....
BOYOING
YOUR BOOBS ARE HUGE SO THIS IS GONNA BE TOUGH, YURIKA.
GIVE ME A HAND, AKIRA-CHAN.
HUH?
HELP ME PUSH THEM IN.
HURRY UP.
HUH? BUT I—
GULP

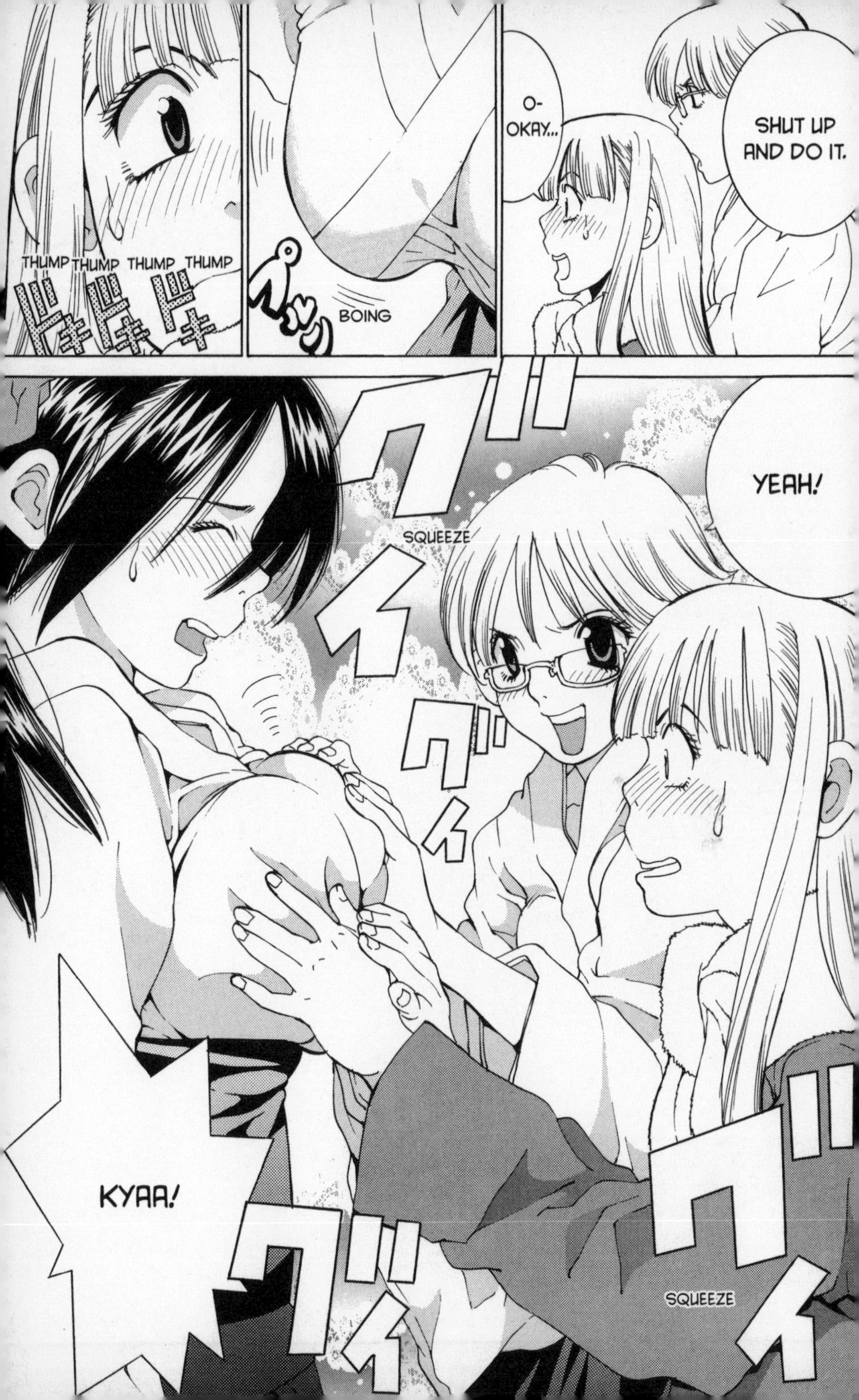
SHUT UP AND DO IT.
O- OKAY...
BOING
THUMP THUMP THUMP THUMP
YEAH!
SQUEEZE
SQUEEZE
KYAA!

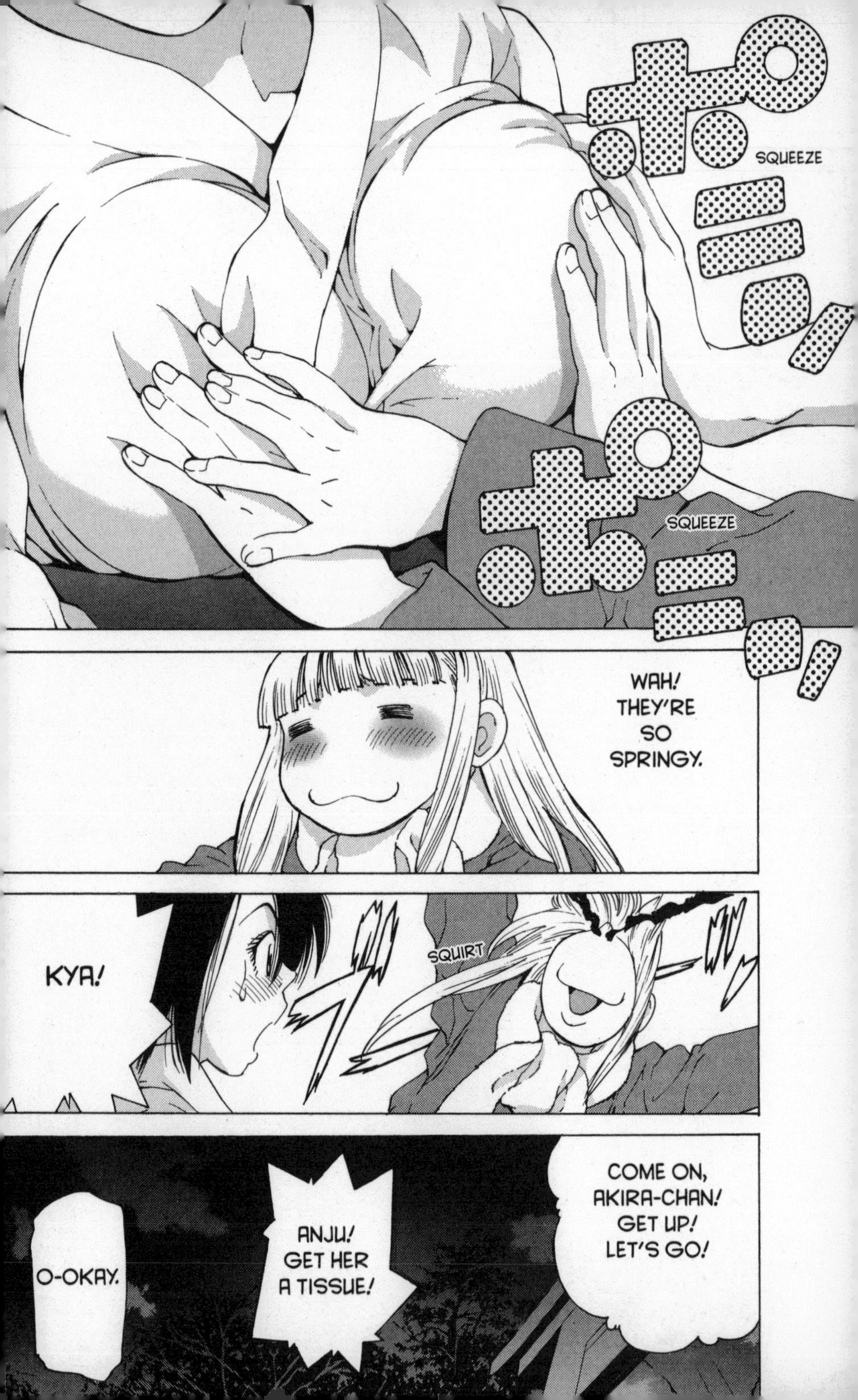
SQUEEZE
SQUEEZE
WAH! THEY'RE SO SPRINGY.
SQUIRT
KYA!
COME ON, AKIRA-CHAN! GET UP! LET'S GO!
ANJU! GET HER A TISSUE!
O-OKAY.

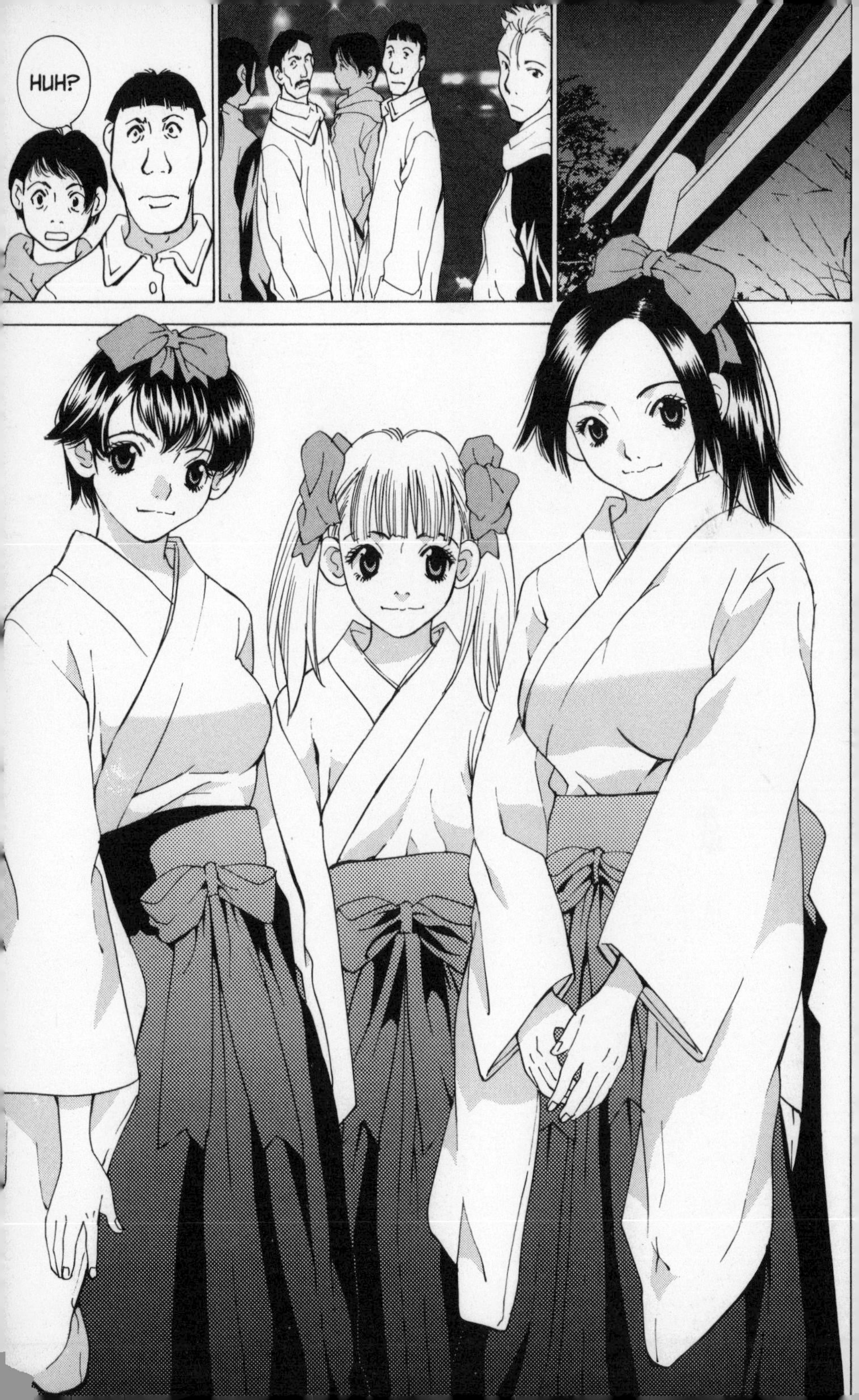
HUH?

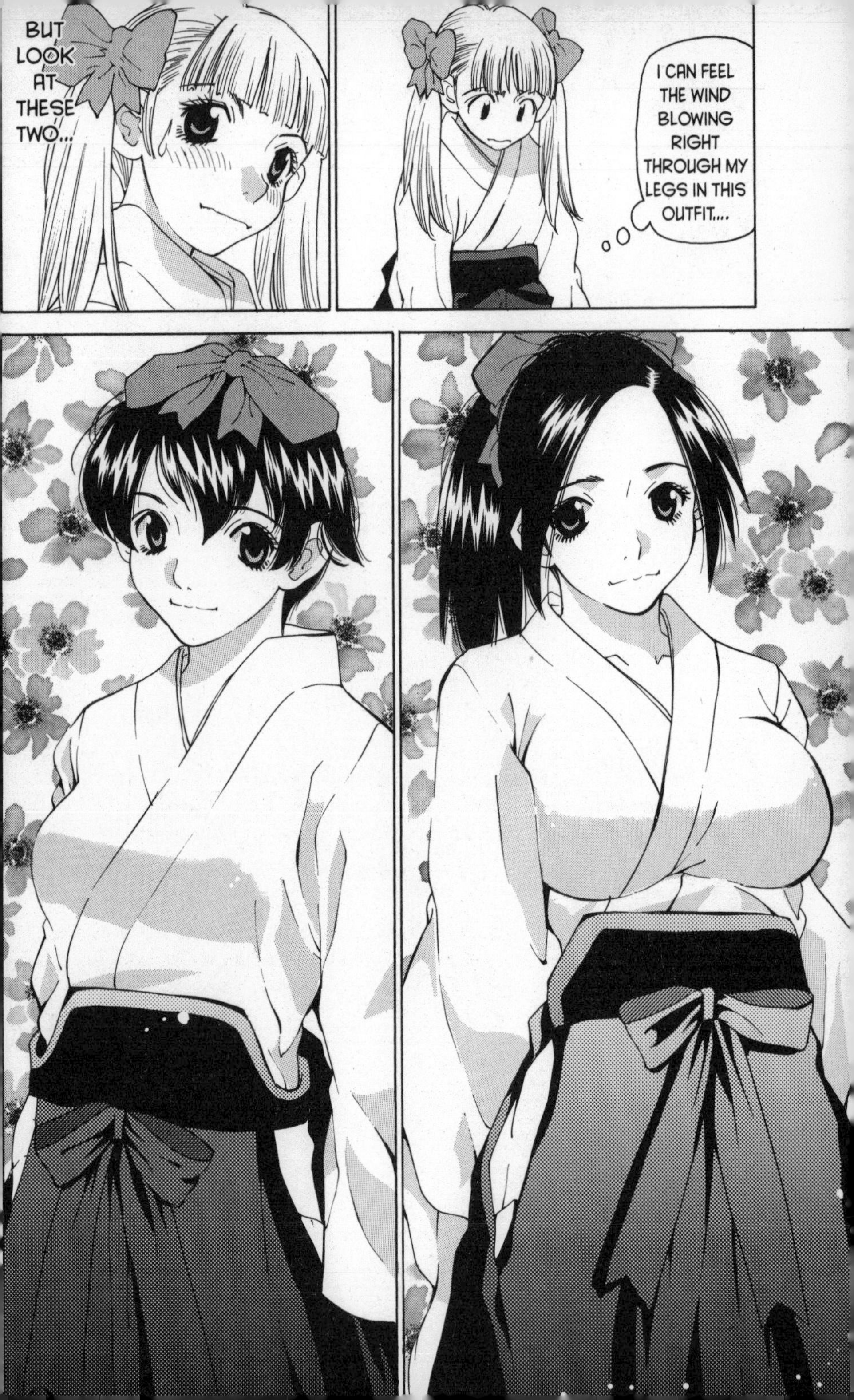
I CAN FEEL THE WIND BLOWING RIGHT THROUGH MY LEGS IN THIS OUTFIT....
BUT LOOK AT THESE TWO...

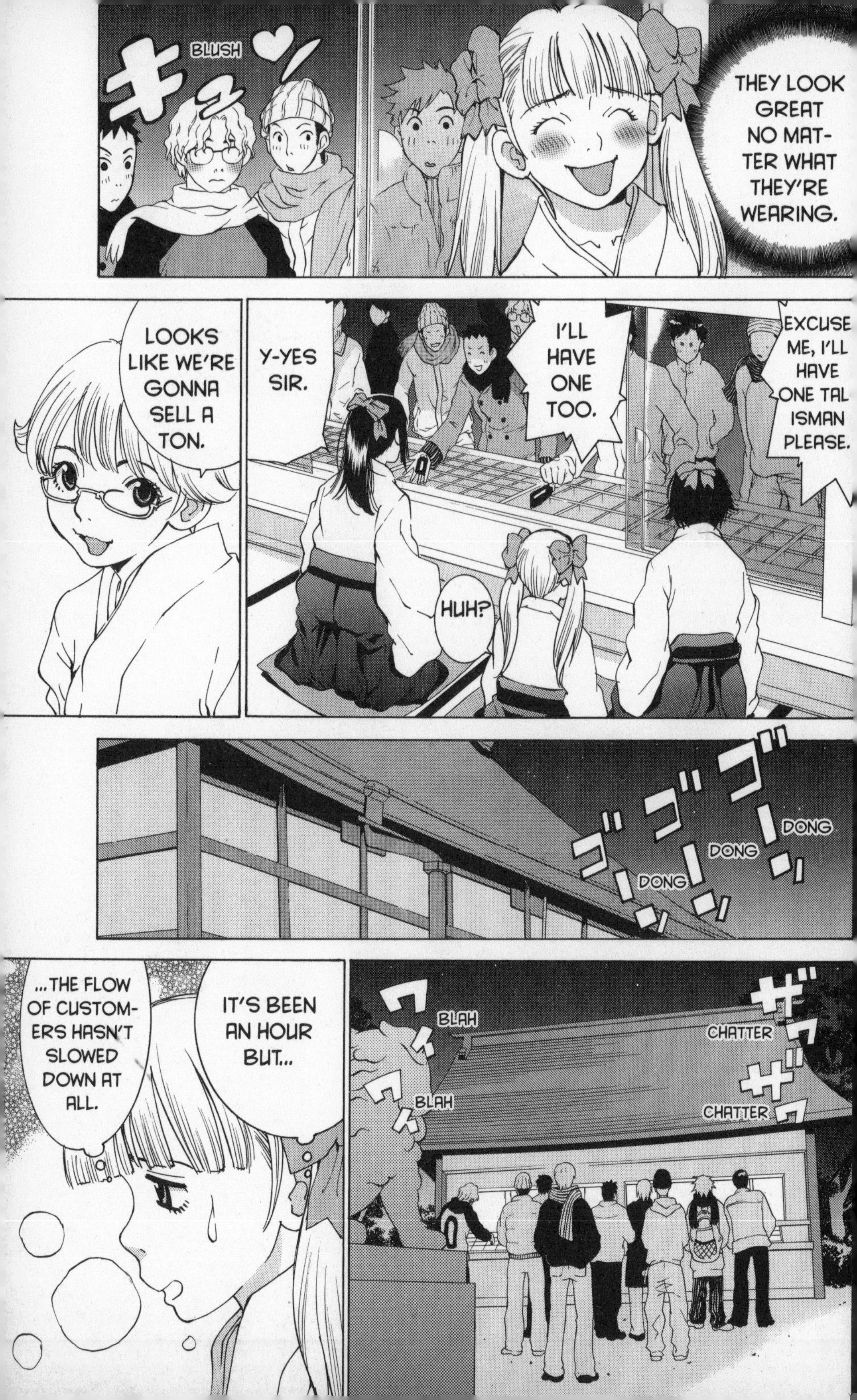
THEY LOOK GREAT NO MAT-TER WHAT THEY'RE WEARING.
BLUSH
EXCUSE ME, I'LL HAVE ONE TAL ISMAN PLEASE.
I'LL HAVE ONE TOO.
Y-YES SIR.
HUH?
LOOKS LIKE WE'RE GONNA SELL A TON.
DONG
DONG
DONG
CHATTER
CHATTER
BLAH
BLAH
IT'S BEEN AN HOUR BUT...
...THE FLOW OF CUSTOM-ERS HASN'T SLOWED DOWN AT ALL.

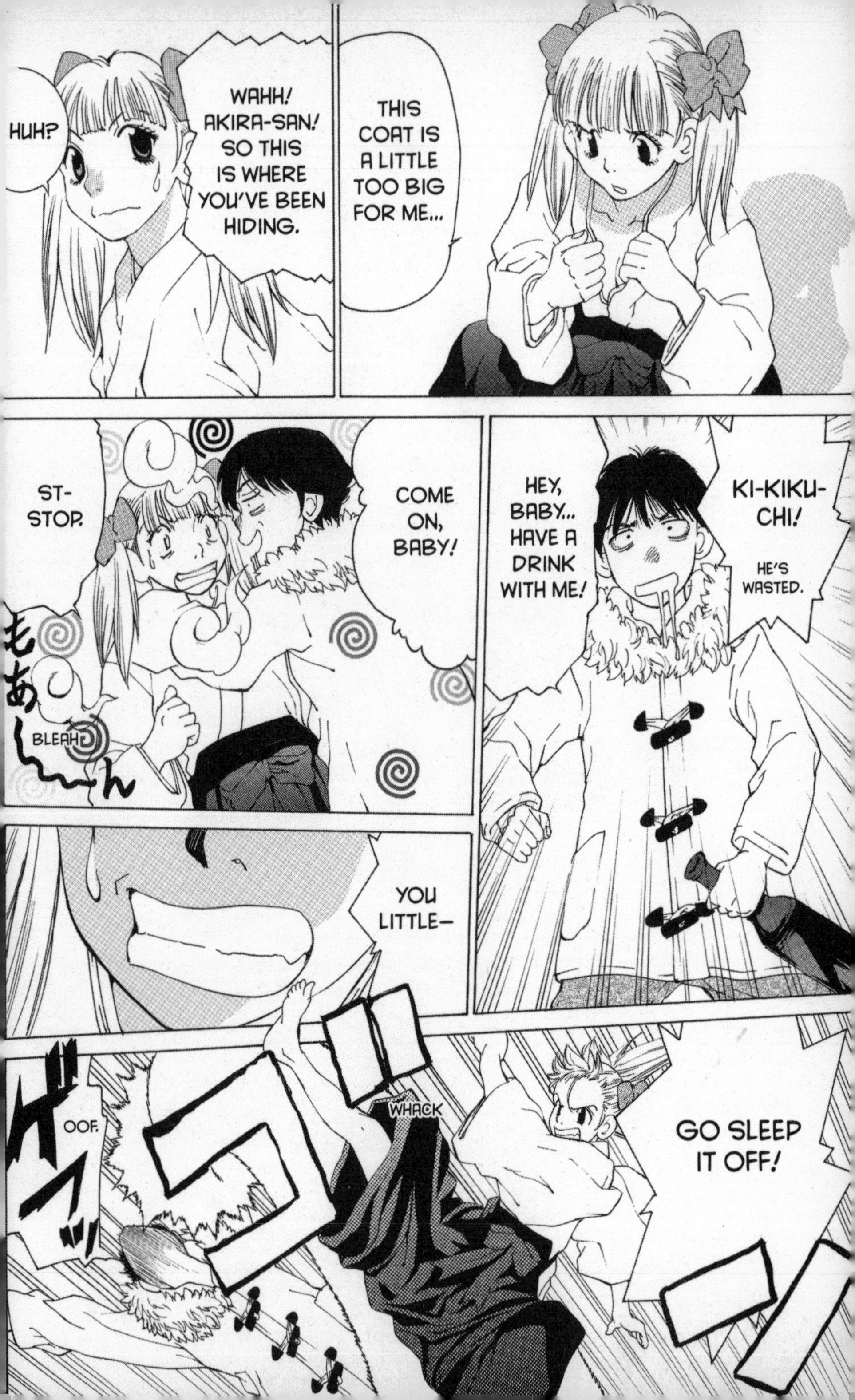
THIS COAT IS A LITTLE TOO BIG FOR ME...
WAHH! AKIRA-SAN! SO THIS IS WHERE YOU'VE BEEN HIDING.
HUH?
KI-KIKUCHI!
HE'S WASTED.
HEY, BABY... HAVE A DRINK WITH ME!
COME ON, BABY!
ST- STOP.
BLEAH
YOU LITTLE–
GO SLEEP IT OFF!
WHACK
OOF.

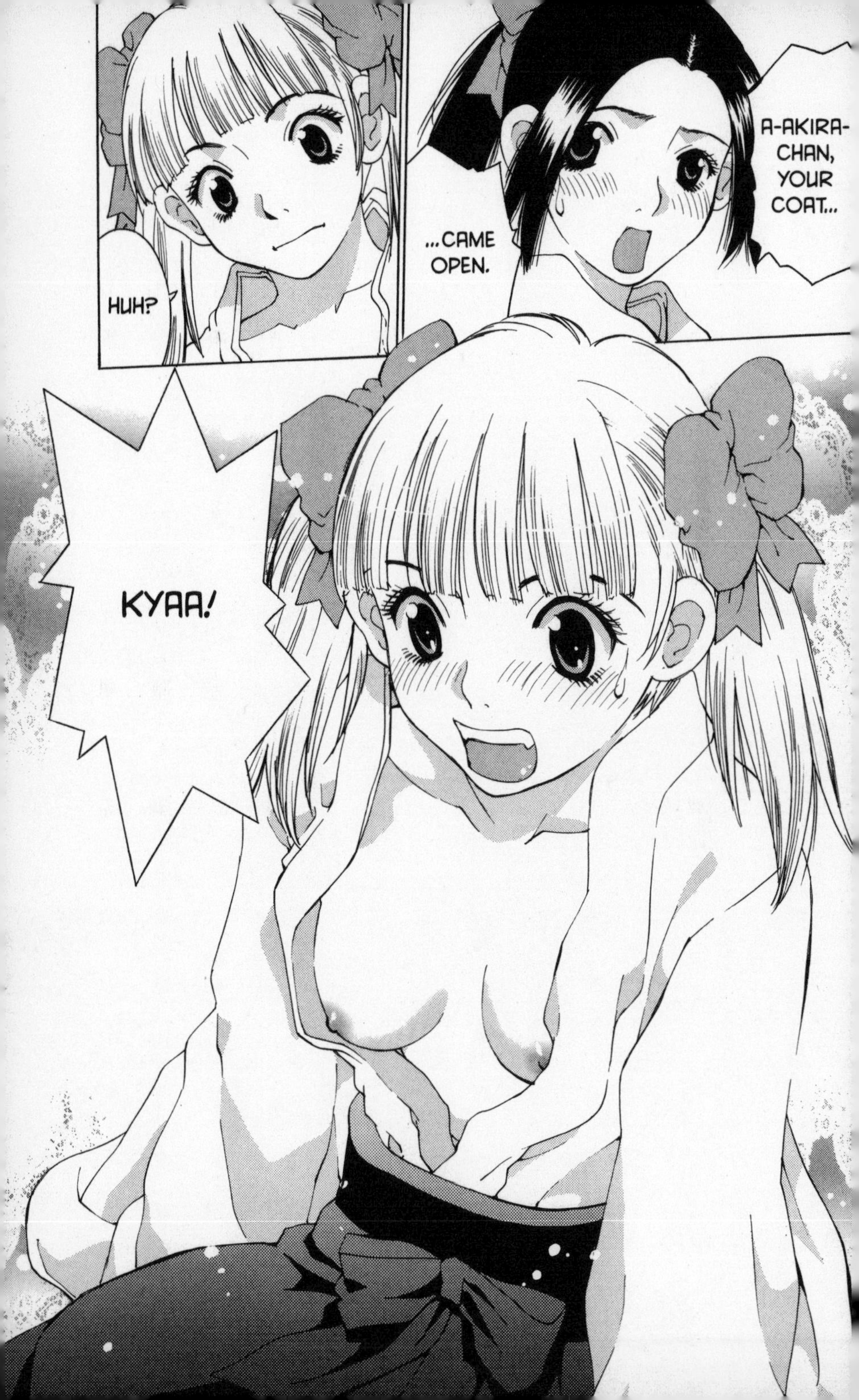
A-AKIRA-CHAN, YOUR COAT...
...CAME OPEN.
HUH?
KYAA!

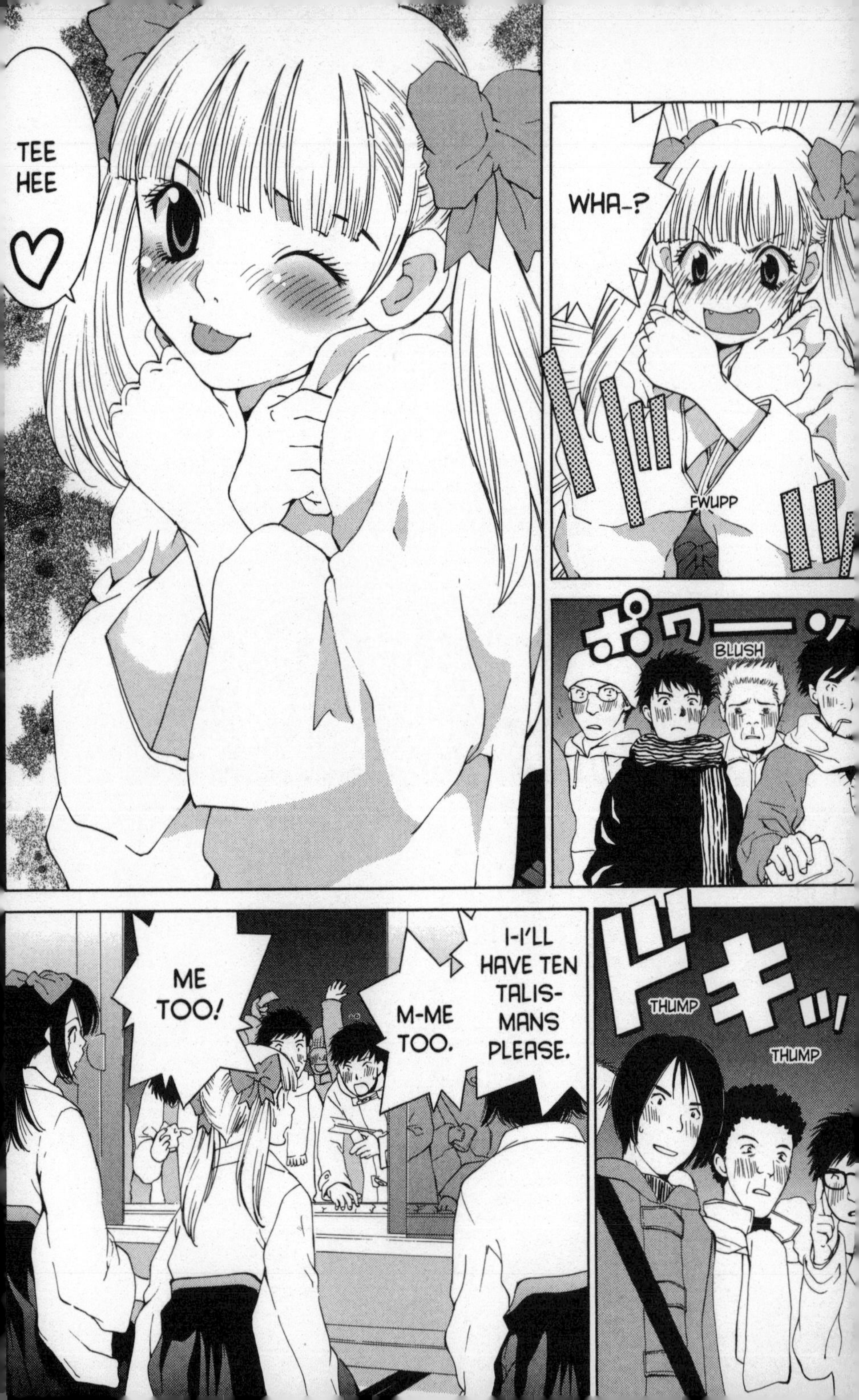

WHA-?
FWUPP
ポワーン
BLUSH
TEE HEE ♡
ドキッ
THUMP
THUMP
I-I'LL HAVE TEN TALIS-MANS PLEASE.
M-ME TOO.
ME TOO!

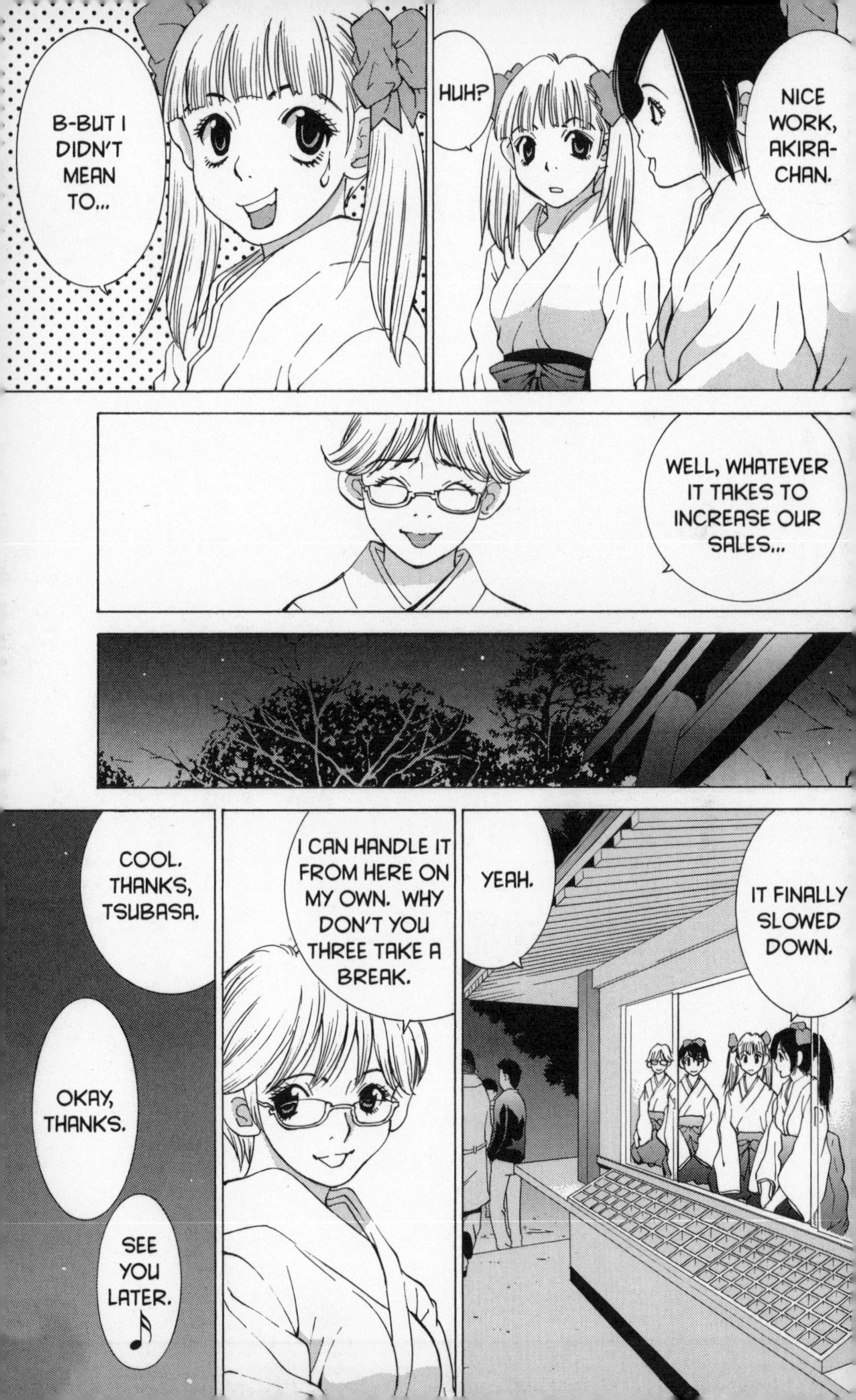
NICE WORK, AKIRA-CHAN.
HUH?
B-BUT I DIDN'T MEAN TO...
WELL, WHATEVER IT TAKES TO INCREASE OUR SALES...
IT FINALLY SLOWED DOWN.
YEAH.
I CAN HANDLE IT FROM HERE ON MY OWN. WHY DON'T YOU THREE TAKE A BREAK.
COOL. THANKS, TSUBASA.
OKAY, THANKS.
SEE YOU LATER. ♪

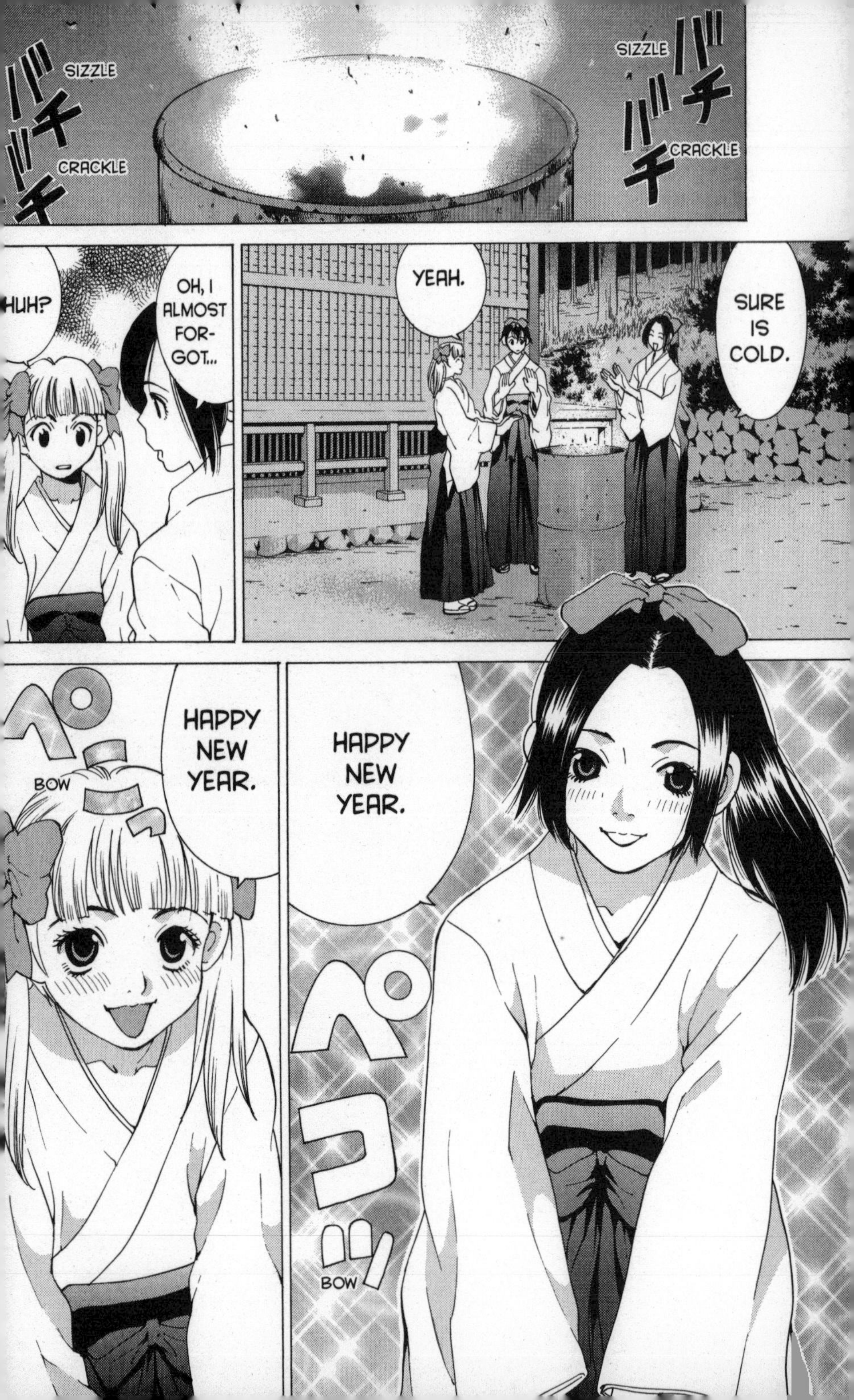

SIZZLE
CRACKLE
SIZZLE
CRACKLE
SURE IS COLD.
YEAH.
OH, I ALMOST FOR-GOT...
HUH?
HAPPY NEW YEAR.
BOW
HAPPY NEW YEAR.
BOW

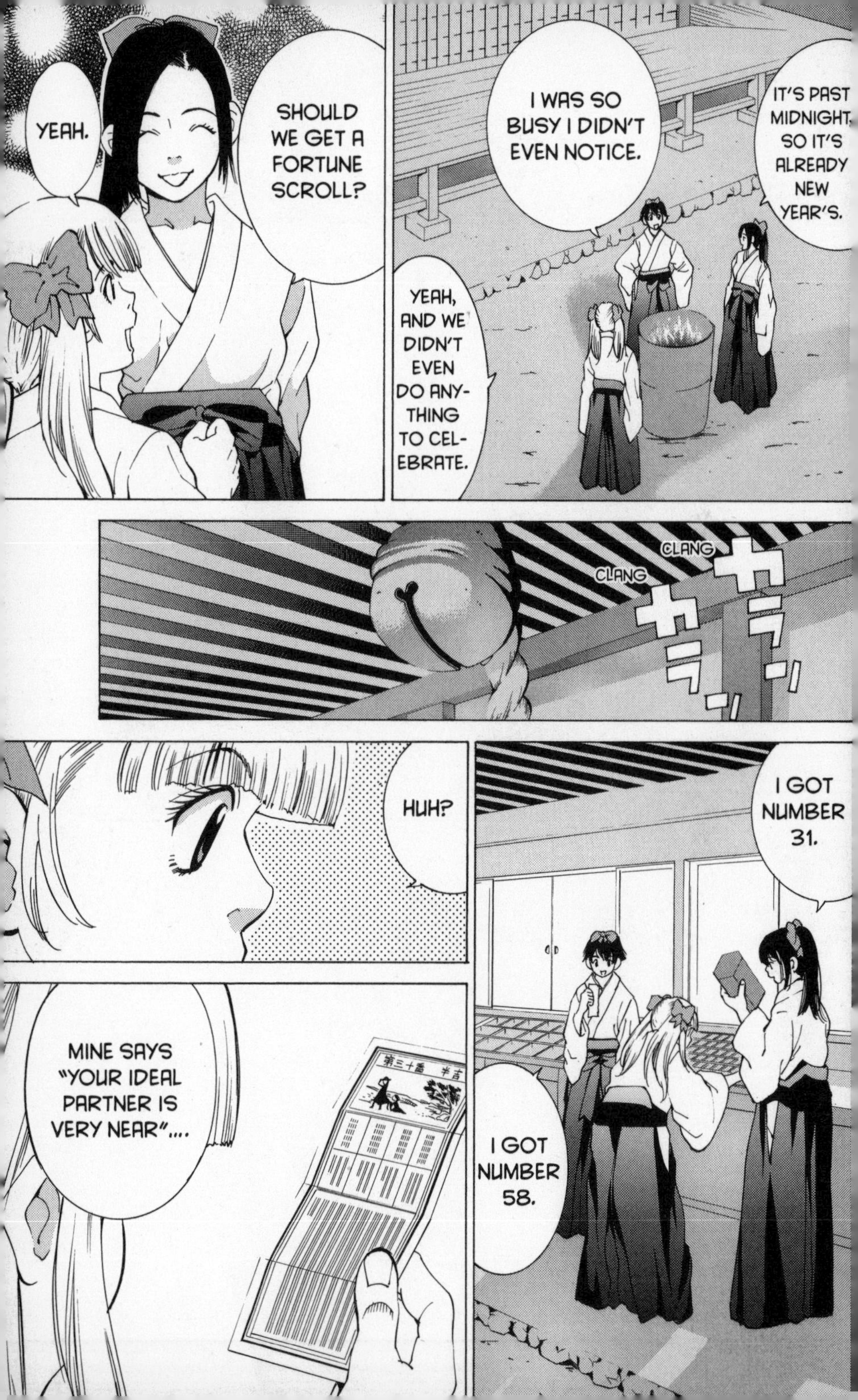
IT'S PAST MIDNIGHT, SO IT'S ALREADY NEW YEAR'S.
I WAS SO BUSY I DIDN'T EVEN NOTICE.
YEAH, AND WE DIDN'T EVEN DO ANY-THING TO CEL-EBRATE.
SHOULD WE GET A FORTUNE SCROLL?
YEAH.
CLANG
CLANG
I GOT NUMBER 31.
I GOT NUMBER 58.
HUH?
MINE SAYS "YOUR IDEAL PARTNER IS VERY NEAR"....

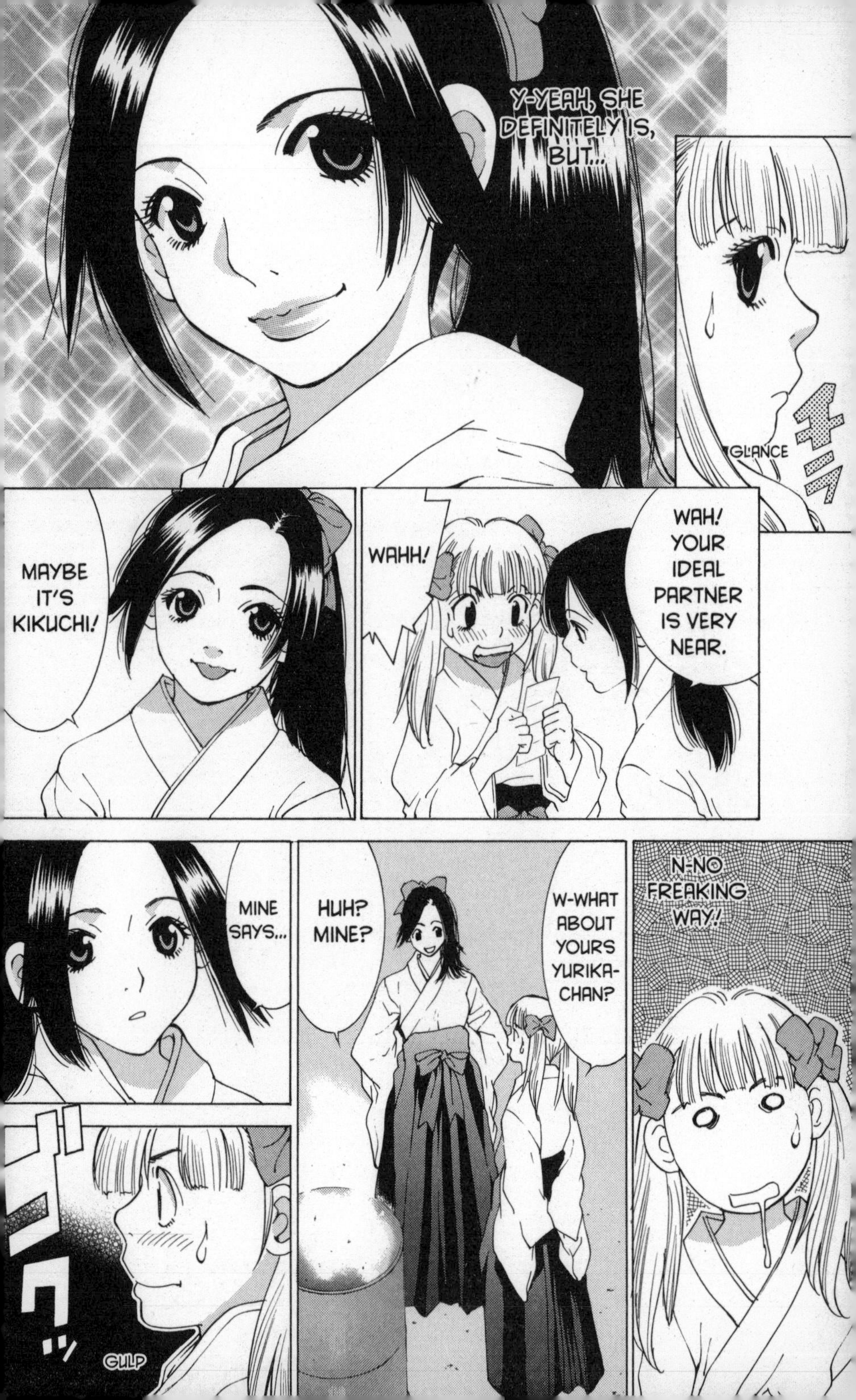
Y-YEAH, SHE DEFINITELY IS, BUT...
GLANCE
WAH! YOUR IDEAL PARTNER IS VERY NEAR.
WAHH!
MAYBE IT'S KIKUCHI!
N-NO FREAKING WAY!
W-WHAT ABOUT YOURS YURIKA-CHAN?
HUH? MINE?
MINE SAYS...
GULP

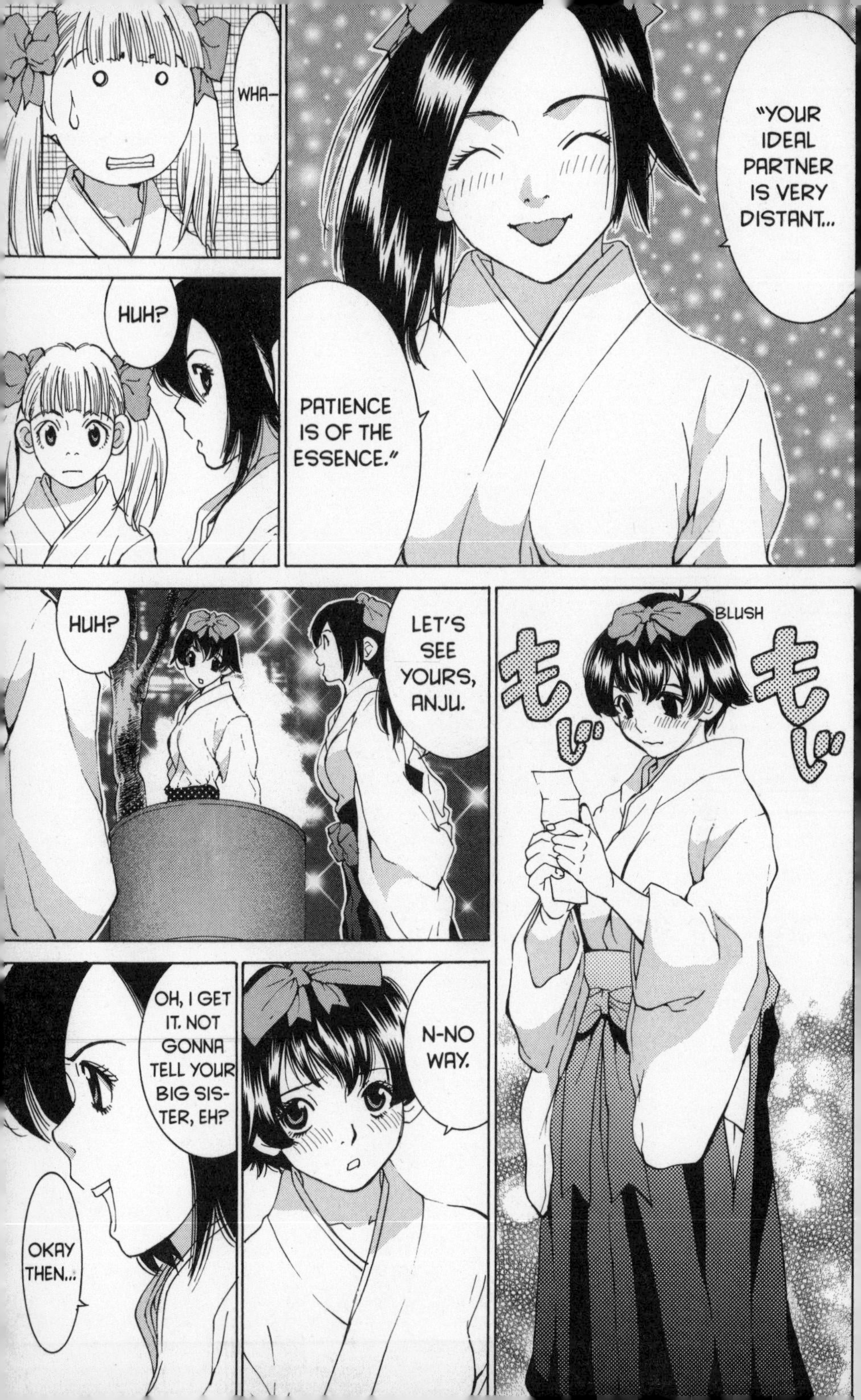
"YOUR IDEAL PARTNER IS VERY DISTANT...
PATIENCE IS OF THE ESSENCE."
WHA–
HUH?
BLUSH
もじもじ
LET'S SEE YOURS, ANJU.
HUH?
N-NO WAY.
OH, I GET IT. NOT GONNA TELL YOUR BIG SIS-TER, EH?
OKAY THEN...

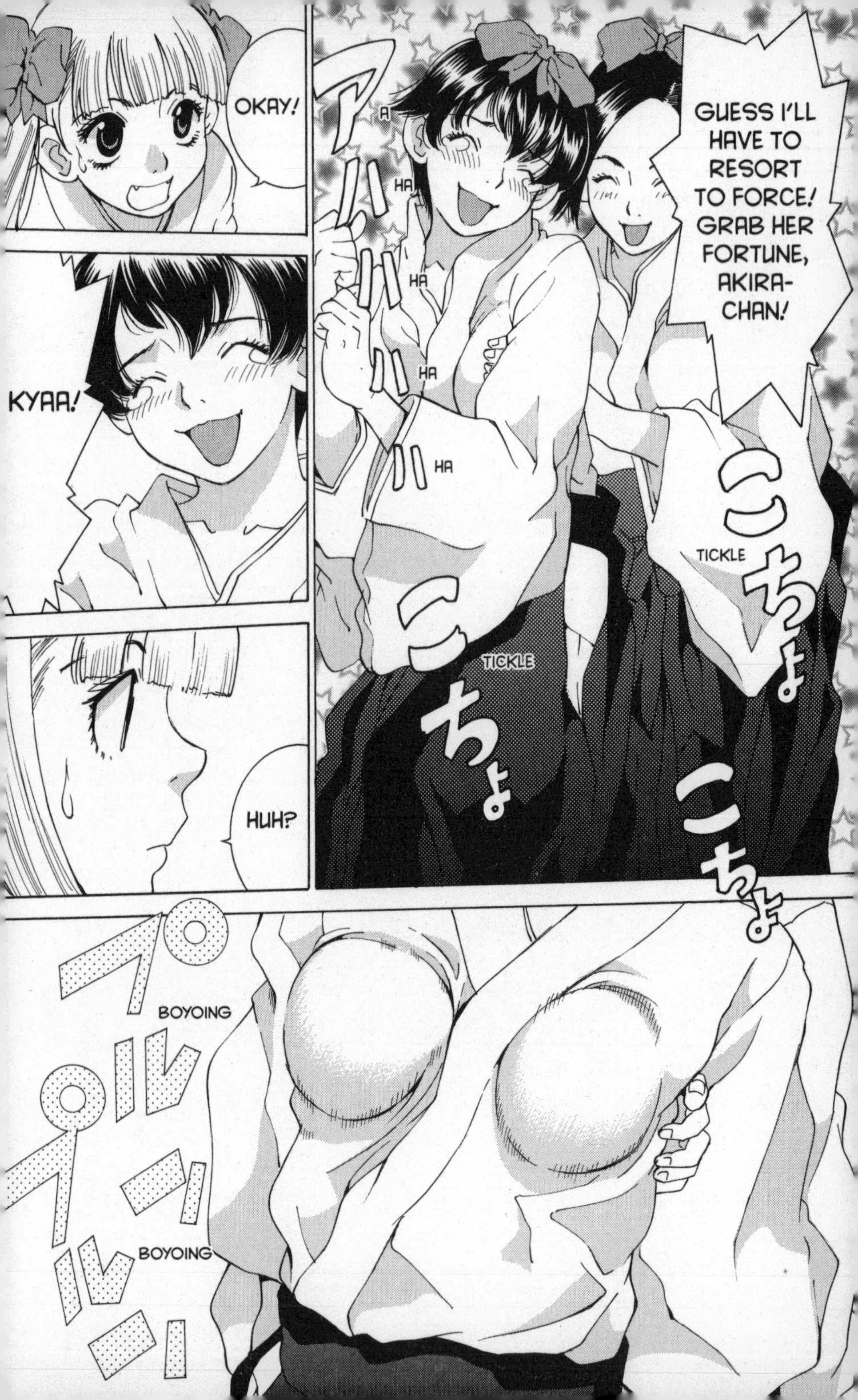
GUESS I'LL HAVE TO RESORT TO FORCE! GRAB HER FORTUNE, AKIRA-CHAN!
アハハハハ
A HA HA HA HA
こちょこちょ
TICKLE
こちょこちょ
TICKLE
OKAY!
KYAA!
HUH?
プルン
BOYOING
プルン
BOYOING

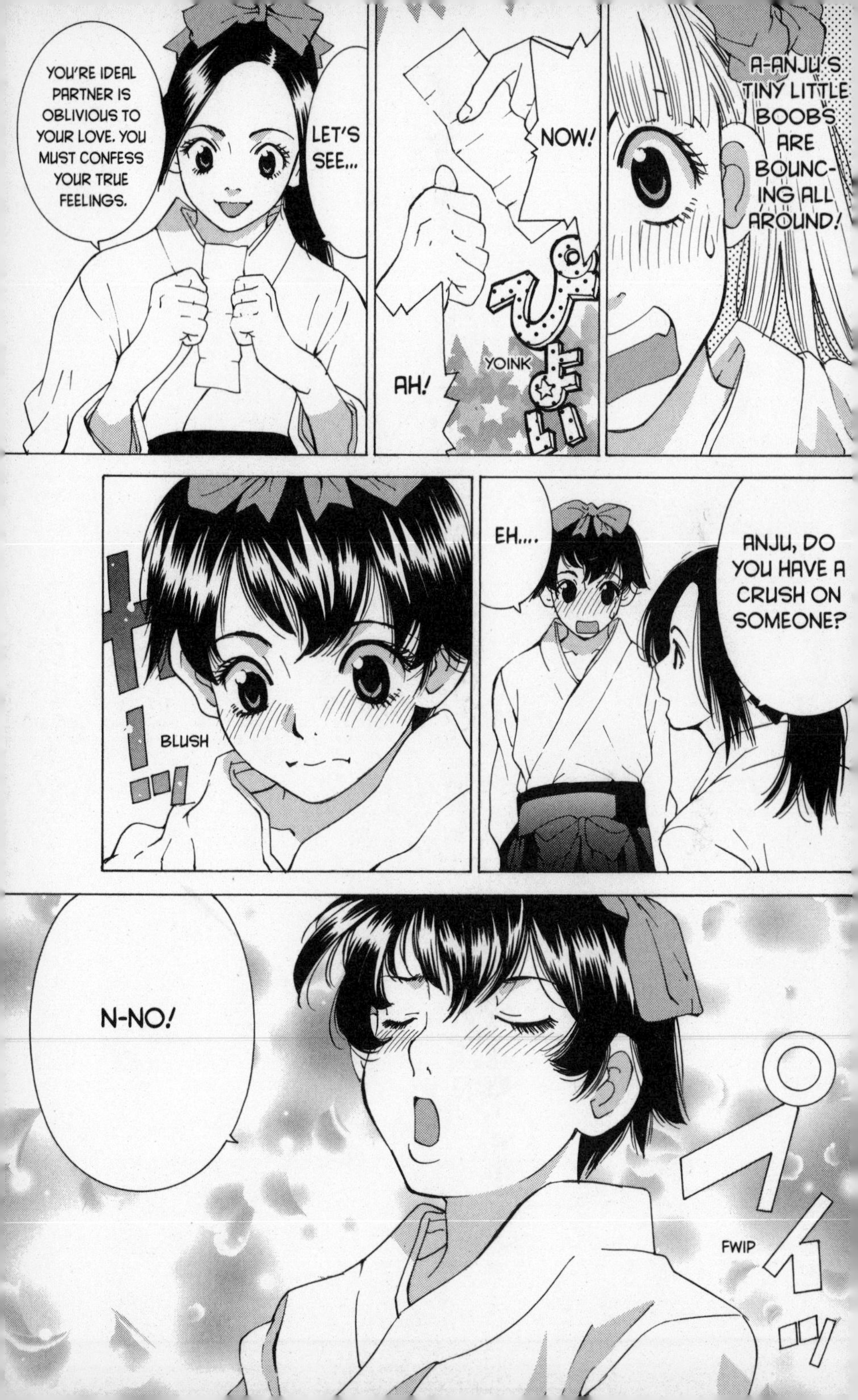
A-ANJU'S TINY LITTLE BOOBS ARE BOUNCING ALL AROUND!
NOW!
AH!
YOINK
LET'S SEE...
YOU'RE IDEAL PARTNER IS OBLIVIOUS TO YOUR LOVE. YOU MUST CONFESS YOUR TRUE FEELINGS.
ANJU, DO YOU HAVE A CRUSH ON SOMEONE?
EH....
BLUSH
N-NO!
FWIP

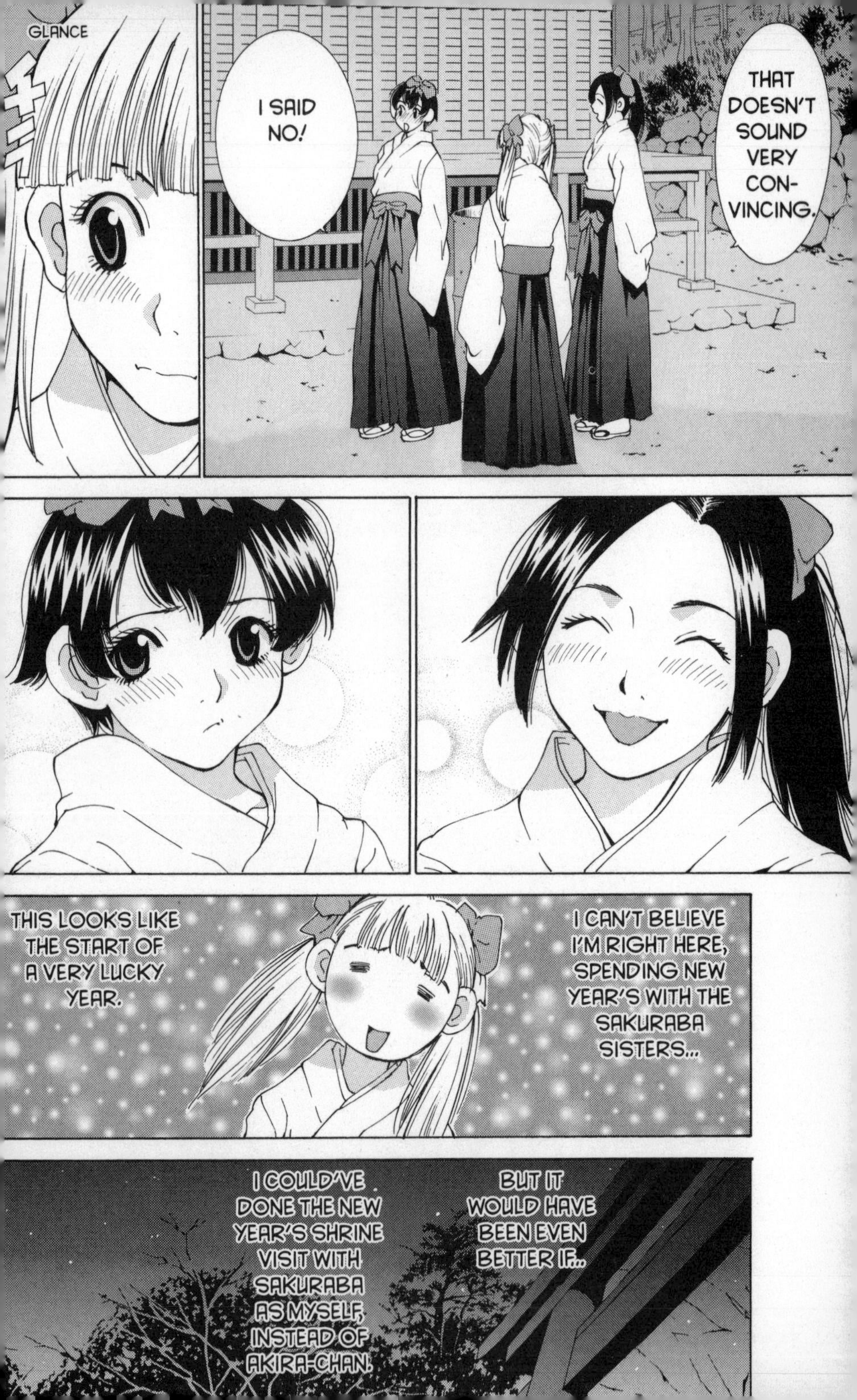
THAT DOESN'T SOUND VERY CON-VINCING.
I SAID NO!
GLANCE
I CAN'T BELIEVE I'M RIGHT HERE, SPENDING NEW YEAR'S WITH THE SAKURABA SISTERS...
THIS LOOKS LIKE THE START OF A VERY LUCKY YEAR.
BUT IT WOULD HAVE BEEN EVEN BETTER IF...
I COULD'VE DONE THE NEW YEAR'S SHRINE VISIT WITH SAKURABA AS MYSELF, INSTEAD OF AKIRA-CHAN.

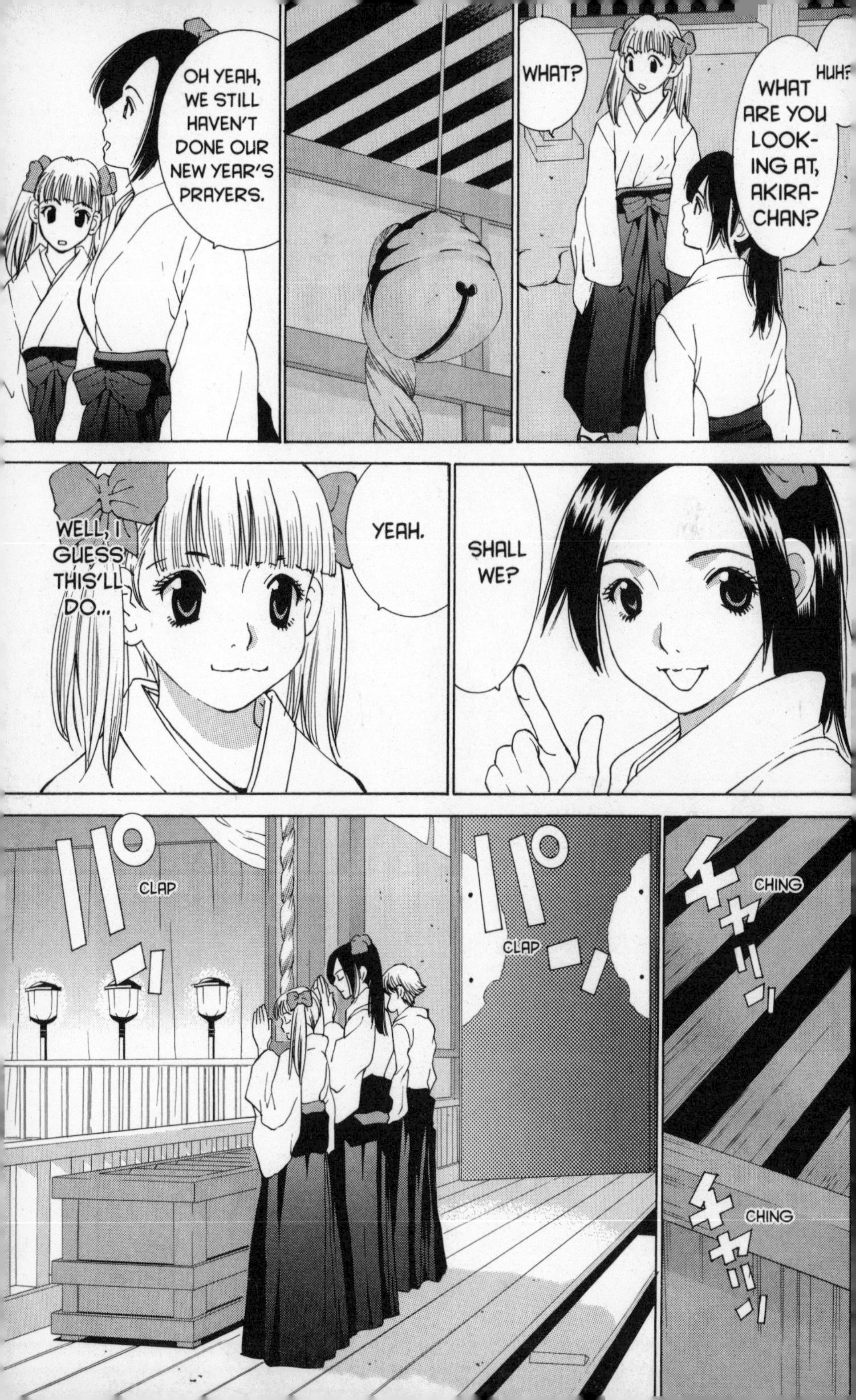
HUH?
WHAT ARE YOU LOOKING AT, AKIRA-CHAN?
WHAT?
OH YEAH, WE STILL HAVEN'T DONE OUR NEW YEAR'S PRAYERS.
SHALL WE?
YEAH.
WELL, I GUESS THIS'LL DO...
CHING
CHING
CLAP
CLAP

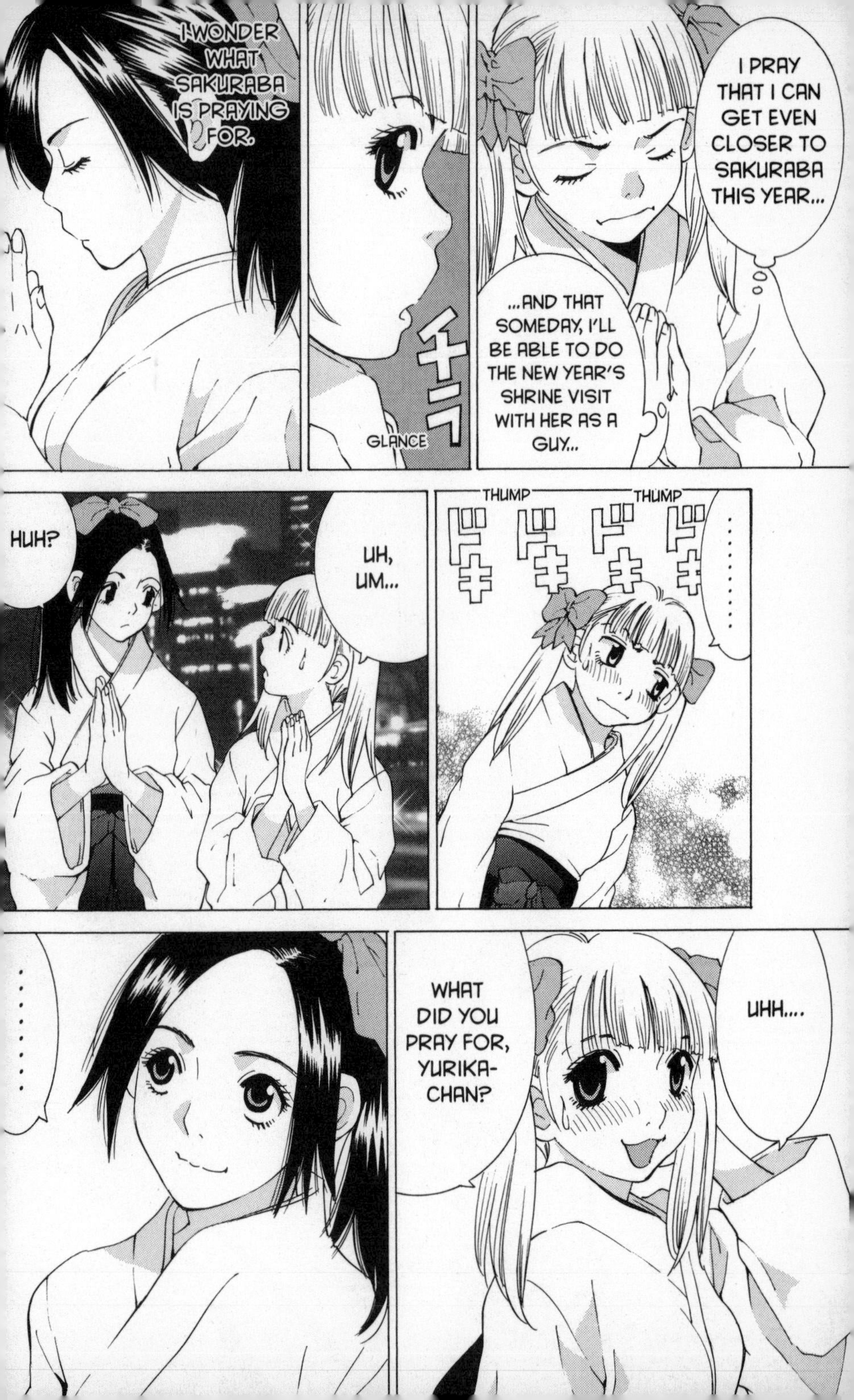
I PRAY THAT I CAN GET EVEN CLOSER TO SAKURABA THIS YEAR...
...AND THAT SOMEDAY, I'LL BE ABLE TO DO THE NEW YEAR'S SHRINE VISIT WITH HER AS A GUY...
チラ
GLANCE
I WONDER WHAT SAKURABA IS PRAYING FOR.
......
ドキドキドキドキ
THUMP THUMP
UH, UM...
HUH?
UHH....
WHAT DID YOU PRAY FOR, YURIKA-CHAN?
....

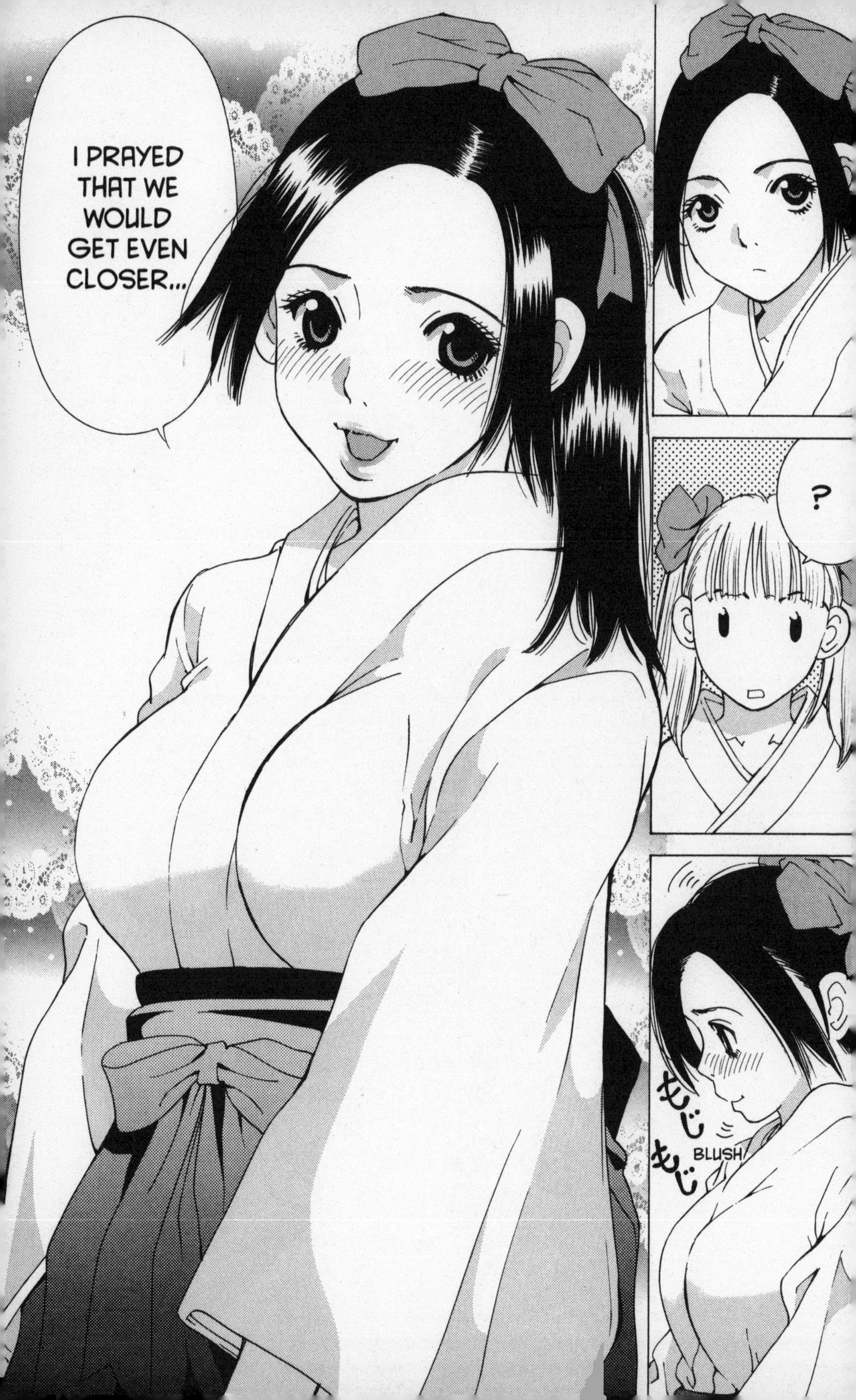
?
もじもじ
BLUSH
I PRAYED THAT WE WOULD GET EVEN CLOSER...

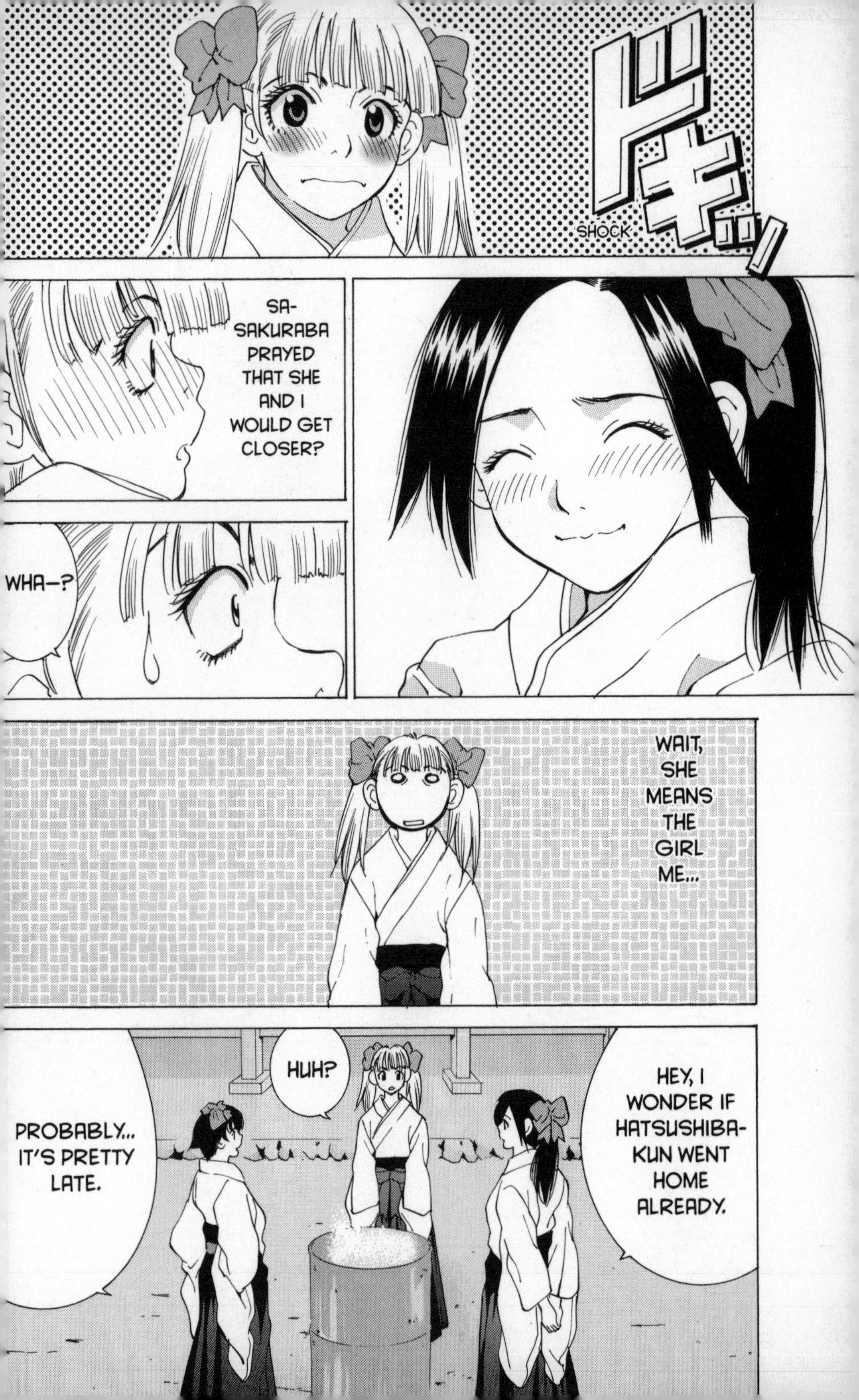
SHOCK
SA-SAKURABA PRAYED THAT SHE AND I WOULD GET CLOSER?
WHA-?
WAIT, SHE MEANS THE GIRL ME...
HEY, I WONDER IF HATSUSHIBA-KUN WENT HOME ALREADY.
HUH?
PROBABLY... IT'S PRETTY LATE.

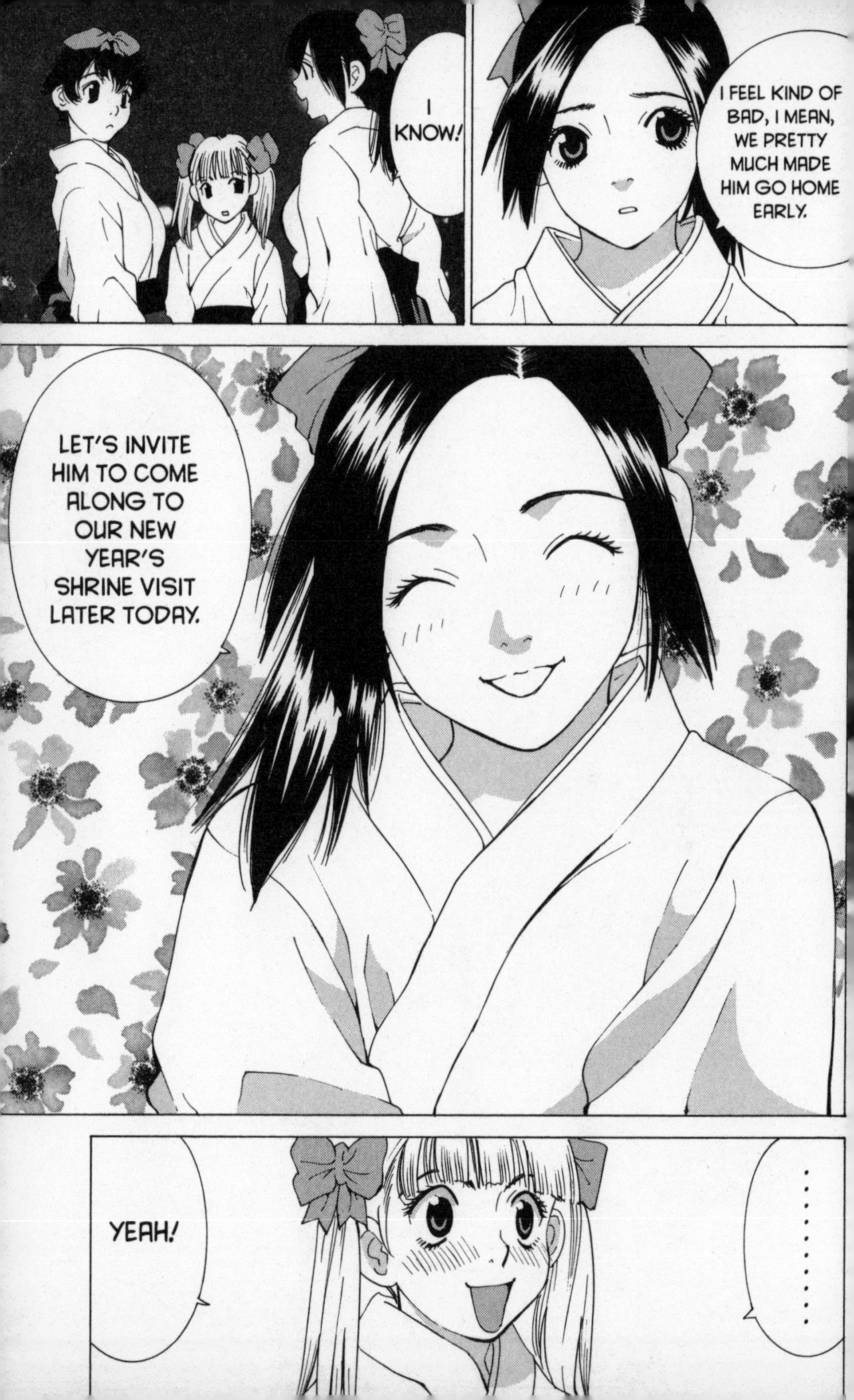
I FEEL KIND OF BAD, I MEAN, WE PRETTY MUCH MADE HIM GO HOME EARLY.
I KNOW!
LET'S INVITE HIM TO COME ALONG TO OUR NEW YEAR'S SHRINE VISIT LATER TODAY.
....
YEAH!

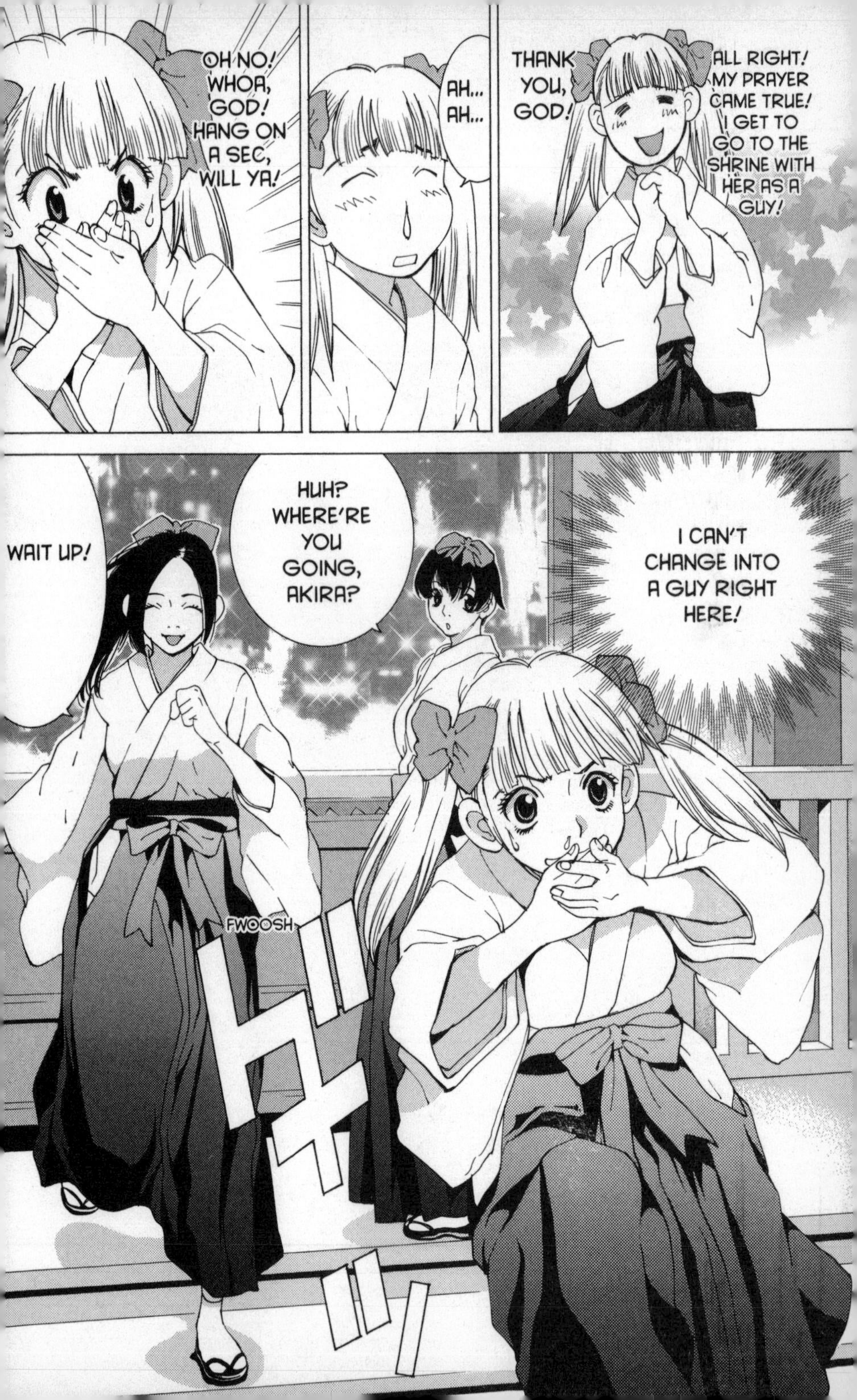
ALL RIGHT! MY PRAYER CAME TRUE! I GET TO GO TO THE SHRINE WITH HER AS A GUY!
THANK YOU, GOD!
AH... AH...
OH NO! WHOA, GOD! HANG ON A SEC, WILL YA!
I CAN'T CHANGE INTO A GUY RIGHT HERE!
HUH? WHERE'RE YOU GOING, AKIRA?
WAIT UP!
FWOOSH

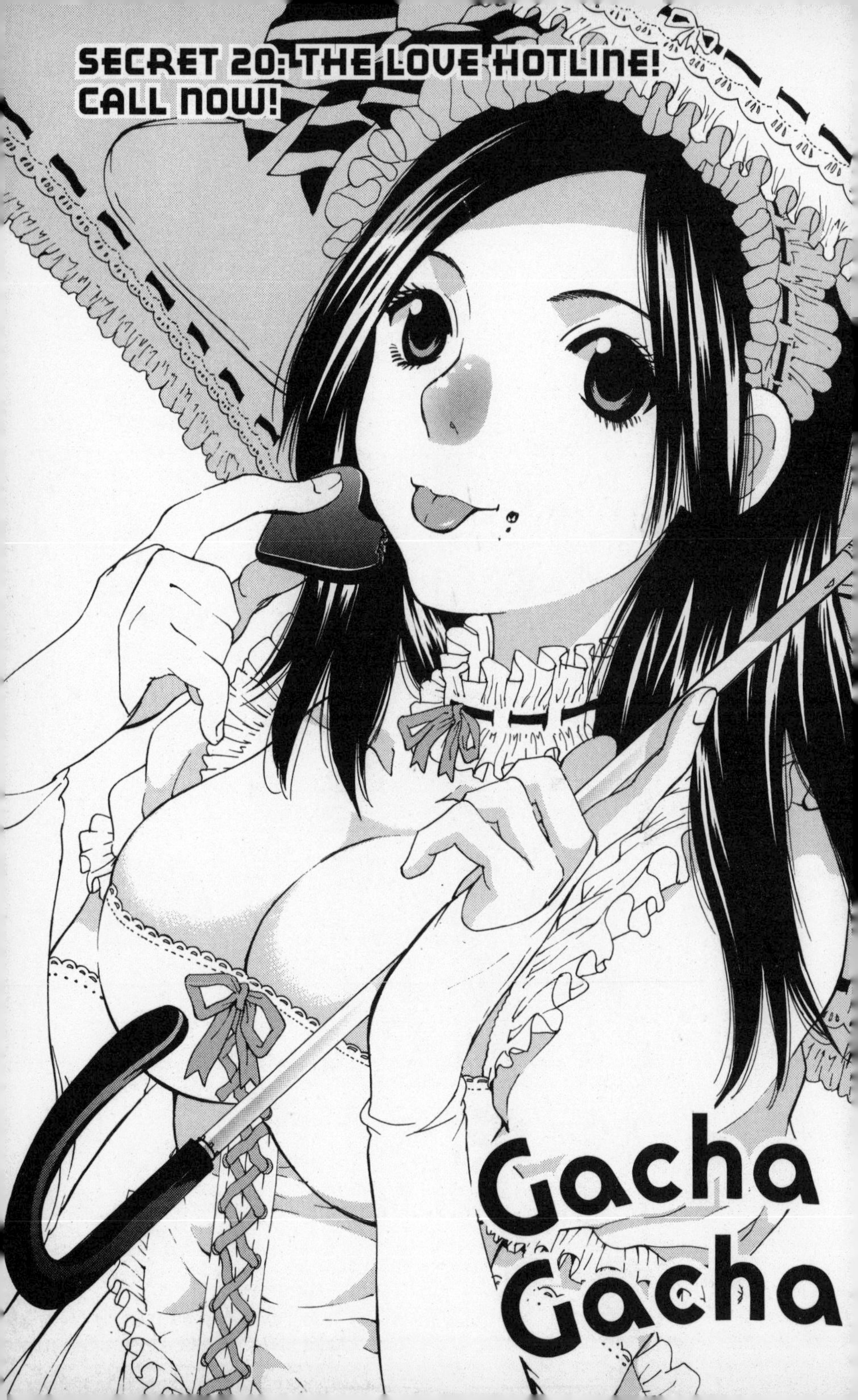
SECRET 20: THE LOVE HOTLINE!
CALL NOW!
Gacha
Gacha

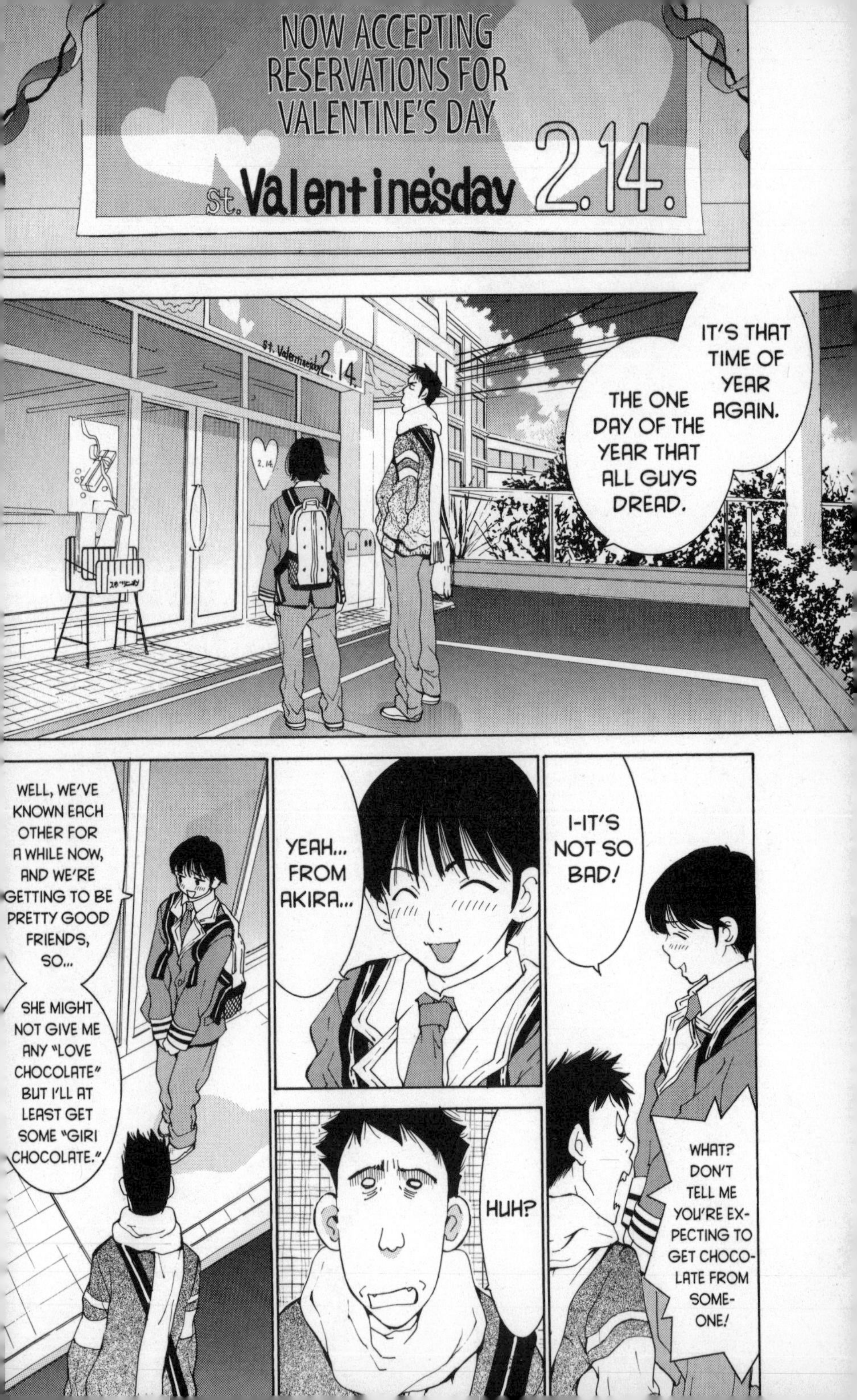
NOW ACCEPTING RESERVATIONS FOR VALENTINE'S DAY
st. Valentine'sday 2.14.
st. Valentine'sday 2.14.
2.14.
IT'S THAT TIME OF YEAR AGAIN.
THE ONE DAY OF THE YEAR THAT ALL GUYS DREAD.
I-IT'S NOT SO BAD!
WHAT? DON'T TELL ME YOU'RE EX-PECTING TO GET CHOCO-LATE FROM SOME-ONE!
YEAH... FROM AKIRA...
HUH?
WELL, WE'VE KNOWN EACH OTHER FOR A WHILE NOW, AND WE'RE GETTING TO BE PRETTY GOOD FRIENDS, SO...
SHE MIGHT NOT GIVE ME ANY "LOVE CHOCOLATE" BUT I'LL AT LEAST GET SOME "GIRI CHOCOLATE."

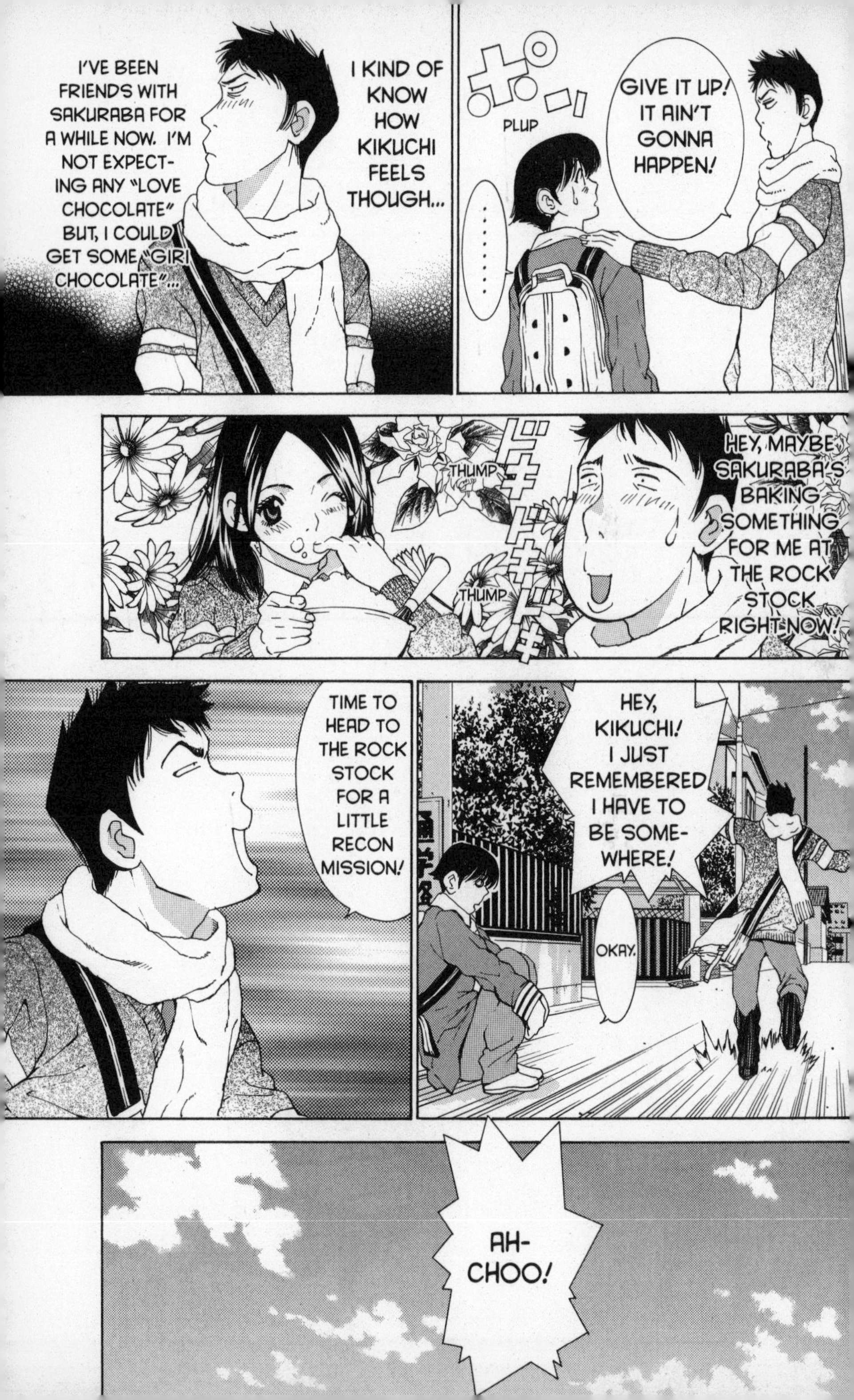
ポ-ン
PLUP
GIVE IT UP! IT AIN'T GONNA HAPPEN!
......
I KIND OF KNOW HOW KIKUCHI FEELS THOUGH...
I'VE BEEN FRIENDS WITH SAKURABA FOR A WHILE NOW. I'M NOT EXPECTING ANY "LOVE CHOCOLATE" BUT, I COULD GET SOME "GIRI CHOCOLATE"...
HEY, MAYBE SAKURABA'S BAKING SOMETHING FOR ME AT THE ROCK STOCK RIGHT NOW!
ドキドキドキドキ
THUMP
THUMP
HEY, KIKUCHI! I JUST REMEMBERED I HAVE TO BE SOMEWHERE!
OKAY.
TIME TO HEAD TO THE ROCK STOCK FOR A LITTLE RECON MISSION!
AH-CHOO!

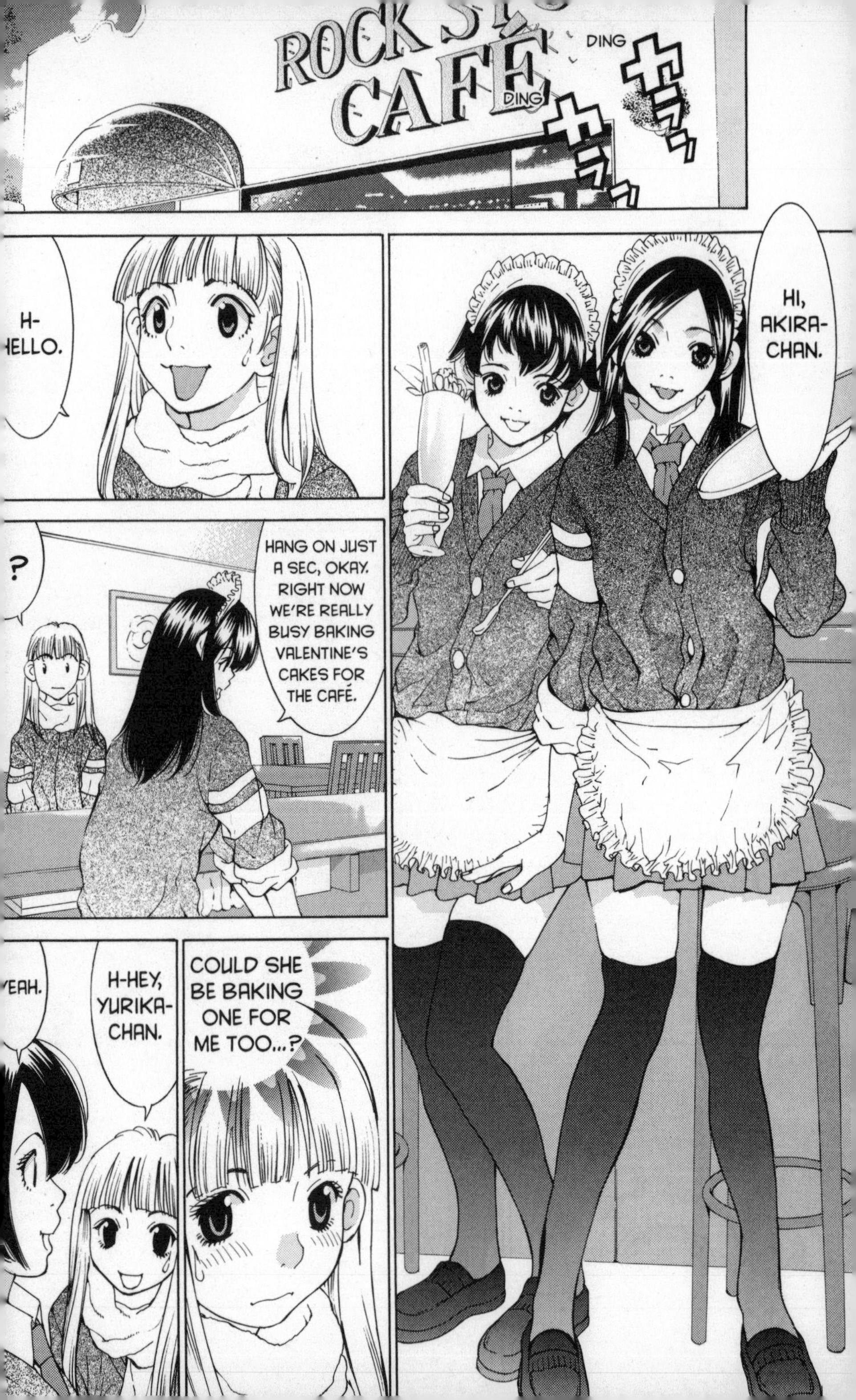
ROCK
CAFÉ
DING
DING
HI, AKIRA-CHAN.
H-HELLO.
HANG ON JUST A SEC, OKAY. RIGHT NOW WE'RE REALLY BUSY BAKING VALENTINE'S CAKES FOR THE CAFÉ.
?
COULD SHE BE BAKING ONE FOR ME TOO...?
H-HEY, YURIKA-CHAN.
YEAH.

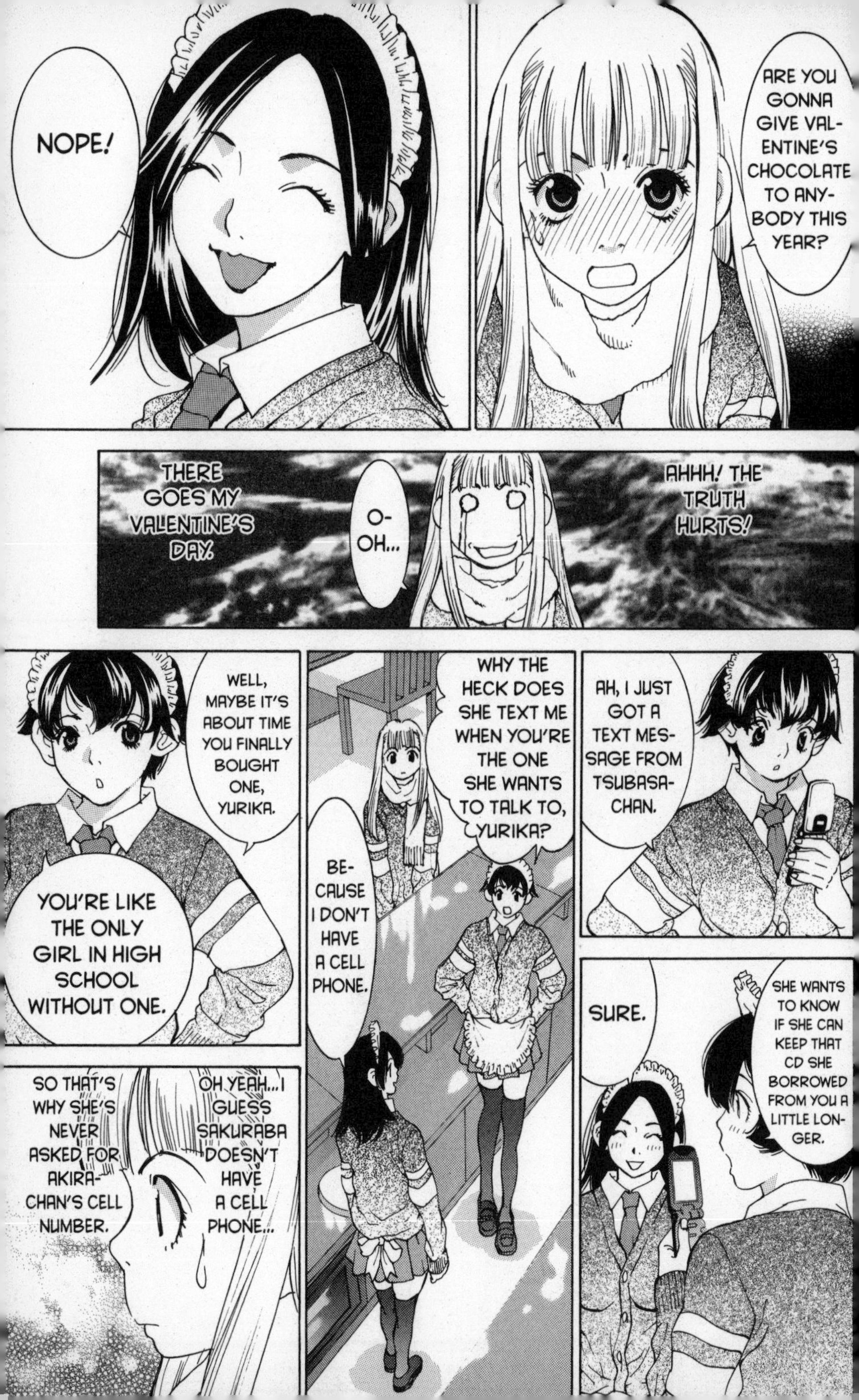
ARE YOU GONNA GIVE VAL-ENTINE'S CHOCOLATE TO ANY-BODY THIS YEAR?
NOPE!
AHHH! THE TRUTH HURTS!
O-OH...
THERE GOES MY VALENTINE'S DAY.
AH, I JUST GOT A TEXT MES-SAGE FROM TSUBASA-CHAN.
SHE WANTS TO KNOW IF SHE CAN KEEP THAT CD SHE BORROWED FROM YOU A LITTLE LON-GER.
SURE.
WHY THE HECK DOES SHE TEXT ME WHEN YOU'RE THE ONE SHE WANTS TO TALK TO, YURIKA?
BE-CAUSE I DON'T HAVE A CELL PHONE.
WELL, MAYBE IT'S ABOUT TIME YOU FINALLY BOUGHT ONE, YURIKA.
YOU'RE LIKE THE ONLY GIRL IN HIGH SCHOOL WITHOUT ONE.
OH YEAH... I GUESS SAKURABA DOESN'T HAVE A CELL PHONE...
SO THAT'S WHY SHE'S NEVER ASKED FOR AKIRA-CHAN'S CELL NUMBER.

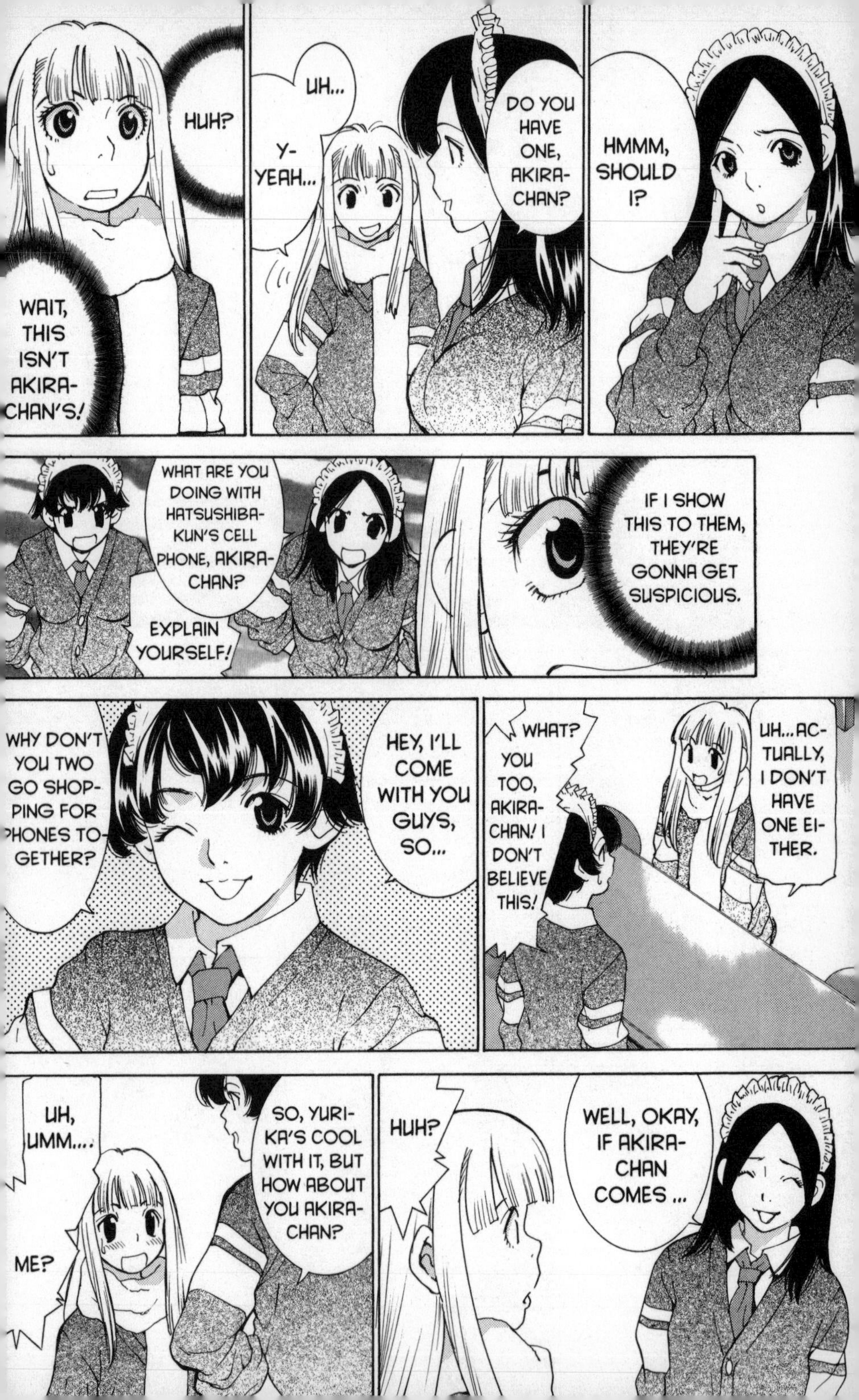
HMMM, SHOULD I?
DO YOU HAVE ONE, AKIRA-CHAN?
UH...
Y-YEAH...
HUH?
WAIT, THIS ISN'T AKIRA-CHAN'S!
IF I SHOW THIS TO THEM, THEY'RE GONNA GET SUSPICIOUS.
WHAT ARE YOU DOING WITH HATSUSHIBA-KUN'S CELL PHONE, AKIRA-CHAN?
EXPLAIN YOURSELF!
UH...ACTUALLY, I DON'T HAVE ONE EITHER.
WHAT? YOU TOO, AKIRA-CHAN! I DON'T BELIEVE THIS!
HEY, I'LL COME WITH YOU GUYS, SO...
WHY DON'T YOU TWO GO SHOPPING FOR PHONES TOGETHER?
WELL, OKAY, IF AKIRA-CHAN COMES ...
HUH?
SO, YURIKA'S COOL WITH IT, BUT HOW ABOUT YOU AKIRA-CHAN?
UH, UMM....
ME?

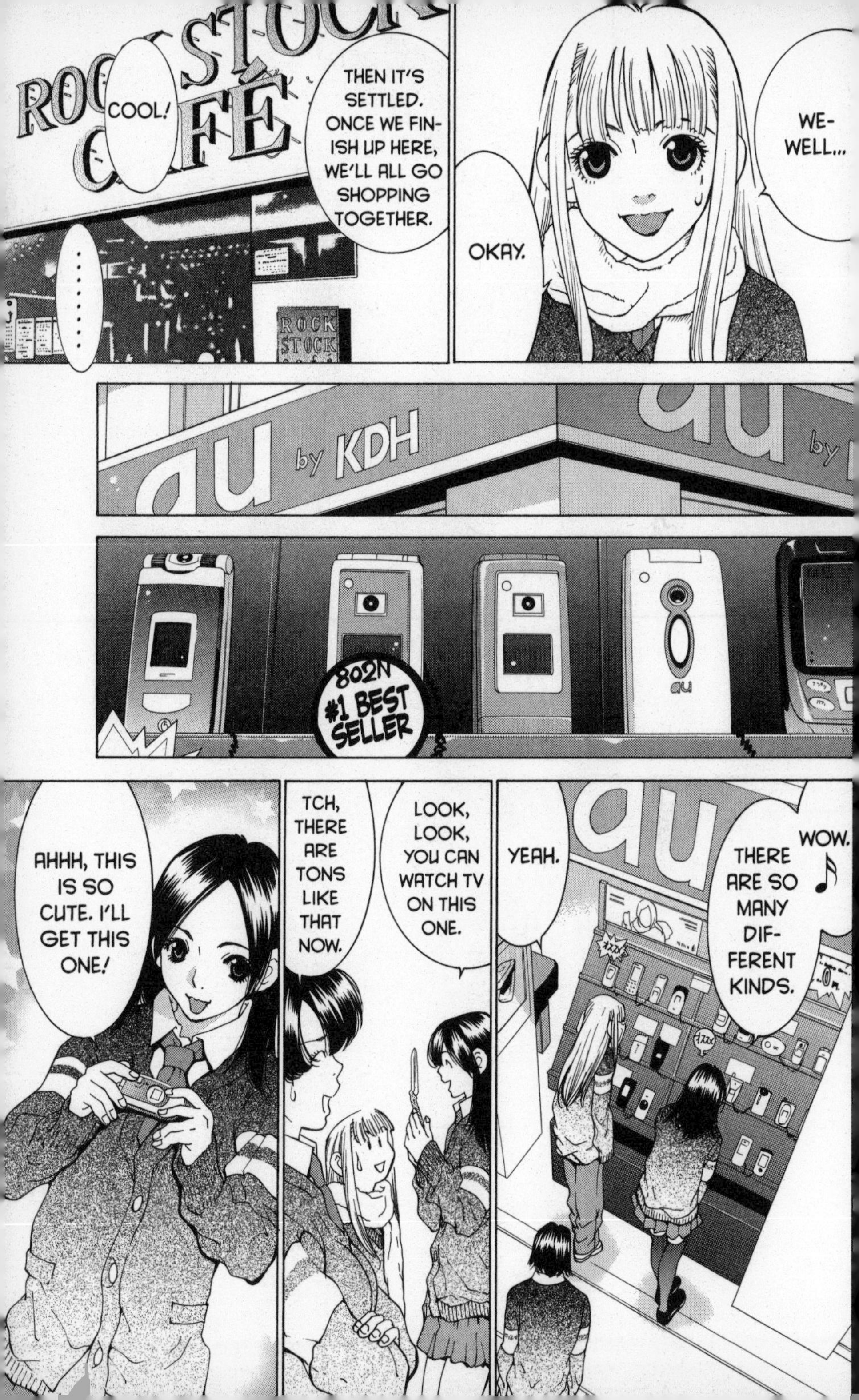
WE-WELL...
OKAY.
ROCK STOCK CAFÉ
THEN IT'S SETTLED. ONCE WE FINISH UP HERE, WE'LL ALL GO SHOPPING TOGETHER.
COOL!
......
au by KDH
802N #1 BEST SELLER
WOW. ♪
THERE ARE SO MANY DIFFERENT KINDS.
YEAH.
LOOK, LOOK, YOU CAN WATCH TV ON THIS ONE.
TCH, THERE ARE TONS LIKE THAT NOW.
AHHH, THIS IS SO CUTE. I'LL GET THIS ONE!

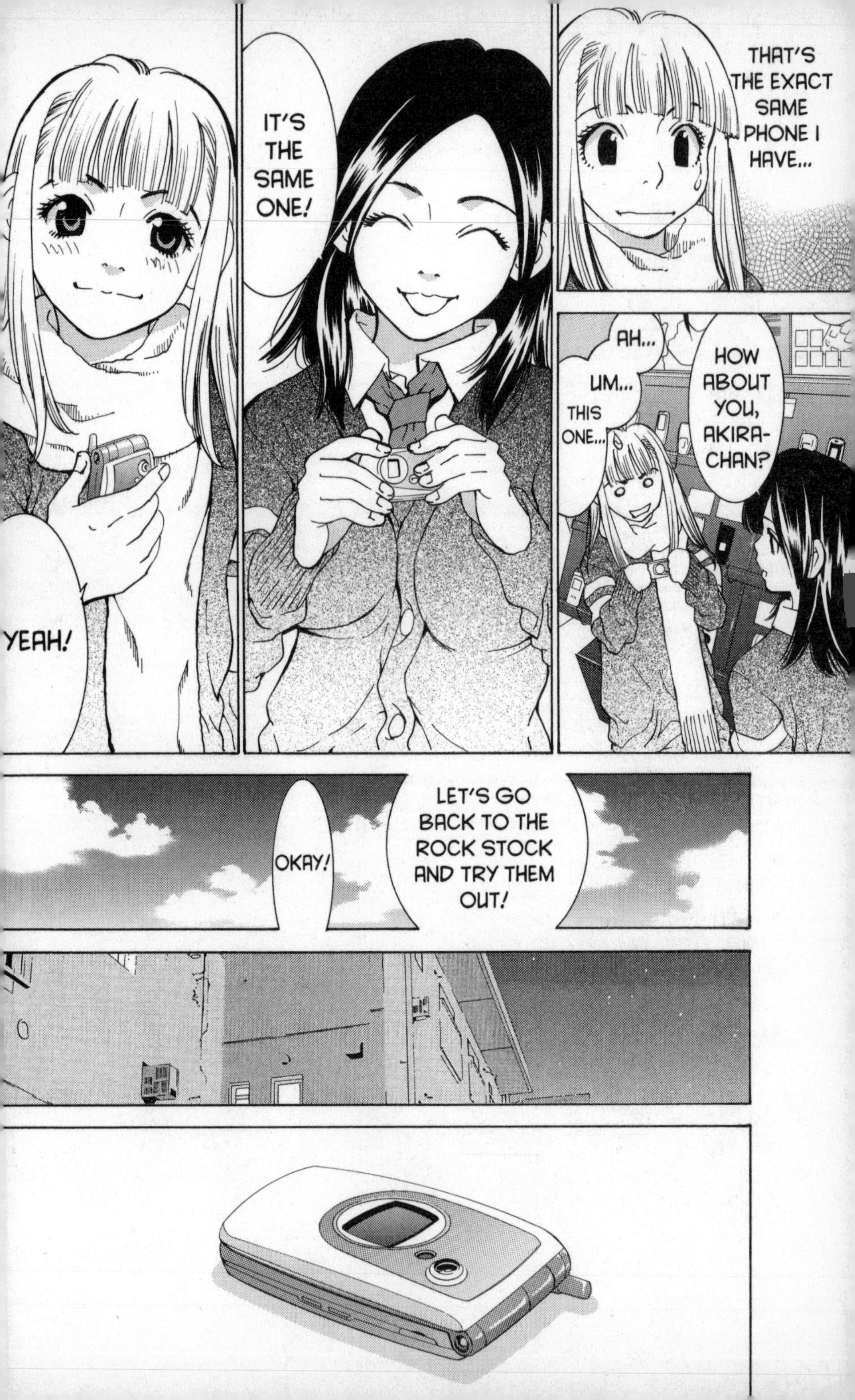
THAT'S THE EXACT SAME PHONE I HAVE...
HOW ABOUT YOU, AKIRA-CHAN?
AH...
UM...
THIS ONE...
IT'S THE SAME ONE!
YEAH!
LET'S GO BACK TO THE ROCK STOCK AND TRY THEM OUT!
OKAY!

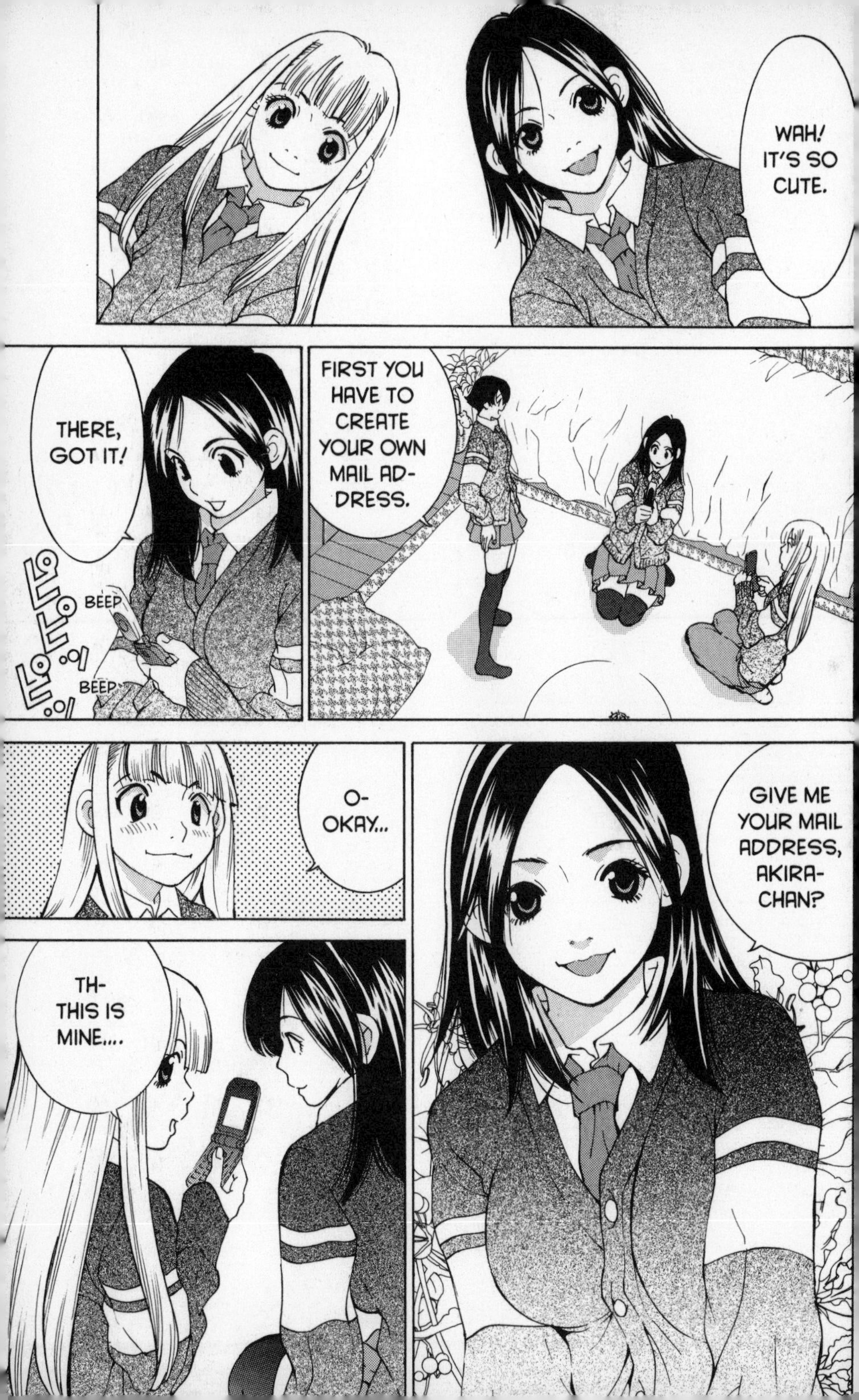
WAH! IT'S SO CUTE.
FIRST YOU HAVE TO CREATE YOUR OWN MAIL AD-DRESS.
THERE, GOT IT!
BEEP
BEEP
GIVE ME YOUR MAIL ADDRESS, AKIRA-CHAN?
O- OKAY...
TH- THIS IS MINE....

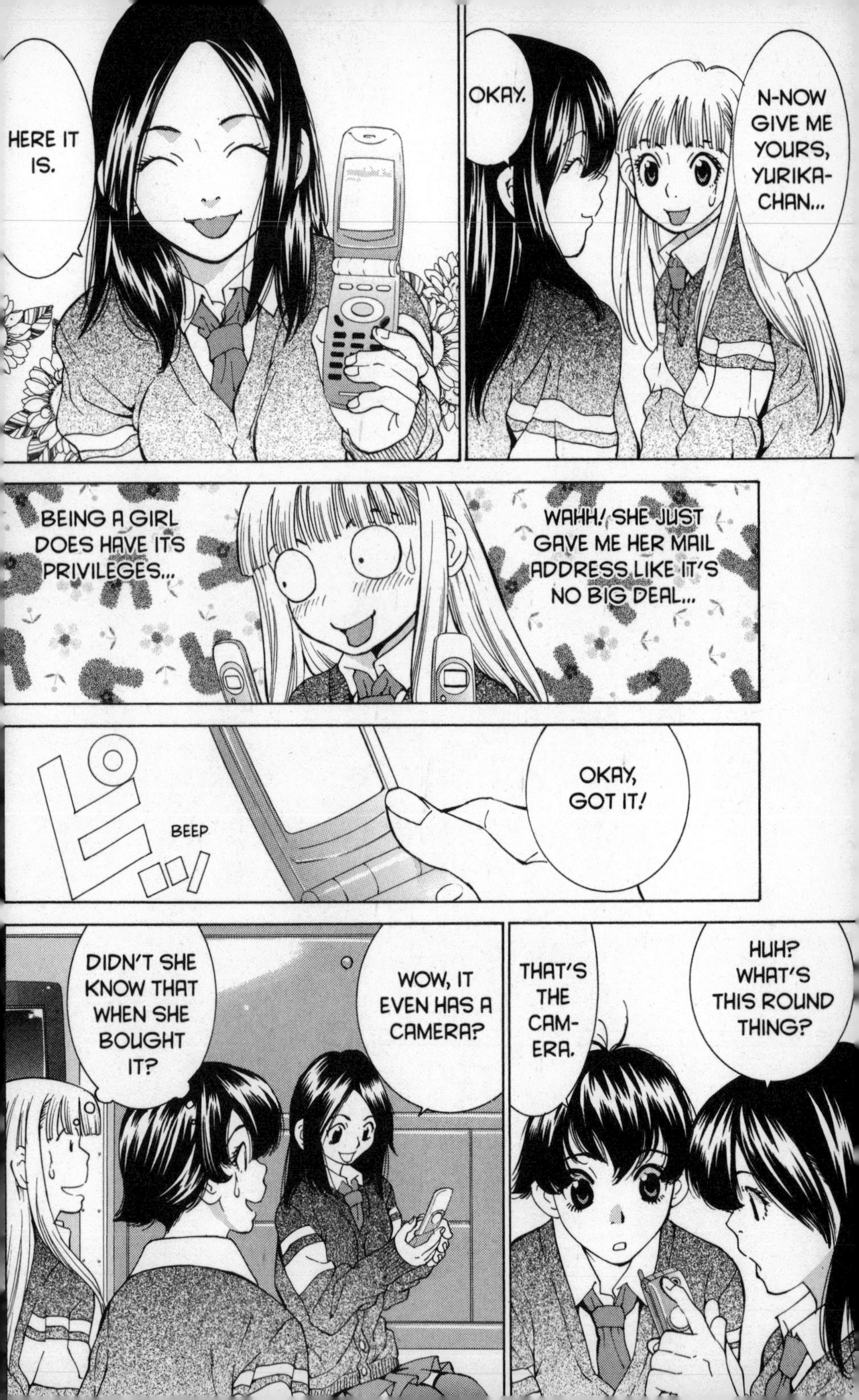
N-NOW GIVE ME YOURS, YURIKA-CHAN...
OKAY.
HERE IT IS.
WAHH! SHE JUST GAVE ME HER MAIL ADDRESS LIKE IT'S NO BIG DEAL...
BEING A GIRL DOES HAVE ITS PRIVILEGES...
OKAY, GOT IT!
BEEP
HUH? WHAT'S THIS ROUND THING?
THAT'S THE CAM-ERA.
WOW, IT EVEN HAS A CAMERA?
DIDN'T SHE KNOW THAT WHEN SHE BOUGHT IT?

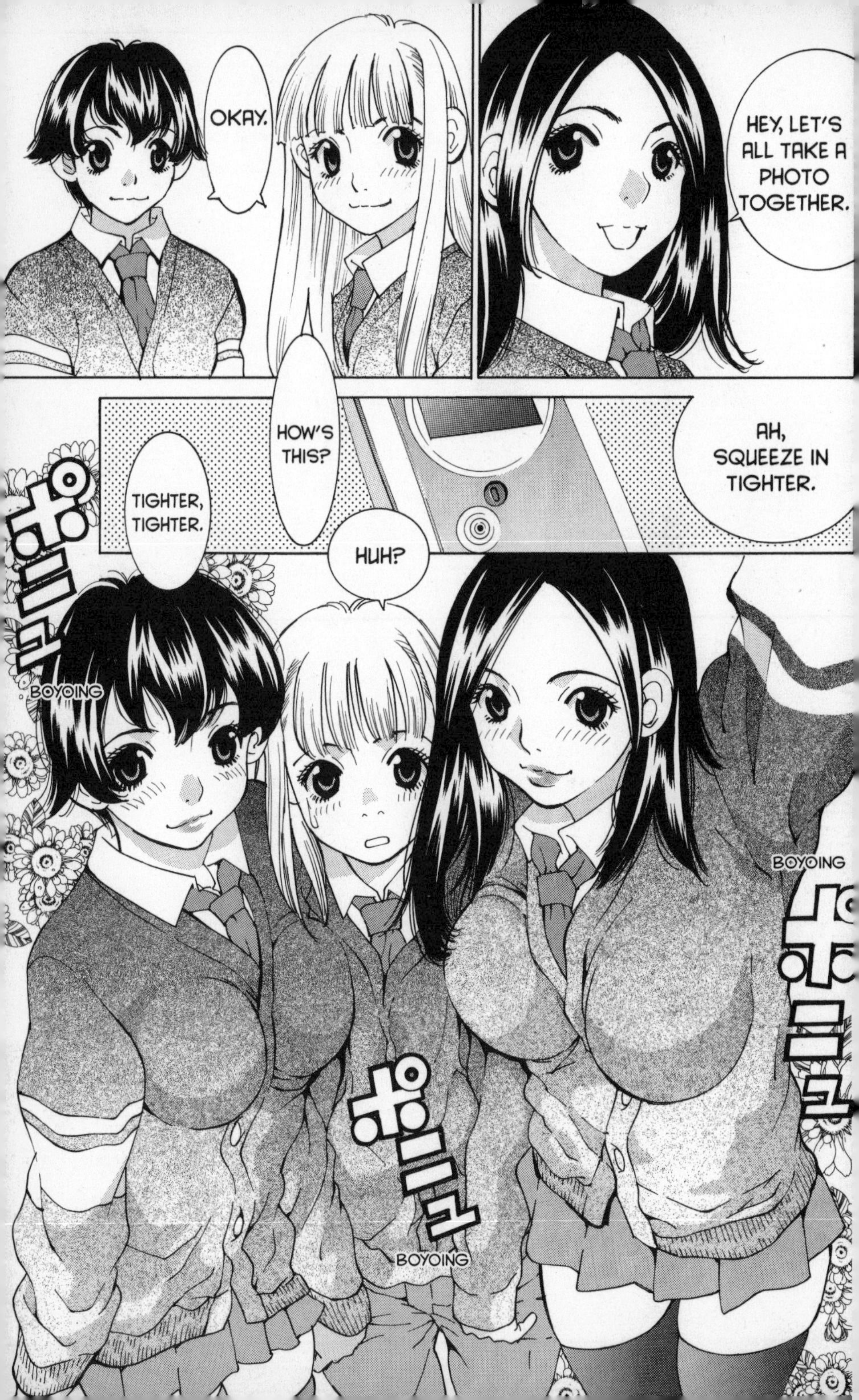
HEY, LET'S ALL TAKE A PHOTO TOGETHER.
OKAY.
AH, SQUEEZE IN TIGHTER.
HOW'S THIS?
TIGHTER, TIGHTER.
HUH?
ポニュ
BOYOING
ポニュ
BOYOING
ポニュ
BOYOING

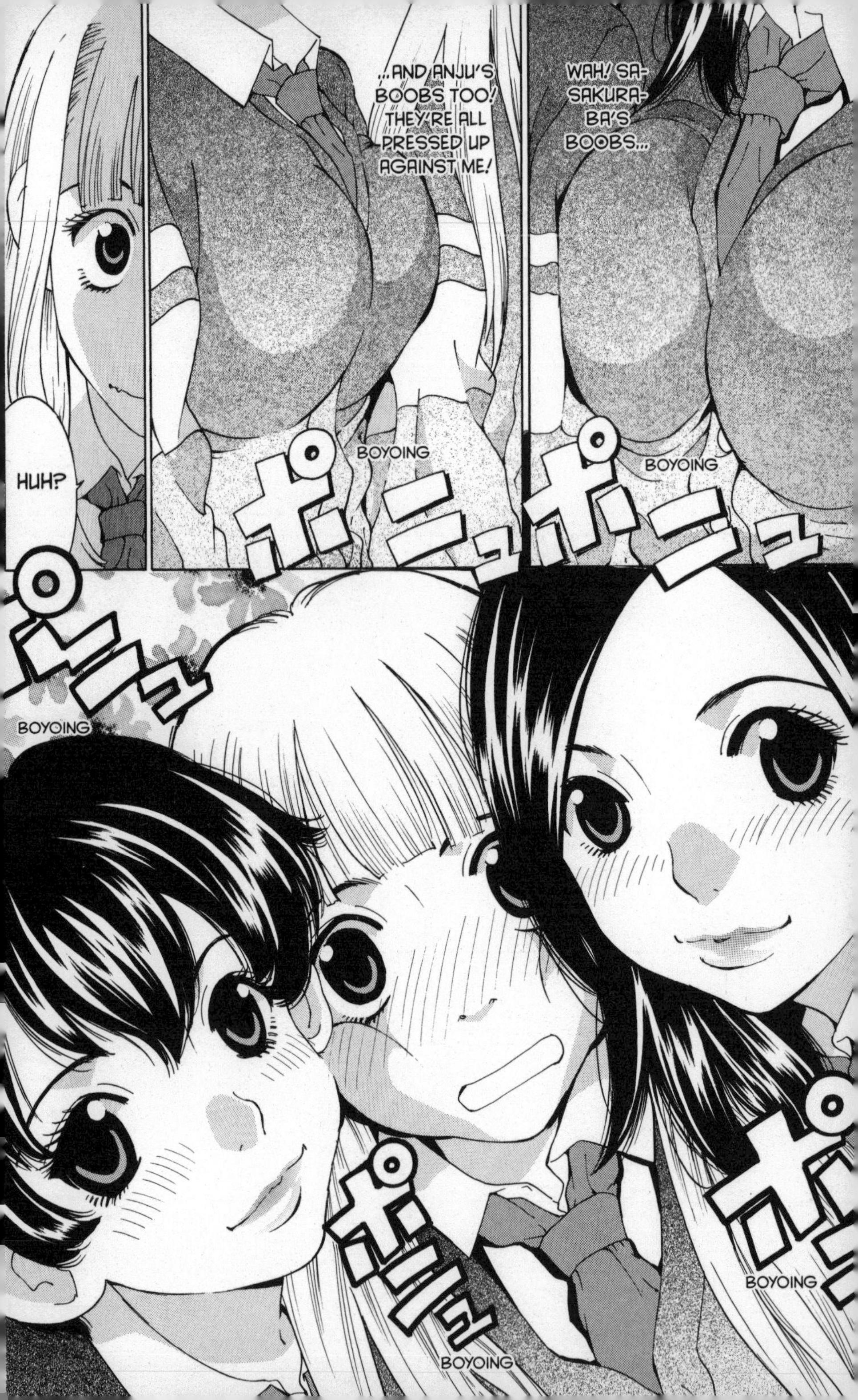

WAH! SA-SAKURA-BA'S BOOBS...
BOYOING
...AND ANJU'S BOOBS TOO! THEY'RE ALL PRESSED UP AGAINST ME!
BOYOING
HUH?
BOYOING
BOYOING
BOYOING

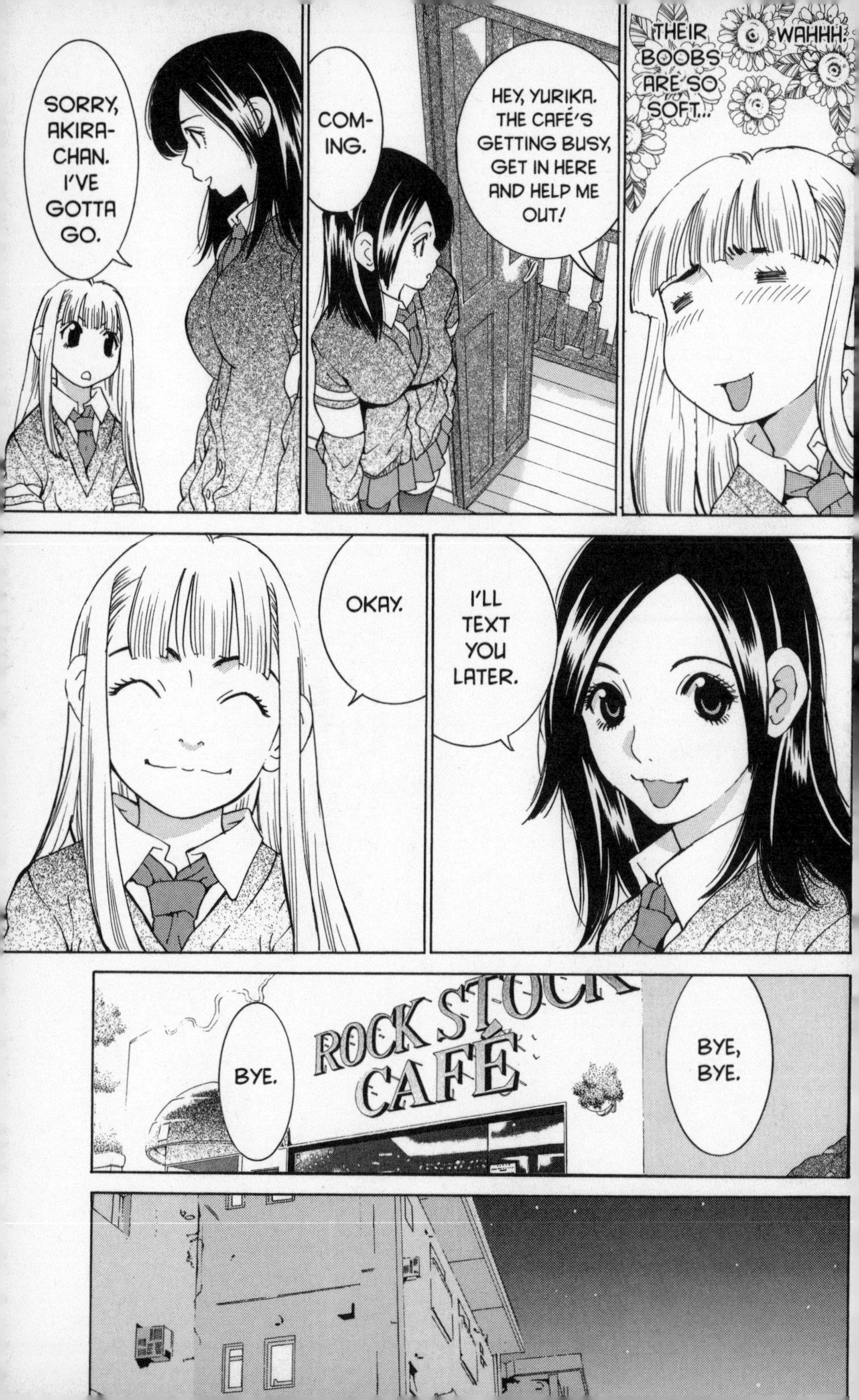
WAHHH
THEIR BOOBS ARE SO SOFT...
HEY, YURIKA. THE CAFÉ'S GETTING BUSY, GET IN HERE AND HELP ME OUT!
COMING.
SORRY, AKIRA-CHAN. I'VE GOTTA GO.
I'LL TEXT YOU LATER.
OKAY.
BYE, BYE.
ROCK STOCK CAFÉ
BYE.

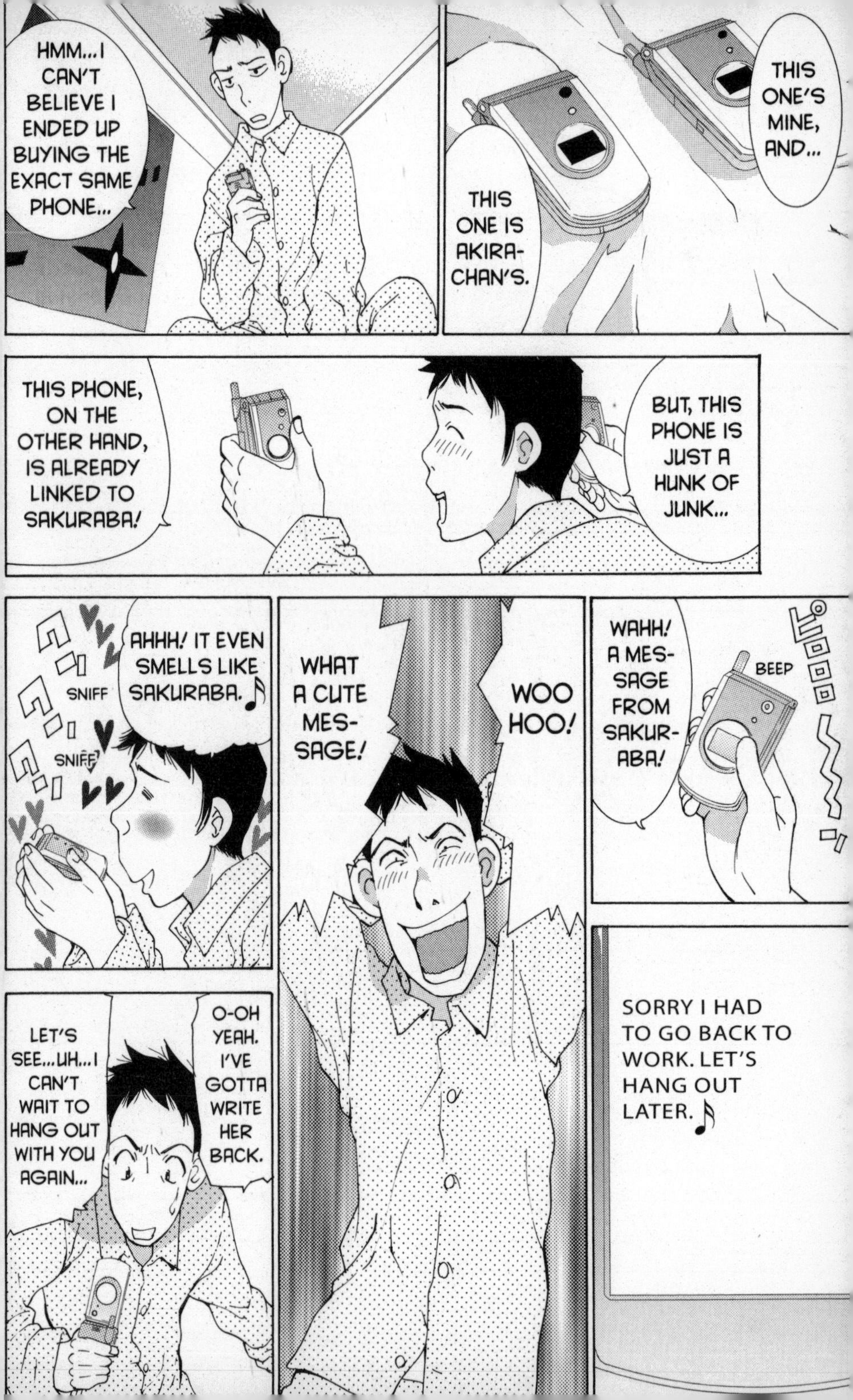
THIS ONE'S MINE, AND...
THIS ONE IS AKIRA-CHAN'S.
HMM...I CAN'T BELIEVE I ENDED UP BUYING THE EXACT SAME PHONE...
BUT, THIS PHONE IS JUST A HUNK OF JUNK...
THIS PHONE, ON THE OTHER HAND, IS ALREADY LINKED TO SAKURABA!
BEEP
WAHH! A MESSAGE FROM SAKURABA!
SORRY I HAD TO GO BACK TO WORK. LET'S HANG OUT LATER.♪
WOO HOO!
WHAT A CUTE MESSAGE!
AHHH! IT EVEN SMELLS LIKE SAKURABA.♪
SNIFF
SNIFF
O-OH YEAH. I'VE GOTTA WRITE HER BACK.
LET'S SEE...UH...I CAN'T WAIT TO HANG OUT WITH YOU AGAIN...

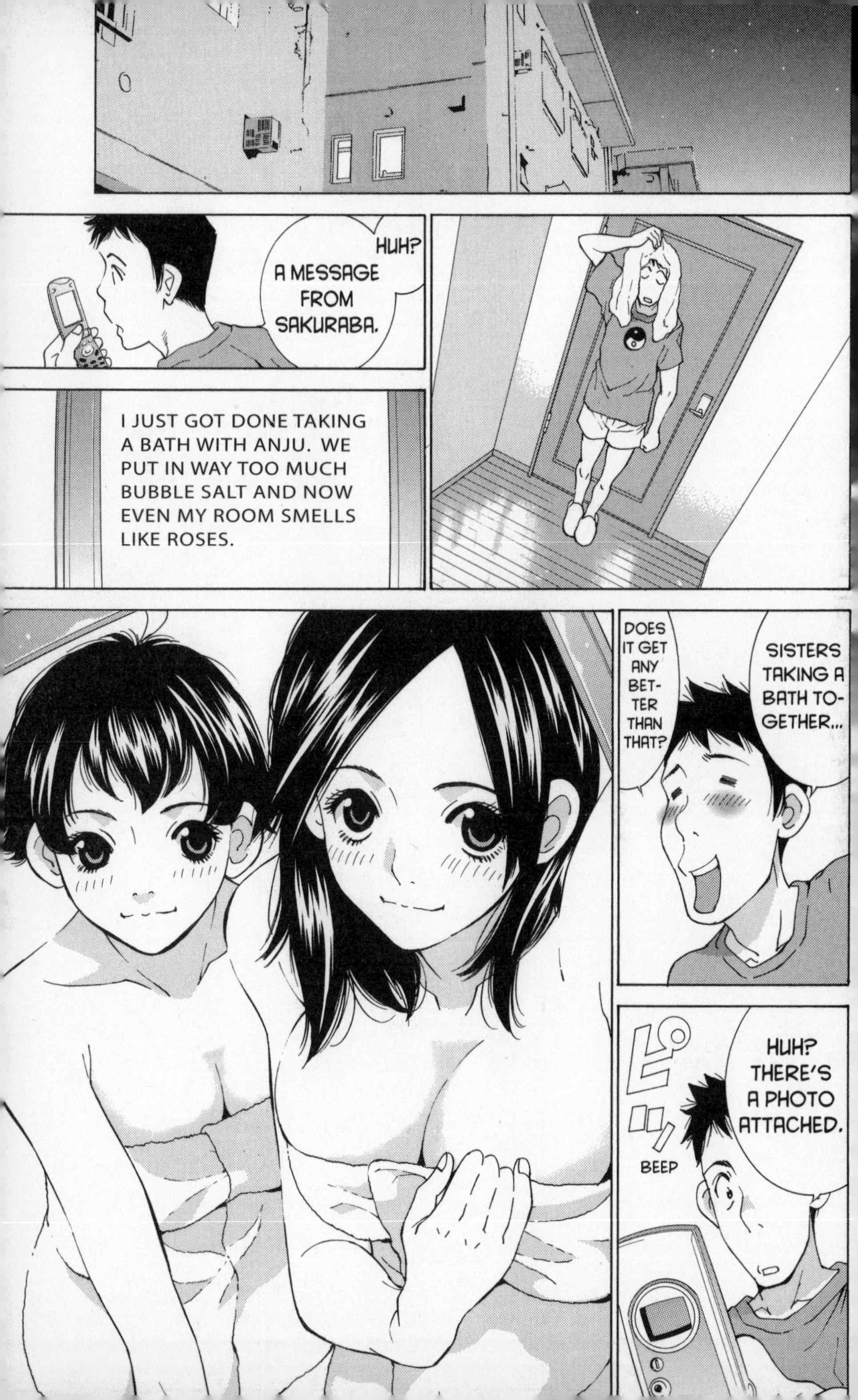
HUH? A MESSAGE FROM SAKURABA.
I JUST GOT DONE TAKING A BATH WITH ANJU. WE PUT IN WAY TOO MUCH BUBBLE SALT AND NOW EVEN MY ROOM SMELLS LIKE ROSES.
SISTERS TAKING A BATH TO-GETHER...
DOES IT GET ANY BET-TER THAN THAT?
ピッ
BEEP
HUH? THERE'S A PHOTO ATTACHED.

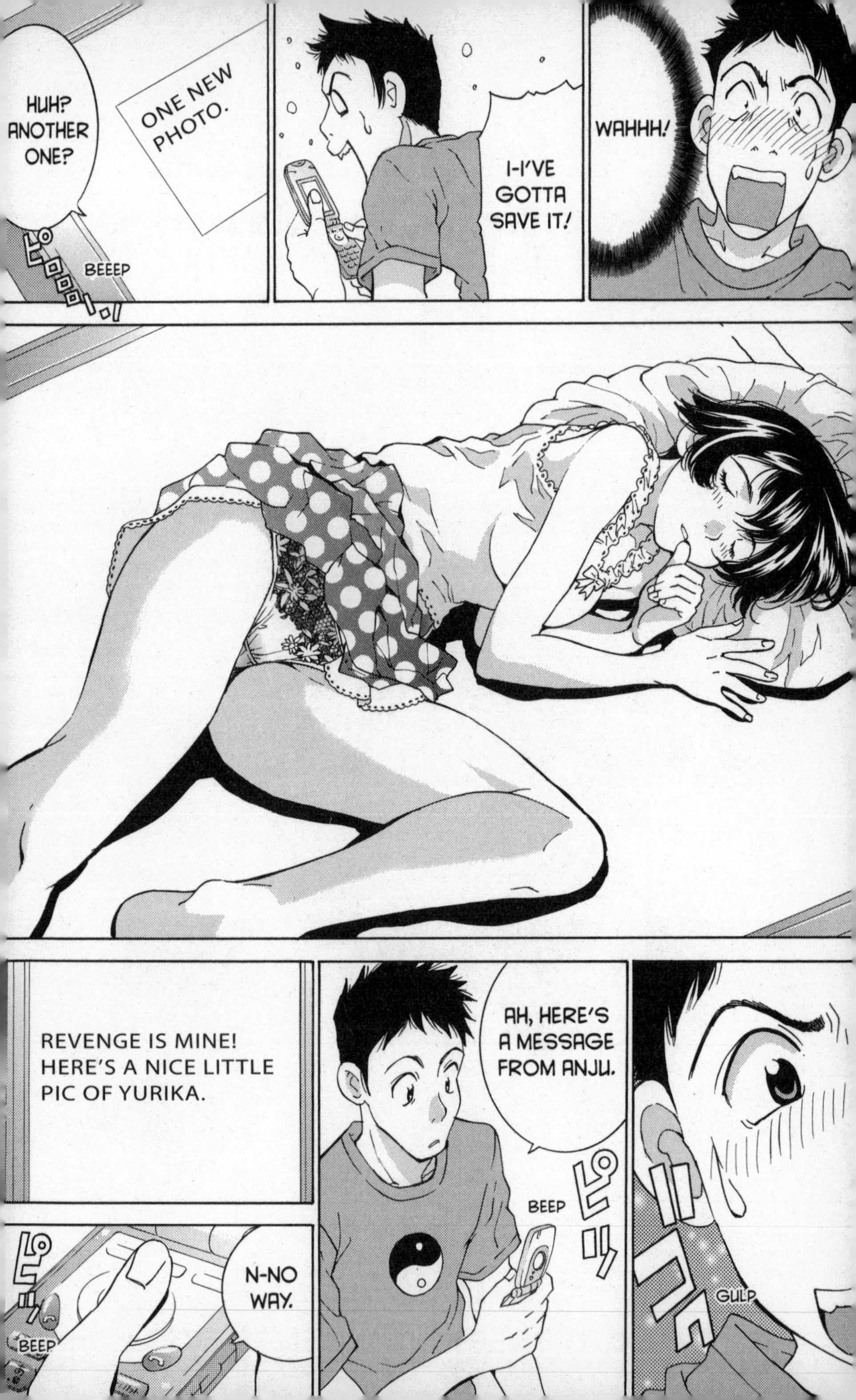
WAHHH!
I-I'VE GOTTA SAVE IT!
HUH? ANOTHER ONE?
ONE NEW PHOTO.
BEEEP
GULP
AH, HERE'S A MESSAGE FROM ANJU.
BEEP
REVENGE IS MINE! HERE'S A NICE LITTLE PIC OF YURIKA.
N-NO WAY.
BEEP

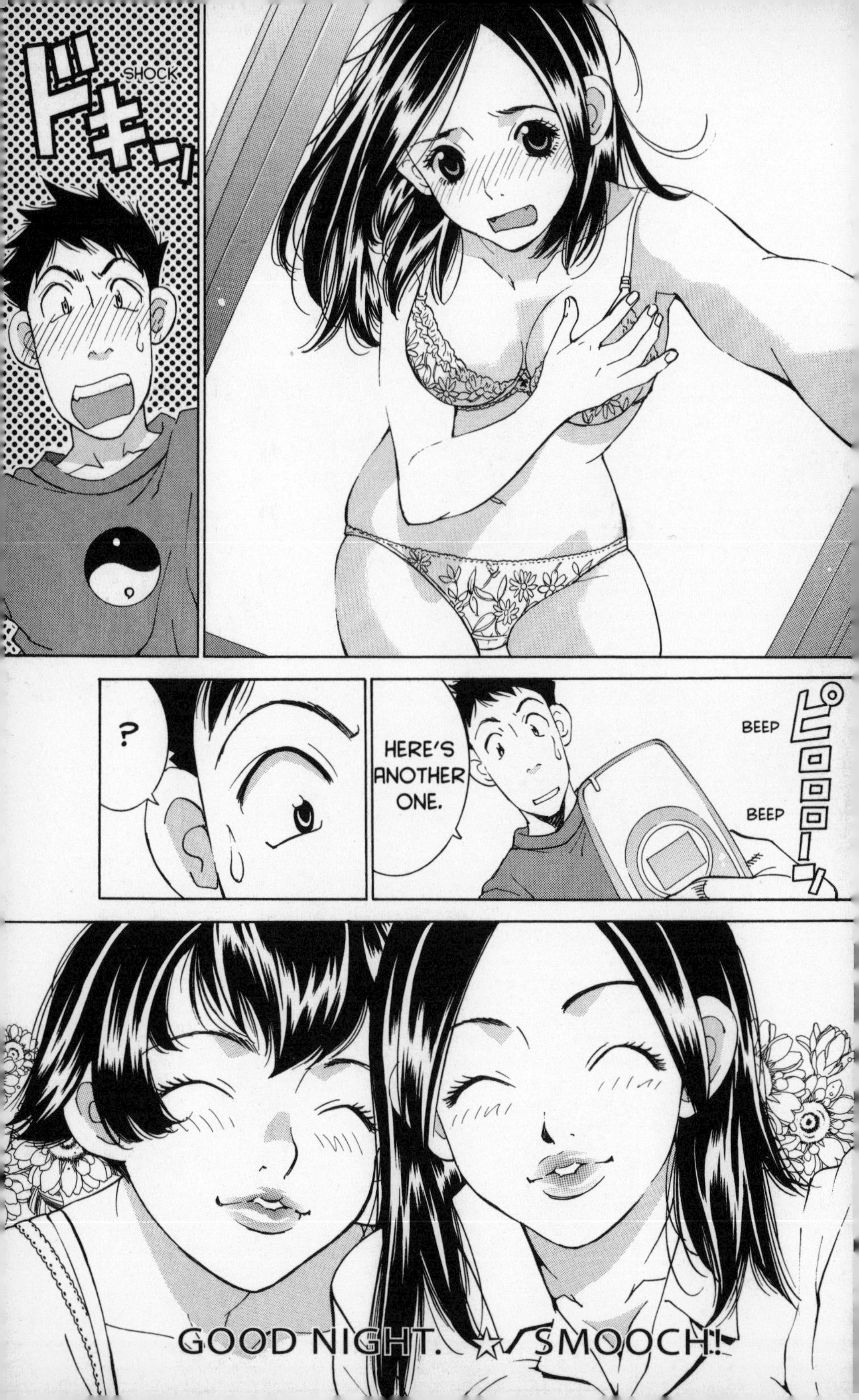
ドキーッ
SHOCK
ピロロロローッ
BEEP
BEEP
HERE'S ANOTHER ONE.
?
GOOD NIGHT. ☆ SMOOCH!

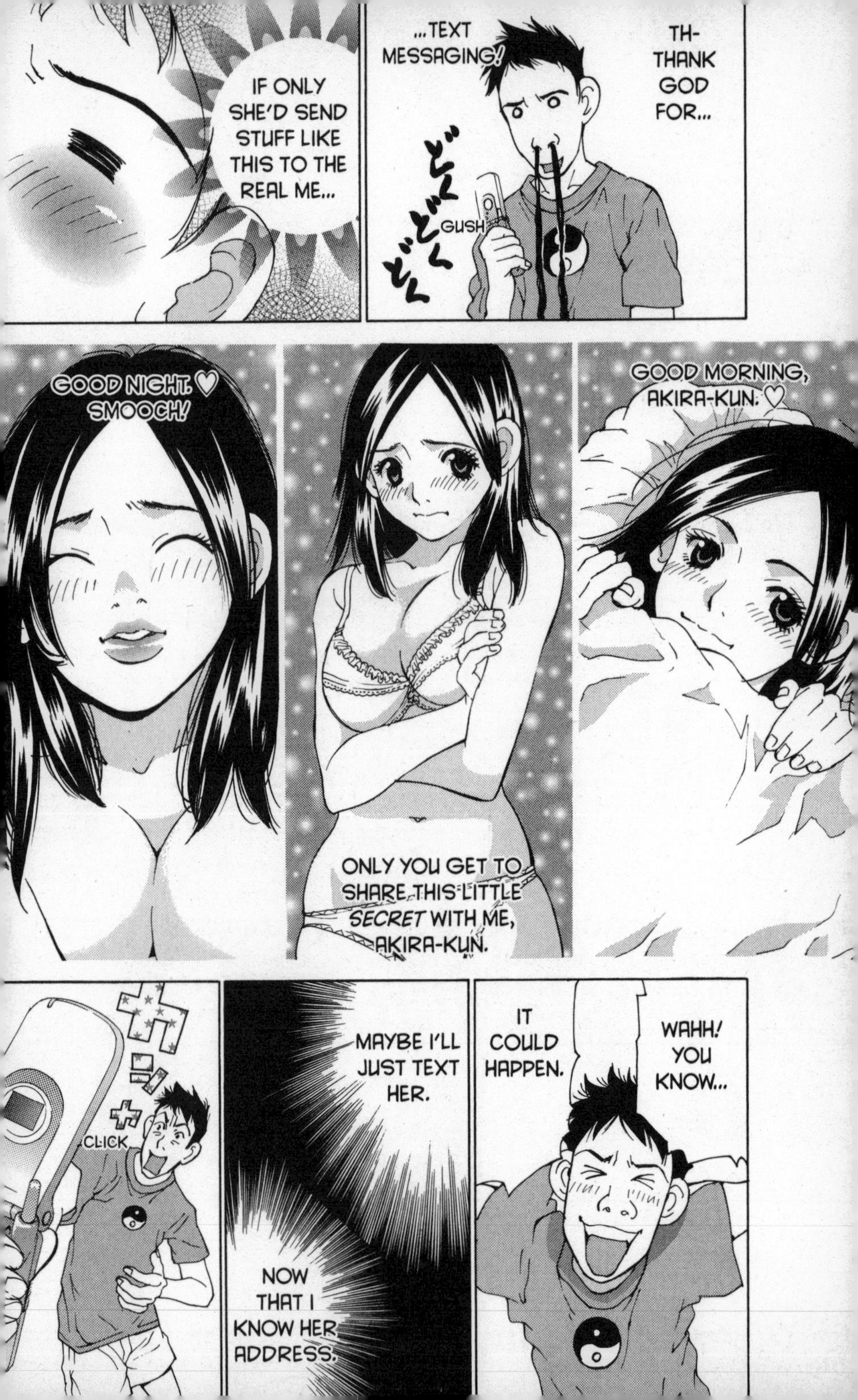
TH-THANK GOD FOR...
...TEXT MESSAGING!
どくどく
どくどく
GUSH
IF ONLY SHE'D SEND STUFF LIKE THIS TO THE REAL ME...
GOOD MORNING, AKIRA-KUN. ♡
ONLY YOU GET TO SHARE THIS LITTLE *SECRET* WITH ME, AKIRA-KUN.
GOOD NIGHT. ♡ SMOOCH!
WAHH! YOU KNOW...
IT COULD HAPPEN.
MAYBE I'LL JUST TEXT HER.
NOW THAT I KNOW HER ADDRESS.
CLICK

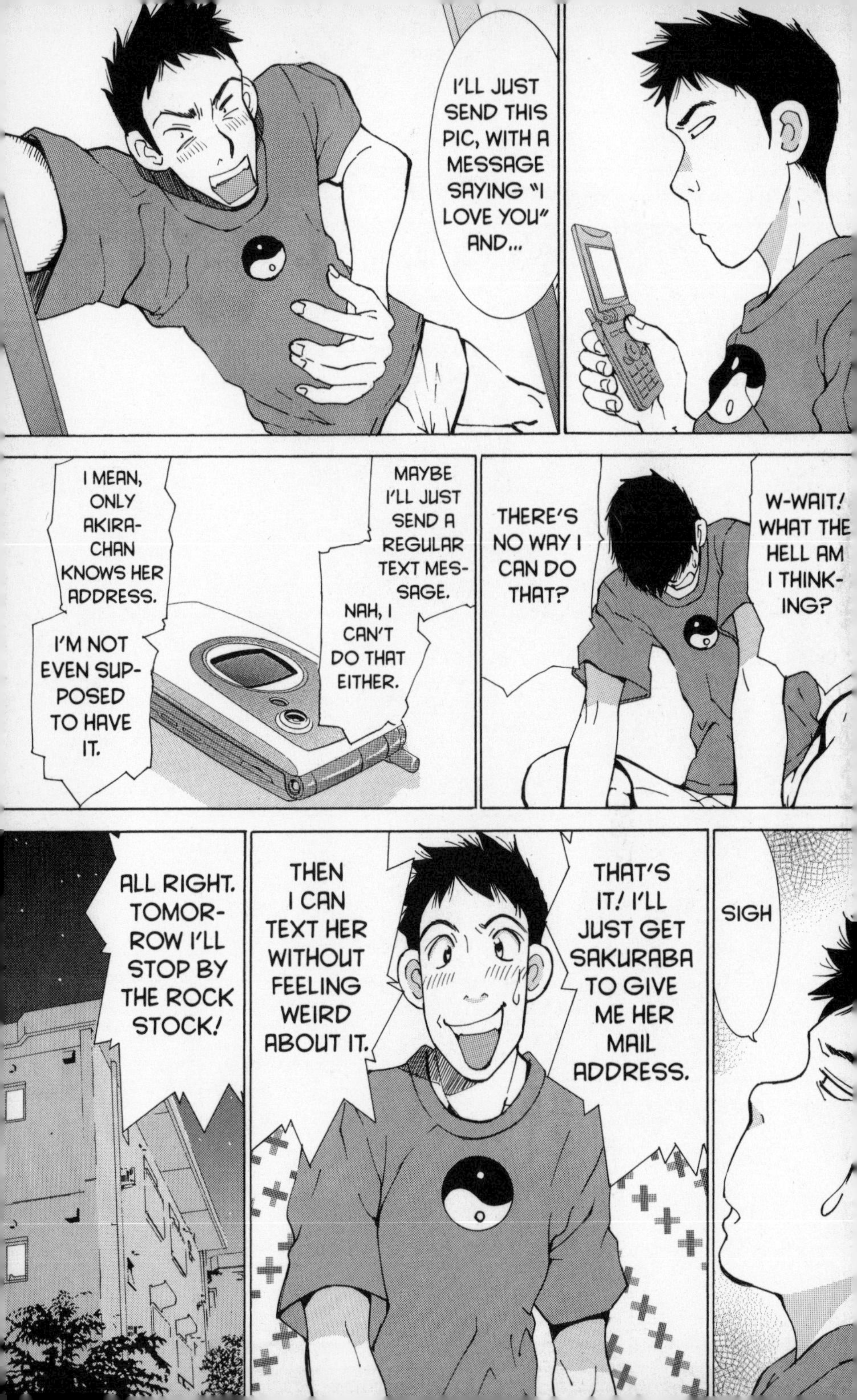
I'LL JUST SEND THIS PIC, WITH A MESSAGE SAYING "I LOVE YOU" AND...
W-WAIT! WHAT THE HELL AM I THINKING?
THERE'S NO WAY I CAN DO THAT?
MAYBE I'LL JUST SEND A REGULAR TEXT MESSAGE.
NAH, I CAN'T DO THAT EITHER.
I MEAN, ONLY AKIRA-CHAN KNOWS HER ADDRESS.
I'M NOT EVEN SUPPOSED TO HAVE IT.
SIGH
THAT'S IT! I'LL JUST GET SAKURABA TO GIVE ME HER MAIL ADDRESS.
THEN I CAN TEXT HER WITHOUT FEELING WEIRD ABOUT IT.
ALL RIGHT. TOMORROW I'LL STOP BY THE ROCK STOCK!

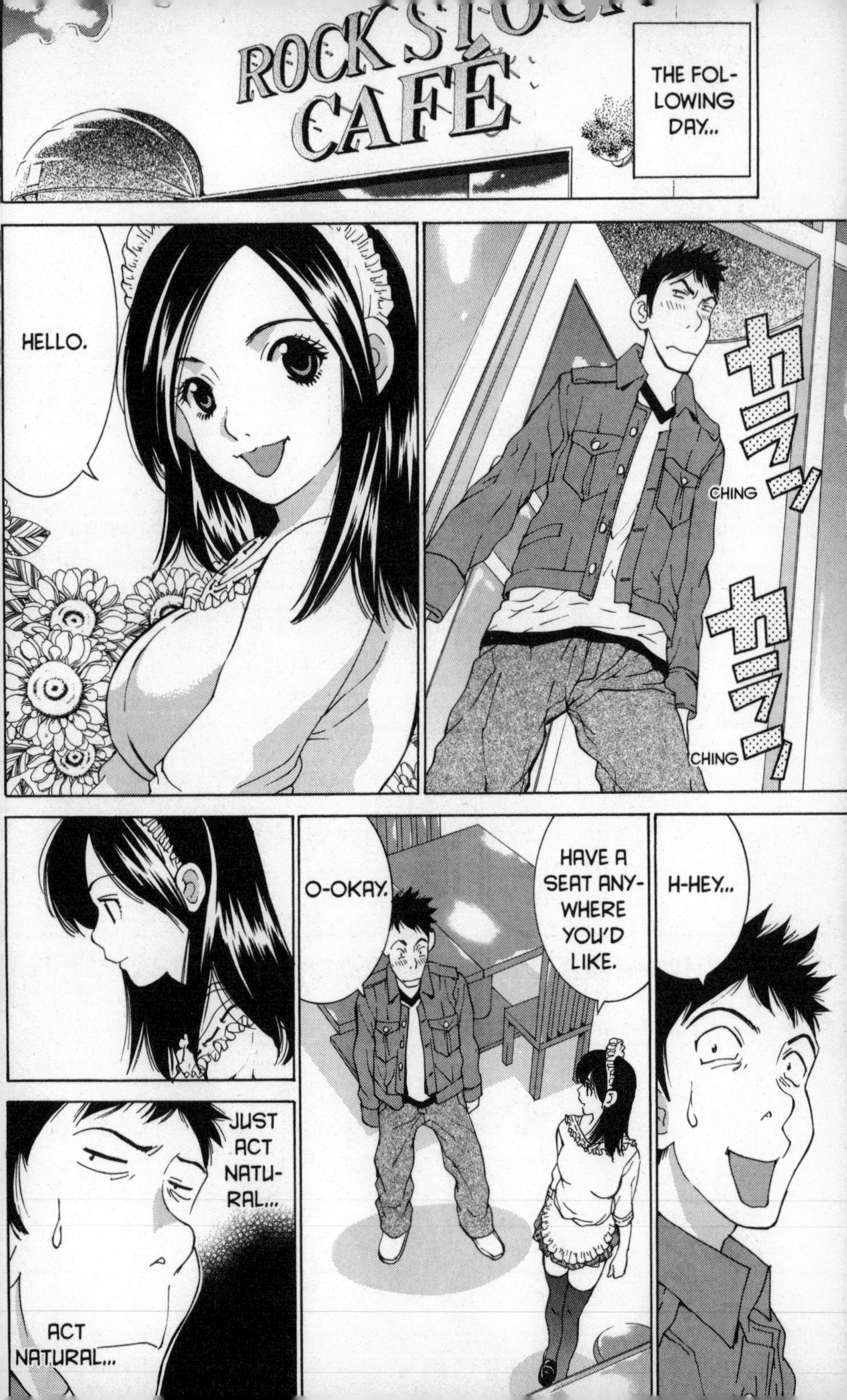
THE FOLLOWING DAY...
ROCK STOC
CAFÉ
CHING
CHING
HELLO.
H-HEY...
HAVE A SEAT ANYWHERE YOU'D LIKE.
O-OKAY.
JUST ACT NATURAL...
ACT NATURAL...

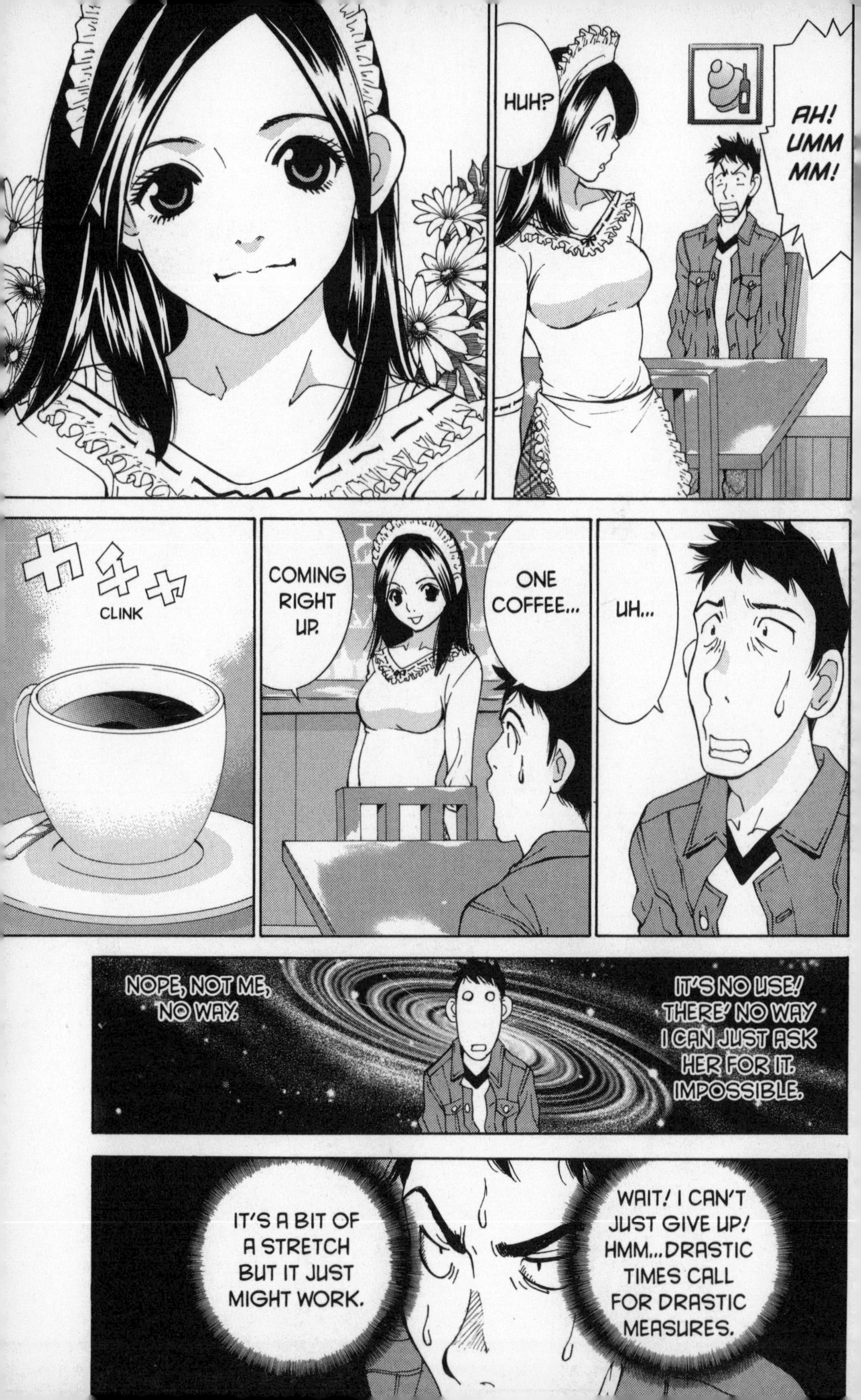
AH! UMM MM!
HUH?
UH...
ONE COFFEE...
COMING RIGHT UP.
CLINK
IT'S NO USE! THERE' NO WAY I CAN JUST ASK HER FOR IT. IMPOSSIBLE.
NOPE, NOT ME, NO WAY.
WAIT! I CAN'T JUST GIVE UP! HMM...DRASTIC TIMES CALL FOR DRASTIC MEASURES.
IT'S A BIT OF A STRETCH BUT IT JUST MIGHT WORK.

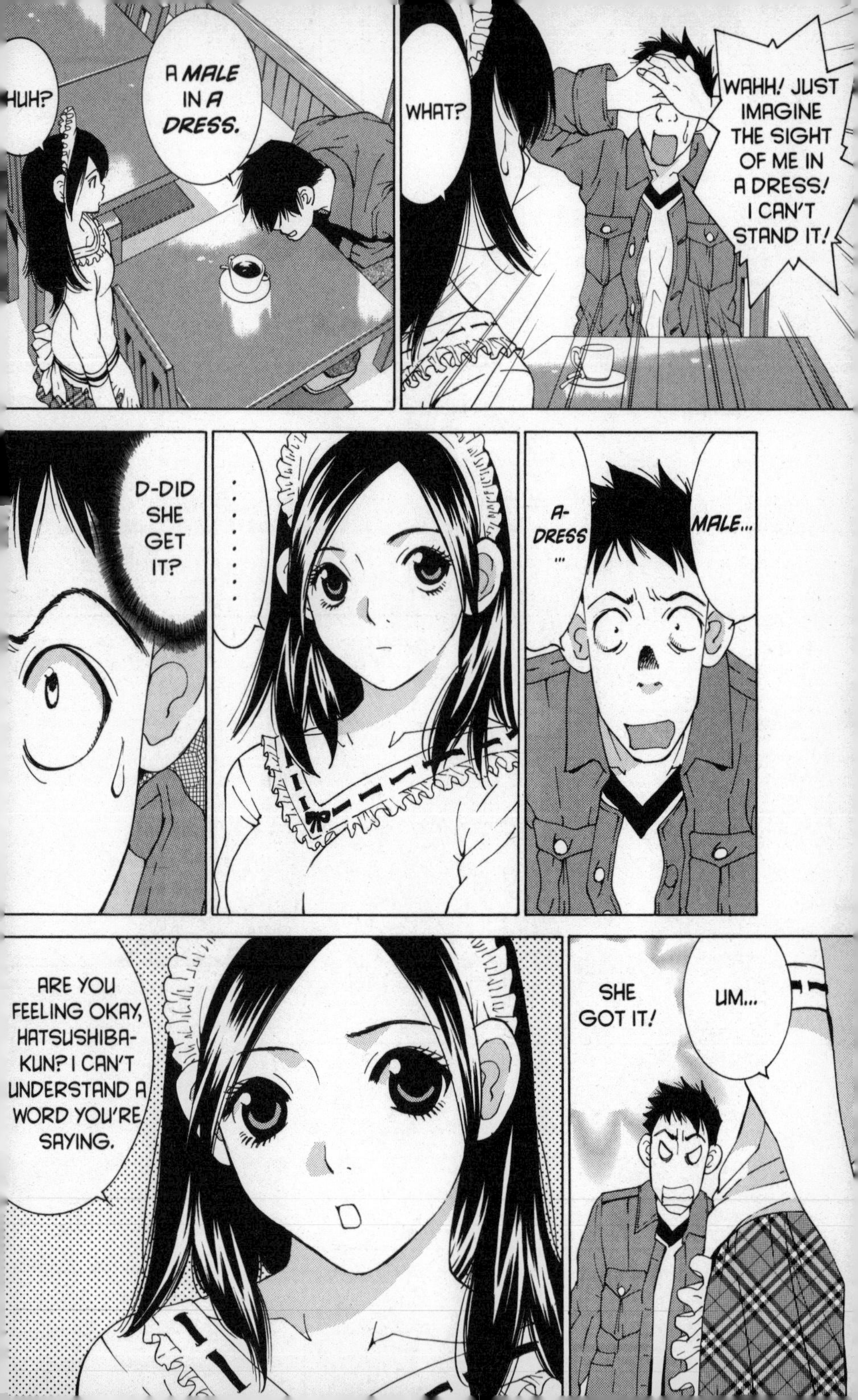
WAHH! JUST IMAGINE THE SIGHT OF ME IN A DRESS! I CAN'T STAND IT!
WHAT?
A MALE IN A DRESS.
HUH?
MALE...
A-DRESS...
......
D-DID SHE GET IT?
UM...
SHE GOT IT!
ARE YOU FEELING OKAY, HATSUSHIBA-KUN? I CAN'T UNDERSTAND A WORD YOU'RE SAYING.

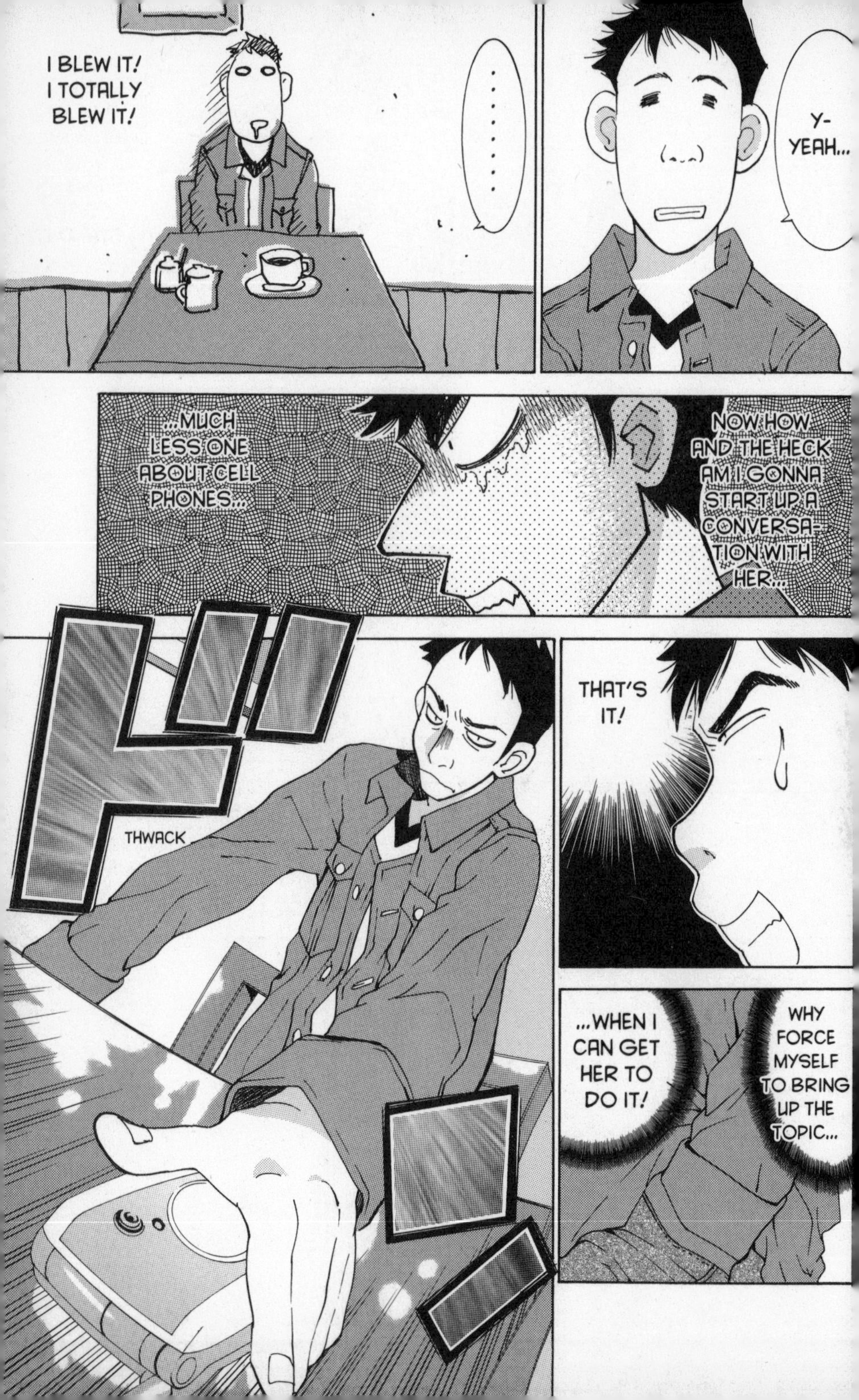
Y-YEAH...
......
I BLEW IT! I TOTALLY BLEW IT!
NOW HOW AND THE HECK AM I GONNA START UP A CONVERSA-TION WITH HER...
...MUCH LESS ONE ABOUT CELL PHONES...
THAT'S IT!
WHY FORCE MYSELF TO BRING UP THE TOPIC...
...WHEN I CAN GET HER TO DO IT!
THWACK

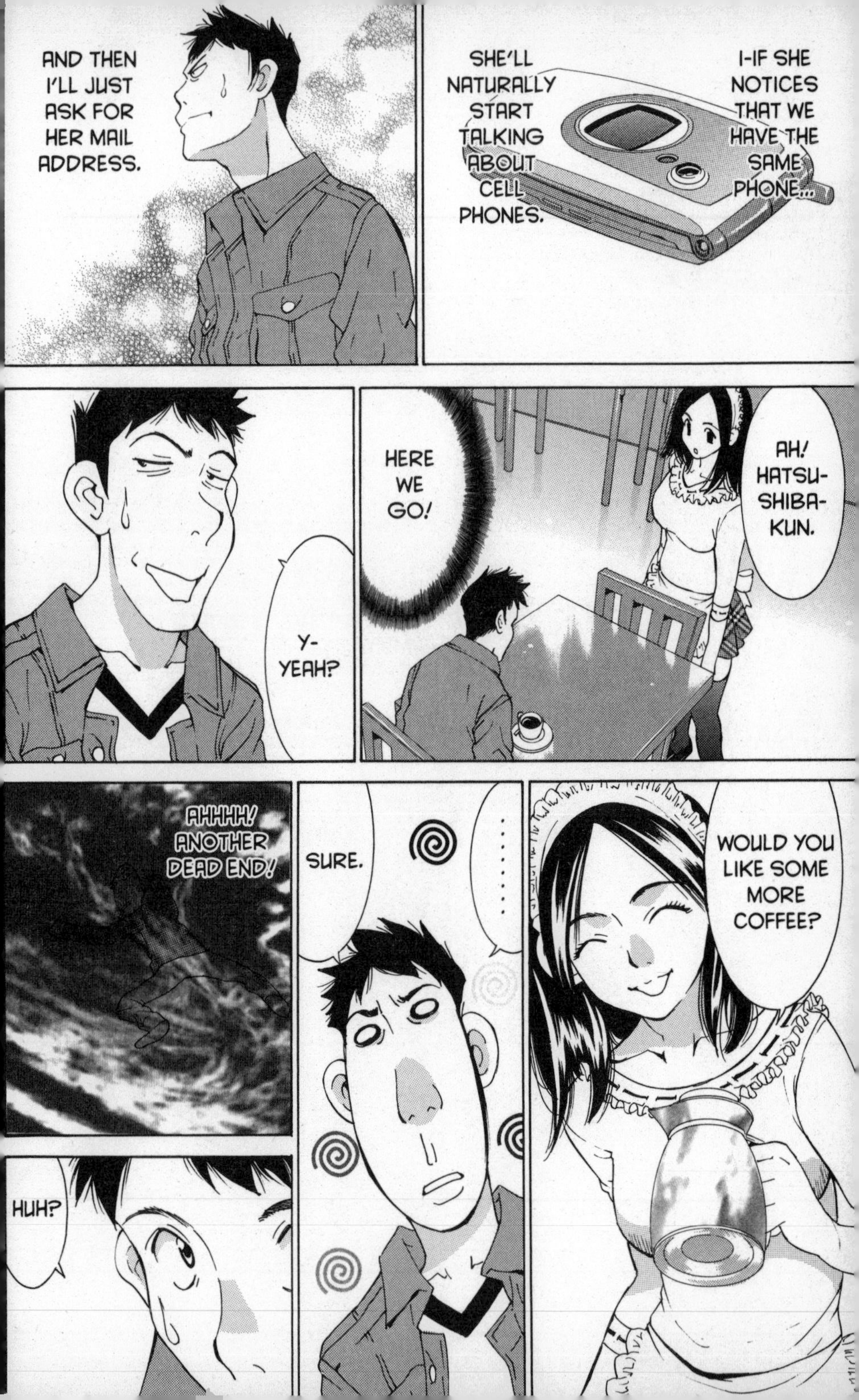
I-IF SHE NOTICES THAT WE HAVE THE SAME PHONE...
SHE'LL NATURALLY START TALKING ABOUT CELL PHONES.
AND THEN I'LL JUST ASK FOR HER MAIL ADDRESS.
AH! HATSU-SHIBA-KUN.
HERE WE GO!
Y-YEAH?
WOULD YOU LIKE SOME MORE COFFEE?
......
SURE.
AHHHH! ANOTHER DEAD END!
HUH?

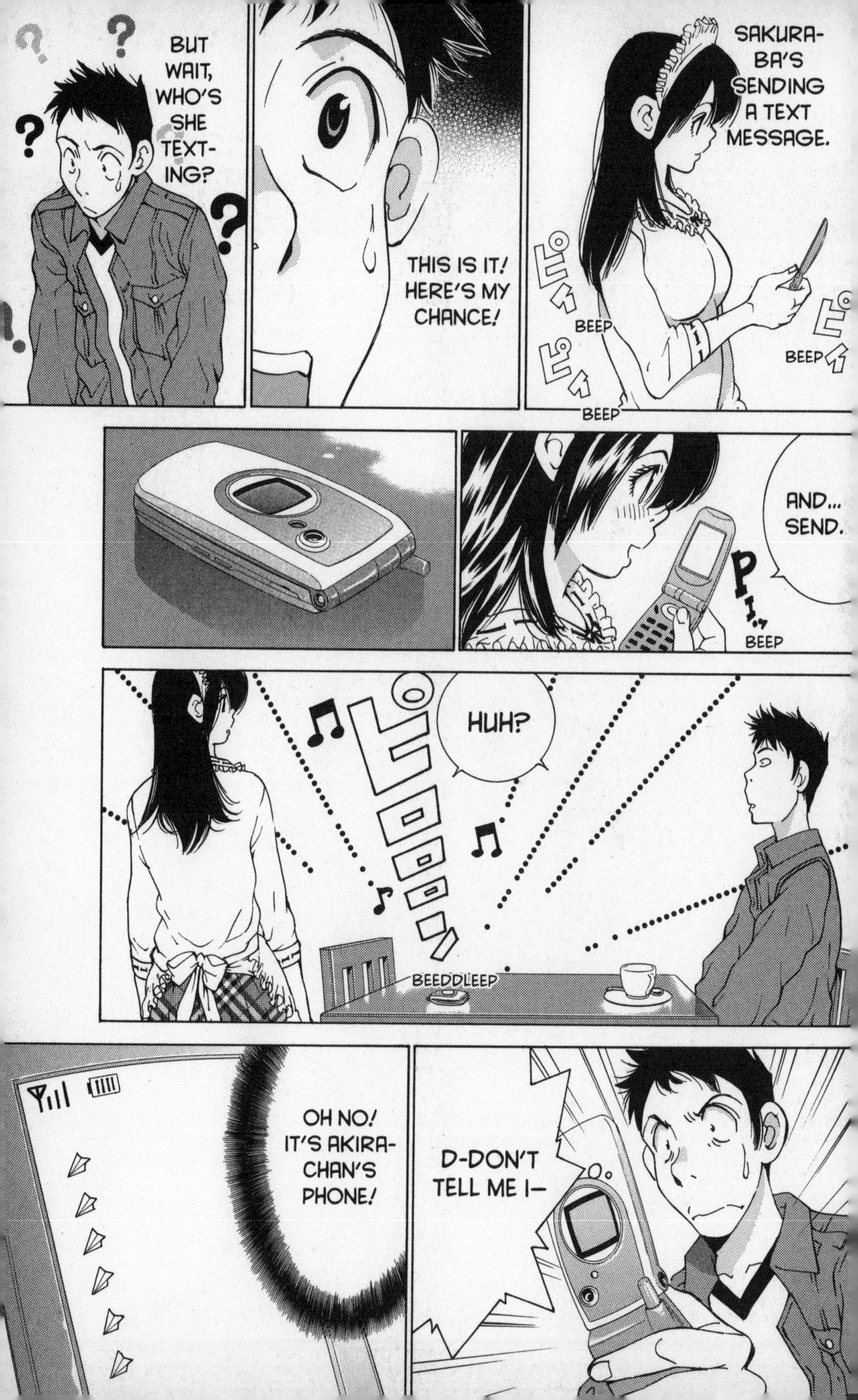
SAKURA-BA'S SENDING A TEXT MESSAGE.
BEEP
BEEP
BEEP
THIS IS IT! HERE'S MY CHANCE!
BUT WAIT, WHO'S SHE TEXT-ING?
AND... SEND.
BEEP
HUH?
BEEDDLEEP
D-DON'T TELL ME I—
OH NO! IT'S AKIRA-CHAN'S PHONE!

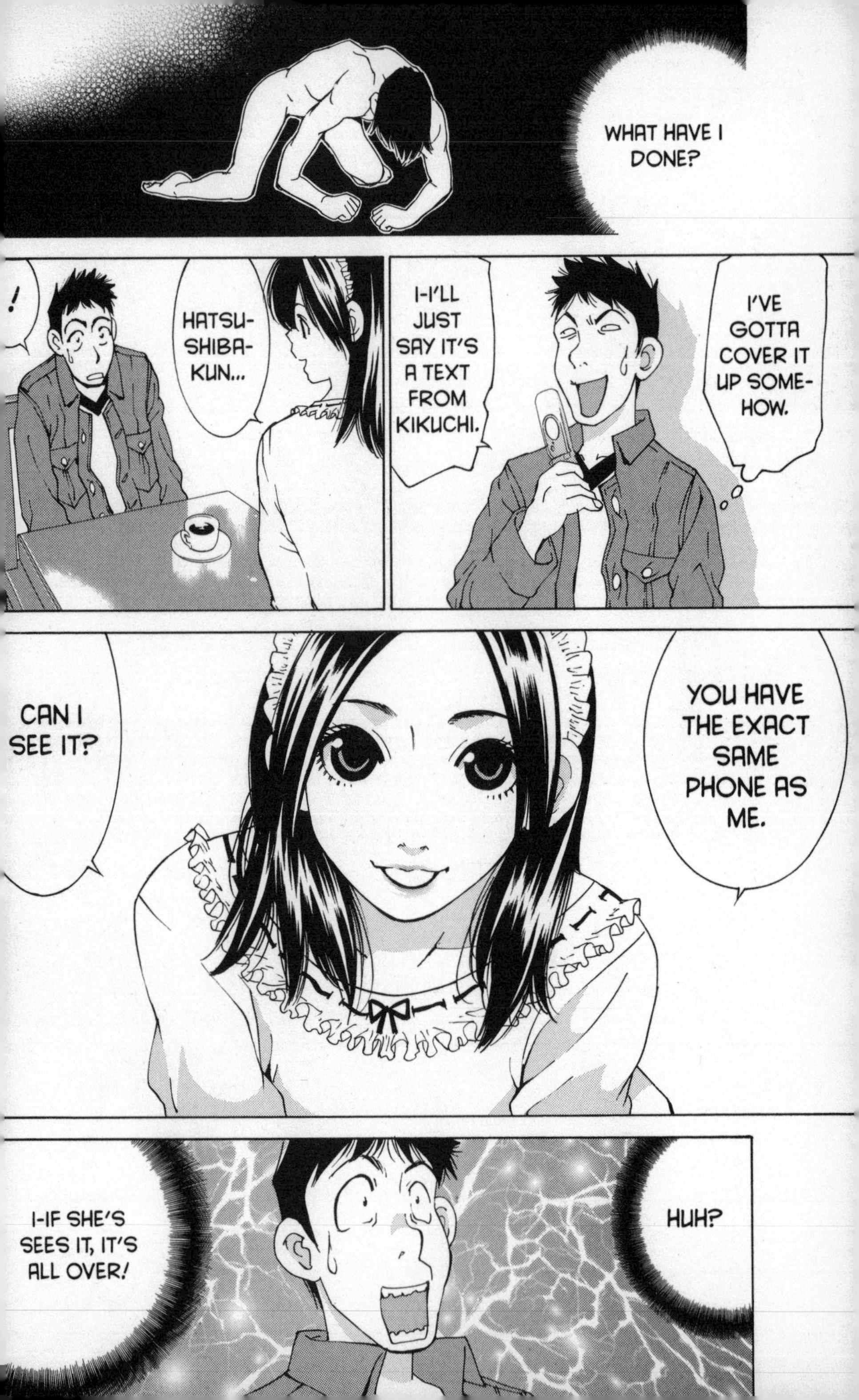
WHAT HAVE I DONE?
I'VE GOTTA COVER IT UP SOME-HOW.
I-I'LL JUST SAY IT'S A TEXT FROM KIKUCHI.
HATSU-SHIBA-KUN...
!
YOU HAVE THE EXACT SAME PHONE AS ME.
CAN I SEE IT?
HUH?
I-IF SHE'S SEES IT, IT'S ALL OVER!

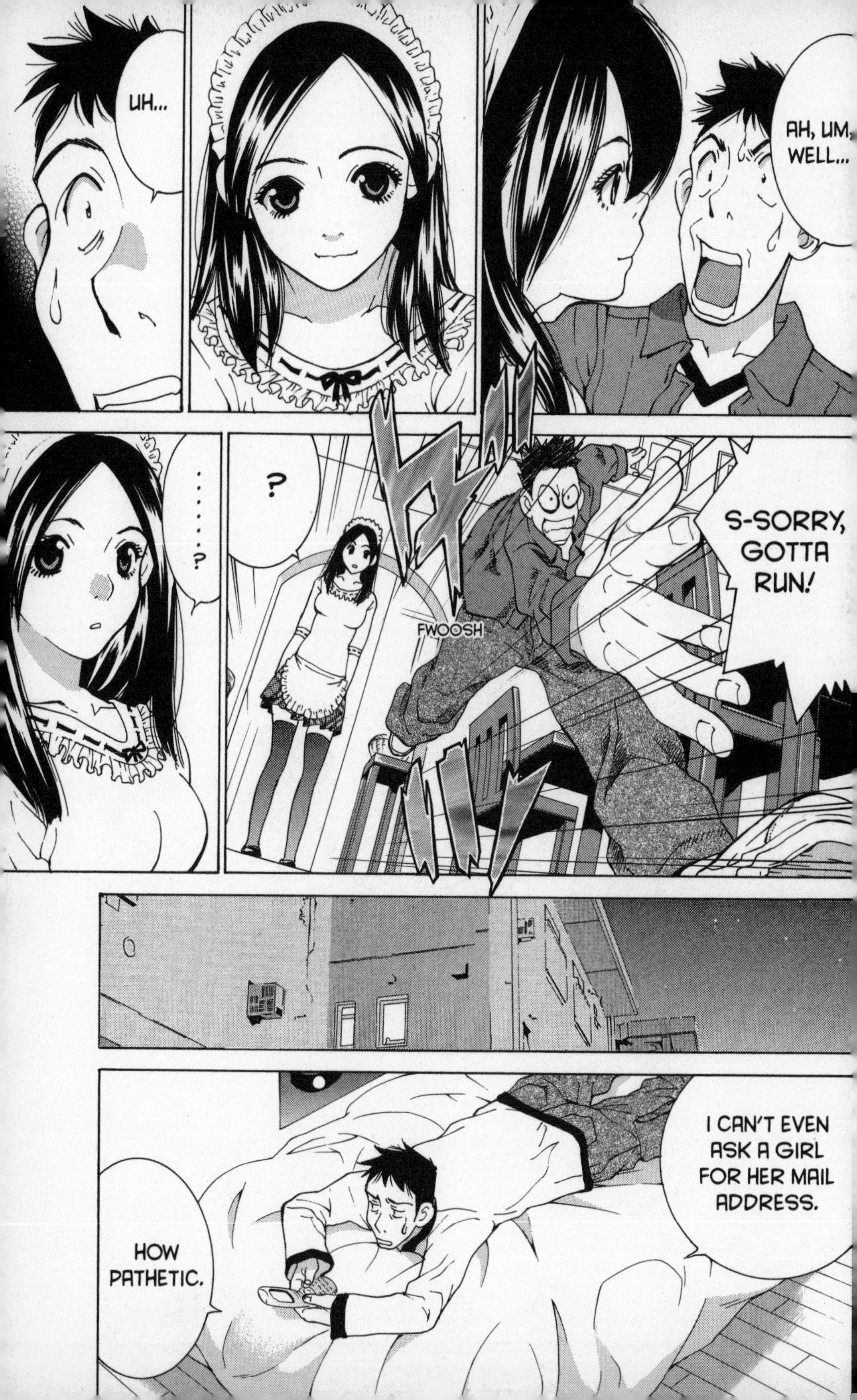
AH, UM, WELL...
UH...
S-SORRY, GOTTA RUN!
FWOOSH
?
......?
I CAN'T EVEN ASK A GIRL FOR HER MAIL ADDRESS.
HOW PATHETIC.

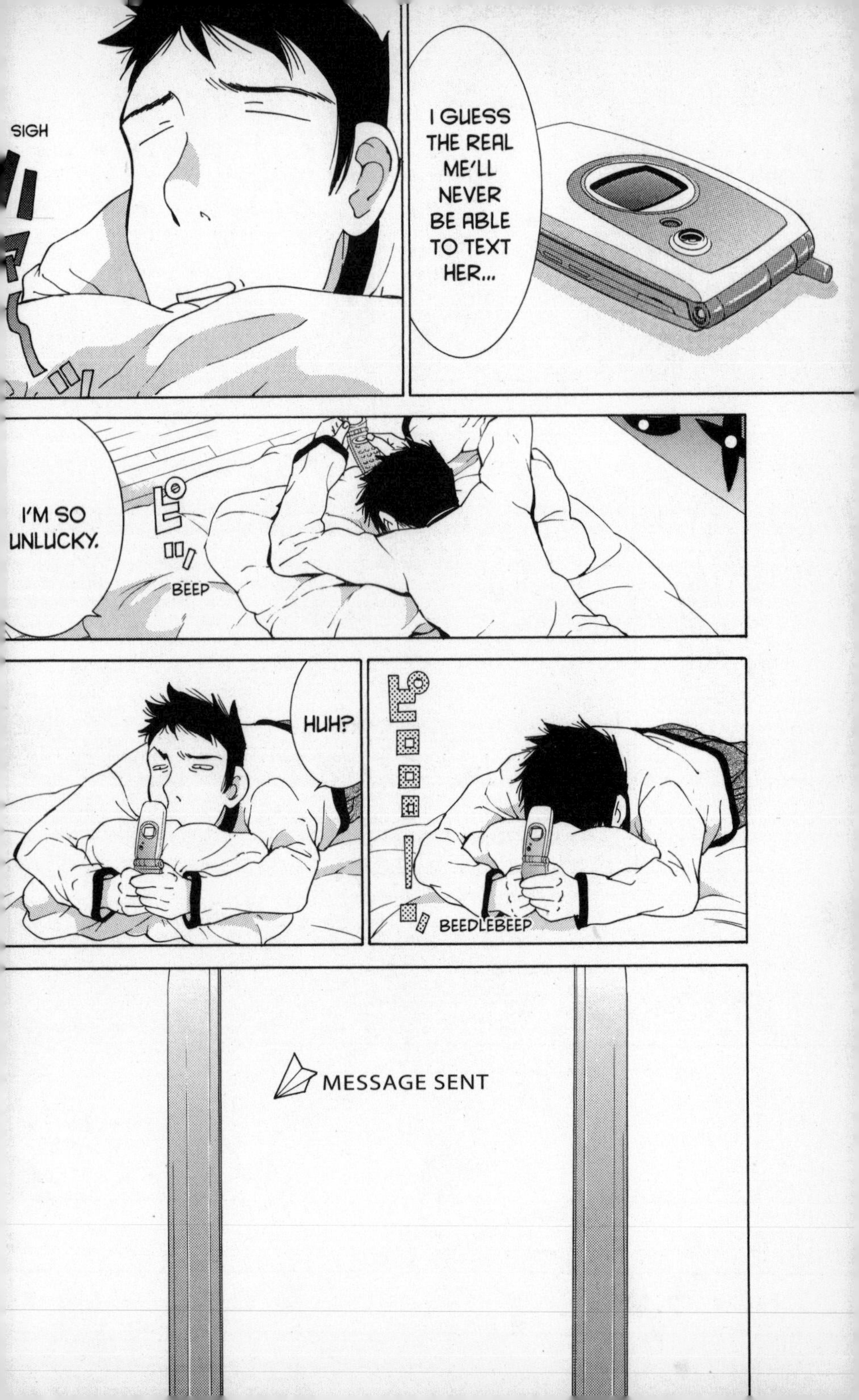
I GUESS THE REAL ME'LL NEVER BE ABLE TO TEXT HER...
SIGH
I'M SO UNLUCKY.
BEEP
BEEDLEBEEP
HUH?
MESSAGE SENT

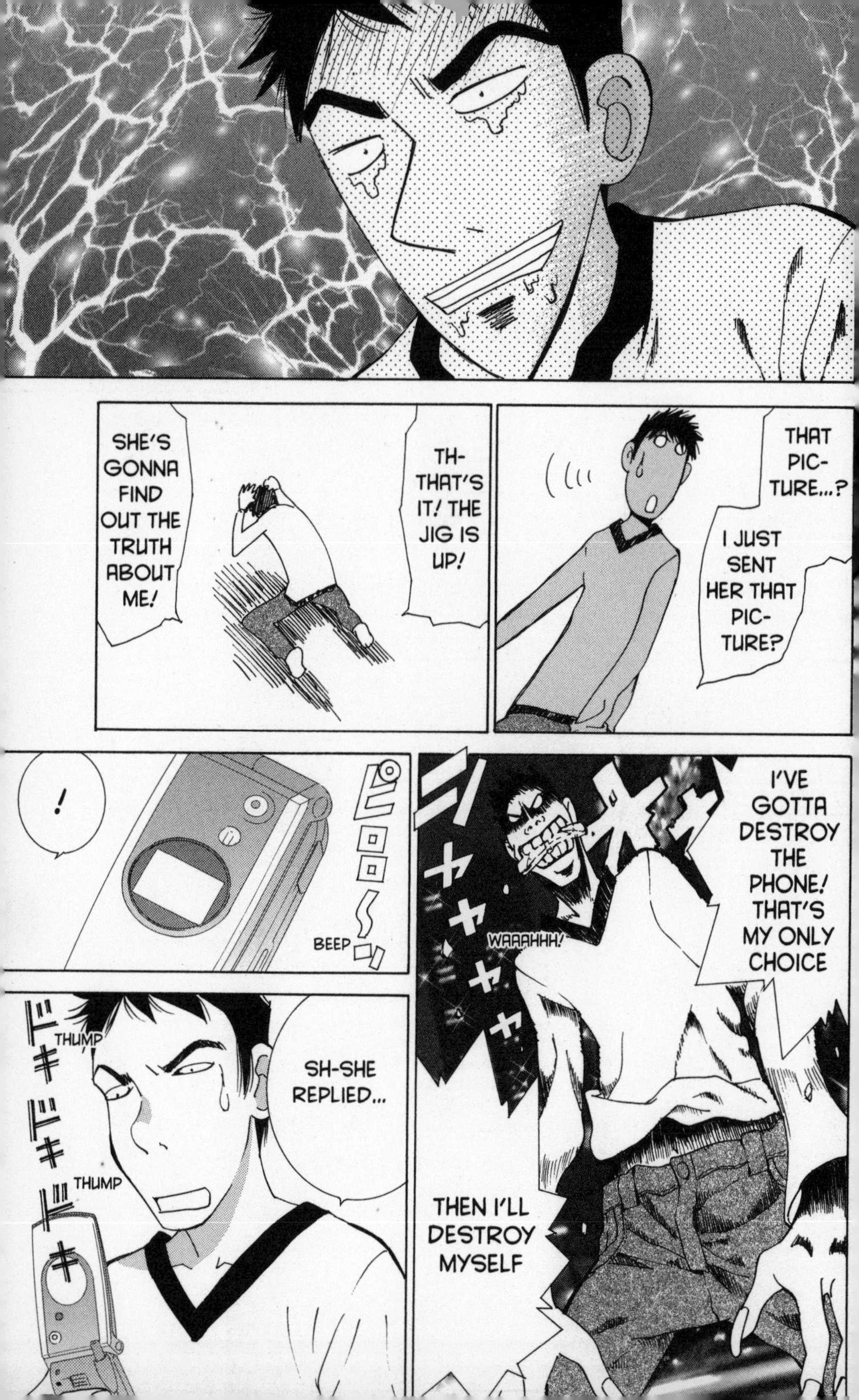
THAT PICTURE...?
I JUST SENT HER THAT PICTURE?
TH-THAT'S IT! THE JIG IS UP!
SHE'S GONNA FIND OUT THE TRUTH ABOUT ME!
I'VE GOTTA DESTROY THE PHONE! THAT'S MY ONLY CHOICE
WAAAHHH!
THEN I'LL DESTROY MYSELF
!
BEEP
SH-SHE REPLIED...
THUMP
THUMP

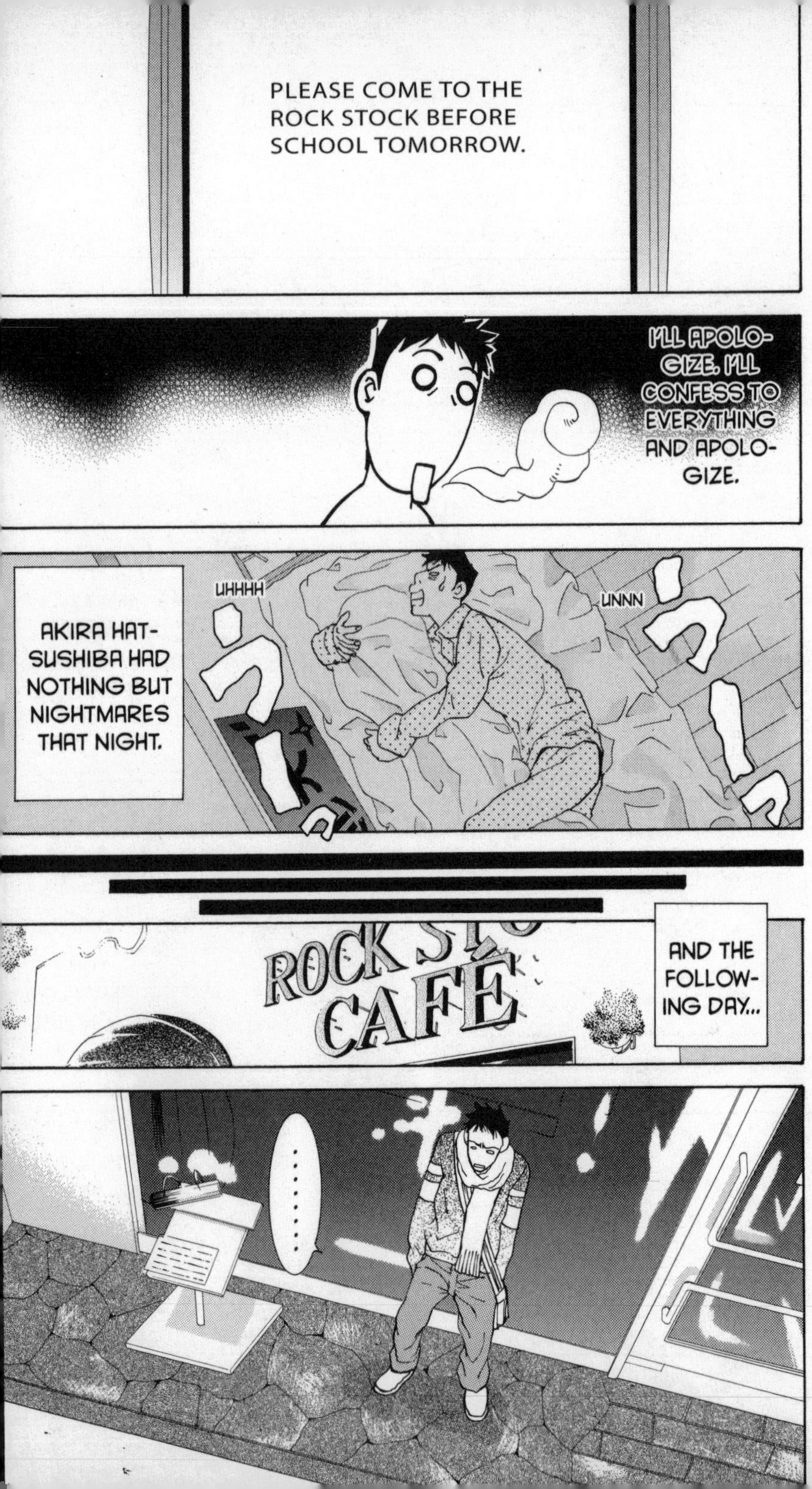
PLEASE COME TO THE ROCK STOCK BEFORE SCHOOL TOMORROW.
I'LL APOLOGIZE. I'LL CONFESS TO EVERYTHING AND APOLOGIZE.
UNNN
UHHHH
AKIRA HATSUSHIBA HAD NOTHING BUT NIGHTMARES THAT NIGHT.
AND THE FOLLOWING DAY...
ROCK STO
CAFÉ
....

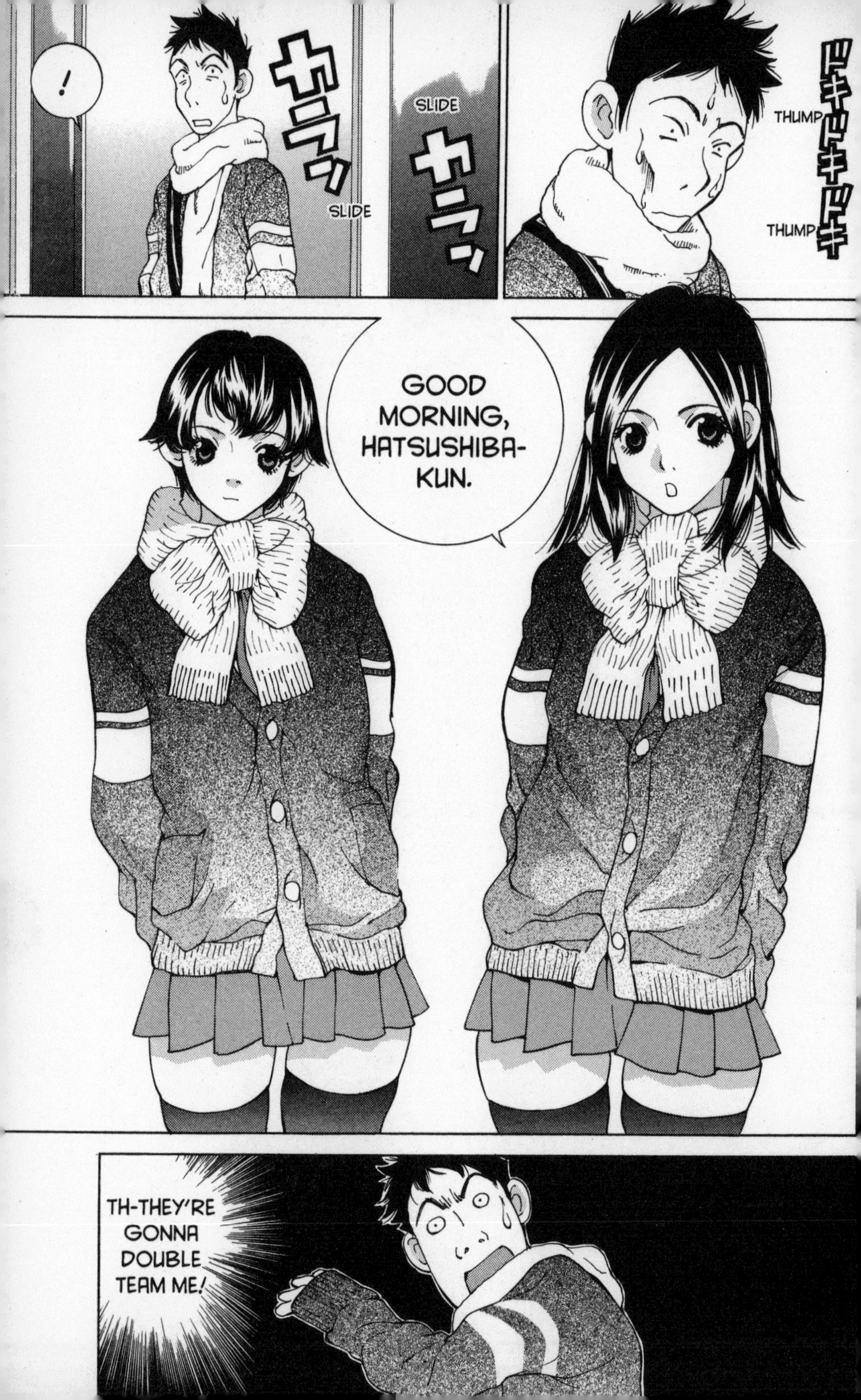
THUMP
THUMP
SLIDE
!
SLIDE
GOOD MORNING, HATSUSHIBA-KUN.
TH-THEY'RE GONNA DOUBLE TEAM ME!

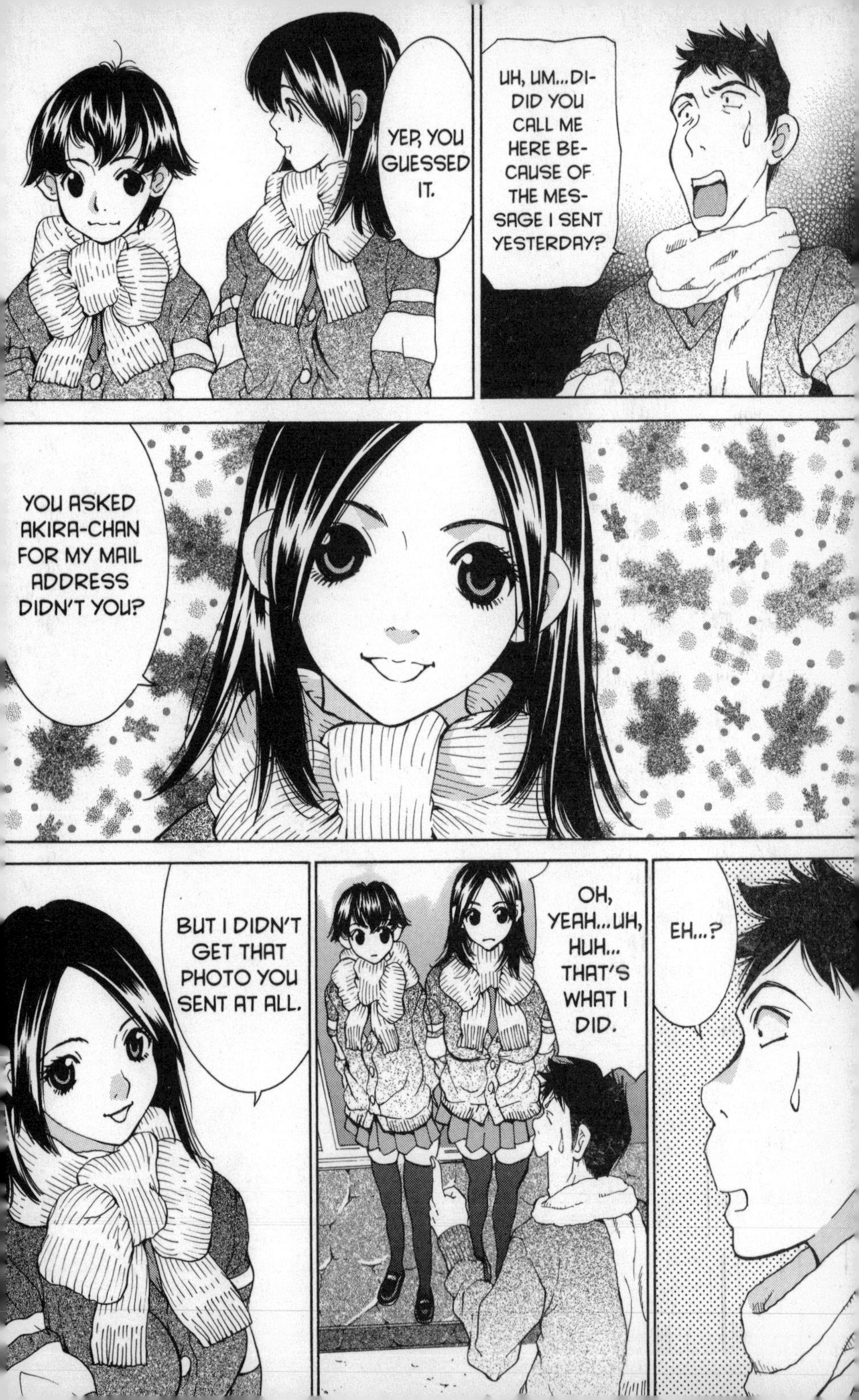
UH, UM...DI-DID YOU CALL ME HERE BECAUSE OF THE MESSAGE I SENT YESTERDAY?
YEP, YOU GUESSED IT.
YOU ASKED AKIRA-CHAN FOR MY MAIL ADDRESS DIDN'T YOU?
EH...?
OH, YEAH...UH, HUH... THAT'S WHAT I DID.
BUT I DIDN'T GET THAT PHOTO YOU SENT AT ALL.

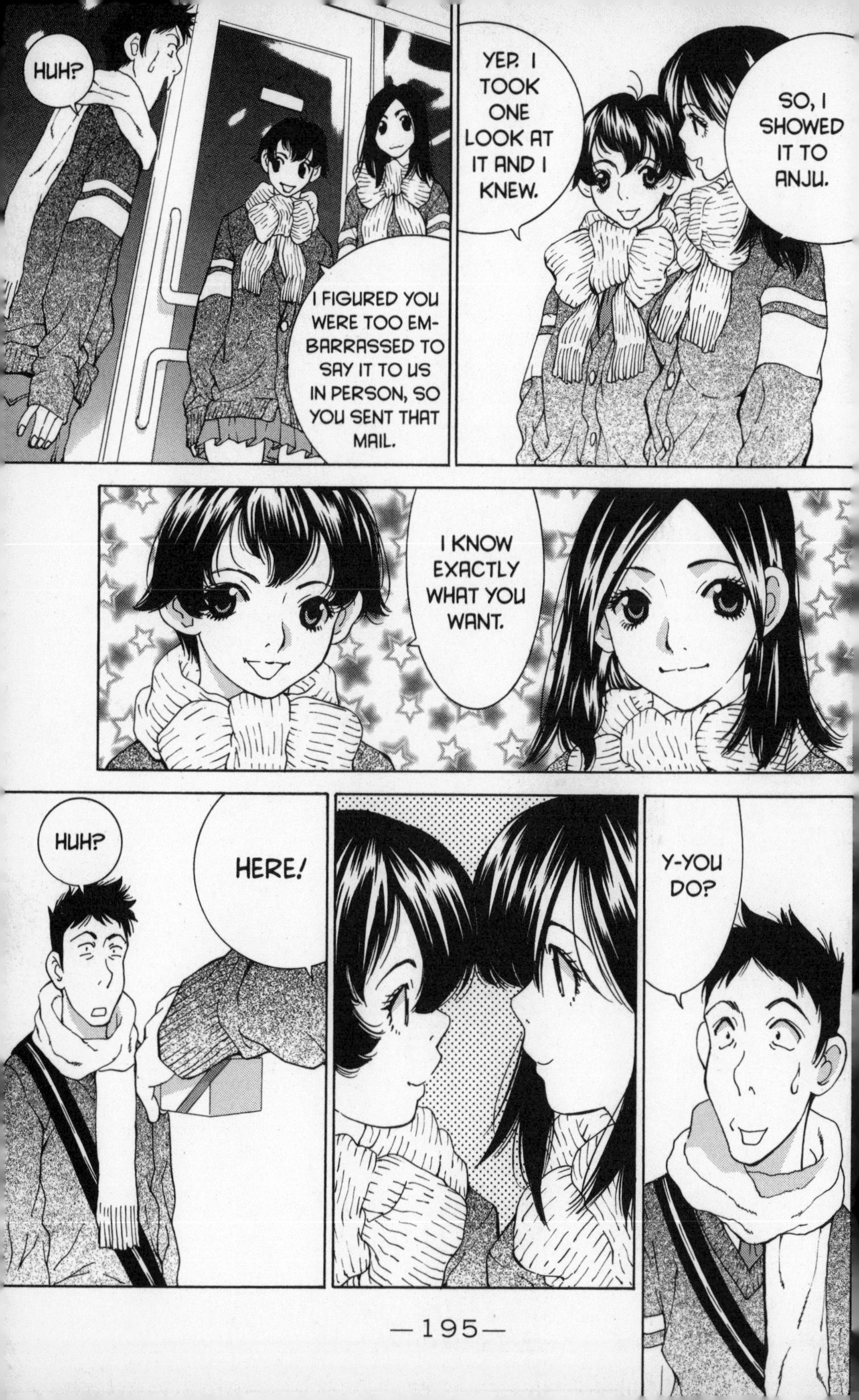
SO, I SHOWED IT TO ANJU.
YEP. I TOOK ONE LOOK AT IT AND I KNEW.
HUH?
I FIGURED YOU WERE TOO EM-BARRASSED TO SAY IT TO US IN PERSON, SO YOU SENT THAT MAIL.
I KNOW EXACTLY WHAT YOU WANT.
Y-YOU DO?
HERE!
HUH?

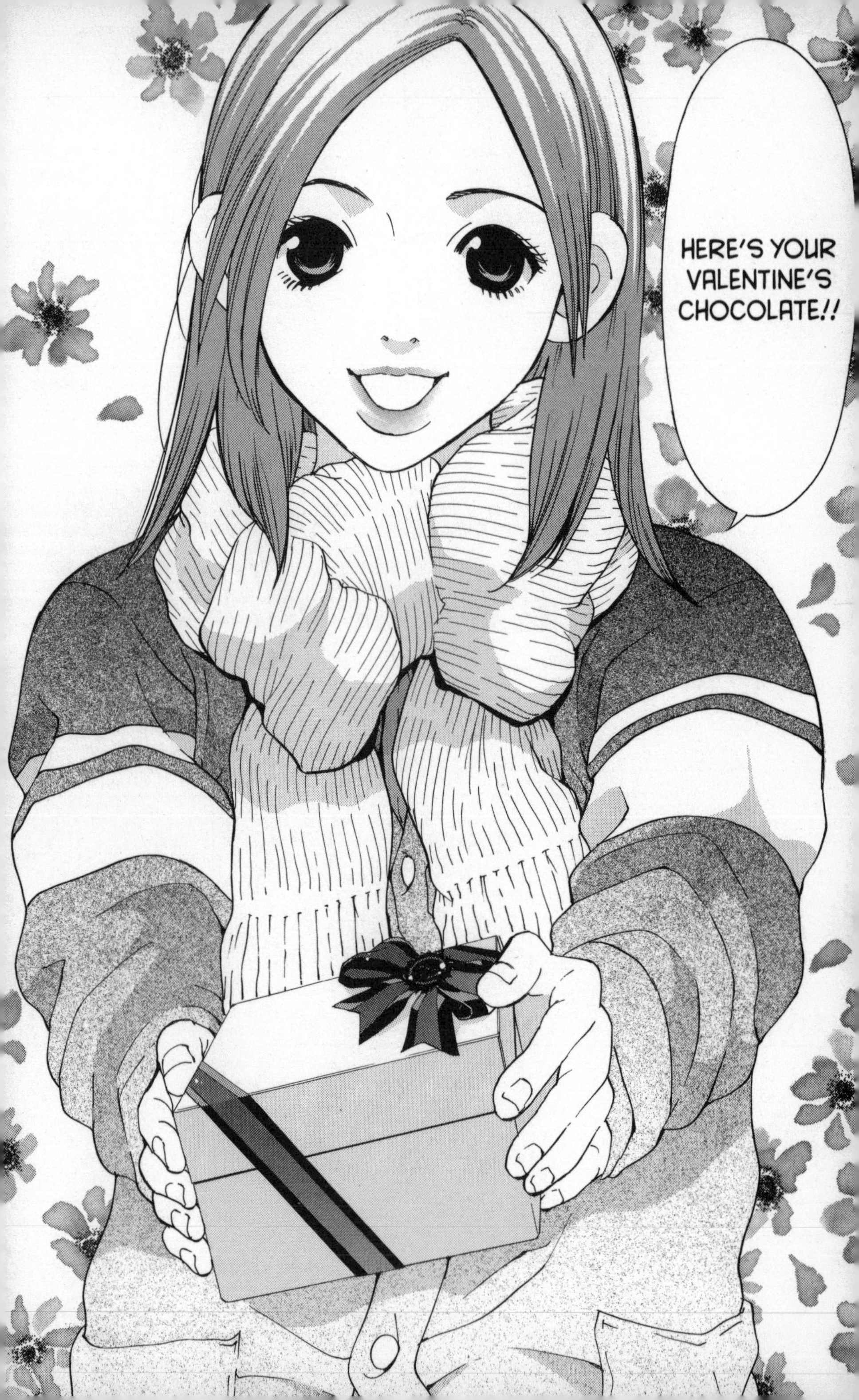
HERE'S YOUR VALENTINE'S CHOCOLATE!!

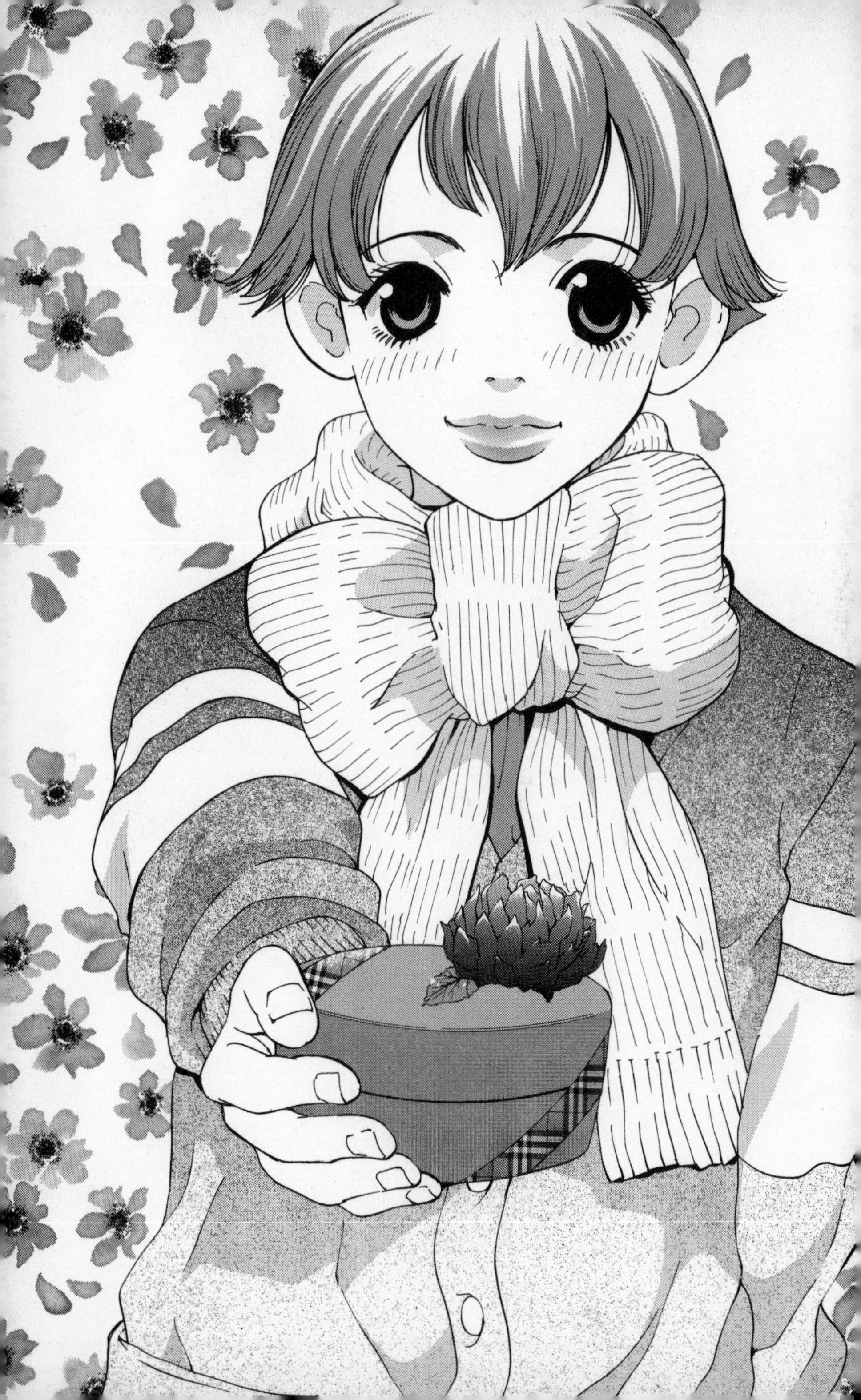

HUH?

TRY SOME.

IT'S JUST GIRI CHOCO-LATE, SO...

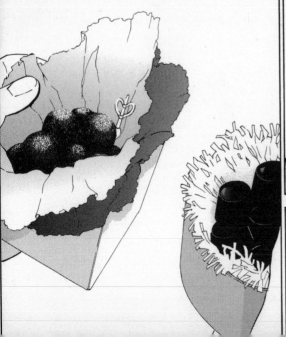

OH, SO THEY SOMEHOW DECIDED THAT THE PHOTO I SENT WAS MY WAY OF ASKING FOR VALENTINE'S CHOCOLATE.

O-OKAY.

HUH?

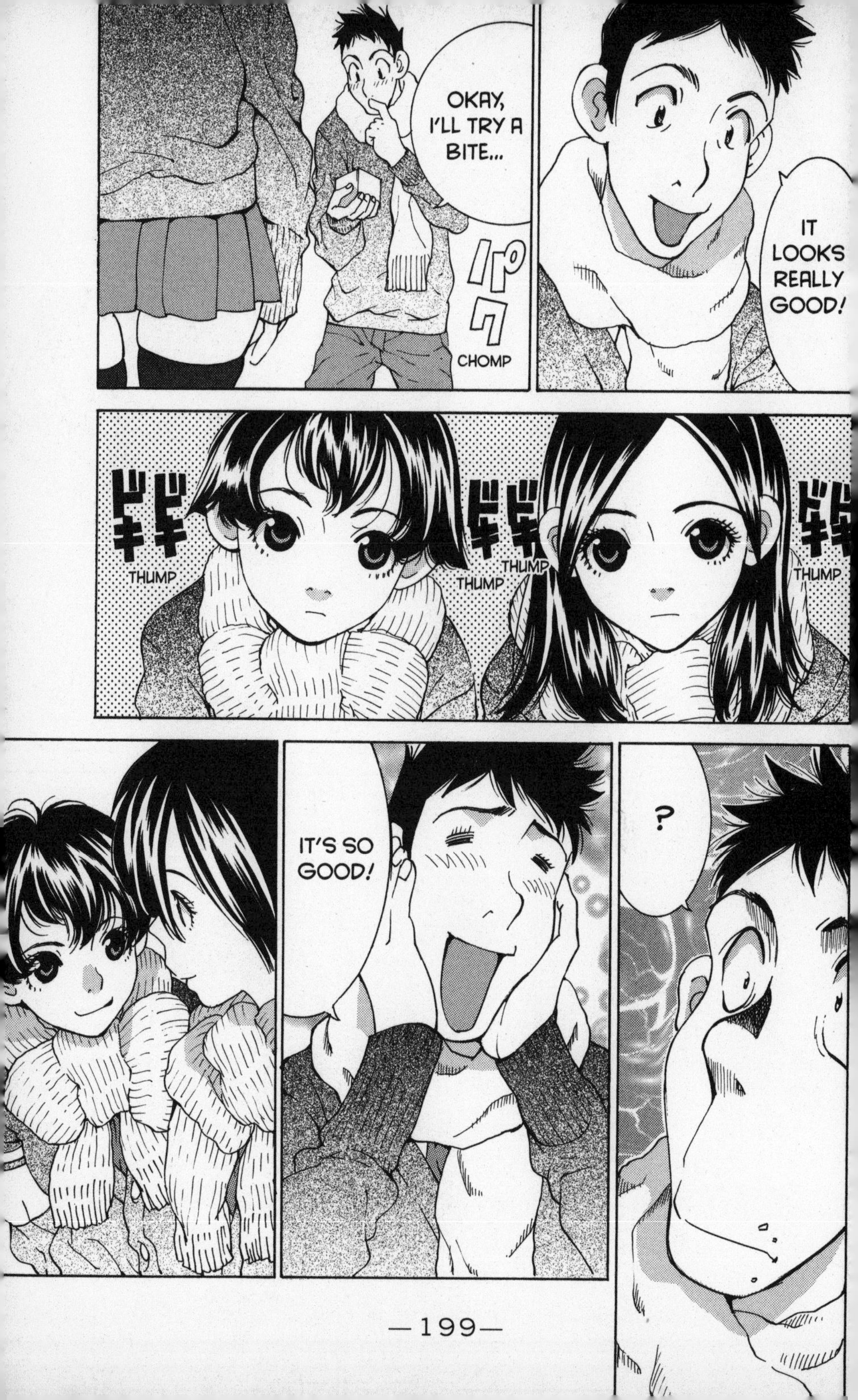
IT LOOKS REALLY GOOD!
OKAY, I'LL TRY A BITE...
パク
CHOMP
ドキドキ
THUMP
ドキドキ
THUMP
THUMP
ドキドキ
THUMP
?
IT'S SO GOOD!

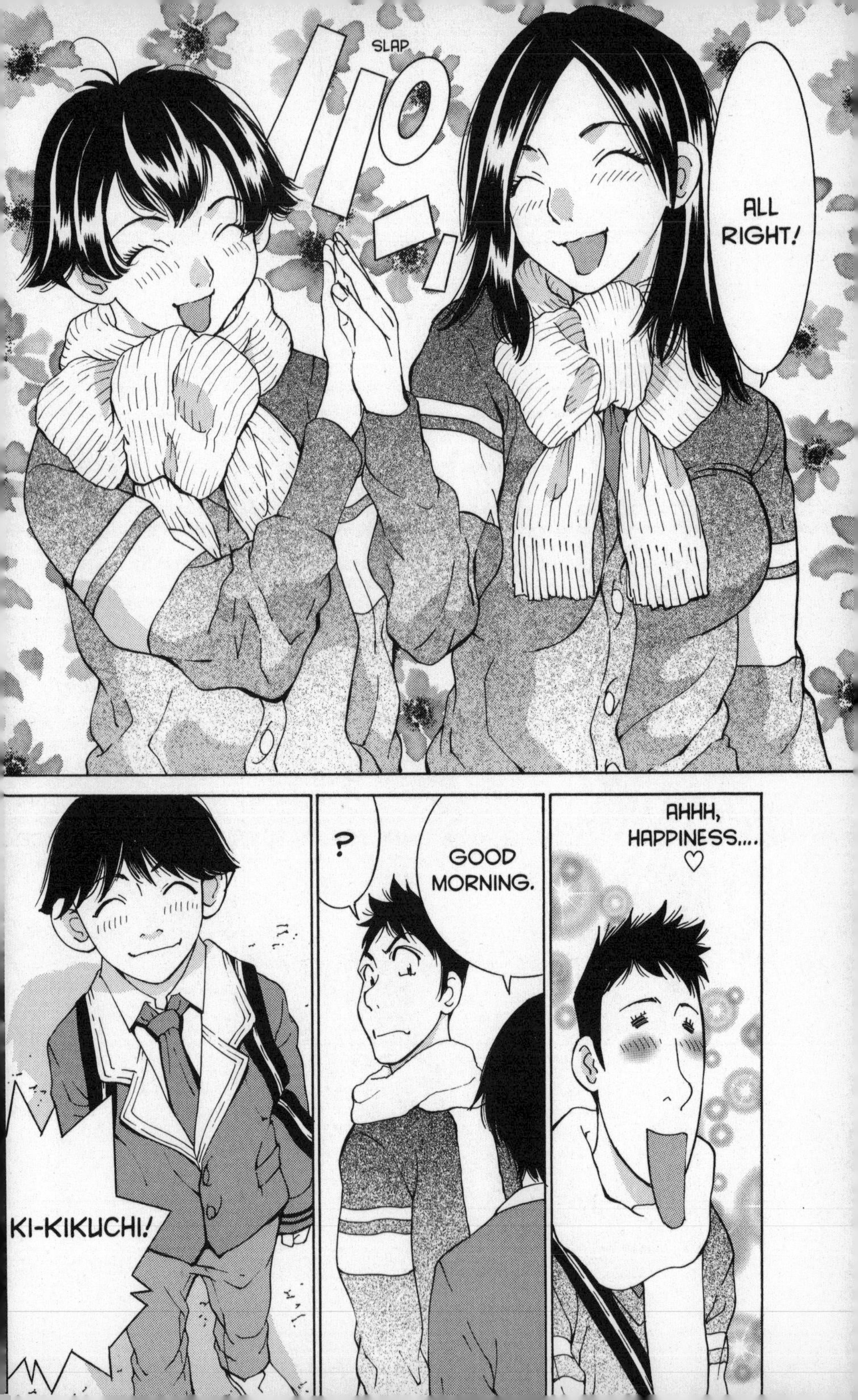
ALL RIGHT!
SLAP
AHHH, HAPPINESS.... ♡
GOOD MORNING.
?
KI-KIKUCHI!

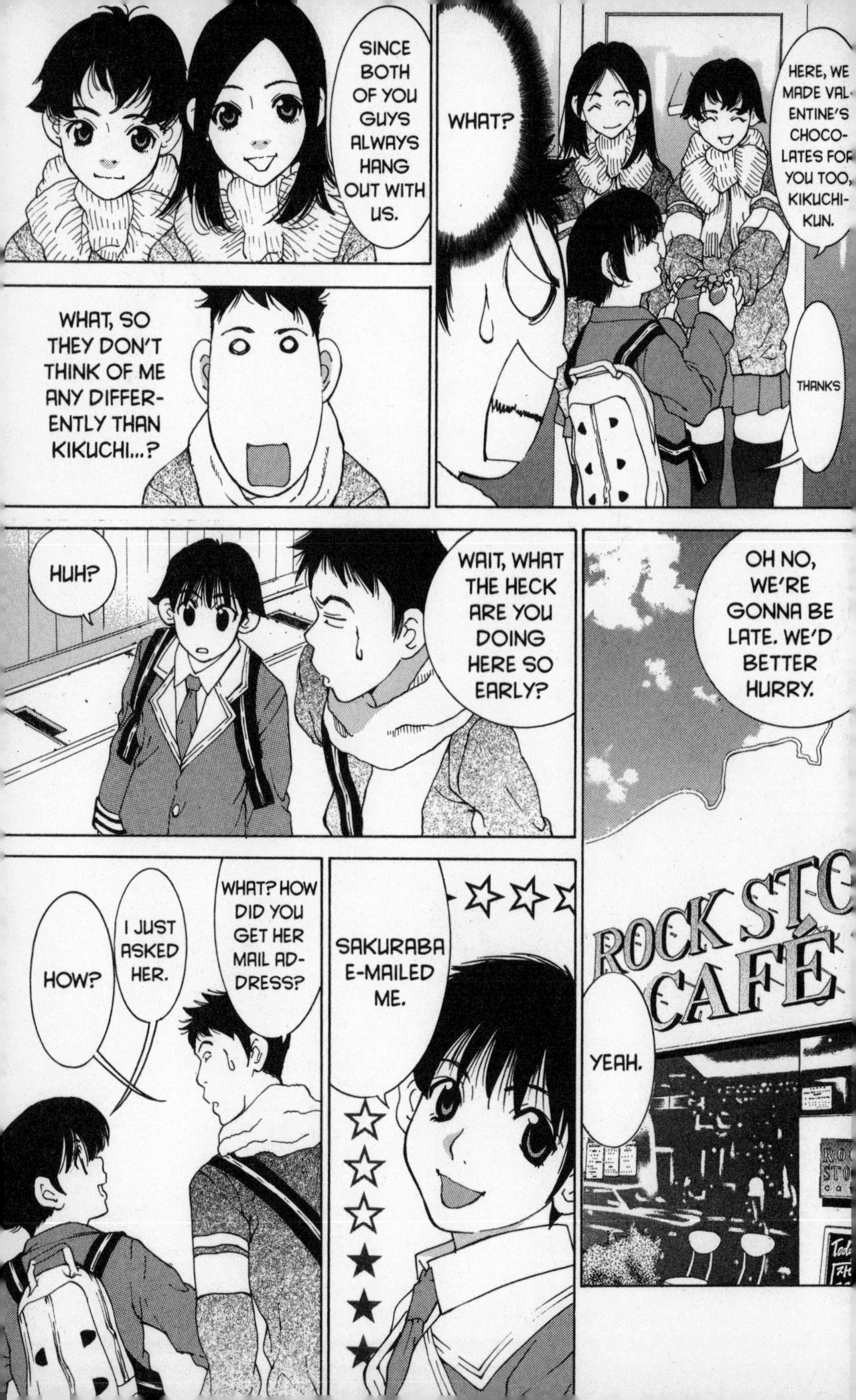
HERE, WE MADE VALENTINE'S CHOCOLATES FOR YOU TOO, KIKUCHI-KUN.
THANKS
WHAT?
SINCE BOTH OF YOU GUYS ALWAYS HANG OUT WITH US.
WHAT, SO THEY DON'T THINK OF ME ANY DIFFERENTLY THAN KIKUCHI...?
OH NO, WE'RE GONNA BE LATE. WE'D BETTER HURRY.
ROCK STO
CAFÉ
YEAH.
WAIT, WHAT THE HECK ARE YOU DOING HERE SO EARLY?
HUH?
SAKURABA E-MAILED ME.
WHAT? HOW DID YOU GET HER MAIL ADDRESS?
I JUST ASKED HER.
HOW?

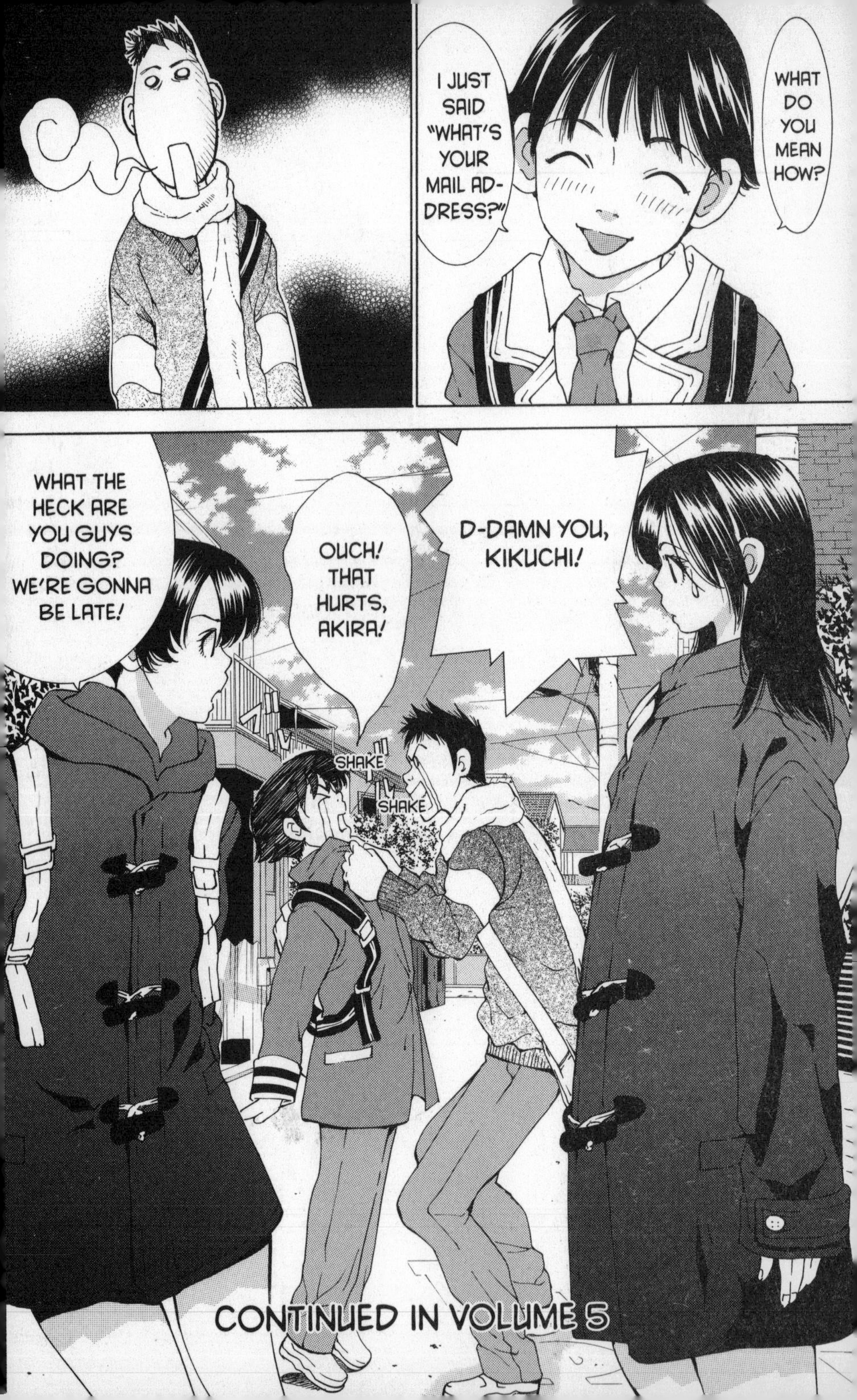
WHAT DO YOU MEAN HOW?
I JUST SAID "WHAT'S YOUR MAIL AD-DRESS?"
D-DAMN YOU, KIKUCHI!
OUCH! THAT HURTS, AKIRA!
WHAT THE HECK ARE YOU GUYS DOING? WE'RE GONNA BE LATE!
SHAKE
SHAKE

CONTINUED IN VOLUME 5

GACHA GACHA ILLUSTRATION CORNER

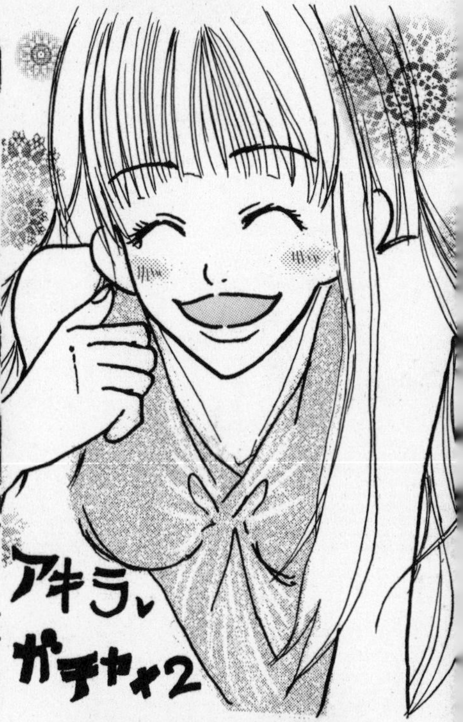
アキラ、
ガチャャ2

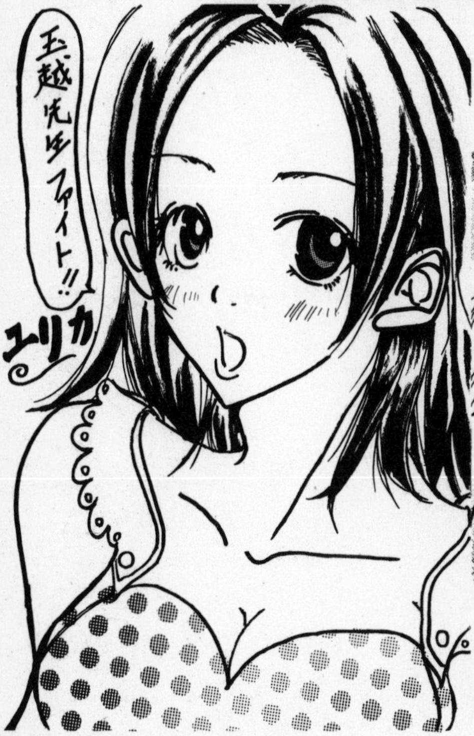
玉越先生ファイト!!
ユリカ

今回のイラスト大賞は
P.N羽夢さんに決定!!

おめでとう！ サイン色紙お送りします！

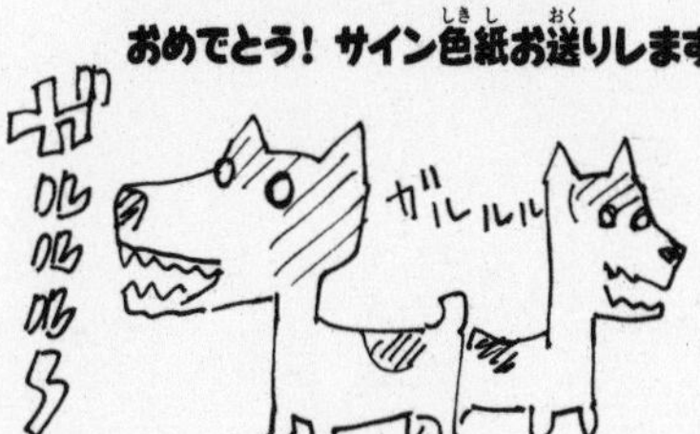
ガルルル
ガルルル

まだまだイラスト大募集!!
みんな送ってくれくれ☆
←あて先はこちら!!

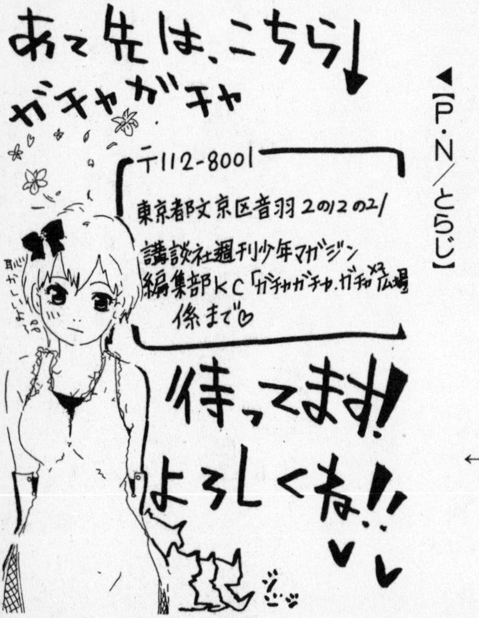
あて先は、こちら↓
ガチャガチャ
〒112-8001
東京都文京区音羽2の12の21
講談社週刊少年マガジン
編集部KC「ガチャガチャ、ガチャ絵広場」
係まで♡
待ってます!
よろしくね!!
◀【P・N／とらじ】

▼【椎木太史】

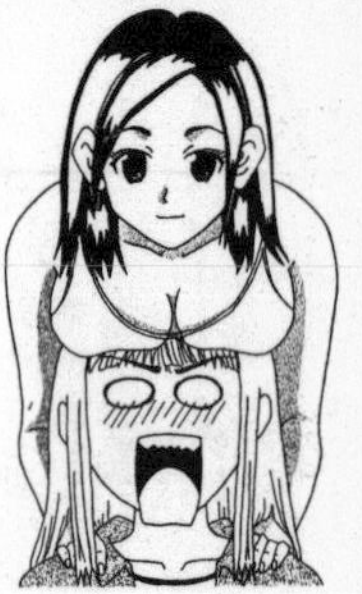

▼【P・N/天地しゃるる】

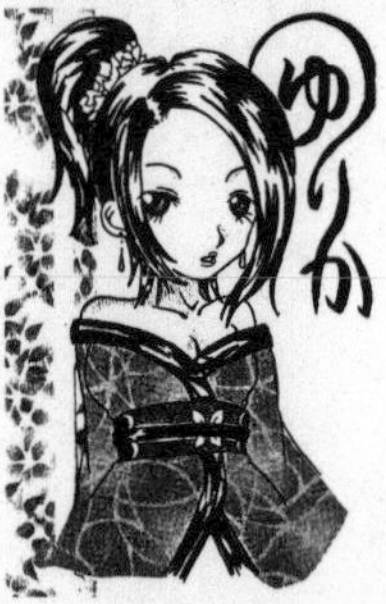
ゆりか

▼【P・N/とらじ】▼

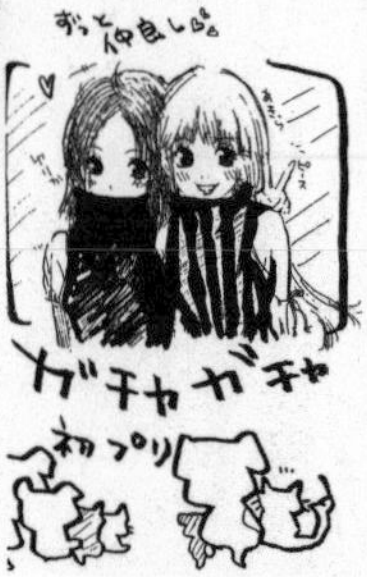
ガチャガチャ

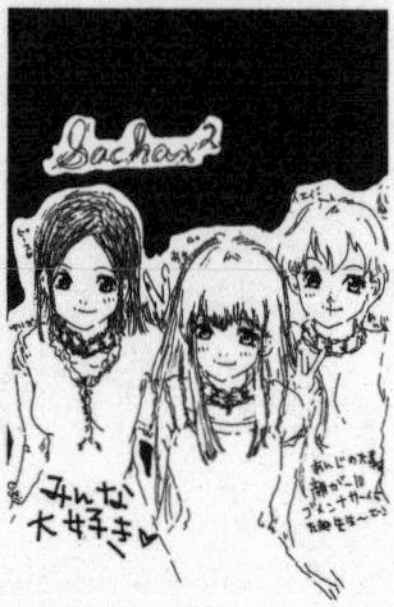
みんな大好き

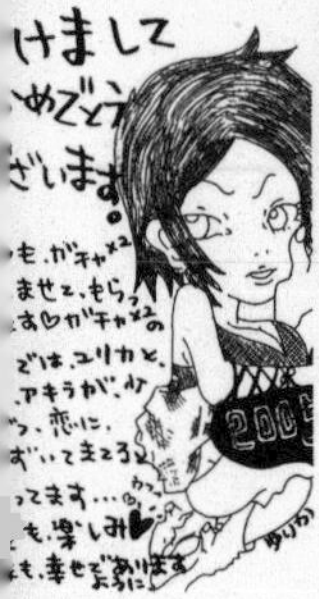

▼【荒川勇斗】

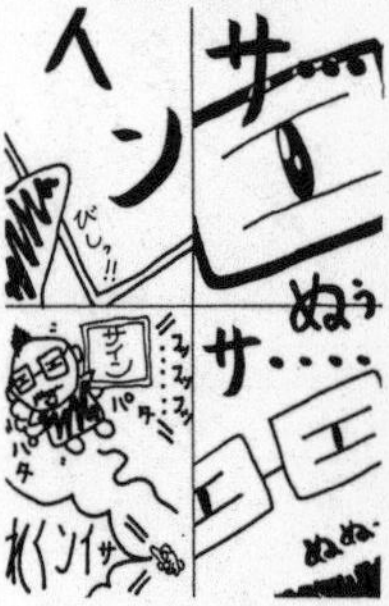
ヘンサ……
サ……

▼【P・N/マールザク】

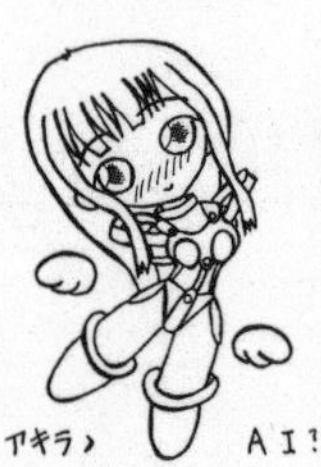
(アキラ)
AI?!

▼【持田 蛍】

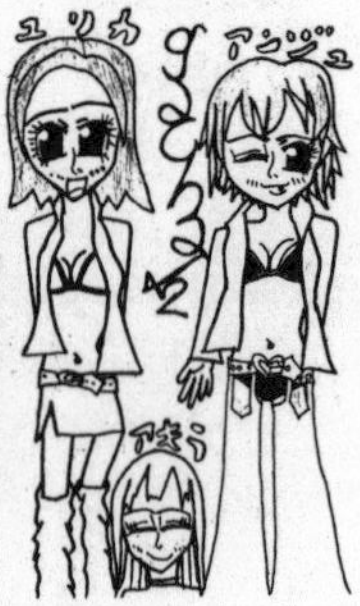
ユリカ
アンジュ

▼【P・N/ヒマラ】

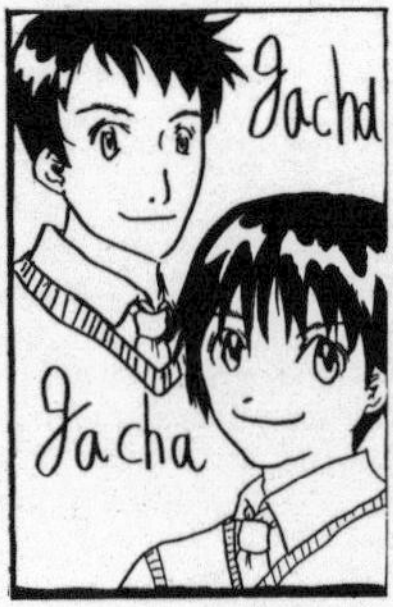
Gacha
Gacha

【P・N/かつぱ】

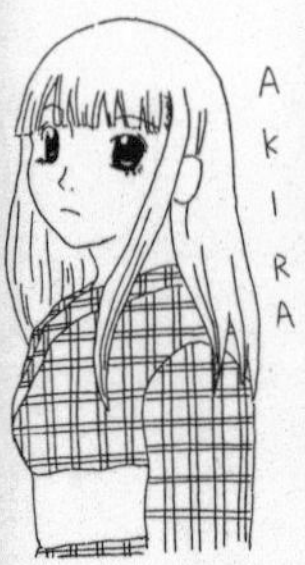
AKIRA

▼【押手祐太】

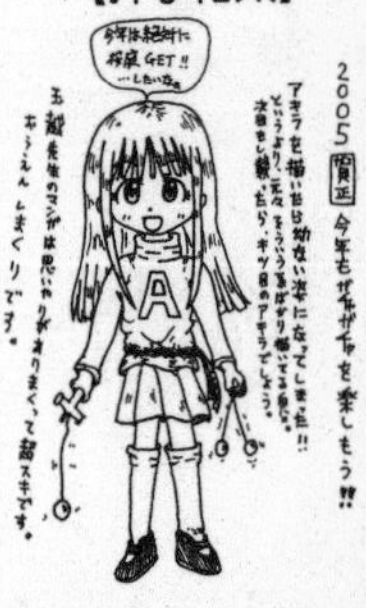
2005 賀正

▼【P・N/スイカ】

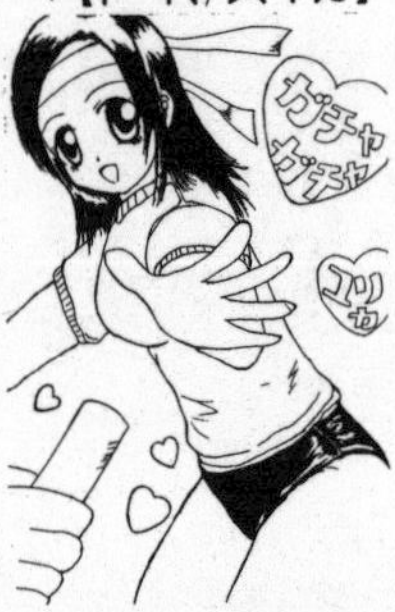
ガチャガチャ
ユリカ

▼【P・N/あじゆさ】▼

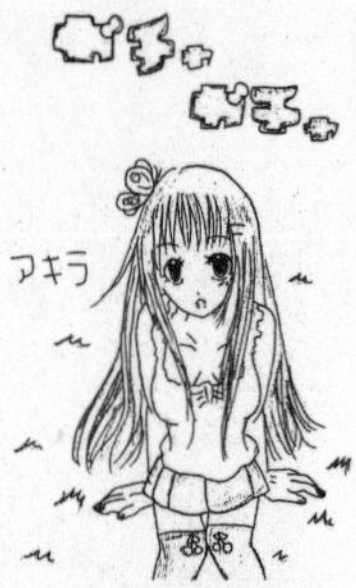
ガチャガチャ
アキラ

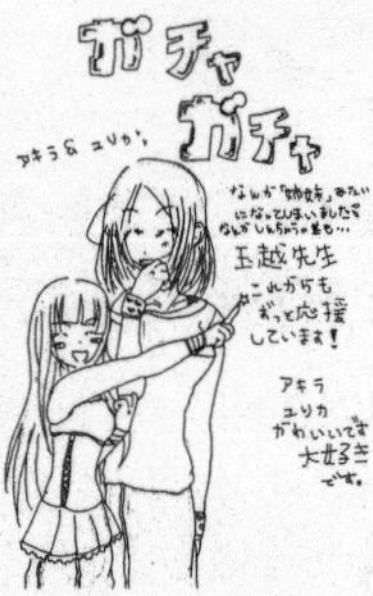
ガチャガチャ
玉越先生
これからもずっと応援しています!

【P・N/つばさ】

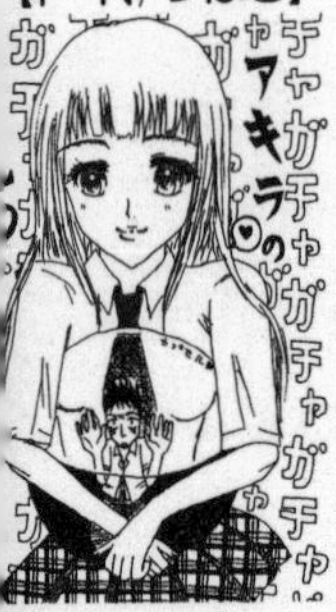
アキラ

▼【P・N/葵しぐれ】

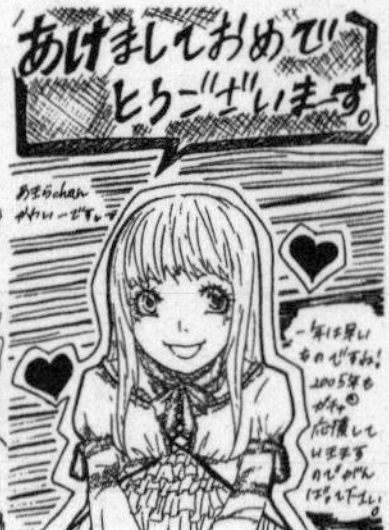
あけましておめでとうございます。

▼【P・N/スイカ】

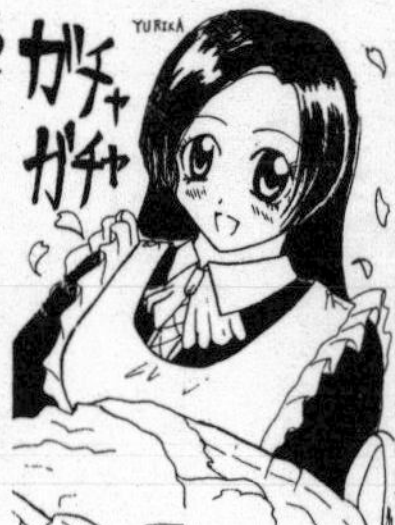
ガチャガチャ

▼【浜 龍史】

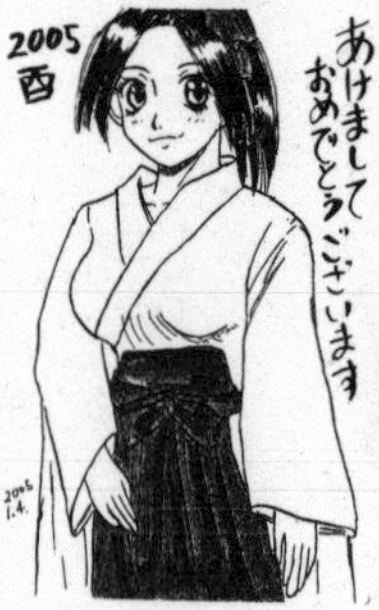
2005 酉
あけましておめでとうございます

▼【P・N/ホワイト】

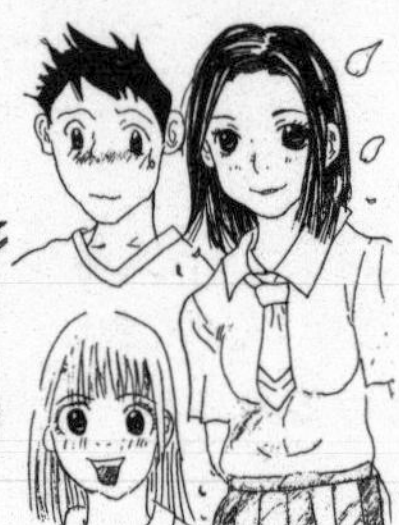

【P・N/マウス】

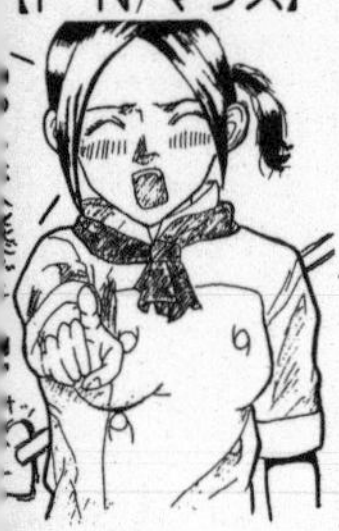
桜庭ユリカ

▼【P・N/ひまら

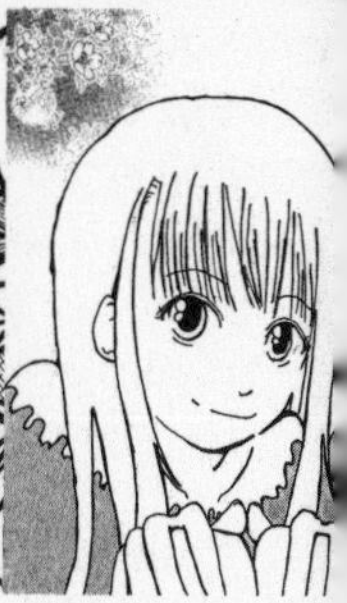

▼【P・N/西中生】

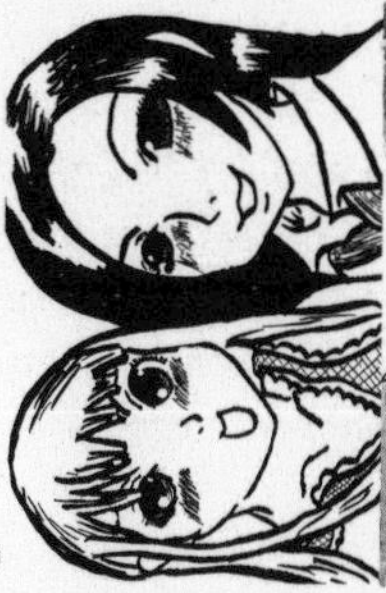

▼【P・N/とらじ】▼

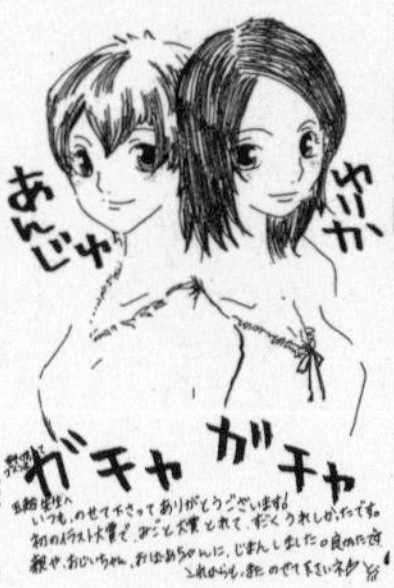
ガチャ ガチャ
あんじゅ
やりか

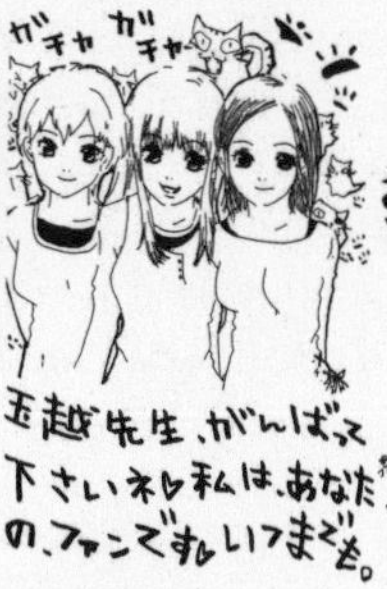
ガチャ ガチャ
玉越先生、がんばって下さいネ♥私は、あなたの、ファンです♥いつまでも。

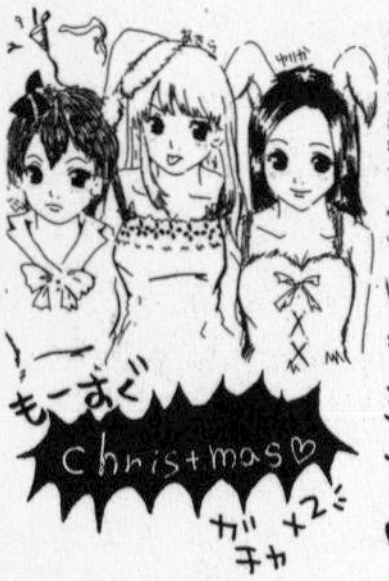
もーすぐ
Christmas♡
ガチャ×2

▼【益子ちはる】

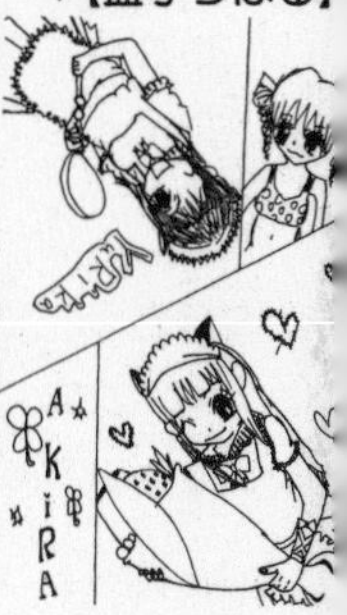
AKiRA

▼【P・N/西中生】

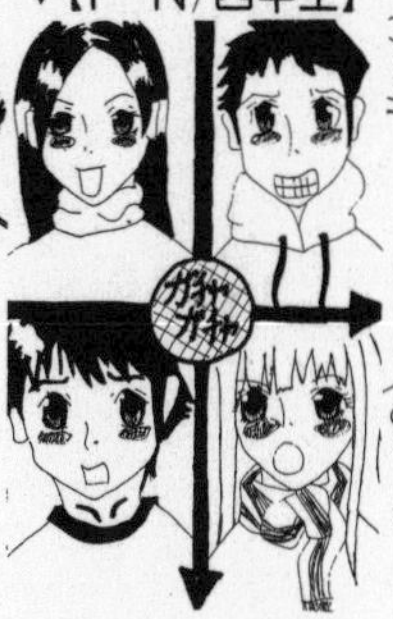

▼【田辺孝一】

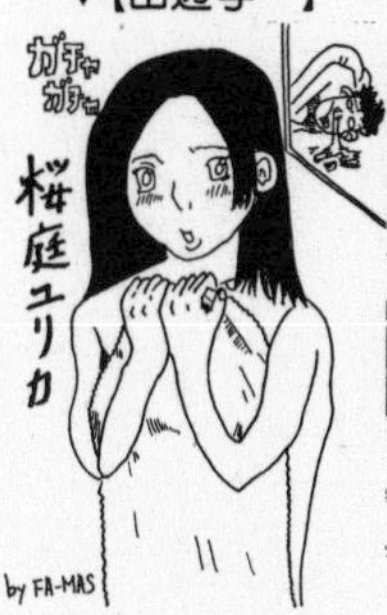
ガチャガチャ
桜庭ユリカ
by FA-MAS

▼【P・N/ひまら】▼

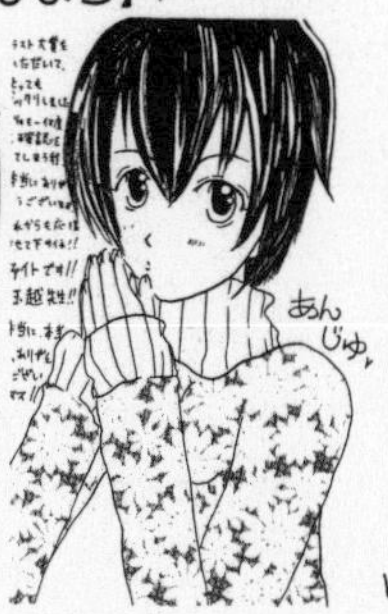
あんじゅ

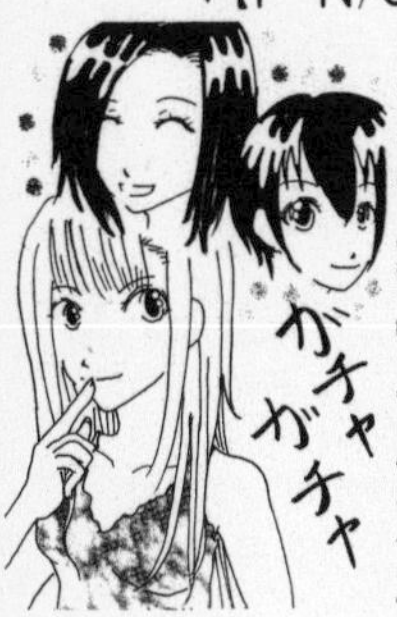
ガチャ
ガチャ

▼【笹崎寛人】

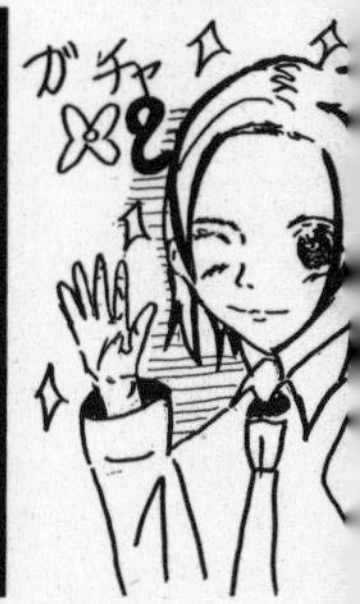
ガチャ

①～④【P・N/天地しゃるる】

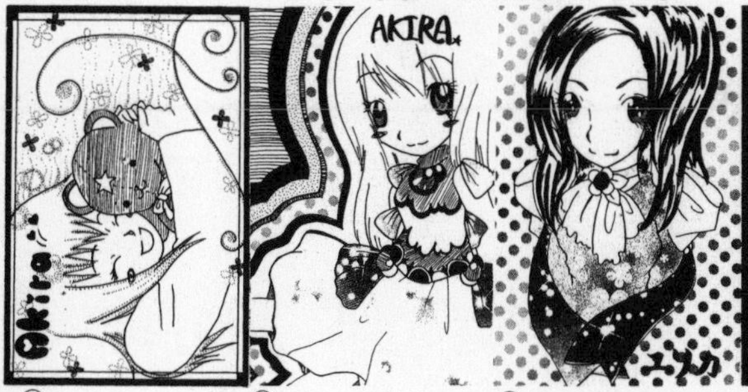
AKIRA
Akira

① ② ③ ④

▼【P・N/めぐちぃ

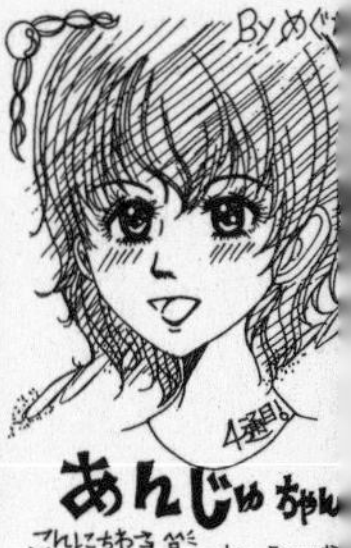
あんじゅちゃん

▼【P・N/しあ】

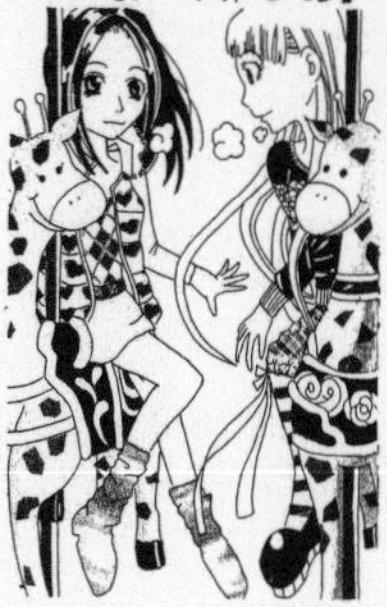

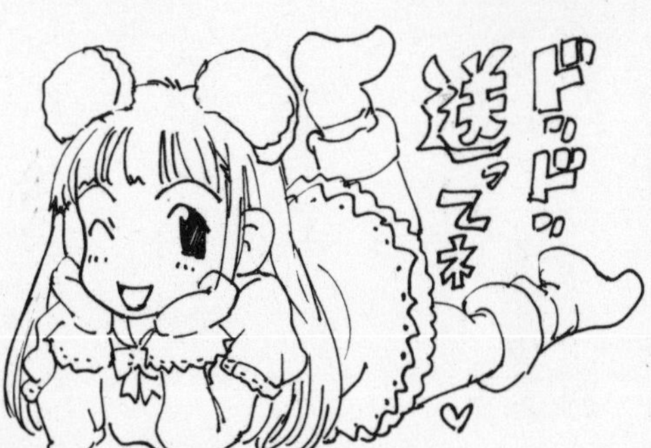
ドッドッ送ってネ

About the Creator

Hiroyuki Tamakoshi was born in 1970. In 1997, he was awarded the Fine Work Prize in the Best New Cartoonist category at *Shonen* magazine's 45th annual competition. His previous work includes *Boys Be . . .* (1991–1997), *Boys Be . . . 2nd Season* (1997–2000), and *Boys Be . . . L Co-op* (2000–2001). Masahiro Itabashi was the cartoonist of the original work. *Gacha Gacha* was published in *Shonen* magazine's double issue 36–37 in 2002, and is currently in the serial magazine beginning with issue 29 in 2003 with *Special No. 8*.

Comics

Boys Be . . . complete in 16 volumes.
Boys Be . . . 2nd Season, complete in 20 volumes
Boys Be . . . L Co-op, complete in 5 volumes
Gacha Gacha, volumes 1–8
Boys Be . . . 1991
Boys Be . . . 1992
Boys Be . . . 1993
Boys Be . . . 1994
Boys Be . . . 1995
Boys Be . . . 1996
Boys Be . . . 1997
Boys Be . . . 1998
Boys Be . . . 1999
Boys Be . . . 2000
Kodansha Manga Collection

Favorite Mobile Suit
RX-78 GUNDAM.
The strongest man in the world
Amuro Ray.
A respectable person
GUNDAM (because I want to be a GUNDAM).
PC environment
Power Mac G4 733 MHz, OS 10.3.5, 19-inch monitor.
Favorite movie
Lock, Stock, and Two Smoking Barrels.
Are you enjoying your life?
So-so.
Favorite animal
Cats, but I have a dog.
Describe yourself with a metaphor
A kettle.
Favorite animation
Evangelion and *FLCL*.

Translation Notes

Japanese is a tricky language for most Westerners, and translation is often more an art than a science. For your edification and reading pleasure, here are notes on some of the places where we could have gone in a different direction in our translation, or where a Japanese cultural reference is used.

Kansetsu kiss, page 14

I-I WAS JUST THINKING...
THAT WAS ALMOST LIKE A KISS.

Akira is actually saying something like "That was a *kansetsu* kiss." A "*kansetsu* kiss" occurs when two people's lips touch the same spot. For example, if Akira took a sip from a straw, and then Yurika took a sip from the same straw, that would be a "*kansetsu* kiss." In this case, Yurika is eating the grain of rice that was stuck to Akira's lips, so it's a somewhat removed *kansetsu* kiss.

Stools, page 21

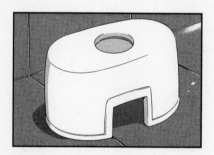

These little stools are a common fixture in Japanese bathrooms. One sits on the stool and showers before soaking in the tub.

Sneezing, page 82

In Japan, they say that when someone talks about you behind your back it makes you sneeze.

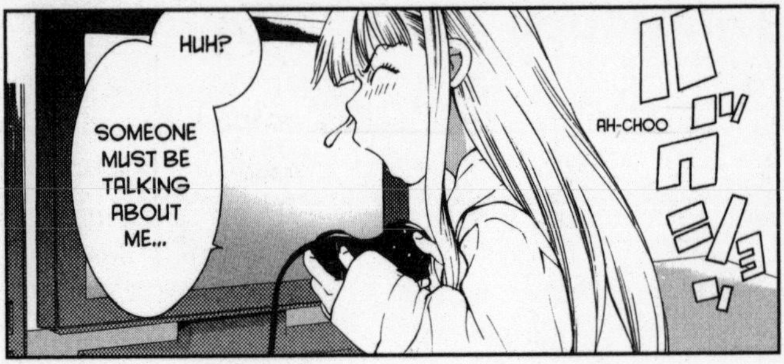
AH-CHOO
HUH?
SOMEONE MUST BE TALKING ABOUT ME...

***No Longer Human,* page 84**

No Longer Human or *Ningenshikaku* is a famous Japanese novel by literary master Osamu Dazai.

***Koohaku,* page 125**

Akira is referring to the *koohaku,* a celebrity showdown in which two teams of pop stars, the red and the white, compete against each other by doing musical numbers. The show airs only on New Year's Eve.

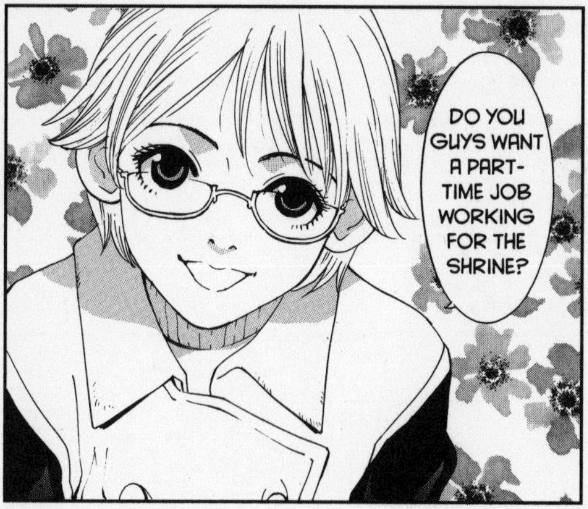
DO YOU GUYS WANT A PART-TIME JOB WORKING FOR THE SHRINE?

Shinto shrines, page 132

In Japan, Shinto shrines are run by families who generally live on the premises. They are staffed by female workers, called "Miko."

Obi, page 139

An obi is a wide belt or sash used to tie a kimono.

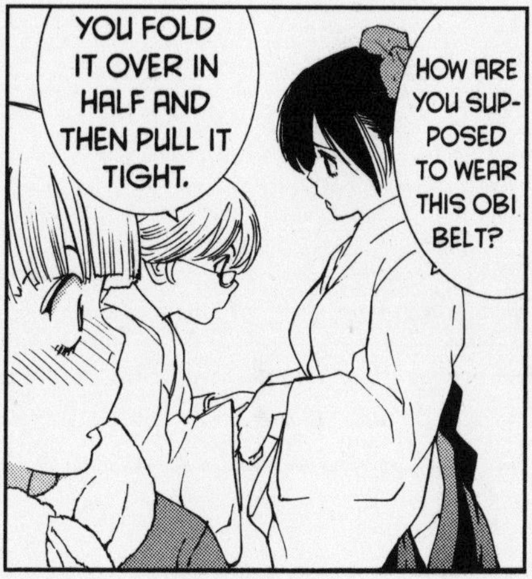
HOW ARE YOU SUP-POSED TO WEAR THIS OBI BELT?
YOU FOLD IT OVER IN HALF AND THEN PULL IT TIGHT.

Mikuji, page 151

Yurika is talking about a *mikuji* which we translated as a fortune scroll. *Mikuji* are fortunes that are sold all year long but are especially popular on New Year's Day.

Valentine's Day, page 164

The Japanese version of Valentine's Day is a bit different than the American tradition. In Japan, Valentine's Day is a day when girls give presents to the boys they like (usually chocolate). There is another holiday, called White Day, when boys give presents to girls.

Giri choco, page 164

You may remember from volume 2 of *Gacha Gacha: The Next Revolution* that *giri choco* literally means something like "obligatory chocolate" or "duty chocolate." *Giri choco* is used to describe the chocolate that girls give to guys on Valentine's Day out of obligation. For example, if a woman gave chocolate to every man in her office, so that no one felt left out, she might refer to it as *giri choco*. However, if a girl gave chocolate to her boyfriend, or a guy she was in love with, that would be considered *Honmei* which we translated as love chocolate.

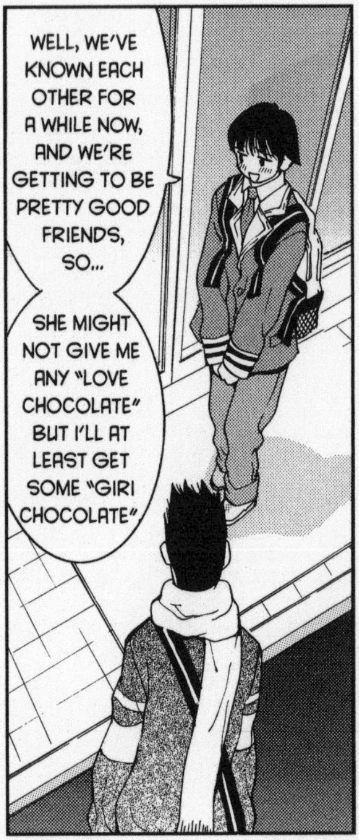
WELL, WE'VE KNOWN EACH OTHER FOR A WHILE NOW, AND WE'RE GETTING TO BE PRETTY GOOD FRIENDS, SO...
SHE MIGHT NOT GIVE ME ANY "LOVE CHOCOLATE" BUT I'LL AT LEAST GET SOME "GIRI CHOCOLATE"

Preview of Volume 5

We're pleased to present you a preview from volume 5. This volume will be available in English on November 27, 2007, but for now you'll have to make do with Japanese!

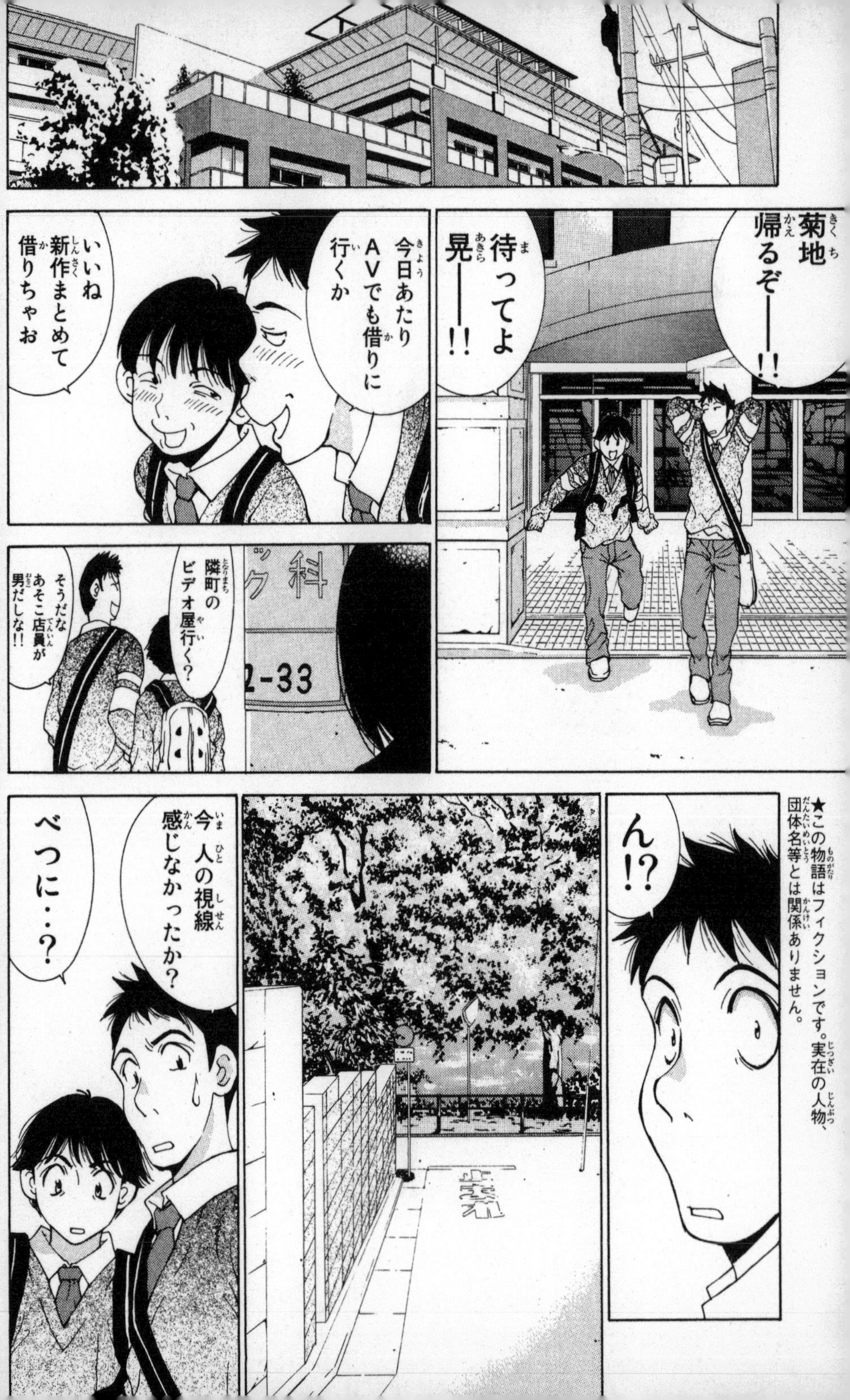
菊地帰るぞー!!
待ってよ晃ー!!
今日あたりAVでも借りに行くか
いいね新作まとめて借りちゃお
隣町のビデオ屋行く?
そうだなあそこ店員が男だしな!!
★この物語はフィクションです。実在の人物、団体名等とは関係ありません。
ん!?
今人の視線感じなかったか?
べつに…?

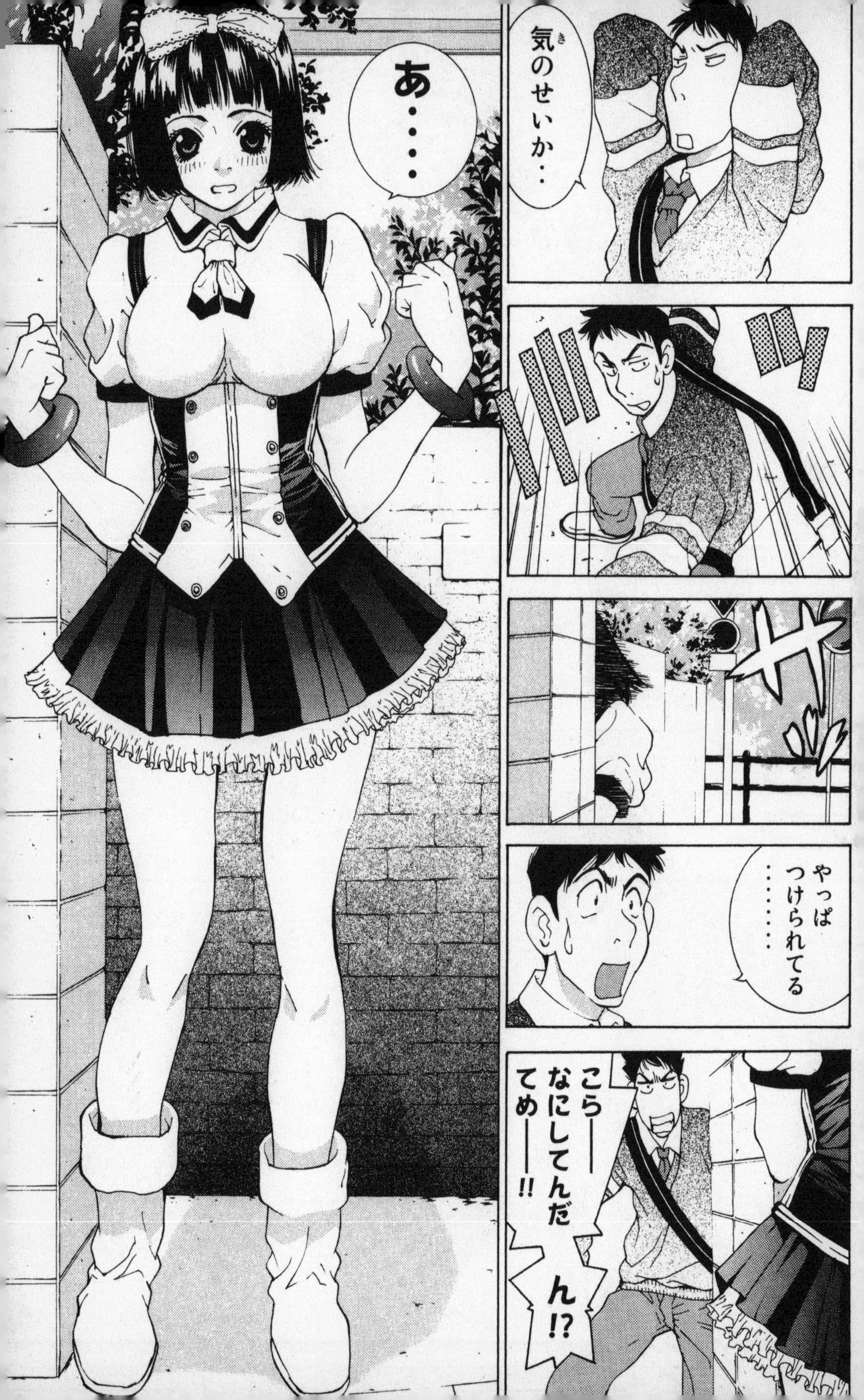
気のせいか・・
やっぱつけられてる・・・・・・
こら——なにしてんだてめ——!!
ん!?
あ・・・・

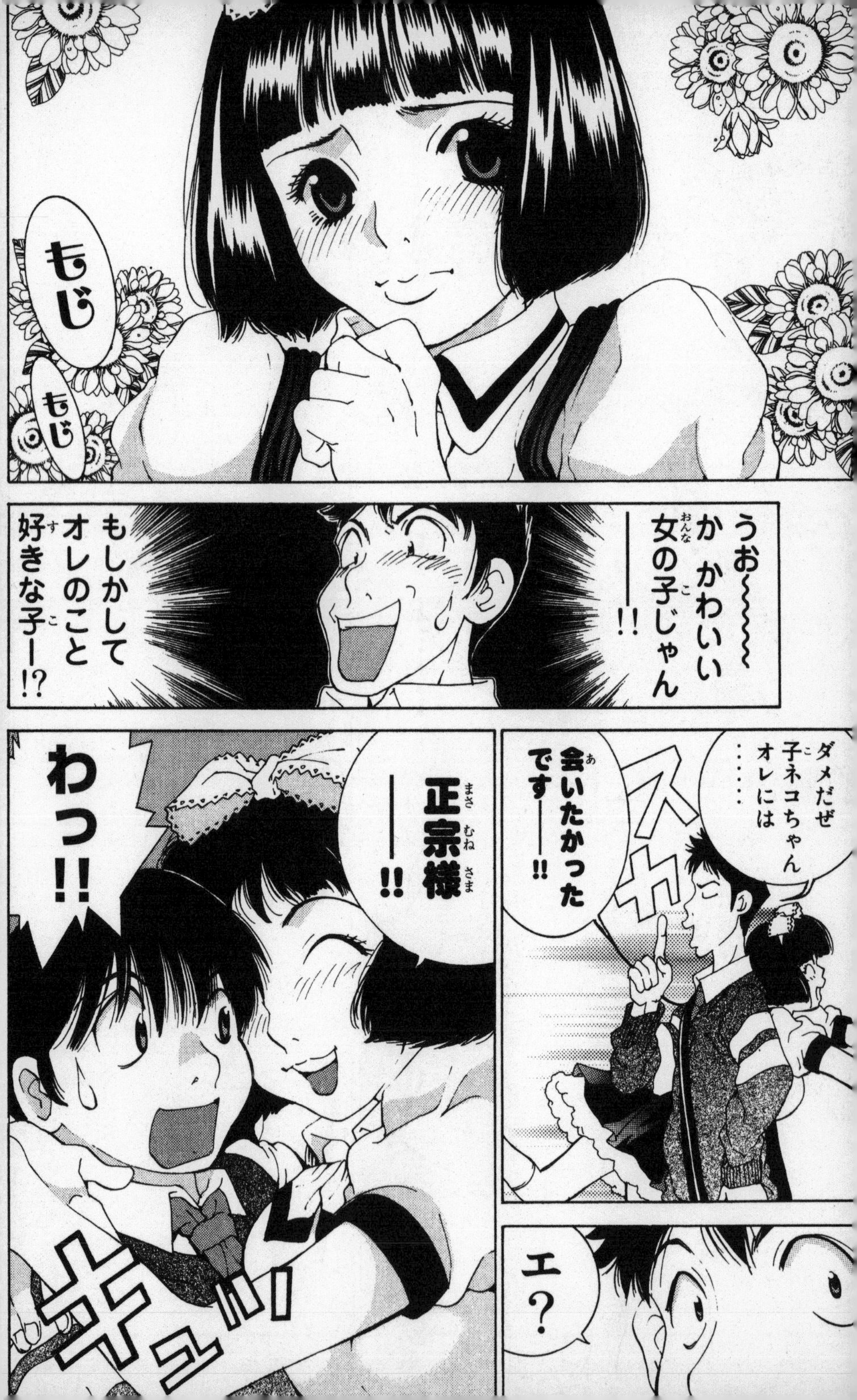
もじ
もじ
うお〜〜〜 かわいい女の子じゃん——!!
もしかしてオレのこと好きな子ー!?
ダメだぜ子ネコちゃんオレには……
スカ
会いたかったです——!!
エ?
正宗様——!!
わっ!!
ギュ!!

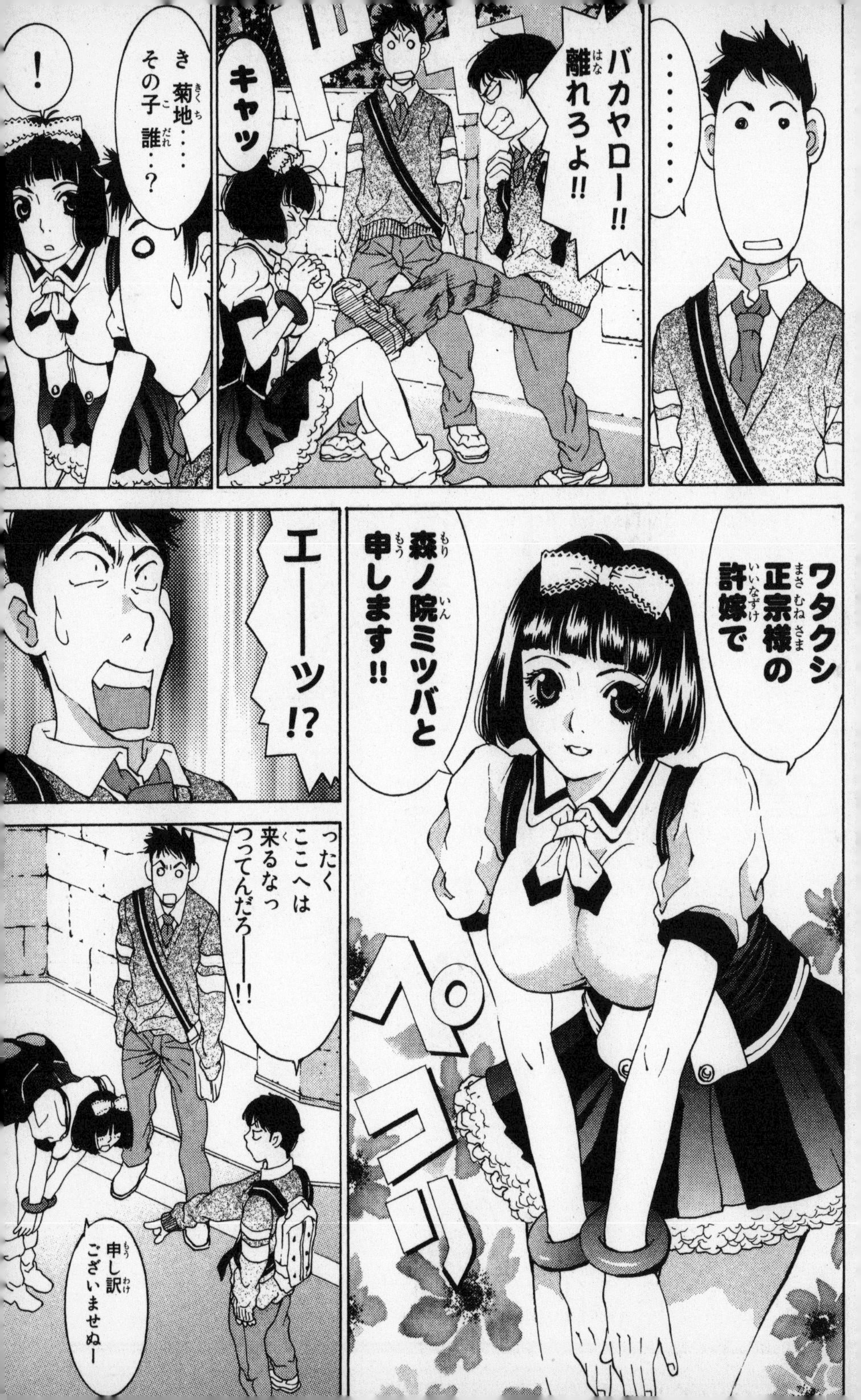
……
バカヤロー!!
離れろよ!!
キャッ
き 菊地……
その子 誰…?
!
ワタクシ
正宗様の
許嫁で
森ノ院ミツバと
申します!!
ペコリ
エーーッ!?
ったく
ここへは
来るなっ
つってんだろーー!!
申し訳
ございませぬー

SUZUKA

Kouji Seo

SHE'S SO COOL

Yamato is ready for a fresh start. So when his aunt invites him to stay rent-free in her big-city boarding-house in hustling, bustling Tokyo, Yamato jumps at the chance. There's just one teensy-weensy catch: It's an all-girl housing complex and spa! Things get even more nerve-racking when Yamato meets his neighbor Suzuka, a beautiful track-and-field star. She's not just the cutest girl Yamato's ever met, she's also the coolest, the smartest, and the most intimidating. Can an ordinary guy like Yamato ever hope to win over a girl like Suzuka?

1
MATURE CONTENT
SUZUKA
KOUJI SEO

Special extras in each volume! Read them all!

VISIT WWW.DELREYMANGA.COM TO:
- Read sample pages
- View release date calendars for upcoming volumes
- Sign up for Del Rey's free manga e-newsletter
- Find out the latest about new Del Rey Manga series

RATING M AGES 18+

DEL REY DEL REY MANGA デルレイ

The Otaku's Choice

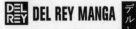

Pastel

by Toshihiko Kobayashi

I LOVE YUU

Poor 16-year-old Mugi Tadano is left heartbroken after his girlfriend moves away. A summer job at his friend Kazuki's beachside snack bar/hotel seems like the perfect way to get his mind off the breakup. Soon Kazuki sets Mugi up on a date with a girl named Yuu, who's supposed to be...well...a little less than perfect. But when Yuu arrives, she's not the monster that either of the boys had imagined. In fact, Yuu is about the cutest girl that Mugi has ever seen. But after Mugi accidentally walks in on Yuu while she's in the bath, Yuu is furious. When Mugi goes to apologize the next day, he learns that Yuu has left the island. Mugi vows to search high and low for her, but will he ever see the beautiful Yuu again?

Ages: 16 +

Special extras in each volume! Read them all!

VISIT WWW.DELREYMANGA.COM TO:
- View release date calendars for upcoming volumes
- Sign up for Del Rey's free manga e-newsletter
- Find out the latest about new Del Rey Manga series

TOMARE!

[STOP!]

You're going the wrong way!

Manga is a completely
different type of reading
experience.

To start at the *beginning,*
go to the *end*!

That's right! Authentic manga is read the traditional Japanese way—from right to left. Exactly the opposite of how American books are read. It's easy to follow: Just go to the other end of the book, and read each page—and each panel—from right side to left side, starting at the top right. Now you're experiencing manga as it was meant to be!